JURY SELECTION IN CRIMINAL TRIALS

SKILLS, SCIENCE, AND THE LAW

CANADIAN LEGAL SKILLS

JURY SELECTION IN CRIMINAL TRIALS

SKILLS, SCIENCE, AND THE LAW

DAVID M. TANOVICH
DAVID M. PACIOCCO
STEVEN SKURKA

JURY SELECTION IN CRIMINAL TRIALS

Published in 1997 by
Irwin Law
1800 Steeles Avenue West
Concord, Ontario
L4K 2P3

ISBN 1-55221-022-7

Canadian Cataloguing in Publication Data
Tanovich, David M.
Jury selection in criminal trials: skills, science and the law

(Canadian legal skills)
Includes bibliographical references and index.
ISBN 1-55221-022-7

1. Jury selection — Canada. 2. Criminal procedure — Canada.
I. Paciocco, David M. II. Skurka, Steven. III. Title. IV. Series.

KE9348.T34 1997 345.71'075 C97-931542-5
KF9680.T3 1997

Printed and bound in Canada.

1 2 3 4 5 00 99 98 97

SUMMARY

TABLE OF CONTENTS

DETAILED TABLE OF CONTENTS

FOREWORD

Until recently, criminal law practitioners in Canada said very little about jury selection. What they did say seldom went beyond "war stories" that, while interesting, had little educational value. Canadian legislators, judges, and academics seemed even less interested in the process. In recent years, however, spurred by the *Canadian Charter of Rights and Freedoms* and insights from the social sciences, the jury selection process has become a "hot" topic in Canadian criminal law.

This text reflects the new-found interest in the jury selection process. It is first and foremost a practitioner's manual. The text takes the reader through each stage of the jury selection process. A wealth of information is presented in a systematic and thoroughly readable fashion. The authors bring together in a single source the numerous legislative and judicial pronouncements that together constitute the applicable substantive and adjectival law. The reader will find careful analysis of all the relevant legislative and judicial pronouncements. Extensive commentary from practitioners adds a further dimension to the text. These commentaries provide insight into the operation of the jury selection process and the numerous tactical considerations that must be addressed when selecting a jury. The appendices also contain valuable precedents for the busy practitioner.

The text is, however, more than a practitioner's manual. It raises and canvasses many as yet unresolved legal issues. In doing so, the text provides grist for the practitioner's mill, enlightens all who are engaged in the study of criminal law, and provokes a careful assessment of many of the principles that lie at the heart of the criminal justice system.

This text will prove invaluable to the practitioner who must be familiar with the "nuts and bolts" of the jury selection process. It will be equally valuable to those who see the criminal justice system as a work in process to be honed and re-honed to better meet the needs of the community.

Thanks to the efforts of the authors, we now have ready access to a valuable resource that both informs as to the current state of the law and alerts as to the issues that lie on the horizon.

The Honourable Mr. Justice David Doherty
Court of Appeal for Ontario

INTRODUCTION

> So that the liberties of England cannot but subsist so long as . . . [the jury] . . . remains sacred and inviolate; not only from all open attacks (which none will be so hardy as to make,) but also from all secret machinations which may sap and undermine it; by introducing new and arbitrary methods of trial . . . And, however *convenient* these may appear at first, (as doubtless all arbitrary powers, well executed, are the most *convenient*) yet let it be again remembered that delays and little inconveniences in the forms of justice are the price that all free nations must pay for their liberty in more substantial matters; that these inroads upon this sacred bulwark of the nation are fundamentally opposite to the spirit of our constitution.

W.R. Blackstone, *Commentaries on the Laws of England*, Vol. 4 (Philadelphia: Rees Welsh & Co., 1900) at 349–59

> Trial by jury is an institution unique to common law countries. It is more than a mere incident of criminal procedure. It has been described as a pillar of the Constitution and praised as a palladium of liberty. This is because the rights and freedoms of individuals in our society have been protected from the power of the state to launch prosecutions and control the appointment of judges by the requirement that guilt on any charge must be proved to the satisfaction of 12 ordinary citizens.

R. v. *Bryant* (1984), 48 O.R. (2d) 732 at 741 (C.A.), Blair J.

These passages reflect the fact that trial by jury is an integral part of the fabric of democracy, as it has been conceived in the English common law system. In many respects, the reverence given to trial by jury is a historical vestige of bygone social realities. There was a time when trial by one's peers meant more than it does today. A jury would be drawn from the same community as the accused, and the accused would most often be known to those jurors, personally or by reputation. Like the old system of "oath-helping," in which witnesses were called to assert the accused's innocence, not on the basis of what they knew about the event but rather according to what they knew about the accused, the jury operated to ensure that good people were not falsely charged. Moreover, in a stratified class system in which the privileged judges had little in common with those most likely to be prosecuted, having the opportunity to be tried by one's "peers" took on special significance. Guilt was to be determined by twelve "ordinary" citizens. The jury system also protected liberty and democracy because jurors had the power to refuse to apply unjust laws. Twelve good citizens could nullify the application of an unjust law in a particular case by refusing to apply it.

Since these halcyon days in which the jury was seen as a bulwark of democracy, much has changed. "Community" is not what it once was. With the urbanization of society, most who live among us will not even know us or our reputations. Trial by our peers is trial by our community only in the loosest sense. Indeed, our conception of a just verdict has changed. At the core of our criminal justice system is the imperative that guilt or innocence be adjudicated by a neutral, impartial trier of fact. We disqualify those who are connected to the accused or to the prosecution from participation in the jury, and our rules of evidence are designed to limit the risk that people will be tried on their reputations and character rather than on the evidence presented. Moreover, resort to trial by one's peers to preserve accused persons from trial by an elitist judge has lost much of its importance. It is now common for judges to be the sons and daughters of "ordinary citizens." And while we recognize the reality that juries can decide not to apply the law, given that they are not asked for reasons for their decisions, we proceed on the understanding that they do not have the right to nullify the law and that they are bound to follow the judge's directions as to what law to apply. In modern times it is probably more common for juries to "nullify" the law, not by making decisions of conscience not to follow it but rather by misunderstanding the law that they are directed to apply. It is no secret that the jury charge often calls on distinctions and legal tests too subtle for the clever law student, let alone for the untrained, ordinary citizen. No matter how much better educated today's jurors are than those from days gone past, there is reason to doubt that the law is applied with technical precision in the jury rooms of our nation.

Despite all of this, our traditional reverence for the jury system and our belief that it is a fundamental part of our democratic system persist. No one was surprised to find that when we sought to describe and protect the fundamental principles of our system of criminal justice in the *Canadian Charter of Rights and Freedoms*, the right to trial by jury was included in section 11(f). Despite its detractors, the jury system remains a central feature of that system, and it is important for criminal lawyers to think about the opportunities that it presents and to understand its rules and its conventions.

Despite our constitutional efforts to ensure equal application of the law, practitioners of criminal law understand how much turns on who the triers of fact and law will be in a given case. "Judge shopping" is one of the unspoken realities in the criminal justice system, but we are less abashed when it comes to jury selection. For most offences that can be tried by a jury, defence lawyers can elect not to have a jury trial, preferring to take their chances in front of a judge. Prosecutors can refuse to consent to a re-election where they feel it advantageous to have a jury trial, when the accused has changed his or her mind and is seeking to be tried by judge alone. When there will be a trial by jury we allow the parties to participate in its selection by rejecting those whom they believe will judge their case harshly. There is substantial controversy about whether this elaborate selection process is worth the time and energy that it takes, given that selection is so often based on unreliable theories and beliefs, often amounting to no more than stereotype and conjecture. Yet most experienced criminal lawyers are quick to claim that the process is a significant one, which can be effective in providing a fairer trial to the accused and to the Crown. Even with the controversy surrounding its effectiveness, jury selection is undoubtedly a crucial feature of the system of trial by jury, and for this reason we felt it worthwhile to provide this concise practice guide to provide assistance to those contemplating, and to those who are conducting, criminal jury trials.

The last few years have witnessed some major changes in the way we look on and conduct the process of jury selection. In *R.* v. *Bain*, [1992] 1 S.C.R. 91, the Supreme Court of Canada abolished the Crown's ability to stand aside jurors, while in *R.* v. *Parks* (1993), 15 O.R. (3d) 324 (C.A.), leave to appeal refused (1994), 28 C.R. (4th) 403n (S.C.C.), and *R.* v. *Wilson* (1996), 47 C.R. (4th) 61 (Ont. C.A.), the Ontario Court of Appeal expanded the challenge for cause process in Ontario by permitting a generic challenge based on racial prejudice as of right for Black accused. In *R.* v. *Biddle* (1993), 14 O.R. (3d) 756 (C.A.), appeal allowed on other grounds [1995] 1 S.C.R. 761, the Ontario Court of Appeal expressed the view that section 15(1) of the *Charter* may prevent prosecutors from using their peremptory challenges in a discriminatory fashion. Given these notable changes to the jury landscape, we decided that it would be useful to the practitioner if we analysed these decisions and outlined their possible implications for the future. We are also convinced that a step-by-step guide to selecting a jury in a criminal trial will be of assistance.

Chapter 1 describes the availability and outlines the purpose of trial by jury. It is also intended to provide counsel with assistance in deciding when the election for a jury trial should be made. The practices and theories of the experienced criminal practitioners who so generously assisted us in preparing this book helped us immensely with this material.

Chapter 2 discusses the contribution that provincial legislation makes to the jury selection process. It examines the creation of the jury panel from which the jury in a particular case will be selected. Provincial eligibility and exemption criteria are examined, as is the limited means available to the litigants to ensure a "qualified" jury. The process of challenging the jury array is also discussed, including the implications of section 15 of the *Canadian Charter of Rights and Freedoms*.

Chapter 3 considers the limited circumstances in which a judge is entitled to pre-screen the jury panel for partiality, in the hope that the fairly widespread practice of trial judges doing so in preference to granting challenges for cause will cease. A challenge for cause occurs where either the Crown or the defence seeks, with reason, to have one or more jurors disqualified from serving on the jury. The challenge to the juror is for "cause" in the sense that there is reason to believe that the juror should not serve, based on one of the approved grounds of disqualification spelled out in the *Criminal Code*. Chapter 4 describes the challenge for cause process, explores its purpose, and discusses its availability in criminal cases. It also provides some modest tactical observations about whether a challenge for cause should be undertaken.

Chapter 5 provides a detailed account of the law relating to challenges for cause and is intended to provide the trial practitioner with the necessary tools to obtain a challenge for cause. It contains an analysis of the threshold test; an examination of the meaning of "air of reality"; a discussion of challenges based on pre-trial publicity, racial bias, and offence-based biases; and a thorough analysis of the means by which the necessary evidentiary foundation can be laid.

Chapter 6 looks at the mechanics of the challenge for cause procedure, examining such matters as who is entitled to challenge for cause, the order of challenges, and the form of the challenge. It also considers the controversial issue of whether the non-challenging party can accept the challenge and thus avoid having the challenge tried by the mini-jury.

Chapter 7 looks at the triers of the challenge for cause, while chapter 8 examines the procedure on a trial of a challenge for cause.

Chapter 9 looks at the mechanics of the peremptory challenge, in which either the Crown or the accused exercises the right to refuse a particular juror, without specifying cause. Depending on the seriousness of the offence, counsel are allotted a predetermined number of such challenges.

Chapter 10 offers practical tips on selecting a jury. It is an attempt to gather together the wisdom and experience of lawyers who have selected jurors. This will, we hope, be of assistance to other counsel in identifying those prospective jurors who should be challenged and those who should not. The contribution of social science is also explored. An attempt is made to highlight and critically assess the social science literature. Despite the efforts that have been made to identify the "ideal juror," there remain divergent views on who the best jurors would be in a particular kind of case, and no fool-proof blueprint emerges. Yet we hope that our discussion will provide food for thought, and it is our view that there is much that is of value in chapter 10.

Finally, chapter 11 examines whether either the prosecutor or the defence can use its peremptory challenges in a discriminatory fashion or whether such action constitutes a violation of section 15(1) of the *Charter*.

We have also provided the practitioner with appendices. Appendix I is a survey of the results of challenges for cause that have been taken in sexual assault cases, showing the extent to which such challenges have resulted in the disqualification of prospective jurors. An affidavit prepared by Professor Neil Vidmar for a sexual assault case is included as Appendix II. Relevant excerpts from the provincial *Jury Act*s and *Criminal Code of Canada* are included as Appendices III and IV.

This work would not have been possible without the assistance of a number of busy, prominent practitioners, who have been generous in donating their time. We wish to give special thanks to Donald Bayne, QC (Ottawa defence counsel); Michael D. Edelson (Ottawa defence counsel); Celynne Dorval (Ottawa Assistant Crown Attorney); Malcolm Lindsay, QC (Ottawa Senior Assistant Crown Attorney); Pat McCann (Ottawa defence counsel); and Patrick J. Ducharme (Windsor defence counsel).

We would like to thank law students Tracey Ross (University of Ottawa), Nadine Courville (Osgoode Hall at York University), Cindy Cross (Osgoode Hall at York University), and Elie Roth (Osgoode Hall at York University) for the quality research assistance they provided.

Finally, we would like to thank William Kaplan and Irwin Law for their incredible patience and strong commitment to legal scholarship. They permitted an inordinate number of changes to the original manuscript so that the book would be kept as current as reasonably possible, and we are grateful.

CHAPTER 1

OVERVIEW OF THE JURY SELECTION PROCESS

1.1 THE PURPOSE AND ROLE OF THE JURY

* Trial by jury is a fundamental part of our criminal justice system. The jury is "one of the great protectors of the citizen because it is composed of twelve persons who collectively express the common sense of the community": *R.* v. *Morgentaler*, [1988] 1 S.C.R. 30 at 77. As one jurist eloquently stated: "Juries give a human side to criminal trials": *R.* v. *Bain*, [1992] 1 S.C.R. 91 at 113, Gonthier J. In *R.* v. *G.(R.M.)* (1996), 110 C.C.C. (3d) 26 at 34 (S.C.C.), Justice Cory noted that

> [t]he jury system is clearly a significant factor in many democratic regimes. This is emphatically true in Canada. It is extremely important to our democratic society that jurors as representatives of their community may make the decision as to the guilt or innocence of the accused before the court based solely on the evidence presented to them. There is a centuries old tradition of juries reaching fair and courageous verdicts. That tradition has taken root and been so well and fearlessly maintained that it has flourished in this country. Our courts have very properly stressed the importance of jury verdicts and the deference that must be shown to those decisions. Today, as in the past, great reliance has been placed upon those decisions. That I think flows from the public awareness that twelve members of the community have worked together to reach a unanimous verdict.

> In reaching a verdict, jurors have heeded the wisdom of the prophet Isaiah whose advocacy of a reasoned approach to solving problems has echoed through the ages in the moving and memorable words "Come now, and let us reason together." Isaiah 1:18. Of course, it is the great strength and virtue of the jury system that members of the community have indeed come together and reasoned together in order to reach their unanimous verdict. It is truly a magnificent system for reaching difficult decisions in criminal cases. It has proven itself in the centuries past and continues to do so today.

* It has also been held that the jury

> serves collective or social interests in addition to protecting the individual. The jury advances social purposes primarily by acting as a vehicle of public education and lending the weight of community standards to trial verdicts. Sir James Stephen underlined the collective interests served by trial by jury when he stated:
>
> > . . . trial by jury interests large numbers of people in the administration of justice and makes them responsible for it. It is difficult to over-estimate the importance of this. It gives a degree of power and of popularity to the administration of justice which could hardly be derived from any other source. (J.F. Stephen, *A History of the Criminal Law of England*, vol. 1, (London: MacMillan, 1883) at 573)

See *R.* v. *Turpin*, [1989] 1 S.C.R. 1296 at 1309–10, Wilson J.; see too *R.* v. *Lee*, [1989] 2 S.C.R. 1384 at 1399–1400, Wilson J., and *R.* v. *Bryant* (1984), 48 O.R. (2d) 732 (C.A.).

* The following rationales for the existence of the jury system were identified in the seminal decision of *R.* v. *Sherratt*, [1991] 1 S.C.R. 509 at 523–24:

- the jury serves as an excellent fact finder as a result of its collective decision making;
- the jury acts as the conscience of the community due to its representative character;
- the jury serves as the final bulwark against oppressive laws or their enforcement; and finally,
- the jury provides a means whereby the public increases its knowledge of the criminal justice system and by doing so increases societal trust in the administration of justice.

See, too, Law Reform Commission of Canada, *The Jury in Criminal Trials* (Working Paper 27) (Ottawa: Supply & Services, 1980), and *R.* v. *Turpin*, [1989] 1 S.C.R. 1296 at 1309–10.

* In providing the opportunity for criminal cases to be tried by a jury of twelve individuals, the framers of the modern jury never intended it to be a tool in the hands of either the Crown or the accused but rather envisioned it to be a trier of fact that constitutes "a representative cross-section of society, honestly and fairly chosen": *R.* v. *Sherratt*, [1991] 1 S.C.R. 509 at 524.

* The jury's role in a criminal trial is to act as the trier of fact. It is instructed that it must be unanimous in its determination of whether the prosecution has proven the guilt of the accused beyond a reasonable doubt: *Harrison* v. *R.* (1974), [1975] 2 S.C.R. 95. The juror's task of determining culpability is a heavy one. As Justice McLachlin recognized in *R.* v. *Sims*, [1992] 2 S.C.R. 858 at 867:

> The jury system places a heavy responsibility in the hands of jury members. Individuals are asked to make grave decisions bearing upon the rights and liberties of their peers. It is a burden which may prey heavily on the minds of some.

1.2 SECRECY AND JURY DELIBERATIONS

* A juror's deliberations are shrouded in secrecy. As Chief Justice Dickson remarked in *R.* v. *Morgentaler*, [1988] 1 S.C.R. 30 at 78:

> We cannot enter the jury room. The jury is never called upon to explain the reasons which lie behind a verdict.

Indeed, section 649 of the *Criminal Code of Canada*, R.S.C. 1985, c. C-46, specifically makes it an offence for a juror to disclose any information relating to the jury's deliberations:

> 649. Every member of a jury who, except for the purposes of
>
> (*a*) an investigation of an alleged offence under subsection 139(2) in relation to a juror, or
>
> (*b*) giving evidence in criminal proceedings in relation to such an offence,
>
> discloses any information relating to the proceedings of the jury when it was absent from the courtroom that was not subsequently disclosed in open court is guilty of an offence punishable on summary conviction.

As Paul Quinlan notes in his excellent article "Secrecy of Jury Deliberations: Is the Cost Too High" (1993) 22 C.R. (4th) 127 at 128: "Although s. 649 was only enacted in 1972, the ban [on disclosure of jury deliberations] had been enforced at common law through contempt of court proceedings available against both the juror and the questioner." See *R.* v. *Dyson* (1971),

[1972] 1 O.R. 744 (H.C.J.). Some of the policy reasons for protecting secrecy include finality of the verdict, preventing jurors from being pressed to expose the reasons for their decision, ensuring and promoting freedom of debate among jurors, and ensuring public confidence in trial by jury: *Ellis* v. *Deheer*, [1922] 2 K.B. 113 (C.A.), *R.* v. *Dyson* (1971), [1972] 1 O.R. 744 (H.C.J.), and *R.* v. *Gumbly* (1996), 112 C.C.C. (3d) 61 at 72–74 (N.S.C.A.)

In *R.* v. *Guess*, [1997] B.C.J. No. 1208 (Prov. Ct.) (QL), the preliminary inquiry judge allowed jurors to testify about the process of deliberation undertaken in a murder charge that they had adjudicated. The preliminary inquiry involved an allegation of obstruction of justice against a fellow juror who had become involved personally with one of the accused in the murder prosecution.

* One of the costs of measures designed to protect the secrecy of jury deliberations, such as section 649 of the *Criminal Code*, has been to preclude the introduction of fresh evidence (i.e., affidavit or testimony of juror) on appeal to attack the verdict because of some impropriety in the jury room so as to avoid a miscarriage of justice. See *R.* v. *Perras (No. 2)* (1974), 18 C.C.C. (2d) 47 (Sask. C.A.) (majority verdict); *R.* v. *Wilson* (1993), 19 C.R. (4th) 132 (Man. C.A.) (alleged communication of juror with RCMP concerning evidence not adduced at trial in relation to accused's co-conspirator); *R.* v. *Thompson* (1961), 46 Cr. App. R. 72 (C.C.A.) (allegation that the jury foreperson had shown jurors a list of the accused's previous convictions, which were not admitted at trial, after a majority of the jury was in favour of acquitting). Indeed, in the well-known English case of *Vaise* v. *Delaval* (1785), 99 E.R. 944 (K.B.), Lord Mansfield did not admit fresh evidence from two jurors showing that the jury verdict had been decided by the casting of lots: cited and summarized in P. Quinlan, "Secrecy of Jury Deliberations: Is the Cost Too High?" (1993) 22 C.R. (4th) 127 at 131–132. But see *R.* v. *Zacharias* (1987), 39 C.C.C. (3d) 280 (B.C.C.A.), where evidence that jurors changed their votes to guilty because they were unaware of the consequences of an inability to reach a verdict obtained from a juror pursuant to an inquiry under section 649(a) was admitted on appeal. Evidence from jurors was also admitted in the cases of *R.* v. *Mercier* (1973), 12 C.C.C. (2d) 377 (Que. C.A.) (Crown Attorney had entered jury room and erased certain writing of the foreperson on the blackboard used by the jurors), and *R.* v. *Mayhew* (1975), 29 C.R.N.S. 242 (Ont. C.A.) (whether conversations by police officers about the criminal record of the accused were possibly overheard by jurors in corridors of the courtroom), although arguably in these latter two cases the evidence did not relate to the deliberations of the jury.

* Another cost to be addressed is the right of social scientists to study jury deliberations for research purposes. Some have suggested that section 649 should be amended to permit the study of jury deliberations: see, for example, Law Reform Commission of Canada, *The Jury in Criminal Trials* (Working Paper 27) (Ottawa: Supply & Services, 1980) at 142, and Doherty J., "Jury Instructions — Effective Communication or Elaborate Camouflage?" (Address to the Criminal Lawyers' Association Conference, Toronto, 1996) at 6. Justice Doherty argues for an exception to section 649 that would enable researchers to study jurors, for example, to determine the extent to which jurors comprehend jury instructions. Doherty J.A. highlights the importance of studying juror comprehension as follows (at 4–5):

> Many who operate within the criminal justice system, including judges, are convinced that the level of juror comprehension is woefully low. They argue that it is unrealistic to think that jurors understand much of what they are told about the law. . . . The social science information, however, provides the most disturbing view of the level of juror comprehension. Studies over the last 25 or 30 years, most of which have been done in the United States indicate the following:
>
> - There are high levels of misunderstanding among jurors on basic issues such as the burden of proof.
> - Judicial instructions do not significantly improve overall juror comprehension, although they do assist in some specific areas.
> - Deliberations among jurors do not appear to significantly improve juror comprehension.
> - Instructions which are presented in "plain English" and which take advantage of other aids (eg. providing the instructions in writing) result in significant improvement in juror understanding.

The issue of juror comprehension is discussed in the following articles, some of which are cited in Justice Doherty's article: K.R. Anderson & B.R. Braun, "The Legal Legacy of John Wayne Gacy: The Irrebuttable Presumption that Juries Understand and Follow Jury Instructions" (1995) 78 Marq. L. Rev. 791; W.W. Steele & E.G. Thornburg, "Jury Instructions: A Persistent Failure to Communicate" (1991) 74 Judicature 249; "Symposium: Making Jury Instructions Comprehensible" (1987) 8 U. Bridgeport L. Rev. 279; G. Kramer & D.M. Koenig, "Do Jurors Understand Criminal Jury Instructions? Analysing the Results of the Michigan Juror Comprehension Project" (1990) 23 U. Mich. J.L. Ref. 401; L.J. Severance, E. Greene & E.F. Loftus, "Toward Criminal Jury Instructions that Jurors Can Understand" (1984) 75 J. Crim. L. & Crim. 198; and R.P. Charrow & V.R. Charrow, "Making Legal Language Understandable: A Psycholinguistic Study of Jury Instructions" (1979) 79 Colum. L. Rev. 1306.

* In addition, it is well established that it is improper for a trial judge to ask the jury to give reasons for its verdict, for example, to particularize the basis of an ambiguous verdict: *R.* v. *Tuckey* (1985), 20 C.C.C. (3d) 502 (Ont. C.A.); *R.* v. *Tempelaar* (14 July 1993), (Ont. C.A.) [unreported], aff'd [1995], 1 S.C.R. 760; *R.* v. *Gauthier* (1996), 108 C.C.C. (3d) 231 (C.A.); *R.* v. *Soloman and Triumph* (1984), 6 Cr. App. R. (S) 120. In *R.* v. *Selles* (20 June 1997), (Ont. C.A.) [not yet reported], the accused was convicted of one count of sexual assault causing bodily harm. Following the verdict, the trial judge asked the jury to answer a number of questions in order to determine which of the six incidents described by the complainant in her evidence had been unanimously accepted as proved. In its argument, the Crown argued that the jury's answer to these questions demonstrated that no prejudice enured to the accused by the non-compliance of the indictment with the provision of s. 581 (1) of the *Criminal Code*. Justice Finlayson, writing for the court, held:

> I do not think that it is appropriate to consider the jury's answer to the question relating to the count on which it was unanimous in order to determine if there has been prejudice. It is well established that it is improper for a trial judge to ask the jury to give reasons for its verdict. The reason for such a prohibition was set out clearly in the case of *R.* v. *Tuckey, Baynham and Walsh* (1985), 20 C.C.C. (3rd) 502 (Ont. C.A.). . . . Lacourciere J.A., for the majority, found that the trial judge had erred in asking the jury to give reasons for its verdict (at P. 513):
>
>> There is generally no justification in a criminal case to ask the jury to answer questions or to particularize the basis of the verdict, whether it be guilty or not guilty. We adopt what was said by the Court of Appeal in England in the case of *R.* v. *Soloman and Triumph* (1984), 6 Cr. App. R. (S) 120 at 126–7:
>>
>>> It is not difficult to see the reason why it is undesirable to ask a jury to explain an otherwise unambiguous verdict. There are many instances of cases, of which the present is one, in which the offence charged may be supported by more than one view of the evidence given in the case. The jury entirely consistent with their oaths may have reached agreement on the general verdict, though not precisely on the same basis of fact, and to invite them to further refine their decision could only lead to confusion.
>
> I would add that a jury's verdict has always been considered sacrosanct. A jury is protected from having to explain how its members voted and for what reason. The anonymity of the jury verdict safeguards the individual juror from personal scrutiny and accountability. Absent allegations of impropriety, a

public investigation into the adjudicative process behind the collective verdict could well have an inhibiting effect on individual jurors who would otherwise be prepared to take unpopular positions with respect to the case before them. I agree with Lacourciere J.A. when he stated in *R.* v. *Tuckey*, *Supra*, at 514, that:

> To require [the jury] to state particulars of the offence found is a practice fraught with danger and contrary to traditional practice. While it may be helpful to the trial judge in assessing an appropriate sentence, it represents a serious departure from criminal practice which *ought not to be condoned or continued.* [Emphasis added.]

1.3 THE CONSTITUTIONAL DIMENSION

1.3(a) **Is There a Constitutional Right to Trial by Jury?**

* The *Canadian Charter of Rights and Freedoms* recognizes the importance of trial by jury and gives it explicit constitutional status in section 11(f). Section 11(f) states:

> 11. Any person charged with an offence has the right
>
> . . .
>
> (*f*) except in the case of an offence under military law tried before a military tribunal, to the benefit of trial by jury where the maximum punishment for the offence is imprisonment for five years or a more severe punishment.

1.3(a)(i) **When Is Section 11(f) Triggered?**

* By its clear wording, section 11(f) is triggered only by those non-military offences where the accused is liable to be imprisoned for five or more years. Consequently, prior to recent amendments to the *Young Offenders Act*, R.S.C. 1985, c. Y-1, young offenders tried in youth courts had no right to trial by jury since the maximum punishment was less than five years' imprisonment: *R.* v. *B.(S.)* (1989), 76 Sask. R. 308 (C.A.); *R.* v. *L.(R.)* (1986), 52 C.R. (3d) 209 (Ont. C.A.). However, section 20(1) of the *Young Offenders Act* was amended in 1995 to include subsection (k.1)(i)(a), which provides a sentence for first-degree murder of ten years, which includes a sentence of custody not to exceed six years. Consequently, young offenders charged with first-degree murder now have the right to be tried by a jury. However, it is questionable whether youths charged with second-degree murder have a similar right. While the sentence for second-degree murder under subsection 20(1)(k.1)(ii) is seven years, there is a potential to serve

only four of those years in custody, pursuant to 20(1)(k.1)(ii)(a). The remainder of the sentence is served in the community, under conditional supervision: see section 20(1)(k.1)(ii)(b). However, since it appears that the young offender may be required to complete the full disposition in custody if he or she breaches the conditional supervision (see sections 26.3(b) and 26.6(2)(b)), section 11(f) may be triggered.

* It has been held that section 11(f) does not apply:
  - to corporations, since corporations cannot be imprisoned: *PPG Industries Canada Ltd.* v. *Canada (A.G.)* (1983), 146 D.L.R. (3d) 261 (B.C.C.A.);
  - at extradition proceedings: *Waddell* v. *Canada (A.G.)* (23 August 1996), (B.C.S.C.) [unreported] [summarized at 32 W.C.B. (2d) 14];
  - at summary contempt proceedings: *MacMillan Bloedel Ltd.* v. *Simpson* (1993), 84 C.C.C. (3d) 559 (B.C.C.A.). See too *R.* v. *Cohn* (1984), 48 O.R. (2d) 65 (C.A.);
  - to dangerous offender applications under section 754(2) of the *Criminal Code*: *R.* v. *Lyons*, [1987] 2 S.C.R. 309;
  - to confer a right to trial by judge alone: *R.* v. *Turpin*, [1989] 1 S.C.R. 1296 at 1322–23;
  - to invalidate section 265(4) of the *Criminal Code* (dealing with the requirement of an "air of reality" before the defence of honest but mistaken belief in consent is left with the jury) or the more general common law requirement that before a defence is placed before a jury, the trial judge must be satisfied that there is some evidence on which a jury properly instructed could acquit. These are questions of law, properly within the realm of the trial judge: *R.* v. *Osolin*, [1993] 4 S.C.R. 595 at 691;
  - or to proceedings where an accused has, without a legitimate excuse,[1] failed to attend his jury trial and who, by virtue of sections 598(1) and (2) of the *Criminal Code*, is then deemed to have elected trial by judge alone: *R.* v. *Lee*, [1989] 2 S.C.R. 1384.

* In the United States, there are two federal constitutional provisions that provide a right to trial by jury. Article III of the U.S. Constitution, § 2, cl. 3

---

1 In *R.* v. *Harris* (1991), 66 C.C.C. (3d) 536 at 539 (Ont. C.A.), the Court of Appeal held that an honest mistake with respect to the date of the trial constitutes a legitimate excuse and that "nothing less than an intentional avoidance of appearing at trial for the purpose of impeding or frustrating the trial or with the intention of avoiding its consequences, or failure to appear because of a mistake resulting from wilful blindness, should deprive an accused of his constitutional right to trial by jury guaranteed by section 11(f)."

states in part that "[t]he trial of all Crimes, except in Cases of Impeachment, shall be by Jury." The Sixth Amendment also provides in part:

> In all criminal prosecutions, the accused shall enjoy the right to a speedy and public trial, by an impartial jury of the State and district wherein the crime shall have been committed . . .

Unlike section 11(f) of the *Charter*, neither of these constitutional provisions has a limiting punishment clause. However, it has been held that trial by jury is constitutionally mandated only for non-petty or serious offences. Offences that carry a sentence of imprisonment of more than six months are presumed serious, though it is open to the accused to point to additional penalties that indicate that the legislature clearly intended the offence to be a serious one: *Blanton* v. *North Las Vegas*, 489 U.S. 538 (1989) and *U.S.* v. *Nachtigal*, 113 S. Ct. 1072 (1993).

1.3(a)(ii) **Can the Section 11(f) Right Be Waived?**

* The right to trial by jury in section 11(f) is not absolute but qualified by the word "benefit." The significance of this is discussed by the Supreme Court of Canada in *R.* v. *Turpin*, [1989] 1 S.C.R. 1296 at 1312–13:

> The word "benefit", on the other hand, can just as easily be read as importing a qualification on the right to a jury trial, a qualification which recognizes the reality that in some circumstances a jury trial may not be a benefit and may even be a burden on the accused. As Professor Charles Whitebread and Christopher Slobogin observe in their treatise *Criminal Procedure: An Analysis of Cases and Concepts* (2nd ed. 1986), at p. 607:
>
>> The defendant may want to waive a jury trial when he feels that a jury panel composed of members of the community will be prejudiced against his case. This may be especially true when the defendant's alleged crime has received wide publicity or is particularly gruesome. The defendant may also feel that a judge would be less apt than a jury to draw negative conclusions from the defendant's appearance or manner of speech. Or, he may merely prefer that the arbiter of his fate be one person trained in the law rather than twelve laypersons.
>
> In other words, the intent of the provision could be to guarantee an accused the benefit of a jury trial where a jury trial is in fact from his or her perspective a benefit but not to impose it on the accused when it is not. In my view, this . . . interpretation of the s. 11(*f*) right is more in tune with the purpose of the provision if that purpose is correctly perceived as being to protect the interests of the accused. The accused's

> interests would seem to be better served by construing s. 11(*f*) as conferring a "benefit" on the accused which can be waived by him if it seems to be in his best interests to do so.

* Consequently, since section 11(f) confers only the right to "the benefit" of trial by jury, the right can be waived: *R.* v. *Turpin*, [1989] 1 S.C.R. 1296. As Wilson J. held for the Court (at 1313):

> To compel an accused to accept a jury trial when he or she considers a jury trial a burden rather than a benefit would appear, in Frankfurter J.'s words, "to imprison a man in his privileges and call it the Constitution": see *Adams* v. *U.S. ex rel. McCann*, 317 U.S. 269 at 280 (1942).

* Once an accused waives his or her section 11(f) right, the *Criminal Code* provisions setting out the mode of trial govern: *R.* v. *Turpin*, [1989] 1 S.C.R. 1296 at 1322–23. In other words, even if the accused wishes not to be tried by a jury, if he or she is charged with an offence for which the *Criminal Code* requires trial by jury, the *Criminal Code* prevails. As Wilson J. held in *Turpin* (at 1323):

> There is, in my view, nothing in s. 11(*f*) to give the appellants a constitutional right to elect their mode of trial or a constitutional right to be tried by judge alone so as to make s. 11(*f*) inconsistent with the mandatory jury provisions of the *Criminal Code*.

* In the United States, a jury trial can only be waived with the consent of the prosecutor and judge: *Singer* v. *U.S.*, 380 U.S. 24 at 36 (1965); *U.S.* v. *Clark*, 943 F.2d 775 (7th Cir. 1991). See, too, Rule 23(a) of the Federal Rules of Criminal Procedure.

1.3(a)(iii) **Does Section 11(f) Require a Twelve-Person Jury?**

* When one thinks of trial by jury, one no doubt immediately thinks of the movie *Twelve Angry Men* — that is, of a jury composed of twelve individuals. However, it is not all that clear why the common law settled on the number twelve. In *Williams* v. *Florida*, 399 U.S. 78 (1970), Justice White of the U.S. Supreme Court attempted to arrive at an answer but was left to conclude (at 87–90):

> . . . history, however, affords little insight into the considerations that gradually led the size of that body to be generally fixed at 12. Some have suggested that the number 12 was fixed upon simply because that was the number of the presentment jury from the hundred, from which the petit jury developed. Other, less circular but more fanciful reasons for the number 12 have been given, "but they were all brought forward after the number was

> fixed," and rest on little more than mystical or superstitious insights into the significance of "12". Lord Coke's explanation that the "*number of twelve* is much respected *in holy writ*, as 12 *apostles*, 12 *stones*, 12 *tribes, etc.*" is typical. In short, while sometime in the 14th century the size of the jury at common law came to be fixed generally at 12, that particular feature of the jury system appears to have been a historical accident, unrelated to the great purposes which gave rise to the jury in the first place. [Footnotes omitted.]

See too *R.* v. *Genest* (1990), 61 C.C.C. (3d) 251 at 255–59 (Que. C.A.).

* Section 11(f) of the *Charter* does not define what constitutes a "jury." However, by virtue of section 631(5) of the *Criminal Code*, juries in Canada are composed of twelve individuals. Section 631(5) states:

> Where the number of persons who answers to their names under subsection (3) is not sufficient to provide a full jury, the clerk of the court shall proceed in accordance with subsections (3) and (4) *until twelve jurors are sworn*. [Emphasis added.]

In *R.* v. *Chambers* [1990] 2 S.C.R. 1293 at 1304, Justice Cory, for the majority, held: "It has been held by this Court that an accused should not be lightly deprived of the *right to be tried by a jury of 12 persons*. See . . . [*R.* v. *Spek*, [1982] 2 S.C.R. 730 at 741]" [emphasis added]. Since Cory J. did not refer to section 11(f), he was probably referring to the common law (and/or the statutory right by virtue of section 631(5) of the *Criminal Code*), as opposed to a constitutional right. See also the reference to twelve jurors in section 643(1).

* Indeed, it has been held that a jury reduced from twelve to ten during the course of a trial pursuant to section 644(2) of the *Criminal Code* does not violate section 11(f): see *R.* v. *Genest* (1990), 61 C.C.C. (3d) 251 (Que. C.A.), leave to appeal refused (1991), 62 C.C.C. (3d) vi (note) (S.C.C.); *R.* v. *Lessard* (1992), 74 C.C.C. (3d) 552 (Que. C.A.), leave to appeal refused (1992), 145 N.R. 390 (note) (S.C.C.). Section 644(2) states:

> Where in the course of a trial a member of the jury dies or is discharged pursuant to subsection (1), the jury shall, unless the judge otherwise directs and if *the number of jurors is not reduced below ten*, be deemed to remain properly constituted for all purposes of the trial and the trial shall proceed and a verdict may be given accordingly. [Emphasis added.]

In *Lessard*, the Quebec Court of Appeal held (at 559):

> . . . [T]he mere reduction in the number of jurors from 12 to 11 and even to 10, does not prevent it from fulfilling its functions, that is, to decide questions of fact, to reach a verdict reflecting contemporary social values, to act as a watch-dog against state oppression, to maintain the credibility of the judicial system and to serve in the education of the public. I do not see what

> magic connotation can be attributed to the number 12 and how the discharge of one or even two jurors, would put in question the institution itself, having regard to the fundamental values protected by section 11(*f*).

* The *Criminal Code* provisions permitting six-person juries in the Yukon Territory and the Northwest Territories have been declared unconstitutional, pursuant to section 15(1), and were repealed by Parliament in 1992: *R.* v. *Bailey* (1985), 17 C.R.R. 1 (Y.T.S.C.); *R.* v. *Punch*, [1985] N.W.T.R. 373 (S.C.); and *R.* v. *Emile*, [1988] N.W.T.R. 196 (C.A.). While these challenges were made under the equality provisions of section 15(1), the Court of Appeal in *Emile* noted (at 209) that the "public perception is that an accused person suffers disadvantage when he is tried by a jury panel of six persons" and that the "functions of the jury . . . are better fulfilled by a 12-person jury than by a six-person jury."

* In the United States, while all federal juries are composed of twelve members (see Rule 23(b) of the Federal Rules of Criminal Procedure) and require unanimity (Rule 31(b)), the state legislatures are free to tinker with the size of their juries. They can reduce the number of jurors from twelve to six, *Williams* v. *Florida*, 399 U.S. 78 (1970), but not below six: *Ballew* v. *Georgia*, 435 U.S. 223 (1978). In *Williams*, the court offered the following justification, similar to that advanced by the Quebec Court of Appeal in *Lessard*, for its opinion (at 100–1):

> The purpose of the jury trial, as we noted in Duncan, is to prevent oppression by the Government. . . . Given this purpose, the essential feature of a jury obviously lies in the interposition between the accused and his accuser of the commonsense judgment of a group of laymen, and in the community participation and shared responsibility that results from that group's determination of guilt or innocence. The performance of this role is not a function of the particular number of the body that makes up the jury. To be sure, the number should probably be large enough to promote group deliberation, free from outside attempts at intimidation, and to provide a fair possibility for obtaining a representative cross-section of the community. But we find little reason to think that these goals are in any meaningful sense less likely to be achieved when the jury numbers six, than when it numbers 12 — particularly if the requirement of unanimity is retained. And, certainly the reliability of the jury as a fact finder hardly seems likely to be a function of its size. [Footnotes omitted.]

In addition, in *Apodaca* v. *Oregon*, 406 U.S. 404 (1972), the U.S. Supreme Court held that states can abolish the requirement of unanimity. The guilty verdicts in *Apodaca* and a companion case were made by a 10–2 and an 11–1 vote. Seven years later, in *Burch* v. *Louisiana*, 441 U.S. 130 (1979), the U.S. Supreme Court revisited *Apodaca* and held that the verdict must be unanimous where the jury is composed of six individuals.

1.3(b) Does the *Charter* Guarantee Trial by an Impartial Jury?

* The right to be tried by an impartial jury is found in section 11(d) of the *Charter*. Section 11(d) states:

> 11. Any person charged with an offence has the right
>
> . . .
>
> (*d*) to be presumed innocent until proven guilty according to law in a fair and public hearing by an independent and impartial tribunal.

1.4 THE CHARACTERISTICS OF THE JURY

* A number of justices on the Supreme Court of Canada have in various opinions set out the following characteristics that all juries should possess in order for them to accomplish their goals: impartiality, competence, and representativeness. See *R.* v. *Sherratt*, [1991] 1 S.C.R. 509 at 525; *R.* v. *Bain*, [1992] 1 S.C.R. 91 at 159, Stevenson J. and at 114, Gonthier, McLachlin, and Iacobucci JJ.; and *R.* v. *Biddle*, [1995] 1 S.C.R. 761 at 787–90, Gonthier J. and McLachlin J. (L'Heureux-Dubé J. concurring with McLachlin J., but only on this observation). Consequently, it is suggested that all three of these characteristics are constitutional imperatives under sections 11(d) and (f) of the *Charter*.

1.4(a) Impartiality

* There is no question that a jury must be impartial, which, as noted above, is explicitly mandated by section 11(d) of the *Charter*. See *R.* v. *Sherratt*, [1991] 1 S.C.R. 509. As Justice Doherty said in *R.* v. *Parks* (1993), 15 O.R. (3d) 324 at 334 (C.A.), "[a]n impartial jury is a crucial first step in the conduct of a fair trial": see also *R.* v. *Barrow*, [1987] 2 S.C.R. 694 at 710. Moreover, as Justice Le Dain highlighted in *R.* v. *Valente*, [1985] 2 S.C.R. 673 at 689:

> . . . [I]mpartiality . . . [is] fundamental not only to the capacity to do justice in a particular case but also to individual and public confidence in the administration of justice. Without that confidence the system cannot command the respect and acceptance that are essential to its effective operation.

1.4(b) **Competence**

* The characteristic of competence was first introduced in *R.* v. *Bain*, [1992] 1 S.C.R. 91 at 114, by Justice Gonthier (McLachlin and Iacobucci JJ. concurring), in his dissenting opinion. Gonthier J. stated:

> A further quality of a proper jury that has not been discussed in *Sherratt* . . . is competence. Jurors should not only be representative and impartial, they should also be able to understand the trial, their role in the trial, the evidence that is presented, the principles they have to apply, among other things. This requirement of competence is not mentioned in relevant legislation, aside from general requirements of mental health and linguistic capability, but it is implicit. Most trials require the same competence as is involved in the daily pursuit of one's affairs, and the ability to speak and understand one of the official languages will suffice. Some trials are more complex and complicated, however, especially in the area of economic crimes, to name only one, and then a tampering with randomness may be appropriate to achieve a minimal ability to understand the evidence and issues.

* The characteristic of competence was recognized again by Justice McLachlin in her concurring opinion in *R.* v. *Biddle*, [1995] 1 S.C.R. 761 at 788–89 (Justice L'Heureux-Dubé concurring, but only on this observation). To date, only four justices of the Supreme Court of Canada have endorsed competence as essential for a jury.

* While the notion that juries should be competent is not a controversial one, it does raise the important issue of how competence is to be achieved. Justice Gonthier in *Bain* appears to suggest that it may be appropriate in a complex fraud trial, for example, to "tamper with randomness" in order to select jurors able to understand the issues and evidence. But how is this goal to be achieved? Are jurors to be pre-screened for a level of education and/or experience that would enable them to be competent? If this is what Justice Gonthier has in mind, where would the trial judge find the jurisdiction to "tamper with randomness"? One option is for the trial judge to exercise his or her "stand by" power pursuant to section 633 which states:

> The judge may direct a juror whose name has been called pursuant to subsection 631(3) to stand by for reasons of personal hardship or any other reasonable cause.

Under this section, lack of competence could be caught under the ground "any other reasonable cause." See *R.* v. *Holcomb* (1973), 6 N.B.R. (2d) 485 at 492 (C.A), aff'd (1973), 6 N.B.R. (2d) 858 (S.C.C.), where the Court of Appeal interpreted the meaning of "any other . . . cause," albeit in the context of what is now section 644 of the *Criminal Code*, to include "any cause which the

Judge deems reasonable in the conduct of a trial which requires a competent and impartial jury."

1.4(c) **Representativeness**

* The characteristic of representativeness was first introduced by the Supreme Court of Canada in *R.* v. *Sherratt*, [1991] 1 S.C.R. 509, where Justice L'Heureux-Dubé (Justices Sopinka, Gonthier, and Cory concurring) held (at 525):

> [The] perceived importance of the jury and the *Charter* right to jury trial is meaningless without some guarantee that it will perform its duties impartially and represent, as far as is possible and appropriate in the circumstances, the larger community. Indeed, without the two characteristics of impartiality and representativeness, a jury would be unable to perform properly many of the functions that make its existence desirable in the first place. Provincial legislation guarantees representativeness, at least in the initial array. The random selection process, coupled with the sources from which this selection is made, ensures the representativeness of Canadian criminal juries. . . . Thus, little if any objection can be made regarding this crucial characteristic of juries.

* Representativeness is crucial, because it ensures "[a] diversity of views and outlooks," which is part of the "genius of the jury system" and makes "jury verdicts a reflection of the shared values of the community": *R.* v. *Parks* (1993), 15 O.R. (3d) 324 at 336 (C.A.). So, too, in *R.* v. *Sherratt*, [1991] 1 S.C.R. 509 at 523, Justice L'Heureux-Dubé held that "[t]he jury . . . due to its representative character . . . acts as the conscience of the community" and Judge Irving Kaufman, head of the U.S. Federal Judiciary Committee on the Operation of the Jury System (cited in *R.* v. *F.(A.)* (1994), 30 C.R. (4th) 333 at 364, note 50 (Ont. Gen. Div.), Stach J.), similarly remarked:

> If the law is to reflect the moral sense of the community, the whole community — and not just a special part — must help to shape it. If the jury's verdict is to reflect the community's judgment — the whole community's judgment — jurors must be fairly selected from a cross-section of the whole community, not merely a segment of it.

Representativeness is also a means of enhancing the chances of an impartial verdict. As Justice Doherty recognized in *R.* v. *Parks* (1993), 15 O.R. (3d) 324 at 342 (C.A.):

> The "diffused impartiality" produced by the melding of 12 diverse and individual perspectives into a single decision-making body may also counter personal prejudices.

See also the comments of Justice Gonthier in *R.* v. *Bain*, [1992] 1 S.C.R. 91 at 113, and *R.* v. *Biddle*, [1995] 1 S.C.R. 761 at 787–88. In *Biddle*, a case concerning whether the Crown's use of its ability to stand by jurors pursuant to sections 634(1) and (2) of the *Criminal Code* to create an all-female jury amounted to a reasonable apprehension of bias, Justice Gonthier felt compelled to discuss representativeness given the effect of the stand asides on the composition of the jury (at 787–88):

> Representativeness, on the other hand, is more susceptible to being affected by the selection process. The present case is an excellent example of this. As I observed in *R. v. Bain, supra*, representativeness is a characteristic which furthers the perception of impartiality even if not fully ensuring it. While representativeness is not an essential quality of a jury, it is one to be sought after. The surest guarantee of jury impartiality consists in the combination of the representativeness with the requirement of a unanimous verdict. Consequently, an apparent attempt by the prosecution to modify the composition of the jury so as to exclude representativeness, as occurred in this case, in itself undermines the impartiality of a jury.

* With the *Criminal Code* having been amended in 1992 to abolish Crown stand asides following the decision of the Supreme Court in *R.* v. *Bain*, [1992] 1 S.C.R. 91 (see the discussion of this issue below in chapter 11), the issue of representativeness will probably arise in cases involving the discriminatory use of peremptory challenges (see the discussion below in chapter 11) and challenges to the array pursuant to section 629(1) of the *Criminal Code* (see the discussion below in chapter 2) or pursuant to the relevant section of provincial jury acts dealing with the qualifications of jurors.

* There appears, however, to be a growing debate among Supreme Court justices as to the role that representativeness should play in jury selection. In *R.* v. *Sherratt*, [1991] 1 S.C.R. 509, Justices Sopinka, Gonthier, and Cory concurred with Justice L'Heureux-Dubé's majority opinion in which it was stated that (at 525):

> The random selection process, coupled with the sources from which this selection is made, ensures the representativeness of Canadian criminal juries. . . . *Thus, little if any objection can be made regarding this crucial characteristic of juries.* [Emphasis added.]

So, too, in *R.* v. *Bain*, [1992] 1 S.C.R. 91, Justice Gonthier, in his dissenting opinion, with Justices McLachlin and Iacobucci concurring, affirmed *Sherratt* when he noted (at 113):

> In *Sherratt*, . . . this Court has also elaborated on some of the fundamental characteristics a jury *must possess* to exercise its duty properly, that is impartiality and representativeness. [Emphasis added.]

However, some two years later in *R.* v. *Biddle*, [1995] 1 S.C.R. 761, Justices McLachlin and L'Heureux-Dubé reacted to Justice Gonthier's discussion of representativeness with respect to the trial panel and appear to have softened the positions that they took in *Bain* and *Sherratt*. The majority opinion in *Biddle* did not discuss the issue. McLachlin J., in her concurring opinion, stated (at 788–89):

> Gonthier J. . . . suggests that a jury must be "impartial, representative and competent." I agree that a jury must be impartial and competent. But, with respect, the law has never suggested that a jury must be representative. For hundreds of years, juries in this country were composed entirely of men. Are we to say that all these juries were for that reason partial and incompetent?
>
> To say that a jury must be representative is to confuse the means with the end. I agree that representativeness may provide extra assurance of impartiality and competence. I would even go so far as to say that it is generally a good thing. But I cannot accept that it is essential in every case, nor that its absence automatically entitles an accused person to a new trial.
>
> To say that a jury must be representative is to set a standard impossible of achievement. The community can be divided into a hundred different groups on the basis of variants such as gender, race, class and education. Must every group be represented on every jury? If not, which groups are to be chosen and on what grounds? If so, how much representation is enough? Do we demand parity based on regional population figures? Or will something less suffice? I see no need to start down this problematic path of the representative jury, provided the impartiality and competence of the jury are assured. Representativeness may be a means to achieving this end. But it should not be elevated to the status of an absolute requirement.

Moreover, even Justice Gonthier appears to have tempered his opinion on representativeness in *Biddle* where he stated (at 788) that ". . . representativeness is not an essential quality of a jury" but rather a quality that should be sought after.

* It is suggested that these comments by the Supreme Court on representativeness can be to some extent reconciled by differentiating the right to a representative jury array from the right to a representative jury trial panel. It may be impossible, as Justice McLachlin suggests in *Biddle*, to ensure true representativeness in the actual trial jury, but that does not necessarily mean that the characteristic of representativeness does not have a role to play in jury selection. *Sherratt* can be interpreted at a minimum as suggesting that if representativeness is a constitutional

principle under section 11(f), it is satisfied for the jury array as long as the array is chosen in a random manner from the population in the province.[2] However, where a provision of a provincial jury act excludes either expressly or by implication a segment of the population, thereby limiting the source of the random selection, *Sherratt* suggests that such a section is constitutionally infirm by virtue of not only section 11(f) but also section 15(1) of the *Charter*. We are confident that this is a principle that all members of the Supreme Court would endorse in the appropriate case. (We are not so confident what the result would be in a case where the argument attempted to extend representativeness to the actual jury.)

* As is described below, challenges can be made to the pool of jurors from which a particular jury is to be selected. These challenges are known as "challenges to the array." See 2.7 "Challenging the Array." Even in the early challenge to the array cases, the courts held that while accused are not entitled to a jury of their peers, they are entitled to a process that does not "systematically exclude(s), either by design or unwittingly, an identifiable group from serving on a jury": see *R.* v. *Bird* (1984), 1 C.N.L.R. 122 (Sask. C.A.); *R.* v. *Butler* (1984), 3 C.R. (4th) 174 (B.C.C.A.). Similarly, section 629(1) of the *Criminal Code* permits an accused to challenge the representativeness of the jury array where it is alleged that the lack of representation was a result of "partiality, fraud or wilful misconduct on the part of the sheriff or other officer by whom the panel was returned."

* This distinction between a representative "source(s)" for the selection of the jury array as opposed to a representative trial panel is recognized by D. Pomerant in *Multiculturalism, Representation and the Jury Selection Process in Canadian Criminal Cases* (Working Document) (Ottawa: Department of Justice, 1994) at 26 & 39:

> . . . the Court in *Sherratt* referred to representativeness in another sense: in the "initial array," . . . It also observed that such representativeness is "guaranteed" by provincial *legislation* requiring random selection and defining the sources from which the selection is made. It is quite a different matter to

---

2 See H. Fukurai, E.W. Butler, & R. Krooth, "Cross-Sectional Jury Representation or Systematic Jury Representation? Simple Random and Cluster Sampling Strategies in Jury Selection" [1991] J. Crim. Justice 31, cited in D. Pomerant, *Multiculturalism, Representation and the Jury Selection Process in Canadian Criminal Cases* (Working Document) (Ottawa: Department of Justice, 1994) at 38, for an argument that "cluster sampling" may achieve a more representative array than random sampling.

assess representativeness by focussing on the selection of individual jurors for a trial panel, than it is to focus on the *source from which the trial panel is selected* and the *general selection process.* In the United States, which is the only other jury trial jurisdiction to accept the goal of representative juries, the latter focus has been adopted . . .

The sources of selection should be reasonably representative of the community where the offence is alleged to have been committed. The applicable selection procedures and the manner of their execution should not result in the exclusion or under-representation of significant minority groups in the community, and an effective remedy for inappropriate exclusions that do occur should be made available. [Emphasis added.]

* As Pomerant notes, a similar distinction is made in the United States, where it is recognized that while there is no right to a jury of one's peers or a right to a fair cross-section of the community in the actual trial jury panel, there is a fair cross-section requirement of the Sixth Amendment with respect to the jury pool from which the trial jury is chosen: *Holland* v. *Illinois*, 493 U.S. 474 (1990). In *Taylor v. Louisiana*, 419 U.S. 522 at 530–31 (1975), the U.S. Supreme Court held:

> We accept the fair-cross-section requirement as fundamental to the jury trial guaranteed by the Sixth Amendment and are convinced that the requirement has solid foundation. The purpose of a jury is to guard against the exercise of arbitrary power — to make available the commonsense judgment of the community as a hedge against the overzealous or mistaken prosecutor and in preference to the professional or perhaps over conditioned or biased response of a judge . . . This prophylactic vehicle is not provided if the jury pool is made up of only special segments of the populace or if large, distinctive groups are excluded from the pool. Community participation in the administration of the criminal law, moreover, is not only consistent with our democratic heritage but is also critical to public confidence in the fairness of the criminal justice system. Restricting jury service to only special groups or excluding identifiable segments playing major roles in the community cannot be squared with the constitutional concept of jury trial. "Trial by jury presupposes a jury drawn from a pool broadly representative of the community as well as impartial in a specific case . . . [T]he broad representative character of the jury should be maintained, partly as assurance of a diffused impartiality and partly because sharing in the administration of justice is a phase of civic responsibility."

As Professors Saltzburg and Capra highlight in their summary of the case law, in order to establish a *prima facie* violation of the fair cross-section requirement, the accused must demonstrate (i) that the group excluded from the jury array is a distinctive group within the community; (ii) that the representation of the group in the array is not fair and reasonable in relation to the number of such persons in the community; and (iii) that this under-representation was the result of systematic exclusion of the group in the jury selection process. Once a *prima facie* violation is established, the burden shifts to the state to show that the inclusion of the under-represented group would be "incompatible with a significant state interest": S.A. Saltzburg & D.J. Capra, *American Criminal Procedure: Cases and Commentary*, 4th ed. (St. Paul, Minn.: West Publishing Co., 1992) at 907–9, referring to *Duren* v. *Missouri*, 439 U.S. 357 (1979).

* In *R.* v. *Church of Scientology of Toronto and Jacqueline Matz* (1997), 33 O.R. (3d) 65 (C.A.), the Ontario Court of Appeal held (at 120–21):

> The right to a representative jury roll is not absolute in the sense that the accused is entitled to a roll representative of all of the many groups that make up Canadian society. This level of representativeness would be impossible to obtain. There are a number of practical barriers inherent in the selection process that make complete representativeness impossible. The roll is selected from a discrete geographical district which itself may or may not be representative of the broader Canadian society.
>
> Further, the critical characteristic of impartiality in the petit jury is ensured, in part, by the fact that the roll and the panel are produced through a random selection process. To require the sheriff to assemble a fully representative roll or panel would run counter to the random selection process. The sheriff would need to add potential jurors to the roll or the panel based upon perceived characteristics required for representativeness. The selection process would become much more intrusive since the sheriff in order to carry out the task of selecting a representative roll would require information from potential jurors as to their race, religion, country of origin and other characteristics considered essential to achieve representativeness. The point of this is not to demonstrate that a jury panel or roll cannot or should not be representative, but that the right to a representative panel or roll is an inherently qualified one. There cannot be an absolute right to a representative panel or roll.

* However, the Court went on to note (at 121), with reference to the U.S. Cases referred to above, that "[i]t may be, however, that exclusion of certain segments of society from jury service would infringe the requirement of a representative cross-section." According to *Scientology*, in order for section 11 to be engaged, the accused has to demonstrate that a "distinctive" group

was excluded. On the issue of distinctiveness, Justice Rosenberg, for the Court, held (at 122):

> I hesitate to attempt to articulate an all-inclusive test of distinctiveness such as "some immutable characteristic." In my view, it is preferable to deal with each case having regard to the purposes of the representativeness requirement as set out by L'Heureux-Dubé in *Sherratt.* The essential quality that the representativeness requirement brings to the jury function is the possibility of different perspectives from a diverse group of persons. The representativeness requirement seeks to avoid the risk that persons with these different perspectives, and who are otherwise available, will be systematically excluded from the jury roll.

1.4(c)(i) **Exclusions Based on Citizenship**

* In *R.* v. *Church of Scientology of Toronto and Jacqueline Matz* (1997), 33 O.R. (3d) 65 (C.A.), it was argued that the exclusion of non-citizens from the jury pool by the *Juries Act* in Ontario violates sections 7, 11(f), and 15(1) of the *Charter.* Justice Rosenberg, on behalf of the Court, held that the qualification of citizenship for jury duty was not constitutionally infirm.

* The Ontario Court of Appeal confirmed that sections 11(f) and 11(d) of the *Charter* guarantee that the jury pool from which the petit jury will be selected will be representative. However, the Court went on to hold that the exclusion of non-citizens did not offend the entitlement to a representative jury. Justice Rosenberg held (at 121, 122, 123, 124):

> In my view, there is no characteristic that persons bring to the fact-finding process of the jury *based solely on their immigration status.* Canadian citizens are of all races, nationalities, ethnic origin, colour, religion, sex, age, and ability. Immigration status is simply not a relevant characteristic when regard is had to the rationale underlying the right to a representative pool. A jury pool selected from Canadian citizens represents the larger community for the purposes of trial by jury. . . .
>
> The essential quality that the representativeness requirement brings to the jury function is the possibility of different perspectives from a diverse group of persons. The representativeness requirement seeks to avoid the risk that persons with these different perspectives, and who are otherwise available, will be systematically excluded from the jury roll.
>
> Exclusion of non-citizens does not infringe the representativeness or fair cross-section requirement in this sense. There was no evidence that non-citizens as a group share any common thread or basic similarity in attitude, ideas or experience that would not be brought to the jury process, by citizens. . . .

> In the context of jury representativeness, citizenship, like residency in the province is not an improper basis for defining the parameters of the jury roll. As La Forest J. wrote in *Andrews v. Law Society of British Columbia* at p. 196, "[C]itizenship is a very special status that not only incorporates rights and duties but serves a highly important symbolic function as a badge identifying people as members of the Canadian polity." All free and democratic societies have established a unique status like citizenship to which attach certain rights, privileges and obligations closely related to the concept of self-government. It will be recalled that in speaking of the importance of the jury function, L'Heureux-Dubé held in *Sherratt* that the jury can act as the conscience of the community and as the final bulwark against oppressive laws or their enforcement. I see no reason why this important aspect of self-government should not be reserved for citizens, where, as here, exclusion of non-citizens does not affect the representativeness of the jury roll. . . .
>
> In the context of s. 11, the right to a jury trial carries a right to a petit jury selected from a jury roll that is reasonably representative of the community having been selected from a fair cross-section of the community. Exclusion of persons based solely on their immigration status does not detract from the protection afforded an accused by s. 11 of the *Charter*.

The Court of Appeal buttressed its decision with reference to the following statistical evidence presented in the case (at 122–23):

> From my review of the evidence, it seems that the expert tended to use non-citizenship opinion as a proxy for minority opinion. The evidence, however, simply does not bear out the inference that exclusion of non-citizens disproportionately excludes minorities from the jury. As pointed out above, almost one-half of the 1.7 million residents of Metropolitan Toronto over the age of 18 were not born in Canada, but most, close to three-quarters, have become Canadian citizens. . . .
>
> According to the evidence adduced in the *Laws* case itself, including non-citizens in the panel would increase the likelihood of selecting a black person for the panel by only .9%. In my view, this cannot affect the representative nature of the array.

* Statutory juror disqualifications can contravene the equality rights guarantees provided by section 15(l) of the *Charter*. In *R.* v. *Church of Scientology and Jacqueline Matz* (1997), 33 O.R. (3d) 65 (C.A.), the Ontario Court of Appeal did not have to resolve whether the citizenship disqualification did so. The Court held that the appellants, including Matz, a non-citizen, did not have standing to raise the section 15(l) claim on behalf of excluded non-citizens (at 108, 112–13):

> . . . it is my view that the appellants seek to rely upon the s. 15 *Charter* rights of other persons and cannot do so. In the context of this case, the validity of the jury selection process must be measured by the rights guaranteed to accused persons under s. 11 of the *Charter*. . . .
>
> The doctrine in *Big M Drug Mart* gives an accused the right to defend a criminal charge by arguing that *the law under which the accused is charged* is unconstitutional. That is not the defence raised here. In my view, *Big M Drug Mart* does not stand for the proposition that an accused may assert the personal rights of other actors in the proceedings, except where the possible infringement of those rights affects the accused's rights. . . . Their rights as accused flow primarily from s. 11(d) and (f) as persons "charged with an offence" . . .
>
> Further, I see no policy basis to extend *Big M Drug Mart* to permit the appellants to assert the s. 15 rights of potential jurors. The Supreme Court of Canada has repeatedly affirmed the personal nature of s. 15 rights. . . .
>
> The rights asserted by the appellants in this case under s. 15 are entirely different [from the claim made in *R.* v. *Bain*, [1992] 1 S.C.R. 91]. It is a claim not that the jury roll by reason of exclusion of non-citizens deprived them of a trial by an impartial tribunal, but that non-citizens were deprived of *their* rights to participate on a jury.[3]

The Court went further with respect to the appellant Matz and held that, even assuming section 15(l) applied, she failed to make out a restriction of that right (at 113–14):

> As I understand it, Matz also asserts a s. 15 violation on the theory that, as a member of a discrete and insular minority, the disqualification of persons like her from jury service violates her own right to be treated without discrimination as mandated by s. 15. . . .

3 The Court summarily dismissed the section 7 argument, holding (at 115) that "[t]he claim based on s. 7 of the *Charter* is an attempt, indirectly, to acquire standing to argue the equality rights of potential jurors." The Court further rejected an argument that under s. 7, an accused was entitled to a properly constituted jury (i.e., one that did not violate s. 15(l)). The Court held (at 115–16) that "[t]he appellant was entitled to a properly constituted jury, but as the *Juries Act* and the *Criminal Code* stood at the time, this panel was selected according to the law and the jury was properly constituted" and that "[e]ven if s. 7 of the *Charter* incorporates the equality rights under s. 15, it incorporates only the equality rights of the person whose liberty is at stake. It is that person who is entitled to proceedings in accordance with the principles of fundamental justice. The liberty of non-citizens who may be affected by the alleged discriminatory nature of the *Juries Act* was not at stake in this prosecution."

> Matz was in no way subjected to disadvantageous treatment by reason of any distinction on the analguous ground of her immigration status. She received equal benefit and equal protection of the law without discrimination due to her immigration status. The impugned provisions of the *Juries Act* did not withhold any advantage or benefit from, nor impose a disadvantage or burden on her. She was not, and could not, be summoned as a potential juror in her own case and no s. 15 rights of hers were violated by the provisions.

* Justice Rosenberg, in a footnote (at 114, note 3), left open the question as to whether his reasoning on this latter point would apply to a Black accused challenging the exclusion of prospective Black jurors. The issue will be decided by the Court in *R.* v. *Laws*, on appeal from the decision reported at (1994), 19 C.R.R. (2d) 269 (Ont. Gen. Div.). He also left open for *Laws* the issue as to whether a Black accused could successfully make an equality argument that the exclusion of non-citizens has the effect of excluding a "disproportionate number of his peers" from the panel.

* The Court of Appeal's approach to the issue of standing in *Scientology* is disappointing, especially since its effects will be felt in other contexts (i.e., challenging the exercise of discriminatory peremptory challenges). It is important to bear in mind that "standing" is resolved irrespective of the merits of the attempted challenge, and that therefore litigants who are denied standing are prevented from challenging provisions that may, in fact, exist in breach of the *Charter*. As a practical matter in Ontario, the *Scientology* case has foreclosed judicial review of a potential constitutional wrong, as it is extremely unlikely that an excluded non-citizen in Ontario would bring an expensive challenge under section 2(b) of the *Juries Act*. The other troubling facet of the case is that the Court's analysis on the standing issue is incomplete. While Justice Rosenberg considered the issue of standing from the perspective of a series of Supreme Court of Canada cases permitting an accused to challenge the constitutionality of legislation even where the accused was not affected by its unconstitutional effects, he failed to address the seminal constitutional cases on standing.

* In a quartet of cases, the Supreme Court of Canada set out the following test as to when an individual should be entitled to enforce the constitutional right of another person:

  (i) there is a serious question of law to be addressed;
  (ii) the accused has a genuine interest in the determination of the question; and
  (iii) there is no other reasonable and effective manner in which the question may be brought before the Court. See *Thorson* v. *Canada (A.G.)*

> *(No. 2)* (1974), [1975] 1 S.C.R. 138; *Nova Scotia Board of Censors* v. *McNeil*, [1976] 2 S.C.R. 265; *Canada (A.G.)* v. *Borowski*, [1981] 2 S.C.R. 575; *Finlay* v. *Canada (Minister of Finance)*, [1986] 2 S.C.R. 607.

All three prongs of the standing test appear to be met in this context. First, whether a prospective juror's equality right has been violated by the state is a serious and important question of law. Second, an accused who will be judged by the jury has a genuine interest in the composition of the jury pool. According to the Supreme Court of the United States in *Powers* v. *Ohio*, 499 U.S. 400 at 415 (1991), "racial discrimination [and presumably other forms of constitutionally infirm discrimination as well] in the selection of juries casts doubt on the integrity of the judicial process . . . and places the fairness of the criminal proceeding in doubt." Finally, there is no other reasonable and effective manner in which the question may be determined by a court since it is not likely that a challenged juror will hire a lawyer and seek redress.

* In *Batson* v. *Kentucky*, 476 U.S. 79 (1986), albeit in the different context of discriminatory peremptory challenges, the United States Supreme Court has relied upon similar reasoning to grant standing to accused persons to litigate the equality claims of prospective jurors. The Court held that one of the rationales for prohibiting the prosecution from engaging in race-based peremptory challenges in cases involving Black accused was that (at 87) "by denying a person participation in jury service on account of his race, the State unconstitutionally discriminated against the excluded juror." The same court directly addressed the issue of standing in this context in *Powers* v. *Ohio*, 499 U.S. 400 (1991), where a white accused sought to prohibit race-based peremptory challenges by the prosecution. Justice Kennedy, writing for the majority, granted the accused standing to raise the constitutional challenge on the following theory (at 402, 410–15):

> Jury service is an exercise of responsible citizenship by all members of the community, including those who otherwise might not have the opportunity to contribute to our civic life. In a trilogy of cases . . . our Court confirmed . . . the broader constitutional imperative of race-neutrality in jury selection. . . . Invoking the Equal Protection Clause . . . and relying upon well-established principles of standing, we hold that a criminal defendant may object to race-based exclusions of jurors effected through peremptory challenges whether or not the defendant and the excluded juror share the same race. . . .
>
> We must consider whether a criminal defendant has standing to raise the equal protection rights of a juror excluded from service in violation of these principles. In the ordinary course, a litigant must assert his or her own legal rights and interests, and cannot rest a claim to relief premised on the legal

> rights or interests of third parties. . . . We have recognized the right of litigants to bring actions on behalf of third parties, provided three important criteria are satisfied: the litigant must have suffered an "injury-in-fact," thus giving him or her a "sufficiently concrete interest" in the outcome in dispute, . . . the litigant must have a close relation to the third party . . . and there must exist some hindrance to the third party's ability to protect his or her own interest. . . .
>
> The discriminatory use of peremptory challenges by the prosecution causes a criminal defendant cognizable injury, and the defendant has a concrete interest in challenging the practice. . . . This is not because the individual jurors dismissed by the prosecution may have been predisposed to favour the defendant, if that were true, the jurors might have been excused for cause. Rather, it is because racial discrimination in the selection of jurors "casts doubt on the integrity of the judicial process," *Rose v. Mitchell*, 443 U.S. 545 at 556 (1979), and places the fairness of a criminal proceeding in doubt. . . .
>
> Both the excluded juror and the criminal defendant have a common interest in eliminating racial discrimination from the courtroom. A venireperson excluded from jury service because of race suffers a profound personal humiliation heightened by its public character. The rejected juror may lose confidence in the court and its verdicts, as may the defendant if his or her objections cannot be heard. This congruence of interests makes it necessary and appropriate for the defendant to raise the rights of the juror. . . .
>
> We have held that individual jurors subjected to racial exclusion have the legal right to bring suit on their own behalf. . . . As a practical matter, however, these challenges are rare.

* The hallmark of our *Charter* and constitution is its guarantee that for every rights violation there is an opportunity to seek a just and appropriate remedy in all the circumstances of the case. By interpreting standing in a narrow and restrictive manner, *Scientology* has effectively denied redress for those individuals who may be unlawfully excluded from participating in our jury system.

1.4(c)(ii) **Exclusions Based on Occupation and Marital Status**

* In *R.* v. *Church of Scientology of Toronto and Jacqueline Matz* (1997), 33 O.R. (3d) 65 (C.A.), the Court also held (at 124–25) that the exclusion under the *Juries Act* of Ontario of physicians, veterinarians, and coroners did not cause the jury panel to become unrepresentative. The Court reasoned that persons practising these occupations were not a distinctive group and, while they are among the better educated members of society, their exclusion is trivial relative to the many educated persons who are eligible.

* The Court of Appeal also denied that the exclusion of the spouses of judges, lawyers, and other persons engaged in the enforcement of the law under section 3(1)(7) of the *Juries Act* of Ontario [since repealed] undermined the representativeness of the jury. The spouses of such persons do not form a distinctive group, nor would their disqualification cause under-representation of persons either on the basis of marital status or gender, given that a strong majority of married women remain eligible for jury duty despite this provision.

1.5 HOW JURY SELECTION IS CONDUCTED

* As is described in more detail in chapter 2, persons from the community where the trial is being held are summoned to jury duty. Together these persons constitute the jury panel, or "array." The jurors for a particular case are selected from the panel. This is done when the persons composing the jury panel are gathered together, normally in a courtroom. The names of a number of the panel members are drawn randomly from a drum, and those jurors are told to come forward. They line up in the order in which their names are drawn. The accused is normally placed in the prisoner's dock, close to where those jurors are standing. They are then, one by one, "called to the book" (the Bible on which most will be sworn if selected). They are told: "Juror, look at the accused. Accused, look at the juror." Then the Crown and defence counsel, alternating turns, indicate whether they are content with the juror who has come forward or whether they are challenging that juror. If the juror is not challenged by either party, he or she will be sworn in as a juror in the case and will take his or her place in the jury box and await the selection of the balance of the jury. The pattern is repeated for each prospective juror who is called forward.

* Jurors can be challenged for cause, or they can be challenged peremptorily. Before they can be challenged for cause, the party wishing to do so must satisfy the judge that there is an "air of reality" to the concern that the juror may not be an appropriate juror, based on one of the grounds spelled out in the *Criminal Code*. These grounds include partiality or the inability of a prospective juror, resulting from mental or physical disability, to discharge his or her duties as a juror. If there is an air of reality to counsel's concern, the challenge for cause will begin. As is seen in chapters 4 through 8, which discuss the challenge for cause process, the challenge involves appointing two triers of fact, who will act as a mini-jury to decide whether the challenge for cause is true or not. They will base their decision on the response of the challenged juror to pre-approved questions asked by the challenging party after the challenged juror is sworn to tell the truth. If

the mini-jury determines that the challenge is true, the juror is disqualified. If it is not, the juror will be sworn in unless challenged by either of the parties peremptorily.

* A peremptory challenge, unlike a challenge for cause, enables the parties to refuse a number of jurors without articulating cause for doing so. The technical aspects of the peremptory challenge are discussed in chapter 9. Chapter 10 is concerned with the tactical decision to exercise a peremptory challenge, rather than a challenge for cause.

1.6 THE JURISDICTION OF JURY SELECTION

* The selection of jurors falls within the concurrent jurisdiction of both federal and provincial governments: *R.* v. *Sherratt*, [1991] 1 S.C.R. 509 at 519–20 and *R.* v. *Barrow*, [1987] 2 S.C.R. 694 at 712–13.

* Section 91 (27) of the *Constitution Act, 1867* gives Parliament jurisdiction over the "in court" jury selection procedure (i.e., challenge to the jury panel, challenge for cause, and peremptory challenges).

* Section 92 (14) of the *Constitution Act* gives the provincial legislatures jurisdiction over the "out of court" jury selection process (i.e., creation of the jury panel). Indeed, each province has a *Jury Act*, which sets out who is eligible for jury duty: see section 2.1 below, on provincial eligibility requirements. And see, too, section 626(1), which sets out that "[a] person who is qualified as a juror according to, and summoned as a juror in accordance with, *the laws of a province* is qualified to serve as a juror in criminal proceedings in that province." [Emphasis added.]

1.7 THE AVAILABILITY OF TRIAL BY JURY IN THE *CRIMINAL CODE*

* Not all criminal trials are tried by jury; indeed, most are tried by judge alone. For the more serious offences, however, Parliament recognized the importance of trial by jury by enacting section 471 of the *Criminal Code*, which provides that every accused charged with an indictable offence (or a hybrid offence because of section 34(1)(a) of the *Interpretation Act*, R.S.C. 1985, c. I-2, which states that an offence that may be prosecuted by indictment is deemed to be an indictable offence) is to be tried by a jury. Section 471 reads:

> Except where otherwise expressly provided by law, every accused who is charged with an indictable offence shall be tried by a court composed of a judge and jury.

* Section 471 is not absolute and is qualified by the words "except where otherwise expressly provided by law." Indeed, there are a number of *Criminal Code* provisions that allow accused persons charged with indictable or hybrid offences to elect not to be tried by a jury.

* For offences listed in section 469 of the *Criminal Code* — generally considered, at least historically, to be the most serious offences (i.e., murder, conspiring to commit murder, bribery of a judge) — section 473(1) of the *Criminal Code* provides:

  > Notwithstanding anything in this Act, an accused charged with an offence listed in section 469 may, with the consent of the accused and the Attorney General, be tried without a jury by a judge of a superior court of criminal jurisdiction.

  Failing such consent, section 469 offences are tried by jury.

* In *R.* v. *Luis* (1989), 50 C.C.C. (3d) 398 (Ont. H.C.J.), Ewaschuk J., the court held that a Crown Attorney can consent to the election under section 473(1) as agent of the Attorney General and that no election is necessary where an accused intends to plead guilty to a section 469 offence prior to the empanelling of the jury. The constitutionality of section 473(1) was upheld in *R.* v. *Sobotiak* (1994), 155 A.R. 16 (C.A.), though it has been held that the refusal of the Attorney General to consent to an election under section 473(1) is subject to *Charter* scrutiny: *R.* v. *Cardinal* (1996), 105 C.C.C. (3d) 163 (Alta. Q.B.), Jones J. In *Cardinal*, the court held that the decision of the Crown not to consent to a trial by judge alone violated the principles of fundamental justice under section 7 of the *Charter* because the exercise of discretion was capricious and arbitrary, as it was not founded on any reason of substance. See also *R.* v. *Bird* (1996), 49 C.R. (4th) 33 (Alta. Q.B.), Berger J., where the court dispensed with the need for the Crown's consent because it was satisfied that the refusal of the Crown to consent to trial by judge alone was motivated by the Crown's view that it would be disadvantaged if the trial proceeded before the assigned judge. Justice Berger (at 39) held that "[s]uch a consideration constitutes, in all of the circumstances, an improperly motivated exercise of the Crown's discretion to withhold consent and an interference with the integrity of the process of the Court." In *R.* v. *McGregor* (1992), 14 C.R.R. (2d) 155 (Ont. Gen. Div.), Justice Charron, as she then was, also dispensed with the Crown's consent under section 473(1), as the accused had satisfied her that the amount of pretrial publicity in the community surrounding his murder trial was sufficient to trigger sections 7 and 11(d) of the *Charter* if the case were to be tried by a jury.

* Indictable and hybrid offences listed in section 553 of the *Criminal Code* (such as driving while disqualified, keeping a common gaming house or

bawdy house, theft under $5000, obtaining money or property by false pretenses under $5000, and mischief under $5000) fall within the absolute jurisdiction of the provincial court, where jury trials are not possible.

* For indictable offences not listed in either section 469 or section 553, section 536(2) of the *Criminal Code* gives the accused an election to be tried either by a provincial court judge (see also section 554(1)), by a superior court judge alone, or by a superior court judge and jury, following a preliminary inquiry (see also section 558). Section 536(2) states:

> Where an accused is before a justice charged with an offence, other than an offence listed in section 469, and the offence is not one over which a provincial court judge has absolute jurisdiction under section 553, the justice shall, after the information has been read to the accused, put the accused to his election in the following words:
>
>> You have the option to elect to be tried by a provincial court judge without a jury and without having had a preliminary inquiry; or you may elect to have a preliminary inquiry and to be tried by a judge without a jury; or you may elect to have a preliminary inquiry and to be tried by a court composed of a judge and jury. If you do not elect now, you shall be deemed to have elected to have a preliminary inquiry and to be tried by a court composed of a judge and jury. How do you elect to be tried?

* The *Criminal Code* also contains a provision that enables an accused to re-elect his or her mode of trial. Sections 561(1) and (2) read:

> (1) An accused who elects or is deemed to have elected a mode of trial other than trial by a provincial court judge may re-elect
>
> (*a*) at any time before or after the completion of the preliminary inquiry, with the written consent of the prosecutor, to be tried by a provincial court judge;
>
> (*b*) at any time before the completion of the preliminary inquiry or before the fifteenth day following the completion of the preliminary inquiry, as of right, another mode of trial other than trial by a provincial court judge; and
>
> (*c*) on or after the fifteenth day following the completion of the preliminary inquiry, any mode of trial with the written consent of the prosecutor.
>
> (2) An accused who elects to be tried by a provincial court judge may, not later than fourteen days before the day first appointed for the trial, re-elect as of right another mode of trial, and may do so thereafter with the written consent of the prosecutor.

In *R.* v. *Ruston* (1991), 63 C.C.C. (3d) 419 at 424 (Man. C.A.), the Manitoba Court of Appeal noted that "[t]he significance of the preliminary inquiry, as the event from which time for re-election runs, is that it is at that inquiry that the accused ordinarily will be apprised of the case he has to meet. Only when he has that knowledge can his decision not to seek the benefit of a jury trial be described as an informed one." Consequently, in *Ruston*, the Court of Appeal held that section 561(1) should be interpreted so as to provide the accused with a right of re-election under section 561(1)(b), even after the fifteenth day of the preliminary inquiry, in circumstances where the Crown discloses that it intends to adduce additional evidence at trial if that evidence amounts to a substantial change in the Crown's case. A similar result occurred in *R.* v. *Rockey* (6 December 1994), (Ont. Gen. Div.) [unreported] [summarized at 25 W.C.B. (2d) 524], where the court permitted the accused to make a re-election outside the fourteen-day period when disclosure had only recently been obtained by the defence. Finally, in *R.* v. *Mohammed* (1990), 60 C.C.C. (3d) 296 (Man. Q.B.), Kroft J., it was held that the Crown's decision not to consent to re-election will not be reviewed by courts under the *Charter* unless it is alleged that the discretion was exercised for an improper motive or for some other factor amounting to an abuse of process. In *Mohammed*, it was noted (at 301) that "[i]n the exercise of the discretion that has been given to it, the Crown is entitled to consider such things as time involved and public cost. It may also consider any tactical advantages to be gained by having a trial before a judge alone."

* It is beyond the scope of this book to review all of the *Criminal Code* provisions dealing with trial elections and re-elections. For the benefit of the reader, all of the provisions are included below in Appendix IV. These sections include 536(1)–(5), 554(1), 558, 560(1)–(4), 561(1)–(7), 562(1)–(2), 563, 565, 567, 598(1)–(2), and 686(5)–(5.1).

* Finally, Parliament has also enacted a provision that gives the Attorney General the right to proceed by way of trial by jury as long as the offence is punishable by more than five years' imprisonment. This right supersedes any right of the accused to elect trial by judge alone. Section 568 of the *Criminal Code* states:

> The Attorney General may, notwithstanding that an accused elects under section 536 or re-elects under section 561 to be tried by a judge or provincial court judge, as the case may be, require the accused to be tried by a court composed of a judge and jury, unless the alleged offence is one that is punishable with imprisonment for five years or less, and where the Attorney

> General so requires, a judge or provincial court judge has no jurisdiction to try the accused under this Part and a preliminary inquiry shall be held before a justice unless a preliminary inquiry has been held prior to the requirement by the Attorney General that the accused be tried by a court composed of a judge and jury.

This section survived *Charter* scrutiny in *Hanneson* v. *R.* (1987), 31 C.C.C. (3d) 560 (Ont. H.C.J.), O'Driscoll J. As to how an Attorney General may exercise her rights under section 568, see *R.* v. *Musitano* (1982), 39 O.R. (2d) 732 (H.C.J.), aff'd (1982), 39 O.R. (2d) 732 at 733n (C.A.).

1.8 PRACTICAL TIPS ON DECIDING WHETHER TO ELECT TRIAL BY JURY

* One of the most challenging and yet critical tasks for defence counsel is assessing the appropriate mode of trial when an election is available. The right to a jury trial now enshrined in the *Charter* as a constitutional guarantee does not necessarily mean that counsel will always choose to exercise that right when it is available. Some defence lawyers believe that there is a pervasive "law and order" mentality in the community and that the presumption of innocence does not mean to the public what it perhaps did fifteen years ago. They shy away from jury trials, trusting judges who have been trained in the importance of reasonable doubt. Other lawyers disagree and prefer jury trials. One lawyer who was consulted even suggested that judicial education programs and public pressure designed to "sensitize" judges make judge alone trials undesirable in sexual offences or domestic assaults. By contrast, other skilled advocates will avoid jury trials in sex cases at all costs. There is no consensus, then, on when, if ever, to choose a jury trial.

* Few experienced trial lawyers claim that there is any science to deciding whether to elect trial by jury. What follows is a list of considerations for counsel to review as a practical guide in determining whether a jury trial is appropriate:

CAN THE CLIENT AFFORD A JURY TRIAL?

* A practical reality is that jury trials are more expensive than non-jury trials. Opening statements and closing submissions generally take more time to prepare than argument in a judge alone trial, and the trials tend to be longer, including the jury selection and the judge's directions at both the start and the end of the trial. There tend to be more preliminary motions and more *voir dires* conducted. Once the jury begins deliberating, counsel must generally remain available in case the jury has questions or returns with a verdict. All of this increases legal costs. Sadly, not all clients can afford trial by jury.

ARE THERE SIGNIFICANT PRE-TRIAL ISSUES THAT MUST BE VETTED IN ADVANCE OF THE TRIAL?

* There may be issues of admissibility relating to evidence that is damaging to the accused. Examples include similar fact evidence; search and seizure of real evidence in a *Charter* context; inculpatory statements; and a *Corbett*-style application to exclude the accused's criminal record. Even though a trial judge is trained to disregard inadmissible evidence, common sense would suggest that it is best for the trier of fact not to be put in a position where she will have to disregard damaging information. It is generally prudent to insulate the trier of fact from such evidence by having a jury trial in which the judge will exclude the evidence, keeping the jury from ever being exposed to it.

WHAT IS THE ACCUSED LIKE?

* Certainly some accused persons are more attractive to juries than others. It is difficult to generalize, but an accused who is a police officer (who is not alleged to be a "dishonest cop") is in a far better position to elect trial by jury than an accused with a lengthy criminal record. Jurors bring their own biases and prejudices to a courtroom, and while judicial cleansing through jury directions and the challenge for cause process may have a salutary effect, counsel would be remiss in not considering carefully the client and his or her background, appearance, and mannerisms. Even the race and the sexual orientation of the accused should be considered. While the challenge for cause process may assist in reducing the effects of bias, it cannot ensure that racist or homophobic jurors will not feel animosity towards the accused.

IS THE ACCUSED LIKELY TO TESTIFY?

* It is sometimes said that juries expect to hear from the accused and that it is dangerous to elect trial by jury if the accused will not testify. This is undoubtedly true where the Crown's case cries out for an explanation by the accused. However, many jury trials have ended in a resounding acquittal when the tenor of the defence has been that the burden of proof rests with the prosecution and there is no case to respond to.

* When the accused does have to testify, however, careful attention has to be paid to how he or she is likely to appear to the jury. Is the accused presentable and able to articulate the defence, or is the accused likely to be confused or to appear arrogant or aggressive? It is worse for an accused to perform badly in front of a jury than in front of a judge alone, who will be better able to understand and apply the rule in *R.* v. *W.(D.)*, [1991] 1 S.C.R. 742.

IS THE CASE AGAINST THE ACCUSED INFLAMMATORY OR EMOTIONAL?

* Some criminal allegations, by their very nature, are apt to inflame a jury, particularly where identification is not a realistic issue. Crimes of "stark horror" or cruelty, or those that are considered particularly repugnant by society, such as child sexual offences or child abuse, pornography, drug trafficking, and driving under the influence of alcohol, may be so emotionally evocative that a trial by jury can be dangerous. Similarly, some evidence, such as inflammatory photographs or video presentations, can distort the reasoned assessment of evidence, and defence counsel may not succeed in having it excluded. It is generally perceived that judges tend to be better able to decide cases dispassionately.

IS THE DEFENCE CASE WEAKER IN LAW THAN IN EMOTIONAL APPEAL?

* Some cases have compelling emotional appeal, but a very slim legal foundation for acquittal. For example, the accused may be alleged to have assaulted an abusive spouse in circumstances that may not strictly fall within the defence of self-defence, or the accused may be particularly sympathetic at a human level. It is best to give strong consideration to a jury trial in such cases.

* Moreover, jury verdicts are less susceptible to appeal. Jurors return a "general verdict" of "guilty" or "not guilty" and do not provide reasons for their decision. Although there is some controversy about the extent of a trial judge's obligation to provide reasons for decision when sitting alone, the trial judge will almost invariably, at least to some degree, provide reasons for judgment. Even if the judge is influenced by the sympathetic defence case and provides a favourable verdict, the judge's decision is more susceptible to appeal.

DOES THE DEFENCE NEED TO RELY ON A TECHNICAL, LEGAL BASIS FOR AN ACQUITTAL?

* Whereas a judge has legal training and years of experience applying the law, the jury has no training in reasonable doubt or other necessary legal constraints. Juries naturally frown on an "apparently" guilty man or woman being released back to their own community and may share the victim's outrage. They will be very reluctant to acquit in such a case. "Good facts" may support the decision to have a trial by jury. An acquittal dependent on "bad facts" but favourable law may suggest trial by judge alone.

IS THE CROWN CASE BOTH COMPLEX AND STRONG?

* If the Crown case is a technical one, depending on sophisticated forensic evidence, or involving complex commercial transactions, some defence lawyers believe that a jury may be preferable. A jury may get lost in the evidence, whereas a judge may be better able to follow the evidence than is the jury. Judicial experience, legal training, and the judge's ability to stop counsel when she does not understand the evidence reduce the risk that the judge will be lost in a morass of incomprehensible detail. It has to be wondered, however, how ethical it is to attempt to gain an acquittal based on a doubt inspired by confusion rather than reason.

DOES THE PROSECUTION'S CASE DEPEND ON EVIDENCE THAT IS "DANGEROUS" TO THE DEFENCE?

* Almost invariably, a judge alone trial is required in such a case. An unfortunate history of miscarriages of justice tells us that juries place great reliance on eyewitness identification, despite its deficiencies and inherent unreliability. The same principle would apply with the same force if the Crown's case depends on a jailhouse confession.

* Hearsay evidence admitted under an exception to the rule, particularly the *Khan* rule, is apt to be judged more harshly by a trial judge familiar with the dangers of hearsay than by a jury. If key evidence will be presented in this form, a judge alone trial may be preferable.

HOW APPEALING ARE THE CROWN'S WITNESSES?

* If the Crown's case consists largely of accomplices, unindicted co-conspirators, and various witnesses with motives to lie and fabricate, a jury trial may be most appropriate. In addition to the warnings and cautions that the jury will be provided with, there is a sense among experienced counsel that juries are generally loath to rely on the veracity of such witnesses. Trial judges will be far more alert to the reality that the administration of justice relies on such evidence to obtain appropriate convictions.

* Similarly, if the investigators have been incompetent or negligent but the evidence that was obtained is incriminating, a jury trial may be preferable. A jury is more likely to be concerned about the absence of a proper, thorough investigation than is a judge, who is more experienced with the reality that police investigations are often less than ideal.

WILL CROWN WITNESSES BE HOSTILE?

* When key Crown witnesses are likely to be hostile and to be confronted with their prior statements, a jury trial is undesirable. Even if the witness who is being cross-examined on that prior statement by the Crown refuses to adopt it, the jury will have heard it. This will colour the case against the accused even though the prior statements are not technically admissible to prove the truth of their contents.

IS THE PROBABLE TRIAL JUDGE KNOWN PRIOR TO ELECTION?

* "Judge shopping" is frowned on, but it is a reality. Every trial judge brings a history of decision making and a reputation for fairness or unfairness that can be relied on in the election process. If that reputation is "pro-Crown" generally, or in a particular kind of case, it is obviously prudent to avoid that judge if possible. In smaller jurisdictions counsel will often know who the trial judge is likely to be. Juries are selected "fresh" for each case. While the trial judge may be in a position to influence the jury (for example, by expressing a general opinion about the evidence, or by couching the jury direction in a particular fashion), it may be better to try the case before the jury than before a judge who is likely to be unsympathetic.

WHAT IS COUNSEL LIKE?

* It is just as important for counsel to know themselves as to know the judge. Some lawyers are better at jury trials than at judge alone trials. Jurors, it is commonly believed, prefer a lawyer who appears honest, trustworthy, and human to a lawyer who appears "smooth" and clever. Folksy, self-effacing lawyers who are not spell-binding advocates can experience great success with juries because they can establish a rapport with jury members. Slick or unacceptably aggressive lawyers may not be trusted. Jurors may also have unrealistic expectations about what can be done with a cross-examination. Jury trials are safer for good cross-examiners. Experienced counsel who have substantial credibility with the bench often incline towards judge alone trials, where they can trade on their reputations. Moreover, as offensive as it may sound, some lawyers believe that, as with any other segment of society, jurors can be influenced to a degree by the physical attractiveness of the advocate. Thus the persona of defence counsel can be an important consideration.

* By the same token, even the abilities and personality of the prosecutor who is assigned to the case can have a bearing on the decision of defence counsel whether to elect trial by jury.

* When asked for his observations on the issue of whether to elect trial by judge alone or judge and jury, Windsor defence lawyer Patrick J. Ducharme, provided the following worthwhile advice:

> It has often been said that counsel should elect trial by judge alone when in the individual circumstances of the case the law is favourable and trial by judge and jury when the facts are favourable.
>
> In my view, this advice is overly simple and potentially hazardous to the client. Its most serious weakness is that it takes no account whatever of what is arguably the single most important factor of all, the personality of the lawyer who will advocate the case before the trier of fact.
>
> Whatever the law or the facts may be, the lawyer must shape and develop the theme of the argument and ultimately persuade the trier of fact of the sufficiency, the validity, of that argument. And the plain truth is that, while some lawyers have proven themselves quite capable of impressing judges with the "truth" or the cogency of their arguments, they are far less naturally suited to attract and persuade juries.
>
> There is, in short, a phenomenon in advocacy which might be called the "jury personality." Some of the country's most renowned trial lawyers clearly have it. The lawyers most likely to succeed before a jury are not those who are shy or retiring. Although they steadfastly avoid pomposity or arrogance, they have an unmistakable bearing in and subtle control of the courtroom. They know, usually instinctively, that their every word, act, or gesture is being closely observed by the jury. They are magnetic. For them, the trial is elemental human drama and they are invariably "centre stage."
>
> The "jury personality" is also one who has developed some considerable mastery over language. Her words are sharp and crisp and simple and direct. Knowing that the jury members are likely to be in their everyday experiences far removed from those dry spaces in which the law and lawyers reside, she speaks correct informal language free of stilted legal jargon and cliché.
>
> Lawyers with "jury personalities" are also consummate storytellers. They understand, therefore, that the story they tell must always and ultimately please and persuade. They must tell it easily, naturally, without detracting attention from it by making it seem rehearsed or otherwise insincere. For this reason, too, jury lawyers tend to work well without artificial props, without podium or paper. Literally and figuratively, these things serve as barriers, not as bridges, to the jury. They get in the way of communication. By contrast, lawyers with well-developed jury personalities let nothing stand between themselves and the triers of fact. Their body language suggests intimacy and identification rather than cool professional distance.
>
> At the same time, the jury lawyer is a model of civility to everyone assembled in the court. Generally speaking, the best jury lawyers interrupt

and object to the questions or tactics of opposite counsel only as necessary. In every such instance, they are certain of the correctness of their position. Their civility is manifest, too, in the way they address the jury in closing argument. Again, they eschew the podium and the paper. They remove, in other words, the obstacles. They speak directly to the trier, making eye contact, but avoiding the platitudes and irrelevancies and needless, painful, boring repetition. They show respect for the jurors, by avoiding any remark the least bit demeaning. Thus, they do *not* admonish the jurors to "pay close attention," and they do *not* tell them that the decision they are about to make is the most important decision they have ever made, and they do *not* use words such as "winning" or "losing," words with limitless capacity for conjuring all the worst images of lawyers as hired guns and self-aggrandizing, money-grubbing mercenaries.

Above all else, the lawyer with jury personality connotes with every move made in the courtroom a sense of principled belief in and commitment to the rightness of the client's cause. The jury lawyer has, in this sense, an abundance of pathos, the quality or power of evoking a feeling of compassion or pity. There is nothing new in this: as long ago as the fourth century B.C., the Greek philosopher Aristotle said that "pathos" was an essential quality of the skilled rhetorician. Before juries, especially, the lawyer is preeminently a rhetorician and must be capable of inspiring feelings of compassion or pity from his audience.

In light of this, then, it certainly seems that the election of trial by judge alone or by jury requires, in addition to any other considerations regarding the facts or the law, an honest self-appraisal by the lawyer as to whether he or she possesses the kind of personality likely to affect the jury positively, empathetically. If the lawyer is satisfied, upon this self-appraisal, that his or her skills are of a different order than those revealed by the best jury trial lawyers, then for the client's sake the choice should be trial by judge alone. Whatever the decision, it is for the lawyer to make, not the client, because in the final analysis the burden of rhetorical persuasion falls upon the advocate.

The advice, then, to a lawyer weighing his or her election: know the facts; know the law; know yourself.

CHAPTER 2

THE JURY PANEL

2.1 THE JURISDICTION OF THE PROVINCIAL ENACTMENTS AND THE CREATION OF THE JURY PANEL

* Each province and territory has passed legislation dealing with assembling the jury panel from which the jurors who will try a particular case will be selected. These statutes are as follows:

Alberta — *Jury Act*, R.S.A. 1980, c. J-2
British Columbia — *Jury Act*, R.S.B.C 1979, c. 210
Manitoba — *The Jury Act*, R.S.M. 1987, c. J30
New Brunswick — *Jury Act*, R.S.N.B. 1973, c. J-3
Newfoundland — *Jury Act*, R.S.N. 1990, c. J-5
Northwest Territories — *Jury Act*, R.S.N.W.T. 1988, c. J-2
Nova Scotia — *Juries Act*, R.S.N.S. 1989, c. 242
Ontario — *Juries Act*, R.S.O. 1990, c. J.3
Prince Edward Island — *Jury Act*, R.S.P.E.I. 1988, c. J-5
Quebec — *Loi Sur Les Jurés*, R.S.Q., c. J-2
Saskatchewan — *The Jury Act, 1981*, S.S. 1980–81, c. J-4.1
Yukon Territory — *Jury Act*, R.S.Y. 1986, c. 97

* The *Criminal Code* provides:

> 626.(1) A person who is qualified as a juror according to, and summoned as a juror in accordance with, the laws of a province is qualified to serve as a juror in criminal proceedings in that province.

* Both the eligibility and obligation of persons to serve on juries, as well as the process for bringing those persons forward as the jury panel, are therefore determined according to provincial legislation, even in criminal cases.

* This situation is subject to the caveat that, while a province can legislate for the administration of justice within a province, it cannot infringe on matters of criminal procedure, which are reserved to the federal government by section 91(27) of the *Constitution Act, 1867* (U.K.), 30 & 31 Vict., c. 3: *R.* v. *Barrow*, [1987] 2 S.C.R. 694 at 712.

* Thus provincial jurisdiction is confined to the selection and assembly of the panel from which a criminal jury will be drawn and to eligibility criteria for prospective jurors that are unconnected to the criminal case that is to be tried. By contrast, the selection of the individual jurors from that panel who will try a particular criminal case is governed by federal legislation: *R.* v. *Barrow*, [1987] 2 S.C.R. 694 at 713–14. As the *Barrow* court said at 712–13:

> In the case of jury selection, the provincial power over the administration of justice stops and the federal power over criminal procedure begins when the judge's activity is not concerned with the assembly of an array of eligible citizens, but with the precautions necessary to ensure an impartial jury.

* A number of the provincial statutes provide expressly that they are subject to provisions to the contrary in the *Criminal Code* or in any federal enactment (Alberta, s. 13; Prince Edward Island, s. 32(2); Saskatchewan, s. 38). These sections merely record what would be understood to be the law even in their absence.

* Thus, in *R.* v. *Rowbotham* (1988), 63 C.R. (3d) 113 (Ont. C.A.), the trial judge erred in using the procedures in the Ontario *Juries Act*, R.S.O. 1980, c. 226 for supplementing the jury panel when that panel was exhausted without a complete jury having been selected. The *Criminal Code* provides an exclusive procedure for supplementing a panel, which should have been followed. The error was considered serious enough that the verdict at trial, arrived at by an improperly constituted jury, was set aside.

* Federal statutory provisions and the constitutional doctrine of federal paramountcy can affect even the construction of the provisions of a provincial jury enactment. In *R.* v. *Barrow*, [1987] 2 S.C.R. 694, the Court interpreted narrowly a section of the New Brunswick statute so that it

would not operate unconstitutionally. Section 4(2), which has since been repealed, purported to enable the judge presiding at a jury session to exempt jurors from service, even when they did not qualify for exemption pursuant to any of the specific jury exemption provisions contained in the statute. The Court held that, despite its apparent breadth, the general excusing power could not be used to exempt jurors on the grounds of partiality, since partiality is an issue relating to the criminal case that is to be tried. Federal legislation, not provincial legislation, is to be used to determine the effect of partiality on juror eligibility.

2.2 ELIGIBILITY TO BE ON THE JURY PANEL

2.2(a) **Disqualifications and Exemptions**

* Provincial enactments describe the qualifications for, and the grounds for disqualification from, jury service within each province. Though there are substantial similarities in the qualifications for serving on a jury, the eligibility criteria differ from province to province and are described below.

* All jury enactments provide for the exemption of certain persons from jury duty. Most of the statutes contain procedures whereby eligible jurors can apply for those exemptions. The procedures vary, as do the grounds for exemption. Generally, these statutes provide potential jurors with the opportunity to apply to an administrative official, normally the sheriff, for exemption. In Newfoundland application is made to a provincial court judge. If the official is satisfied that the request for exemption falls within those exemptions provided for by the statute, that person will not be required to serve. If the official denies the request, that person may appeal the decision. Appeal procedures differ as between the enactments.

* Some of the provincial statutes make little, if any, functional distinction between disqualification and exemption. In these jurisdictions, when the juror's list is prepared, persons who are exempt and therefore not required to serve are simply omitted from the list as if they were disqualified. See New Brunswick, s. 8; Nova Scotia, s. 7(3); Prince Edward Island, ss. 8 & 9; and Yukon Territory, s. 8(1).

* The disqualification of persons from jury service depends primarily on "self-reporting" by potential jurors. They are provided with a form that presents them with the opportunity to indicate their own disqualification or eligibility for exemption. This dependence on self-reporting can result in the selection of jurors who are not qualified to serve as jurors under the relevant provincial statute. It is not uncommon for routine criminal-record

checks of a jury panel to reveal, for example, that a prospective juror who is on that panel is in fact ineligible because of a criminal conviction.

2.2(b) Limited Challenges Based on Juror Ineligibility under Provincial Legislation

* Since the process of selecting the panel of prospective jurors is seen to be largely administrative, and since the criteria for eligibility are considered to be unconnected to the criminal case to be tried, the definition and application of provincial criteria for juror eligibility and exemption are not generally considered to be matters of central importance to the parties to a criminal prosecution: *R.* v. *Barrow*, [1987] 2 S.C.R. 694 at 712–16.

* With respect to the empanelling of the jury, McIntyre J., dissenting on other grounds, said in *R.* v. *Barrow*, [1987] 2 S.C.R. 694 at 735:

> It can be seen at once that this process of drawing up a jury list and assembling a jury panel for a particular session is designed to create a pool of disinterested jurors. It is a process in which an individual accused plays no part and has no right to intervene. . . . The accused has no interest in the process, save the interest of any citizen in the due administration of the law.

* While this is generally true, where the provincial criteria threaten to undermine the impartiality, competence, or representativeness of the jury, the accused must be seen to have an interest in the provincial criteria and may therefore be in a position to bring a *Charter* challenge to those criteria. See the discussion earlier in section 1.4(c)(i), "Exclusions Based on Citizenship."

* Short of this, neither the Crown nor the accused has the formal right to challenge jurors on the simple basis that they are not eligible according to the provincial legislation or have inappropriately been denied exemption. A number of the provincial statutes provide an express, general right to challenge individual jurors for cause (Manitoba, s. 52; Ontario, s. 32; New Brunswick, s. 4(1); Prince Edward Island, s. 20; Saskatchewan, s. 27), but these provisions must be construed as applying solely to civil proceedings. This is because section 638(2) of the *Criminal Code* provides that no challenge for cause shall be allowed on a ground not mentioned in section 638(1). Section 638(1) does not mention the failure of a juror to qualify according to provincial criteria.

* While formal challenges for cause cannot be taken against individual ineligible jurors, both the accused and the prosecutor may, altogether apart from the *Charter*, challenge the entire jury panel "on the ground

of partiality, fraud or wilful misconduct on the part of the sheriff or other officer by whom the panel was returned": *Criminal Code*, section 629(1). See the discussion below at 2.7, "Challenging the Array."

* Having said this, where counsel is aware of information that would disqualify a particular, prospective juror according to provincial eligibility requirements, judges who are advised of this circumstance will routinely discharge those persons from jury service without the need for a formal challenge for cause to be conducted. The jurisdiction to do so can be found either through the simple application of the provincial legislation, or alternatively in section 632 of the *Criminal Code*, which provides:

> 632. The judge may, at any time before the commencement of a trial, order that any juror be excused from jury service, whether or not the juror has been called pursuant to subsection 631(3) or any challenge has been made in relation to the juror, for reasons of
>
> (*c*) personal hardship or any other reasonable cause, that, in the opinion of the judge, warrants that the juror be excused.

Where the judge has information prior to the commencement of the trial that a prospective juror is ineligible yet does not disqualify that juror, it is arguable that the judge will have erred, though the general view that eligibility to be on the panel is not a matter that the parties have a direct interest in could well prevent a successful appeal.

* Judges also have the discretion to discharge jurors in the course of a trial under section 644 of the *Criminal Code*. That section provides:

> 644. (1) Where in the course of a trial the judge is satisfied that a juror should not, by reason of illness or other reasonable cause, continue to act, the judge may discharge the juror.
>
> (2) Where in the course of a trial a member of the jury dies or is discharged pursuant to subsection (1), the jury shall, unless the judge otherwise directs and if the number of jurors is not reduced below ten, be deemed to remain properly constituted for all purposes of the trial and the trial shall proceed and a verdict may be given accordingly.

This power, discussed in more detail below, has been used during trials to discharge jurors who should have been disqualified under provincial legislation, where their status as disqualified has been discovered during the trial.

* Should a judge exercise this discretion by not discharging an ineligible juror after the trial has commenced, it is unlikely that this alone will constitute

reversible error. That juror has been sworn as a juror, and his discharge will result in a depleted jury. As indicated, the parties are not generally considered to have an interest in the provincial eligibility criteria, which vary from province to province. These considerations may be sufficient to provide a foundation for the judge's decision not to disqualify that juror. The *Criminal Code* does not reflect the view that provincial ineligibility criteria are so crucial as to undermine the integrity of a verdict that has been reached through the participation of ineligible jurors. Section 642 of the *Criminal Code*, for example, providing for increasing the pool of prospective jurors where the panel has been exhausted, empowers the sheriff or other proper officer to summon jurors by mouth. These persons are added to the jury panel for the purposes of the trial, "whether qualified [as] jurors or not." Moreover, section 638(1) could have included provincial ineligibility as a ground of challenge for cause but did not do so.

* As is seen below, some of the provincial ineligibility rules relate to such things as a mental or physical disability that undermines the ability of a juror to discharge his or her duties, language competence, and literacy. Some rules disqualify persons based on occupation, when the nature of that occupation could have a negative effect on jury deliberations — for example, those who work in the administration of justice. In such cases, it is arguable that the failure of the judge to discharge such ineligible jurors when objection has been taken, even after the trial has commenced, constitutes an erroneous exercise of that judge's discretion, notwithstanding the general view that parties do not have an interest in provincial eligibility criteria. The nature of the challenge in such cases would be based on the fact that the participation of such a juror undermines the fairness of the jury trial, thereby violating sections 11(d) and 11(f) of the *Charter*. It would be based not solely on the fact that these jurors are technically ineligible according to provincial criteria but rather on the impact of the provincial criteria on the impartiality, competence, or representativeness of the jury.

* In *R.* v. *S.(M.)* (1996), 111 C.C.C. (3d) 467 (B.C.C.A.), an appeal that was based on the participation of a juror said to be ineligible according to the *Jury Act*, R.S.B.C. 1979, c. 210, failed. The juror was not, in fact, ineligible. She did translation work for the Solicitor General, but was not an employee of the Solicitor General, hence no question of disqualification arose. In any event, counsel did not object when the status of the juror was discovered during the jury selection process, nor did he choose to challenge her peremptorily.

2.2(c) **Effect of Irregularities in Jury Empanelment**

* Two provisions of the *Criminal Code* seek to ensure that irregularities in the jury selection process, including technical defects in applying provincial eligibility criteria, will not invalidate the verdict in criminal trials:

> 670. Judgment shall not be stayed or reversed after verdict on an indictment
>
> (*a*) by reason of any irregularity in the summoning or empanelling of the jury; or
>
> (*b*) for the reason that a person who has served on the jury was not returned as a juror by a sheriff or other officer.
>
> 671. No omission to observe the directions contained in any Act with respect to the qualification, selection, balloting or distribution of jurors, the preparation of the jurors' book, the selecting of jury lists, or the drafting of panels from the jury lists, is a ground for impeaching or quashing a verdict rendered in criminal proceedings.

* As a result, the presence on the jury of a person who is disqualified from service or exempted from service under a provincial enactment is not a ground for interfering with the verdict of a jury that is otherwise legally rendered: *R.* v. *Stewart*, [1932] S.C.R. 612; *R.* v. *Rushton* (1974), 28 C.R.N.S. 120 (Ont. C.A.).

* These curative provisions, sections 670 and 671, are confined to irregularities: *R.* v. *Barrow*, [1987] 2 S.C.R. 694 at 717. The failure to identify an ineligible juror is considered to be an irregularity, though using an inappropriate pool of prospective jurors is not. Hence, in *R.* v. *Rowbotham* (1988), 63 C.R. (3d) 113 (Ont. C.A.), these provisions could not cure the error committed when the judge used provincial procedures, rather than the procedures provided in the *Criminal Code*, for selecting jurors after the jury panel had been depleted.

* Moreover, sections 670 and 671 apply only after a verdict has been rendered: *R.* v. *Barrow*, [1987] 2 S.C.R. 694 at 717. Thus they cannot cure a defect that is discovered and objected to before or during the trial itself. They could not be relied on, therefore, to save an erroneous decision by a judge to permit an ineligible juror to be sworn, or to continue as a juror, if objection is taken prior to the verdicts being rendered and the participation of that juror would undermine the fairness of the trial.

2.3 PROVINCIAL DISQUALIFICATIONS AND ELIGIBILITY RULES

2.3(a) **Sex: A Prohibited Ground of Disqualification**

* The *Criminal Code* provides:

> 626. (2) Notwithstanding any law of a province referred to in subsection (1), no person may be disqualified, exempted or excused from serving as a juror in criminal proceedings on the grounds of his or her sex.

None of the current jury statutes purports to disqualify jurors on the basis of sex, in any event.

2.3(b) **Age**

2.3(b)(i) **Minimum Age Qualifications**

* All the jury statutes provide a minimum age for juror eligibility. The minimum age ranges from eighteen years (Alberta, s. 2(a); Nova Scotia, s. 4(b); and Saskatchewan, s. 3) to twenty-one years in the Yukon Territory, s. 4(a).
* Ontario, s. 2(c), requires that the juror must attain eighteen years of age "in the year preceding the year for which the jury is selected."
* New Brunswick, s. 2, and the Northwest Territories, s. 4(a), require a minimum age of nineteen years.
* A number of the statutes simply provide that eligible jurors must be of the age of majority within the province: British Columbia, s. 3(c); Manitoba, s. 3(c); Newfoundland, s. 3; Prince Edward Island, s. 3; and Quebec, s. 3(b).

2.3(b)(ii) **Age Exemptions**

* Alberta, s. 3, allows exemptions to be claimed by those over the age of sixty.
* British Columbia, s. 6, enables persons over the age of sixty-five to apply to be exempted from jury duty, as does Newfoundland, s. 8, Saskatchewan, s. 5(d), and Quebec, s. 5(c).
* New Brunswick, s. 5(b), does the same for those prospective jurors who are seventy years of age or over.

2.3(c) **Residence Qualifications**

* Most statutes require that to be eligible to serve on a jury, a person must be a resident of the province: British Columbia, s. 3(1)(b); Manitoba, s. 3(b);

New Brunswick, s. 2; Newfoundland, s. 3; Ontario, s. 2(a); and Saskatchewan, s. 3.

* The Northwest Territories, s. 4(b), requires only that the person be permanently resident in Canada, or a citizen of Canada.
* The Yukon Territory has no residency requirement.
* Prince Edward Island, s. 2, requires residence in the province for twelve months prior to being summoned for jury duty.
* Nova Scotia, s. 4(c), requires that the prospective juror must have resided in the jury district within which the trial is being held for twelve months. Similarly, Alberta, s. 2(b), requires that the prospective juror is qualified for those cases tried by a jury in the judicial district in which he resides, though no length of residency is provided for.
* While Quebec does not have a residency requirement *per se*, section 3(c) requires eligible jurors to be included on the voters' list for the province.

2.3(d) **Citizenship Qualifications**

* Most provincial jury statutes also require that jurors, to be eligible, must be Canadian citizens: British Columbia, s. 3(a); New Brunswick, s. 2; Newfoundland, s. 3; Nova Scotia, s. 4(a); Ontario, s. 2(b); Prince Edward Island, s. 3; Quebec, s. 3(a); and Saskatchewan, s. 3.
* In Alberta, s. 2(b), a prospective juror will be eligible to sit on a jury even if not a Canadian citizen, so long as that prospective juror is "a natural born British subject."
* The Northwest Territories, s. 4(b), requires either citizenship or permanent Canadian residence.
* The Yukon Territory, s. 4(b), requires either Canadian citizenship or that the prospective juror be a British subject.

2.3(e) **Language Qualifications**

* The *Criminal Code* deals specifically with language and juror eligibility. Section 530 provides that accused persons are entitled to be tried before a judge or jury, as the case may be, who speak(s) the official language of Canada that is the language of the accused, or, if circumstances warrant, who speak(s) both official languages of Canada. Section 638 (1)(f) provides that jurors who do not speak the language in which the trial will be conducted may be challenged for cause.

* Most provincial statutes also provide expressly, that, to be eligible, the prospective juror must have a designated degree of language competence.

* The Northwest Territories, s. 4(c), requires that jurors be able to speak either English or French, as does Quebec, s. 4(i). Quebec provides, however, that Indians or Inuk jurors may serve where the accused is Indian or Inuk, even though those jurors do not speak French or English, (s. 45).

* The Yukon Territory, in a provision that is of no force or effect because of section 530 of the *Criminal Code*, purports to require all prospective jurors to understand the English language.

* New Brunswick, s. 5(c), provides that persons who are unable to understand, speak, or read the official language in which the proceedings are being conducted "may be exempted," suggesting that an application to the sheriff for exemption is required. Persons who do not apply for exemption and cannot speak the language of the trial can be challenged for cause under section 638(1)(f) of the *Criminal Code*.

2.3(f) **Literacy**

* British Columbia, s. 4; Manitoba, s. 4; and Prince Edward Island, s. 5, require eligible jurors to be able to "understand, speak . . . [and] read" the language in which the trial is to be conducted. As indicated above, an inability to read the language is a grounds for exemption in New Brunswick, s. 5(c).

* In Newfoundland there is no requirement that prospective jurors be able to read in the language in which the trial is conducted. Section 5 refers solely to the ability of the juror to understand or speak the language.

* Saskatchewan, s. 4(i), does not require literacy in the language of the trial since the statute provides only that persons who are unable to understand the language in which the trial is to be conducted are ineligible.

2.3(g) **Disqualifications Based on Criminal Antecedents**

* All of the provincial jury statutes, except Saskatchewan's, prohibit certain persons with criminal records from serving on juries, though the criteria vary substantially.

  • Alberta, s. 5(a): persons convicted of a criminal offence who have been sentenced to death or to a term of imprisonment exceeding twelve months.
  • British Columbia, s. 3(1)(o): persons convicted within the previous five years of an offence punishable by a fine of greater than $2000, or imprisonment of one year or more, for which no pardon has been received.

- Manitoba, s. 3(p) & (q): persons convicted of an indictable offence for which no pardon has been received, or of an offence within the previous five years for which the punishment could be a fine of $5000, or imprisonment of one year or more, for which no pardon has been received.
- New Brunswick, s. 3(r): persons convicted of offences under the *Criminal Code*, *Food and Drugs Act*, or *Narcotic Control Act*.
- Newfoundland, s. 4(n): persons convicted within the previous five years of an offence punishable by a fine of $1000 or more, or of imprisonment for one year or more.
- Northwest Territories, s. 5(a): persons convicted of an offence who have been sentenced to a term exceeding one year, for which no pardon has been received.
- Nova Scotia, s. 5(4): persons convicted of any offence punishable by death, or for which he or she was sentenced to a term of imprisonment of two years or more.
- Ontario, s. 4(b): persons convicted of an indictable offence, for which no pardon has been received.
- Prince Edward Island, s. 4(l): persons convicted within the previous five years of an offence for which the punishment could have been a fine of $1000 or more, or imprisonment for one year or more.
- Quebec, s. 4(j): persons convicted of any criminal offence.
- Yukon Territory, s. 5(a): persons convicted of an offence who received a sentence of imprisonment exceeding one year, for which no pardon has been received.

2.3(h) **Outstanding Charges**

* Some statutes provide that those who face outstanding charges are disqualified from serving on juries.

- British Columbia, s. 3(1)(p): persons under charge of an offence punishable by a fine of greater than $2000, or imprisonment of one year or more.
- Manitoba, s. 3(r): persons under charge of an offence punishable by a fine of $5000 or more, or imprisonment of one year or more.
- Newfoundland, s. 4(o), and Prince Edward Island, s. 4(m): persons under charge of an offence punishable by a fine of $1000 or more, or imprisonment of one year or more.

  Quebec, s. 4(j): persons under any criminal charge.

2.3(i) **Physical or Mental Disability**

* Most statutes disqualify persons with mental or physical infirmity incompatible with the discharge of their duties as a juror: Alberta, s. 5(b); British

Columbia, s. 3(1)(n); Manitoba, s. 3(o); Newfoundland, s. 4(m); Northwest Territories, s. 5(b); Ontario, s. 4(a); Prince Edward Island, s. 4(k); and Yukon Territory, s. 5(b).

* Nova Scotia does not disqualify such jurors.

* Quebec, s. 4(h), disqualifies only jurors who suffer from mental illness or deficiency. Persons suffering from physical disability can be exempt, but are not disqualified, s. 5(f).

* New Brunswick, s. 5(d), provides that persons who are suffering from a mental or physical infirmity "may be exempted." This wording suggests that they are not ineligible despite their disability, but must apply to be exempted. However, exempt persons are not included on the jury list in New Brunswick. In substance, then, this exemption amounts to a disqualification in most cases. Subsection 5.1(1) provides, however, that section 5(d) does not apply to those who suffer from a physical infirmity and who wish to serve, where adequate assistance can be provided to enable them to discharge their duties as jurors. Thus, the provision, while worded as a permissible exemption, amounts to a disqualification when the juror suffers from a mental infirmity or when a physically disabled juror does not express a wish to serve, or when adequate assistance cannot be provided to enable a physically disabled juror to discharge his or her obligations.

* In British Columbia, s. 4(1), as in New Brunswick, the disqualification does not apply to persons with hearing or visual impairments that can be overcome by such assistance as the court considers adequate to enable the juror to serve.

* Saskatchewan disqualifies only those whose mental disabilities have caused them to be confined to institutions (s. 4(g)) or certified incompetent (s. 4(h)), and allows those who are otherwise incapable of discharging their duties as jurors to apply for exemption (s. 5(2)(f)).

* The *Criminal Code*, s. 638(1)(e), allows jurors who are physically unable to perform properly their duties as a juror to be challenged for cause.

2.3(j) **Residence Distance**

* In the Yukon Territory, persons who reside more than twenty miles from the place fixed for the Supreme Court sittings shall not be entered on the jury list if there are an adequate number of persons within the twenty-mile radius to provide a list of at least forty-eight names: section 8(2) & (3).

* In Quebec, in a number of designated districts, persons living in municipalities more than sixty kilometres from the place fixed for the jury sittings are ineligible: section 4(k).

2.3(k) **Occupational Disqualifications**

* Members of a number of occupations are disqualified or exempted from jury duty, in some cases because it is believed that the nature of the occupation could interfere with the proper conduct of jury deliberations — for example, practising lawyers or judges. In other cases jurors are disqualified or exempted because their occupation was, at least at the time the relevant statute was passed, considered to constitute an essential service that should not be disrupted by jury duty. This would be the case, for example, with the disqualification and exemption of firefighters and some telecommunication workers in some statutes.

* Disqualification rather than exemptions is used to deal with concerns about the occupation of jurors in British Columbia, s. 3(1); Manitoba, s. 3; Nova Scotia, s. 3; Newfoundland, s. 4; Ontario, s. 3; Prince Edward Island, s. 4; and Saskatchewan, s. 4.

* Exemptions are granted, but jurors are not formally disqualified according to occupation, in Alberta, s. 4; Northwest Territories, s. 6; and Yukon Territory, s. 6.

* Quebec uses disqualification for some occupations, (s. 4), and relies on exemptions for others, (s. 5).

* Occupational disqualifications and exemptions provided for in the jury statutes fall into the following categories: politicians and public officials; civil servants; those who administer justice; and others.

2.3(k)(i) **Politicians and Public Officials**

* Parliamentarians and/or senators and/or members of the Privy Council of Canada: Alberta, s. 4(a); British Columbia, s. 3(1)(d); Manitoba, s. 3(d); New Brunswick, s. 3(a); Newfoundland, s. 4(a); Northwest Territories, s. 6(a); Nova Scotia, s. 5(1)(b); Ontario, s. 3(1).1 & 2; Prince Edward Island, s. 4(a); Quebec, s. 4(b); Saskatchewan, s. 4(a); and Yukon Territory, s. 6(a).

* Members of the Provincial Legislature and officers: Alberta, s. 4(b); British Columbia, s. 3(1)(e); Manitoba, s. 3(e); New Brunswick, s. 3(b); Newfoundland, s. 4(a); Northwest Territories, s. 6(b); Nova Scotia, s. 5(1)(c); Prince Edward Island, s. 4(b); Quebec, s. 4(c); Saskatchewan, s. 4(a); and Yukon Territory, s. 6(b).

* Employees of the National Assembly can apply for exemption in Quebec: s. 5(a.1)

* Municipal politicians and/or board members: Alberta, s. 4(d); Saskatchewan, s. 4(c) & (d).

* Lieutenant Governor of the Province: Nova Scotia, s. 5(1)(a).

2.3(k)(ii) **Civil Servants**

* Alberta exempts all salaried officials of the governments of Canada and Alberta: section 4(c).

* Alberta also exempts salaried municipal employees: section 4(d).

2.3(k)(iii) **Employment Related to the Administration of Justice**

* Judges and/or provincial judges and justices of the peace and/or other adjudicators: Alberta, s. 4(f); British Columbia, s. 3(1)(f); Manitoba, s. 3(f); New Brunswick, s. 3(c); Newfoundland, s. 4(c) & (j); Northwest Territories, s. 6(d); Nova Scotia, s. 5(1)(d) & (l); Ontario, s. 3(1)3; Prince Edward Island, s. 4(c); Quebec, s. 4(d); and Yukon Territory, s. 6(d). Saskatchewan expressly disqualifies retired judges and justices of the peace: section 4(d)(i) & (iv).

* Lawyers: British Columbia, s. 3(1)(i); Manitoba, s. 3(i); New Brunswick, s. 3(d); Newfoundland, s. 4(f); Northwest Territories, s. 6(e); and Nova Scotia, s. 5(1)(f). Saskatchewan expressly disqualifies retired and non-practising lawyers: s. 4(d)(ii). The Yukon Territory, s. 6(e), exempts only practising lawyers, as does Quebec, s. 4(e). A number of provinces include students-at-law: Alberta, s. 4(l); Ontario, s. 3(1)4; and Prince Edward Island, s. 4(f).

* Employees of provincial ministries responsible for the administration of justice: British Columbia, s. 3(1)(g); New Brunswick, s. 3(g); Newfoundland, s. 4(e); Prince Edward Island, s. 4(e); and Saskatchewan, s. 4(e)(i).

* Legal aid employees: British Columbia, s. 3(1)(h.1).

* Probation workers and social workers employed by the Yukon Territory: s. 6(j).

* Employees of the Department of Justice or of the Solicitor General of Canada and/or Provincial Justice Departments: British Columbia, s. 3(1)(g); Manitoba, s. 3(g) & (h); New Brunswick, s. 3(g) & (h); Newfoundland, s. 4(d); Prince Edward Island, s. 4(d); and Saskatchewan, s. 4(e)(ii).

* Persons working in the administration of justice can apply for exemption in Quebec: s. 5(b).

* Various peace officers: Alberta, s. 4(g) & (h); British Columbia, s. 3(1)(l); Manitoba, s. 3(l); New Brunswick, s. 3(e) & (f); Newfoundland, s. 4(i); Northwest Territories, s. 6(c); Nova Scotia, s. 5(1)(h); Ontario, s. 3(1)6; Prince Edward Island, s. 4(h); Quebec, s. 4(f); and Yukon Territory, s. 6(c). Saskatchewan provides expressly for the disqualification of retired police officers: s. 4(d)(iii).

* Various court officers and/or sheriffs and sheriffs' officers: Alberta, s. 4(1)(e); British Columbia, s. 3(1)(j) & (k); Manitoba, s. 3(j) & (k); Newfoundland, s. 4(g) & (h); Northwest Territories, s. 6(h); Nova Scotia, s. 5(1)(g); Ontario, s. 3(1)6; Prince Edward Island, s. 4(g); and Yukon Territory, s. 6(h).

* Correctional officers or penitentiary employees and those involved in the custody of prisoners: British Columbia, s. 3(1)(m); Manitoba, s. 3(m); Newfoundland, s. 4(k); Northwest Territories, s. 6(m); Ontario, s. 3(1)6; Prince Edward Island, s. 4(i); and Yukon Territory, s. 6(i).

2.3(k)(iv) **Other**

* Firefighters: Alberta, s. 4(i); New Brunswick, s. 3(p); Northwest Territories, s. 6(g); Quebec, s. 4(g); and Yukon Territory, s. 6(g).

* Professors, teachers, and school officials: Alberta, s. 4(j).

* Clergy: Alberta, s. 4(k); New Brunswick, s. 3(j) & (k); Newfoundland, s. 6(f); Nova Scotia, s. 5(1)(k); Quebec, s. 5(a); and Yukon Territory, s. 6(f).

* Various health care workers, including, in some cases, dentists and nurses: Alberta, s. 4(l); New Brunswick, s. 3(l) & (m); Northwest Territories, s. 6(k); Nova Scotia, s. 5(1)(i) & (j); Ontario, s. 3(1)5; and Yukon Territory, s. 6(n) & (o).

* Chemists and druggists and their apprentices: Alberta, s. 4(l); and Northwest Territories, s. 6(k).

* Land surveyors: Alberta, s. 4(l).

* Editors and journalists: Alberta, s. 4(m).

* Ferry operators, mail carriers and postmasters: Alberta, s. 4(n).

* Pilots in actual service: Alberta, s. 4(o).

* Certain transportation workers: Alberta, s. 4(p); and Yukon Territory, s. 6(p)(i).

* Certain communication workers: Alberta, s. 4(p); Ontario, s. 6(i); and Yukon Territory, s. 6(k) & (l).

* Millers: Alberta, s. 4(q).

* Employees in electrical power plants and water distribution plants: Yukon Territory, s. 6(k)(ii) & (iii).

* Veterinary surgeons: New Brunswick, s. 3(n); Ontario, s. 3(1)5.

* Canadian military officers and/or enlisted personnel: Alberta, s. 4(r); Manitoba, s. 25(1)(c); New Brunswick, s. 3(o); Nova Scotia, s. 5(1)(e); Ontario, s. 6(j); Quebec: s. 5(d); and Yukon Territory, s. 6(m).

* Medical examiners under the *Fatality Inquiries Act*: Manitoba, s. 3(n).

* Coroners: Ontario, s. 3(1)5; and Saskatchewan, s. 4(d)(v), including those who at any time have been coroners.

* Members of a jury committee (established and described in s. 6): Nova Scotia, s. 5(1)(m).

* Consuls and consular agents: New Brunswick, s. 3(q).

2.3(l) **Religious Grounds**

* Some statutes allow persons to apply for exemption on religious grounds: British Columbia, s. 5(1)(a); Manitoba, s. 24(1); Newfoundland, s. 7; Ontario, s. 23(1); and Saskatchewan, s. 5(2)(c).

2.3(m) **Recent Jury Service**

* Some statutes provide that, after having served on a jury, persons are not eligible to do so again for designated periods, absent special circumstances: Alberta, s. 6 (2 years); British Columbia, s. 12 (2 years); Newfoundland, s. 16 (3 years); Northwest Territories, s. 7 (2 years); Nova Scotia, s. 5(3) (3 years): Ontario, s. 3(4) (3 years); Prince Edward Island, s. 7 (2 years); and Yukon Territory, s. 7 (2 years).

* Some statutes do not disqualify, but rather exempt, such persons: Manitoba, s. 25(3) (2 years); New Brunswick, s. 5(a) (5 years); Quebec, s. 5(e) (5 years); and Saskatchewan, s. 5(2)(e) (2 years).

2.3(n) **Connection to Other Prospective Juror**

* No more than one family member or employee of a firm can serve as a juror at a single jury session: Nova Scotia, s. 5(5) & (6).

2.3(o) **Connection to Cases Being Tried during the Session**

* Persons who are witnesses, or who have an interest in an action, are disqualified from serving during that sitting: Ontario, s. 3(3).

2.3(p) **Spouses**

* Spouses of certain enumerated persons who are disqualified are also disqualified: New Brunswick, s. 3(i); Newfoundland, s. 4(l); Prince Edward Island, s. 4(j); Quebec, s. 6; and Saskatchewan, s. 4(f).

2.3(q) **Hardship**

* Section 632(c) of the *Criminal Code* confers on judges the power to excuse jurors on the grounds of personal hardship.

* Most provincial statutes allow potential jurors to apply for exemption at an earlier stage, when serving would cause serious hardship or loss to them, and in some cases to others: British Columbia, s. 5(1)(b); Manitoba, s. 25(1)(b); New Brunswick, s. 5(e) & (f); Newfoundland, s. 6(1); Northwest Territories, s. 15; Ontario, s. 19(2); Prince Edward Island, s. 6; and Saskatchewan, s. 5(2)(a).

* In Alberta, the sheriff is to report to the clerk whether serving on the jury will inflict great hardship or inconvenience on a prospective juror: section 21(3). The judge, having received the report from the clerk, may excuse any such person for good cause: section 26. To the same effect, see Northwest Territories, ss. 16(2) & 15.

* Quebec and Nova Scotia do not have specific "hardship" provisions, but each includes a general power in judges to excuse jurors for good cause, which would include hardship: see below.

* Newfoundland, s. 6(2), provides expressly for those having sole care of young persons, the aged, or those with incapacities. New Brunswick, s. 5(e), and Quebec, s. 5(f), also provide for the exemption of some care-givers.

* Ontario, s. 19(2), and Saskatchewan, s. 5(2)(b), specify "illness" as a ground for exemption, as does Quebec, ss. 5(f) & (g).

2.4 GENERAL EXEMPTING POWERS

* A number of the provincial statutes provide judges with the general power to excuse or exempt prospective jurors for "good cause" when they have not yet been sworn. These include Alberta, s. 26; Northwest Territories, s. 22; and Yukon Territory, s. 20.

* Nova Scotia, s. 5(2), provides power to the judge to excuse any person from jury duty, without the judge having to specify the grounds for such decision.

* Quebec, s. 5, provides an omnibus power in the sheriff and the court to exempt jurors for reasonable grounds not enumerated in the statute, where the public interest permits.

* It has been held that such general powers of exemption must be exercised consistently with the limits on provincial jurisdiction in matters of jury selection. Criteria particular to a specific case, such as juror partiality, cannot be taken into account when exercising this provincial power: *R.* v. *Barrow*, [1987] 2 S.C.R. 694. Technically, this point is now moot. These provincial powers become inoperative in a criminal case once the selection of particular jurors is underway because, since *Barrow*, the federal government has passed legislation dealing with the power of judges to excuse jurors. Section 632 of the *Criminal Code* provides:

> 632. The judge may, at any time before the commencement of a trial, order that any juror be excused from jury service, whether or not the juror has been called pursuant to subsection 631(3) or any challenge has been made in relation to the juror, for reasons of
>
> (*a*) personal interest in the matter to be tried,
> (*b*) relationship with the judge, prosecutor, accused, counsel for the accused or a prospective witness; or
> (*c*) personal hardship or any other reasonable cause that, in the opinion of the judge, warrants that the juror be excused.

See section 2.8(b)(i), "Excusing Jurors," and section 3.3, "Section 632 of the *Criminal Code*," below.

2.5 HOW THE JURY PANEL IS ASSEMBLED

* It is the responsibility of the sheriff, or other judicial officer(s), in each province to create a jury list at the commencement of the court's sitting. Some provinces leave the selection of potential jurors to the sole discretion of the sheriff or other official, offering no guidance as to what sources should be made available in the selection process (i.e., British Columbia); other provinces, while still leaving the assembling of the panel to the discretion of the sheriff or other official, provide access to various sources (i.e., Alberta); and some specify the source from which the prospective jurors are to be selected (i.e., Saskatchewan and Ontario):

  - Alberta: provides sheriff with access to list of electors, assessment rolls, any other public papers (s. 8(1))
  - British Columbia: sole discretion of sheriff (s. 7)

- Manitoba: provides chief sheriff with access to lists (including computer database) of any department or agency of the government (ss. 7(1) & (2))

  specifically requires random selection from appropriate lists (s. 6(1))
- New Brunswick: sheriff shall randomly select names from list provided for in the regulations
- Newfoundland: sole discretion of a provincial court judge (s. 9(1))
- Northwest Territories: provides sheriff with access to voter's lists, assessment rolls and other public documents (s. 9)
- Nova Scotia: the jury committee is to use the latest available list of electors, but if this is not practical it may use assessment rolls and other information respecting persons qualified to serve as jurors (s. 7(5))

  selection must be by random choice (s. 7(1))
- Ontario: director of assessment selects at random potential jurors from information obtained at the most recent enumeration under section 15 of the *Assessment Act* (s. 6(2))

  in the selection of potential jurors in a county where an Indian reserve is situated, the sheriff selects names of eligible persons in the same manner as if the reserve were a municipality and may obtain the names of inhabitants of the reserve from any record available (s. 6(8))
- Prince Edward Island: sole discretion of sheriff (s. 8)
- Quebec: sheriff must select potential jurors from voters' lists (s. 8)
- Saskatchewan: inspector of legal offices randomly selects names from register of names prepared in accordance with s. 13(1) of *The Saskatchewan Hospitalization Act* (s. 6)

- Yukon Territory: provides sheriff with access to voters' lists, assessment rolls, and other public documents (s. 9)

* Some provinces provide access to the jury list prior to the sitting of the court: for example, section 20 of the Ontario *Juries Act* permits inspection of the list by accused or her lawyer ten days prior to the sittings of the court. See also s. 29 (Manitoba); s. 12 (Newfoundland); s. 9(7) (Nova Scotia); and s. 11 (Saskatchewan).

2.6 RECOMMENDATIONS FOR ENSURING A MORE REPRESENTATIVE SELECTION SOURCE

* In *Multiculturalism, Representation and the Jury Selection Process in Canadian Criminal Cases* (Working Document) (Ottawa: Department of Justice, 1994), D. Pomerant makes the following suggestions to "better realize the goal of empanelling representative juries and to improve the public perception that the goal is being seriously pursued" (at 53–54):

> Discretion in the selection process should be completely eliminated. Selection sources that can be accessed by computer should be prescribed. As the rules in Saskatchewan demonstrate, representative sources for selection can be prescribed. The list of persons registered under each provincial health insurance program is regularly updated and is likely to be the most representative available.[1] In provinces such as Alberta, where access is restricted by legislation, the legislation could be amended for this limited purpose, with safeguards for confidentiality such as those imposed in Saskatchewan. Public access to the names on the source list should be permitted and facilitated, as it is in Saskatchewan. Anyone in the community who is interested

1 A similar recommendation was made in the *Report of the Commission on Systemic Racism in the Ontario Criminal Justice System* (Toronto: Queen's Printer, 1995) in 1995. The Commission noted (at 252–53) that in Ontario the source of potential jurors for non-Aboriginal persons is collected from the Ministry of Revenue's database, which lists every property in the province, by district. The problem with this approach is that it is organized around property, which creates a bias for age and income levels. While information about homeownership is quickly updated, information about tenants occurs only by virtue of municipal enumeration which takes place only every three years, and thus tenants are less likely to receive the questionnaire used to select the jury pool. The Commission points out that both Manitoba and Saskatchewan now use provincial health insurance plans as sources for the jury pool.

in jury service and otherwise qualified should be able to access the list in order to confirm that he or she potentially may be chosen, or that members of the group to which he or she belongs, whatever it may be, are not being unreasonably excluded. Anyone qualified and interested in service who is excluded from the list should be able to learn why, and to determine the steps they might take to have their names included or their group better represented.

In addition, no provincial legislation appears to provide clear and simple direction to officials responsible for selection that the purpose of the selection process is to produce jury panels from sources representing a fair cross-section of the community. Each jury act should clearly set out the purpose of the selection process. In Saskatchewan, the absence of such clear direction may not be crucial, as the legislation is structured so as to eliminate the ability of selectors to exercise discretion that might interfere with this goal. However, in other provinces, the absence of clear direction may lead selectors to believe that their discretion is the only guideline to be applied.

Furthermore, provincial legislation could be re-examined with a view to broadening the categories of persons eligible for jury service and narrowing the categories of persons disqualified or exempt from service. This report has focussed on the qualification categories of citizenship and inclusion on a provincial electoral list, and deficiencies in the grounds for exemption, as being matters that might be proper subjects of reform. Whatever the categories may be, they should, ideally, be uniform across the country, as there would appear to be little justification for some to be disqualified or exempt in one province, but not in others.

2.7 CHALLENGING THE ARRAY

2.7(a) **Introduction**

* The second stage of the jury selection process, involving in-court selection, begins when those summoned to be on the jury panel pursuant to provincial legislation assemble in court. The *Criminal Code* provides a number of avenues in which counsel can strive for an impartial, competent, and representative jury: *R.* v. *Sherratt*, [1991] 1 S.C.R. 509, L'Heureux-Dubé. The statutory right to challenge the array pursuant to section 629 of the *Criminal Code* is one such procedure. The challenge to the array involves a review of the manner in which the jury panel was assembled.

* Section 629(1) of the *Criminal Code* provides that:

> 629.(1) The accused or the prosecutor may challenge the jury panel only on the ground of partiality, fraud or wilful misconduct on the part of the sheriff or other officer by whom the panel was returned.

Thus, once the jury panel has been assembled, either the accused or the Crown may challenge the entire panel (usually referred to as the array) on the limited grounds that the sheriff or other officer who returned the panel engaged in (a) partiality; (b) fraud; or (c) wilful misconduct.

2.7(b) **Grounds for Challenging the Array**

2.7(b)(i) **The Statutory Grounds**

* The section 629(1) jurisprudence reveals an unmistakable trend. Only a clear and deliberate policy on the part of the sheriff or other officer to exclude segments of the population will constitute a valid challenge to the array: *R.* v. *Chipesia* (1991), 3 C.R. (4th) 169 (B.C.S.C.). The mere absence of members of a racial or cultural group from the jury panel will not support a conclusion of partiality so long as the procedure in the relevant provincial jury act that is designed to ensure randomness has been followed.

* For example, in *R.* v. *Nahdee* (1993), 26 C.R. (4th) 109 (Ont. Gen. Div.), the sheriff failed to comply with section 6(8) of the Ontario *Juries Act*, which requires selection of names from Indian reserves situated within the county "in the same manner as if the reserve were a municipality" and "[by use of] any record available." Section 6(8) was enacted to take into account the fact that on Indian reserves the property is owned by the band and there are no assessment or enumeration lists. In *Nahdee*, the bands did not respond to the sheriff's request to provide the names of the inhabitants of the reserve. However, the court was of the view that the sheriff had nevertheless failed in his statutory duty, as there was only a single request made by mail, with no further attempt by personal communication or otherwise to obtain the lists from the band or from another source, such as the federal ministry having responsibility for Indian Affairs. The court held that because the Ontario *Juries Act* was designed to facilitate impartiality and to ensure that the jury will be representative of the community in which the trial takes place, the deliberate failure to comply with the mandatory statutory obligations sustained the challenge to the array. Justice Donnelly held (at 118):

> The selection process for the array is fatally flawed ab initio. If the panel is found to be wanting at the outset, that deficiency is not cured by the happenstance that the two native persons on the panel were selected and were challenged. The non-compliance with s.6(8) does constitute partiality under section 629. The partiality of the person performing the function of the sheriff is not founded in an act of bias. There is simply a total absence of evidence of any such attitude. The partiality is found in the acquiescence in a known and repeated failure of the process through which it was sought to comply with the statutory obligation. That acquiescence excluded the target group to be

> included. The actions are not inadvertent. They must result from a conscious decision to do no more — to leave well enough alone. In the face of the statutory duty, that does speak an absence of impartiality. Individual jurors within the targeted segment are denied the opportunity to participate and thereby constitute a truly representative reflection of the community as a whole as dictated by statute. The failure to comply with the duty has resulted in a form of discrimination, a lack of opportunity to contribute to the shared values of the community. . . . A mistrial is hereby declared for that reason. This jury will be discharged.[2]

* Similarly, in *R.* v. *Butler* (1984), 3 C.R. (4th) 174 (B.C.C.A.), the British Columbia Court of Appeal held that a deliberate policy to exclude Native Indians from being summoned, based on the reasoning that Native people make unreliable jurors, was a clear violation of section 629(1). The court held that in the presence of a deliberate policy of exclusion, there is a presumption of partiality. Indeed, even though the actual panel may not differ significantly from panels chosen without any such exclusion, the appearance of partiality arises as a result of its non-random selection.

* Consequently, an accused will not succeed under section 629(1) of the *Criminal Code* where he or she challenges the array simply on the basis of the absence of jurors of his or her cultural or racial background: *R.* v. *Diabo* (1974), 30 C.R.N.S. 75 (Que. C.A.). In *R.* v. *Bradley (No. 1)* (1973), 23 C.R.N.S. 33 (Ont. H.C.J.), the accused alleged partiality because of the absence of Black jurors. The court dismissed the application, holding that the mere fact that no Black jurors were summoned did not constitute evidence of partiality. This principle has been extended to challenges based on gender: *R.* v. *LaForte* (1975), 25 C.C.C. (2d) 75 (Man. C.A.). But see *R.* v. *Catizone* (1972), 23 C.R.N.S. 44 (Ont. Co. Ct.), in which a panel of seventy jurors contained only three women for the trial of a female accused and where the accused successfully challenged the array. The court found that an attempt should be made to include as closely as possible an equal number of females. It is, however, difficult to reconcile this decision with the majority of cases in the area.

2.7(b)(ii) The *Charter* Grounds

* While the *Criminal Code* provides a statutory basis and remedy for challenging the array, the *Charter* provides another means of challenge. In

---

2 In a short endorsement giving no reasons, Justice Clarke in *R.* v. *Marsden* (22 January 1993), (Ont. Gen. Div.) [unreported] struck down section 6(8) as a violation of sections 11(d) and 11(f) of the *Charter*.

most of the cases that have litigated the adequacy of the array under the *Charter*, the accused has advanced one of two constitutional arguments. The first is that the composition of the jury panel is not truly representative of the larger community and that this lack of representativeness is a violation of the *Charter*. Reference is made to *R.* v. *Sherratt*, [1991] 1 S.C.R. 509, where L'Heureux-Dubé J. held (at 525):

> The perceived importance of the jury and the *Charter* right to jury trial is meaningless without some guarantee that it will perform its duties impartially *and represent, as far as is possible and appropriate in the circumstances, the larger community*. Indeed, without the two characteristics of impartiality and representativeness, a jury would be unable to perform properly many of the functions that make its existence desirable in the first place. [Emphasis added.]

As noted above in section 1.4(c), it is unclear the extent to which representativeness is a constitutional characteristic of the jury under either section 11(d) or section 11(f) of the *Charter*. However, most of the decisions have interpreted *Sherratt* as holding that as long as the provincial legislation is complied with by the sheriff, and that legislation ensures the random selection of a representative source (i.e., by not improperly excluding a segment of the population), then the characteristic of representativeness is satisfied. See, for example, *R.* v. *Born With A Tooth* (1993), 139 A.R. 394 (Ont. Gen. Div.) (Q.B.); *R.* v. *Church of Scientology of Toronto and Jacqueline Matz* (1997), 33 O.R. (3d) 65 (C.A.).

* Indeed, courts have held that deliberately "padding" the jury panel with members of a particular race or colour would be improper: *R. v. Born With A Tooth* (1993), 139 A.R. 394 (Q.B.); *R.* v. *Bradley (No. 2)* (1973), 23 C.R.N.S. 39 (Ont. H.C.J.). In *Born With A Tooth*, the court held (at 397–98):

> Artificially skewing the composition of jury panels to accommodate the demands of any of the numerous distinct segments of Canadian society would compromise the integrity of the jury system. The effectiveness of the criminal jury system is based on its widespread acceptance by the community as a fair and just method of deciding issues of criminal responsibility. That confidence, and thus the value of the system, would be seriously eroded if manipulation of the composition of juries were permitted, regardless of how well-intentioned the practice might be.
>
> An unarticulated premise of the argument supporting affirmative action in the jury selection process is that some otherwise qualified members of Canadian society are incapable of judging the conduct of other members of the same community in a fair and impartial manner in accordance with the solemn oath taken by jurors. There is no justification for such an assumption.

> In my view, the condonation of a process other than a random selection from a representative population will lead inevitably to the demise of the jury system. The selective inclusion of members of one group of citizens in a jury panel necessarily discriminates against others. It is a small step from the calculated inclusion of members of one distinct group to the express exclusion of those of other such groups.
>
> There is no provision in the present law for jury panels which are "tailor-made" to suit the race, national or ethnic origin, colour, religion, sex, age, mental or physical disability or other discrete characteristics of accused persons. The ruling sought by the accused could not be made without rejecting a cardinal principle of the criminal jury system. Such a fundamental change should be made only by legislation.

See similar comments by Justice McLachlin in *R.* v. *Biddle*, [1995] 1 S.C.R. 761 at 788–89, albeit in a different context.

* A second constitutional argument that has been advanced is that the absence of jurors who share the same ethnic or cultural background as the accused denies the accused of a fundamental right to a jury of his or her peers under sections 11(d) and (f) of the *Charter*. However, Canadian courts have consistently held that an accused does not have a right to be tried by a jury of his or her peers: *R.* v. *Nepoose* (1988), 93 A.R. 32 (C.A.); *R.* v. *F.(A.)* (1994), 30 C.R. (4th) 333 (Ont. Gen. Div.); *R.* v. *Butler* (1984), 3 C.R. (4th) 174 (B.C.C.A.); and *R.* v. *Kent* (1986), 27 C.C.C. (3d) 405 (Man. C.A.). The U.S. Supreme Court has also taken this approach: *Holland* v. *Illinois*, 493 U.S. 474 (1990).

* In *R.* v. *F.(A.)* (1994), 30 C.R. (4th) 333 (Ont. Gen. Div.), appeal dismissed [1997] O.J. No. 2521 (C.A.) (QL), the accused asserted a constitutional right to be tried by a jury of his cultural peers randomly selected from a smaller cross-section of the community, rather than being obliged to follow the provincial statutory process, which requires random selection from the entire population of the judicial district. The court rejected the constitutional argument of the accused, stating that (370–71):

> The premise underlying jury selection for truth-finding purposes is that the process is better served by a diversity of potential jurors representative of the wider community. It is this very diversity which more readily gains public acceptance as being conducive to an objective and fair verdict in the trial, and is therefore more likely to inspire widespread public confidence in the process.

In his considered decision, Stach J. relied on the decision of *R.* v. *West* (10 January 1992), (B.C.S.C.) [unreported], in which the British Columbia Supreme Court held that in instances where the accused would feel discriminated against because of a lack of cultural peers on the jury, it was the responsibility of counsel, through evidence, to inform the jury of the relevant circumstances, thereby overcoming the jurors' lack of knowledge about relevant geographical or cultural circumstances. See also *R.* v. *Yooya* (1994), [1995] 2 W.W.R. 135 (Q.B.)

* Canadian courts have also been consistent in holding that the equality guarantee in section 15(1) of the *Charter* does not require a jury of peers to be composed substantially of individuals belonging to the same race, culture, or language group as the accused. It has been noted that any such limitation on the use of the diverse and varied societal cross-section outlined in the provincial legislation would permit victims of crime to argue that they were being denied equal protection under the law because of exclusion of a relevant cultural group: *R.* v. *F.(A.)* (1994), 30 C.R. (4th) 333 (Ont. Gen. Div.), appeal dismissed [1997] O.J. No. 2521 (C.A.) (QL). In addition, it has been held that to allow a challenger of the array to demand that a member of his or her cultural group be substantially and disproportionately represented on the jury panel would undermine Canada's multicultural heritage and subvert the right of any otherwise qualified individual to serve as a juror. See *R.* v. *Redhead* (1995), 42 C.R. 4th 252 (Man. Q.B.); *R.* v. *Kent* (1986), 27 C.C.C. (3d) 405 (Man. C.A.).

* The complaint that a jury is not representative, even though it may have been selected by a random cross-section of the community, is distinct from a complaint that a provincial jury act disqualifies, directly or indirectly, certain classes of individuals from eligibility. As noted above in part 1.4(c), the disqualification of otherwise competent and impartial individuals from serving as jurors because of individual eligibility criteria may violate sections 15(1) and 11(f) of the *Charter.* To date, even these types of challenges have met with little success.

2.7(c) **The Procedure for Challenging the Array**

* The *Criminal Code* requires a challenge to the array to be in writing: section 629(2). The challenge must allege that the sheriff or officer who returned the panel was partial, fraudulent, or engaged in wilful misconduct. It has long been accepted that in a written challenge there is no need to include the particulars of the ground relied on, provided that one of the three appropriate grounds is specified: *R.* v. *Ward*, [1972] 3 O.R. 665 (C.A.).

* It has been held that the onus of proof lies on the challenging party to adduce evidence on the balance of probabilities that the sheriff or other officer used partiality, fraud, or wilful misconduct in assembling the array: *R.* v. *LaForte* (1975), 25 C.C.C. (2d) 75 (Man. C.A.).

* Any challenge to the array must be brought before the empanelling of the jury begins, and definitely prior to the swearing in of any juror: *R.* v. *Thomas* (1973), 23 C.R.N.S. 41 (Ont. H.C.J.). This principle is in accordance with the language of section 631(3) of the *Criminal Code*, which directs that the calling of jurors begins (a) when the array of jurors is not challenged, or (b) when the array of jurors is challenged but the judge does not direct a new panel to be returned. Challenges should be conducted in the absence of the jury panel, as there is a possibility that prejudice could ensue against either party: B.Q.H. Der, *The Jury: A Handbook of Law and Procedure* (Toronto: Butterworths, 1989), at 2–12.

* A challenge to the array is heard by the trial judge: section 630 of the *Criminal Code*. The judge must then determine the validity of the challenge, and if the alleged ground is found to be true, he or she shall direct a new panel to be returned. There is also some authority to suggest that if both parties challenge the array a new panel must be returned: *Halsbury's Laws of England*, vol. 11(2), 4th ed. (London: Butterworths, 1990) at para. 985.

2.8 HOW THE JURY IS EMPANELLED

* It should be pointed out, before embarking on a discussion of how particular juries are empanelled, that the entire jury selection procedure, starting with the opening of court where the panel has assembled, constitutes part of the accused's trial for the purposes of section 650(1) of the *Criminal Code*. That section provides the accused with a right to be present throughout the entirety of his or her trial: *R.* v. *Barrow*, [1987] 2 S.C.R. 694. Therefore, the accused must be present for any and all parts of the empanelling process. Any action of the court that denies the accused his or her right to be present for any aspect of jury selection constitutes reversible error.

2.8(a) **Names of Jurors on Cards**

* Once the prospective jurors are within the body of the courtroom, section 631 of the *Criminal Code* sets out the general procedure for selecting potential jury members. Provided that the array of jurors is not challenged or that the challenge to the array is unsuccessful (i.e., the judge has not directed a new panel), the clerk of the court selects cards at random, calling out the name and number on each card as it is drawn, until the number of persons who have answered to their names is, in the opinion of the judge, sufficient to provide a full jury, after allowing for orders to excuse, challenges, and directions to stand by: section 631(3) of the *Criminal Code*. This entire process takes place in open court in the presence of the accused.

* As each juror steps forward, the parties will declare whether they are "content" or whether they "challenge" the prospective juror. If a challenge for cause is being undertaken, it will be resolved according to the procedures described below in chapters 4–8, after which the parties may exercise their peremptory challenges. A peremptory challenge is exercised simply by saying "challenge," which instantly eliminates the prospective juror. No reason need be given. If both parties are content with a juror, he or she will then be sworn and take a seat in the jury box: section 631(4) of the *Criminal Code*. If the initial number of persons called forward after their cards were drawn is not sufficient to provide a full jury, the process will be repeated as many times as is necessary: section 631(5) of the *Criminal Code*.

* The case law suggests that the court has little, if any, discretion to depart from the procedure established in section 631 of the *Criminal Code*. For example, in *R.* v. *Alward* (1976), 15 N.B.R. (2d) 551 (C.A.), the trial judge directed the clerk to select four jurors at a time and to draw no more cards until all challenges of the first four were disposed of. The New Brunswick Supreme Court Appellate Division found that the trial judge should not have departed from the specific directions contained in section 560 (now section 631(3)) of the *Criminal Code*. Based on the facts of this case, the Court held that such a departure from the provisions of the *Criminal Code* did not justify setting aside the murder conviction, though it might provide a ground for an order of *mandamus*. However, in this regard, see *R.* v. *Lee* (12 December 1989), (Ont. H.C.J.) [unreported] [summarized at 8 W.C.B. (2d) 700].

2.8(b) **The Statutory Powers of the Trial Judge**

2.8(b)(i) **Excusing Jurors**

* As indicated above, section 632 of the *Criminal Code* allows the trial judge to order that any juror be excused from jury service, whether or not the juror has been called pursuant to subsection 631(3) or any challenge has been made in relation to the juror, for reasons of:

  (*a*) personal interest in the matter to be tried;

  (*b*) relationship with the judge, prosecutor, accused, counsel for the accused or a prospective witness; or

  (*c*) personal hardship or any other reasonable cause that, in the opinion of the judge, warrants that the juror be excused.

  Section 632 of the *Criminal Code* is fully discussed below at 3.3.

* This provision does not allow the judge to delegate his or her statutory power to excuse jurors to other parties such as the sheriff, since the accused and the public have the right to know why a juror has been excused: *R.* v. *Mid Valley Tractor Sales Ltd.* (1995), 101 C.C.C. (3d) 253 (N.B.C.A.).

2.8(b)(ii) **Standing by Jurors**

* In addition to the power of the trial judge to excuse jurors, section 633 of the *Criminal Code* gives the trial judge the power to stand by jurors. Section 633 provides:

> 633. The judge may direct a juror whose name has been called pursuant to subsection 631(3) to stand by for reasons of personal hardship or any other reasonable cause.

* However, once the accused has been given in charge to the jury, then the procedure for discharging jurors is governed by section 644 of the *Criminal Code*, discussed below at part 2.9.

2.8(b)(iii) **Calling Jurors Who Have Been Stood By**

* Section 641 of the *Criminal Code* states:

> 641.(1) Where a full jury has not been sworn and no names remain to be called, the names of those who have been directed to stand by shall be called again in the order in which their names were drawn and they shall be sworn, unless excused by the judge or challenged by the accused or the prosecutor.
>
> (2) Where, before a juror is sworn pursuant to subsection (1), other jurors in the panel become available, the prosecutor may require the names of those jurors to be put into and drawn from the box in accordance with section 631, and those jurors shall be challenged, directed to stand by, excused or sworn, as the case may be, before the names of the jurors who were originally directed to stand by are called again.

* As the section states, in the event that a full jury has not been sworn and no names from the panel remain to be called, jurors who have been stood by under section 633 of the *Criminal Code* should be called again in the order in which their names were originally drawn. The jurors who have originally been stood by should then be resworn unless they are excused by the judge or challenged by the accused or prosecutor: section 641(1). Where the judge directs additional jurors to be summoned once the panel is exhausted pursuant to section 642 of the *Criminal Code*, but prior to calling

back the jurors who were originally stood by, there is authority which suggests that the accused will not be considered to have been tried by a lawfully constituted jury: *James* v. *R.* (1968), [1969] 1 C.C.C. 278 (B.C.C.A.).

* In addition, according to subsection 641(1), jurors who were originally stood aside and called again once the panel was exhausted cannot be stood aside a second time. However, if other jurors in the panel become available before a juror who has been previously stood by is sworn, the prosecutor may require the names of these jurors to be drawn before drawing the names of the jurors who were stood aside. Jurors in the panel who have not been sworn or stood aside can potentially become available if they were in the same original panel but were involved in another trial during the time that the initial jurors were drawn.

2.8(b)(iv) Summoning Other Jurors When the Panel is Exhausted

* Section 642 of the *Criminal Code* provides:

> 642.(1) Where a full jury cannot be provided notwithstanding that the relevant provisions of this Part have been complied with, the court may, at the request of the prosecutor, order the sheriff or other proper officer forthwith to summon as many persons, whether qualified jurors or not, as the court directs for the purpose of providing a full jury.
>
> (2) Jurors may be summoned under subsection (1) by word of mouth, if necessary.
>
> (3) The names of the persons who are summoned under this section shall be added to the general panel for the purposes of the trial, and the same proceedings shall be taken with respect to calling and challenging those persons, excusing them and directing them to stand by as are provided in this Part with respect to the persons named in the original panel.

* Pursuant to this section, when the panel, including the original stand asides, is exhausted and a jury of twelve has not yet been sworn, the trial judge may, at the Crown's request, order the sheriff or officer to summon from the street or elsewhere as many people as are necessary to constitute a complete jury. These persons may be qualified jurors, or they may be unqualified. These jurors are known as talesmen or tales, and the *Criminal Code* pursuant to subsection 642(2) permits them to be summoned by word of mouth. Jurors who are summoned in this way are added to the general panel for the purposes of the trial and are then dealt with procedurally in the same fashion as the potential jurors in the original panel were dealt

with. For example, the same proceedings will be taken towards the tales with respect to calling and challenging them, excusing them, and directing them to stand by: section 642(3).

* In *R.* v. *Mid Valley Tractor Sales Ltd.* (1995), 101 C.C.C. (3d) 253 (N.B.C.A.), the trial judge ordered the sheriff not to summon simply twenty tales but twenty tales who were eligible for jury duty. This order in effect gave the sheriff authority to pre-screen potential jurors. The Court of Appeal held that the trial judge cannot delegate the power to excuse jurors to another party, as this discretionary power is exclusive to the judicial authority. The court noted that to permit the sheriff or his or her delegates to excuse potential jurors out of the sight and hearing of the accused sullies the public expectation of the judicial role (at 257). The court went on to suggest that the sheriff could perhaps pre-screen candidates, provided that this process is merely a recommendation that leaves the legal act of the decision to the trial judge. Finally, the court held that this deviation from proper procedure could not be saved by section 670(a) of the *Criminal Code*, which provides that a verdict should not be overturned by virtue of "any irregularity in the summoning or empanelling of the jury."

* It has been held that where the summoning of tales is directed, the judge must specify the number of persons to be summoned by the sheriff. This number will depend on the number of people required to complete a twelve-person jury in accordance with section 641(1). Where a full jury has not been selected after the number of tales summoned by the judge has been exhausted, the judge must order the tales who have been stood by to be called again and sworn (unless challenged) before directing that an additional set of talesmen be summoned: *R.* v. *Rowbotham* (1988), 63 C.R. (3d) 113 (Ont. C.A.).

* Tales must be selected in a random fashion and not from an arbitrarily prearranged list: *Smider* v. *Millar* (1964), 50 W.W.R. 108 (B.C.S.C.). In addition, there is English authority to suggest that the entire jury panel cannot be composed of tales: *R.* v. *Solomon* (1957), [1958] 1 Q.B. 203 (C.C.A.). The failure of one of the tales to meet the juror qualifications outlined in the relevant provincial legislation does not in and of itself bar the juror from serving on the jury: *R.* v. *Rowbotham* (1988), 63 C.R. (3d) 113 (Ont. C.A.).

* Finally, in the event that the trial judge decides not to use the tales provision because it appears at the outset that there is a complete shortage of jurors on the panel, he or she may discharge the jurors and order the sheriff to return an entirely new jury panel: R.E. Salhany, *Canadian Criminal Procedure*, 6th ed. (Aurora: Canada Law Book, 1994), para. 6.3110.

2.8(c) **Who Shall Be the Jury**

* Section 643 of the Criminal Code provides:

> 643.(1) The twelve jurors whose names are drawn and who are sworn in accordance with this Part shall be the jury to try the issues of the indictment, and the names of the jurors so drawn and sworn shall be kept apart until the jury gives its verdict or until it is discharged, whereupon the names shall be returned to the box as often as occasion arises, as long as an issue remains to be tried before a jury.
>
> (2) The court may try an issue with the same jury in whole or in part that previously tried or was drawn to try another issue, without the jurors being sworn again, but if the prosecutor or the accused objects to any of the jurors or the court excuses any of the jurors, the court shall order those persons to withdraw and shall direct that the required number of names to make up a full jury be drawn and, subject to the provisions of this Part relating to challenges, orders to excuse and directions to stand by, the persons whose names are drawn shall be sworn.
>
> (3) Failure to comply with the directions of this section or section 631, 635 or 641 does not affect the validity of a proceeding.

* As stipulated by section 643 of the *Criminal Code*, the twelve jurors whose names are drawn and who are sworn in accordance with the procedure outlined in the *Criminal Code* are designated to be the jury to try the criminal case. The names of these twelve jurors are removed from the jury panel, and these individuals are not assigned to sit on the jury of any other case until either the verdict of their particular case is delivered or until the jury is otherwise discharged. In the event of a verdict or discharge, the names of the twelve jurors are resubmitted to the panel ballot box to be redrawn in the event of another trial necessitating jurors: section 643(1). The use of jurors for service in more than one trial is determined largely by local practice. There is no provision for an alternate jury in Canada.

* Section 643(2) of the *Criminal Code* does not require a jury that has been chosen to serve in a second trial (in whole or in part) to be sworn again. However, if the Crown or accused objects to any of the jurors or the court excuses any of the jurors, the court must order the jurors to withdraw. In that event, the court will further direct that the number of persons required to complete a full jury be drawn according to the standard procedure, including challenges and stand asides, until a full jury is sworn: section 643(2).

* The *Criminal Code* provides that failure to comply with the procedure in section 643 will not affect the ultimate validity of the proceedings. This allowance for irregularity extends also to non-compliance with the directions of sections 631 (names of jurors on cards and drawing of cards), 635 (order of challenges), and 641 (calling jurors who have been stood by): section 643(3). This provision has been used to save a proceeding from being invalidated in the case where the remainder of the jury was filled by the inadvertent calling of potential jurors who were stood by before the final member of the original panel had been called: *R.* v. *McLachlan* (1924), 56 N.S.R. 413 (C.A.). However, this "saving provision" has been deemed inoperative when the trial judge summons talesmen prior to calling the jurors who have been stood aside, as this deprives the accused of both a statutory right and a trial by a lawfully constituted jury: *R.* v. *Rowbotham* (1988), 63 C.R. (3d) 113 (Ont. C.A.).

2.9 DISCHARGE OF A JUROR

* Section 644 of the *Criminal Code* outlines the circumstances in which a juror may be discharged during the course of a trial and the ensuing procedure to be resorted to in his or her absence. The section provides:

> 644.(1) Where in the course of a trial the judge is satisfied that a juror should not, by reason of illness or other reasonable cause, continue to act, the judge may discharge the juror.
>
> (1.1) A judge may select another juror to take the place of a juror who by reason of illness or other reasonable cause cannot continue to act, if the jury has not yet begun to hear evidence, either by drawing a name from a panel of persons who were summoned to act as jurors and who are available at the court at the time of replacing the juror or by using the procedure referred to in section 642. *Criminal Law Improvement Act, 1996*, S.C. 1997 c. 18, s. 75, in force June 16, 1997.
>
> (2) Where in the course of a trial a member of the jury dies or is discharged pursuant to subsection (1), the jury shall, unless the judge otherwise directs and if the number of jurors is not reduced below ten, be deemed to remain properly constituted for all purposes of the trial and the trial shall proceed and a verdict may be given accordingly.

* A judge may discharge a juror during the course of a trial upon being satisfied that the juror should not continue to act because of illness or other reasonable cause: section 644(1). If a member of the jury is discharged for

one of these reasons or dies during the course of the trial, the trial may proceed and a verdict can lawfully be rendered by that jury, unless

(a) the judge directs otherwise, or
(b) there are less than ten members remaining on the jury: section 644(2).

* An accused has an initial right to be tried by a twelve-person jury. Until the trial commences, the court must ensure that, if any juror is excused for any reason, another juror be called to complete the twelve-person jury panel: *R.* v. *Spek*, [1982] 2 S.C.R. 730; *R.* v. *Wellman* (1996), 108 C.C.C. (3d) 372 (B.C.C.A.).

* Where a juror is discharged "during the course of a trial," the situation is different. The recent amendment in section 644(1.1) governs. The judge is not required to replace the discharged juror but may do so if the jury has not yet commenced hearing evidence. The section also describes the procedure to be used if the judge does decide to replace the discharged juror. If a jury panel is available, a new name can simply be drawn. If the jury panel is not available, the judge may order the sheriff to summon other persons for jury duty, using the procedure provided for in section 642. This procedure is described above at 2.8(b)(iv).

* The most contentious issue involving section 644 is when it will be appropriate for a trial judge to decide to proceed with a jury of less than twelve jurors. The answer turns on the meaning of the phrase "where in the course of the trial," since it is that phrase that gives rise to both the power to discharge jurors under section 644, and to continue the trial with less than twelve jurors.

* Prior to the passage of section 644(1.1), the "weight of the case authority support[ed] the view that a trial commences when the accused has been put in charge of the jury": *R.* v. *Socobasin* (1996), 110 C.C.C. (3d) 535 at 552 (N.S.C.A.), leave to appeal refused (1997), 113 C.C.C. (3d) vi (note) (S.C.C.). In *R.* v. *Varcoe* (1996), 104 C.C.C. (3d) 449 (Ont. C.A.), the Court held that the trial judge had not erred by proceeding with eleven jurors after discharging a juror after the judge had given the opening instructions and the Crown had made its opening address. In *R.* v. *Wellman* (1996), 108 C.C.C. (3d) 372 (B.C.C.A.), the Court took the same position, saying that the power under section 644 to continue with less than twelve jurors arises after the accused has been put in charge of the jury. See also *R.* v. *Hurley*, [1997] N.S.J. No. 53 (C.A.) (QL), and *R.* v. *Piche* (1997), 113 C.C.C. (3d) 149 (B.C.C.A.).

* Other cases held that the trial commences only where evidence has been presented to the jury and that until this time, discharged jurors should be

replaced because the power under section 644 to continue with less than twelve jurors has not yet arisen. There is dictum in *R.* v. *Barrow*, [1987] 2 S.C.R. 694, that can be read to support this view. The Supreme Court of Canada had held in *R.* v. *Spek*, [1982] 2 S.C.R. 730 [also known as *R.* v. *Basarabas*], that the circumstances in which the accused should be deprived of his common law right to a unanimous verdict of twelve persons should be limited. In *R.* v. *Lo*, [1995] B.C.J. No. 1528 (C.A.) (QL), the British Columbia Court of Appeal relied on the *Spek* decision to support the proposition that "in the course of trial" in section 644 should be interpreted restrictively and confined to cases where presentation of evidence has begun. On this view, a replacement juror should be selected where the jury has not yet begun to hear evidence. Any steps that have been taken up until that time that involve the jury, such as jury instructions and opening statements, must be repeated, either during the trial itself or by declaring a mistrial and starting again. The inconvenience of having to do this encouraged the Court in *R.* v. *Varcoe* (1996), 104 C.C.C. (3d) 449 (Ont. C.A.), to conclude that a trial commences when the accused has been put in the charge of the jury.

* Section 644(1.1) has now settled matters. It follows necessarily from the wording of s. 644(1.1) that the phrase, "where in the course of a trial," must include a period prior to the commencement of the presentation of evidence to the jury. This is because the power to replace a discharged juror under s. 644(1.1) lapses by the time the jury has "begun to hear evidence." That power must therefore necessarily arise at an earlier time, contrary to the decision in *R.* v. *Lo*, [1995] B.C.J. No. 1528 (C.A.) (QL). The *Socobasin* (1996), 110 C.C.C. (3d) 535 (N.S.C.A.) view that the trial commences when the accused has been put in charge of the jury is correct. That being so, a jury shall be deemed to remain properly constituted if it is not reduced below ten, even though evidence has not yet commenced and the trial judge chooses not to replace a discharged juror.

* It follows that the decision in *R.* v. *Singh* (1996), 108 C.C.C. (3d) 244 (B.C.C.A.) is also correct. The trial judge chose to replace a discharged juror after evidence had been presented in a *voir dire*, but before any evidence was led before the jury. The accused claimed that because the trial had commenced, jurisdiction to replace the juror had been lost. Section 644(1.1) affirms that judges have the power to replace discharged jurors, even "in the course of the trial," so long as the jury has not commenced hearing evidence.

* In *R.* v. *Genest* (1990), 61 C.C.C. (3d) 251 (Que. C.A.), the court held that even though section 644 permits the number of jurors to be reduced to ten

in the course of the trial, this provision does not violate section 11(f) of the Charter, which guarantees the benefit of trial by jury. This is because a jury of ten can still fulfil its functions, adequately decide questions of fact, and deliver a fair and impartial verdict that reflects contemporary societal values and maintains the credibility of the jury system: see also *R.* v. *Lessard* (1992), 74 C.C.C. (3d) 552 (Que. C.A.).

* The courts have interpreted "other reasonable cause" for discharge of a juror in a liberal manner that is broad enough to encompass situations when a juror may not be manifestly impartial: *R.* v. *Tsoumas* (1973), 11 C.C.C. (2d) 344 (Ont. C.A.). A juror can be discharged on this ground for any cause that the judge deems reasonable that may have a negative effect on the competence or impartiality of the jury: *R.* v. *Holcomb* (1973), 6 N.B.R. (2d) 485 (C.A.), aff'd (1973), 6 N.B.R. (2d) 858 (S.C.C.). However, in *R.* v. *Sophonow* (1986), 50 C.R. (3d) 193 (Man. C.A.), the court decided that a juror should not be discharged for refusing to deal with the evaluation of the evidence because she felt it unnecessary because of her alleged psychic powers. The Manitoba Court of Appeal held that the suggestion that the juror had a psychic power with regard to the assessment of evidence was insufficient cause for depriving the accused of the right to a twelve-person jury.

* Jurors have been discharged in cases where they have had personal contact with a party to the proceedings, including driving to court: *R. v. Holcomb* (1973), 6 N.B.R. (2d) 485 (C.A.), aff'd (1973), 6 N.B.R. (2d) 858 (S.C.C.), or having lunch with the accused: *R.* v. *MacKay* (1980), 53 C.C.C. (2d) 366 (B.C.C.A.), or asking defence counsel for directions: *R.* v. *Tsoumas* (1973), 11 C.C.C. (2d) 344 (Ont. C.A.).

* The appearance of partiality on the part of a juror has led to a discharge in cases where the juror was a witness in another case involving the same police officer: *R.* v. *Parker* (1981), 23 C.R. (3d) 282 (Ont. H.C.J.); where the juror was a fellow employee of the brother of the murder victim: *R.* v. *Spek*, [1982] 2 S.C.R. 730; where the juror smiled inordinately at the accused during jury selection and admitted that she could not be impartial: *R.* v. *Andrews* (1984), 13 C.C.C. (3d) 207 (B.C.C.A.); and in cases where the juror knew the accused: *R.* v. *Plato* (1985), 60 A.R. 73 (C.A.); or one of the witnesses: *R.* v. *Hall* (6 March 1986), (B.C.C.A.) [unreported] [summarized at 16 W.C.B. 195]. A juror's inability to meet the financial needs of his family constitutes reasonable grounds for discharge under section 644 of the *Code*, as such a concern could have a negative impact and lead to partiality on the part of the jury: *R.* v. *Samson (No. 2)* (1982), 36 O.R. (2d) 719 (Co. Ct.).

* In addition, jurors have been discharged on compassionate grounds that arose during the course of the trial. In *R.* v. *Genest* (1990), 61 C.C.C. (3d) 251 (Que. C.A.), a juror was discharged to comfort his mother after the death of his brother.

* If, during the course of a trial, it is discovered that a member of the jury had been previously convicted of an offence, contrary to the qualifications of a juror under provincial legislation, this will not require discharge of the juror or affect the validity of the verdict: *R. v. Lessard* (1992), 74 C.C.C. (3d) 552 (Que. C.A.).

* In *R.* v. *M.(A.)* (13 September 1994), (Ont. C.A.) [unreported] [summarized at 24 W.C.B. (2d) 498], the Court, by endorsement, held that the trial judge had not erred in refusing to discharge a juror who proved to be on the board of governors of a "crime stoppers" group. She was not considered to be ineligible as "engaged in the enforcement of the law," and the judge had not erred in the exercise of his discretion.

* If any information reaches the trial judge that may indicate the need to discharge a juror, the judge must conduct a personal inquiry. The proceedings to determine if a juror should be discharged are optimally done on the official record and in the presence of the Crown and the accused. The remaining jurors may not be present during the process of examination of an alleged partial juror: *R.* v. *Chambers*, [1990] 2 S.C.R. 1293. Though the juror cannot be cross-examined directly by counsel or put on oath, counsel is invited to make submissions to the court and to suggest appropriate questions for the trial judge to put to the juror: *R.* v. *Hanna* (1993), 80 C.C.C. (3d) 289 (B.C.C.A.). See also *R.* v. *Sophonow* (1986), 50 C.R. (3d) 193 (Man. C.A.), where the accused was permitted by the trial judge to make submissions and cross-examine the juror. Though the judge allowed this because in his opinion the accused had a vital interest in the discharge, the British Columbia Court of Appeal in *Hanna* specifically disregarded the *Sophonow* decision. The court held that counsel was prohibited from cross-examining a juror, as the role of a juror is not that of witness but rather that of an impartial party who will be responsible for rendering a verdict.

* In the event that a juror is discharged, the trial is not automatically declared a mistrial. The determination of whether the trial should be deemed a mistrial or continued with fewer than twelve jurors is entirely within the discretion of the trial judge. To make this determination, the judge must consider a number of factors that were established in *R.* v.

Lessard (1992), 74 C.C.C. (3d) 552 (Que. C.A.), leave to appeal refused (1992), 145 N.R. 390 (note) (S.C.C.), and *R.* v. *Taillefer* (1995), 40 C.R. (4th) 287 (Que. C.A.), leave to appeal refused (1996), 103 C.C.C. (3d) vi (note) (S.C.C.). The judge must consider:

- the nature of the incident leading to the discharge of the juror in light of the evidence at trial;
- the conduct of the parties;
- the whole of the circumstances particular to the trial;
- whether the incident caused prejudice to the parties;
- the appropriate remedy to repair the prejudice;
- whether the incident affected the right of the accused to a fair trial;
- the reaction of the jurors on learning of the incident.

* In addition, the trial judge can investigate if the impartiality of the remaining jurors has been negatively affected by the discharge of a juror: *R.* v. *Musitano* (1985), 53 O.R. (2d) 321 (C.A.). Because of the significant possibility that the jurors will speculate about why a fellow juror was discharged, the judge should give an explanation for the discharge to the remaining jurors: *R.* v. *MacKay* (1980), 53 C.C.C. (2d) 366 (B.C.C.A.). See too *R.* v. *Andrews* (1984), 13 C.C.C. (3d) 207 (B.C.C.A.).

* Once the trial judge makes a determination about whether to discharge a juror or declare a mistrial based on the above factors, an appellate court will not lightly interfere with the exercise of this discretion: *R.* v. *Fabrikant* (1995), 39 C.R. (4th) 1 (Que. C.A.), leave to appeal refused (1995), 42 C.R. (4th) 411 (note) (S.C.C.); *R.* v. *Lessard* (1992), 74 C.C.C. (3d) 552 (Que. C.A.), leave to appeal refused (1992), 145 N.R. 390 (note) (S.C.C.); and *R.* v. *Hahn* (1995), 62 B.C.A.C. 6 (C.A.). Indeed, in *R.* v. *Taillefer* (1995), 100 C.C.C. (3d) 1 (Que. C.A.), leave to appeal refused (1996), 103 C.C.C. (3d) vi (note) (S.C.C.), the Court of Appeal refused to interfere with the judge's decision not to discharge a juror or declare a mistrial where that juror had a discussion with a Crown witness about an aspect of her testimony and reported what she had discovered to the balance of the jury. It was enough, in all of the circumstances given the nature of the information obtained, in light of the evidence at trial, to address the matter by cautioning the jury to render a verdict solely on the evidence heard in the courtroom.

CHAPTER 3

PRE-SCREENING THE JURY PANEL

3.1 INTRODUCTION

* An important issue that arises prior to the challenge for cause and peremptory challenge stages of jury selection is whether the trial judge can pre-screen the jury panel and excuse prospective jurors on the basis of partiality. The Supreme Court of Canada, in *R.* v. *Barrow*, [1987] 2 S.C.R. 694, and now Parliament, in enacting section 632 of the *Criminal Code*, have provided an answer.

3.2 PRE-SCREENING THE JURY IN CASES INVOLVING OBVIOUS PARTIALITY

* The Supreme Court of Canada, in *R.* v. *Barrow*, [1987] 2 S.C.R. 694 at 709–10, and *R.* v. *Sherratt*, [1991] 1 S.C.R. 509 at 527–28 & 532, held that the power of a trial judge to pre-screen prospective jurors is limited to only those cases of obvious or non-controversial cases of partiality. Obvious partiality includes such things as a personal interest in the case, or a relationship with one of the trial participants (i.e., the judge, prosecutor, accused, or a witness). In *Barrow*, Justice Dickson explained that the reason for limiting the trial judge's ability to pre-screen prospective jurors is that, according to section 640(2) of the *Criminal Code*,

the trier of partiality is not the judge but two potential jurors. He further added (at 714):

> Any addition to this process from another source would upset the balance of the carefully defined jury selection process. This is especially the case of any attempt to add to the powers of the judge. . . . The judge's role is to supervise trials of partiality, not to decide them.

* In most cases, the trial judge will pre-screen the jury panel by reading a witness list and by introducing the Crown and the defence as well as him or herself. He or she will then ask jurors with a personal interest or identifiable relationship to any of these persons to stand up. The trial judge may then summarily excuse jurors after having identified the basis for the partiality. As Justice Dickson stated in *R.* v. *Barrow*, [1987] 2 S.C.R. 694 at 709:

  > [A]n initial question by the judge to the jury array is best seen as a summary procedure to speed up the jury selection.

  Occasionally, the trial judge may ask the prospective juror a question to identify a potentially disqualifying personal interest, relationship, or hardship when the individual juror is called to be challenged or accepted.

* The pre-screening of the panel must be conducted in the presence of the accused and with his or her consent: *R.* v. *Barrow*, [1987] 2 S.C.R. 694 at 709–10. However, the explicit consent of the accused or Crown is not necessary before jurors are pre-screened, since prescreening is to be conducted only in cases of obvious partiality, when the consent of the parties can be presumed: *R.* v. *Sherratt*, [1991] 1 S.C.R. 509 at 534.

* It is possible, as an exception to the general rule, that the pre-screening must be done in the presence of the accused, and that prospective jurors may be excused in the absence of the accused where the grounds for doing so relate to the personal hardship of the juror or to other reasonable causes that do not affect the vital interests of the accused. In *R.* v. *Hurley*, [1997] N.S.J. No. 53 (C.A.) (QL), the accused stepped out of the court because there were no seats. By the time he returned and before he could be arraigned, four jurors were excused by reason of personal hardship, and another four were excused because they knew the accused. The trial judge was held not to have erred by continuing with the jury selection. The Court of Appeal cited the practice in Nova Scotia of excusing jurors before arraignment and "not in the presence of the accused" where the grounds

for excusing the juror are based on personal hardship or other reasonable cause, such as a medical disability. The Court noted that even if it was wrong in this regard, section 686(1)(b)(iv) of the *Criminal Code* enabled the appeal to be dismissed because the accused suffered no prejudice as the result of a "procedural irregularity." Prudence would suggest, despite *Hurley*, that the judge responsible for empanelling the jury should ensure that accused persons are present before prospective jurors are excused.

3.3 SECTION 632 OF THE *CRIMINAL CODE*

* Section 632 of the *Code* came into force in 1992 in order to codify the limited power to pre-screen that was recognized in *R.* v. *Barrow*, [1987] 2 S.C.R. 694, and *R.* v. *Sherratt*, [1991] 1 S.C.R. 509. Section 632 states:

> 632. The judge may, at any time before the commencement of a trial,[1] order that any juror be excused from jury service, whether or not the juror has been called pursuant to subsection 631(3) or any challenge has been made in relation to the juror, for reasons of
>
> (*a*) personal interest in the matter to be tried;
> (*b*) relationship with the judge, prosecutor, accused, counsel for the accused or a prospective witness; or
> (*c*) personal hardship or any other reasonable cause that, in the opinion of the judge, warrants that the juror be excused.

---

1 In *R.* v. *Barrow*, [1987] 2 S.C.R. 694 at 703–4, and *R.* v. *Spek*, [1982] 2 S.C.R. 730, the Supreme Court of Canada held that the meaning of the "commencement of a trial" will vary with the context (i.e., which section of the *Code* is involved and what interest that section seeks to protect). In *Barrow*, Chief Justice Dickson held, for the majority, that the meaning of "trial" for the purposes of section 650 of the *Code*, which gives an accused the right to be present in court for the "whole of . . . [his] trial," includes the jury selection process, given the importance of an impartial jury to a fair trial. However, this definition of trial cannot apply to section 632, since if the trial commenced with jury selection, it would preclude the judge from excusing jurors during the jury selection process. In *Spek*, which dealt with the discharge of a juror during the trial pursuant to section 644 of the *Code*, Justice Dickson, as he then was, held that the meaning of the commencement of trial should be narrowly construed, given the importance of an accused's common law right to the unanimous verdict of twelve persons. Dickson J. thus held that a trial has commenced when the accused is put in "charge of the jury." This same meaning of the commencement of a trial should apply to section 632, given its purpose, which is to provide the judge with a summary manner in which to excuse prospective jurors in cases of obvious partiality or personal hardship.

* Section 632 goes further than *Barrow* in that it enables a trial judge also to pre-screen the jury panel for personal hardship (i.e., self-employment, single parent) or "any other reasonable cause." Presumably "other reasonable cause" would also extend to cases of infirmity, provincial ineligibility, and to those rare cases when a juror comes forward and gives a statement that reveals an obvious bias. For example, in one sexual assault case a juror came forward after the challenge for cause and stated to the judge: "I have already convicted the man. I cannot be impartial." It is suggested that the trial judge properly exercised his jurisdiction in excusing the juror pursuant to this section: *R.* v. *Lalonde* (24 April 1995), (Ont. Gen. Div.) [unreported].

* In *R.* v. *Betker* (1997), 115 C.C.C. (3d) 421 at 442–43 (Ont. C.A.), it was recognized that, apart altogether from any consideration of bias, sexual offence victims who are called as jurors in sexual offence cases may be so psychologically scarred and traumatized that it would be inhuman to require them to serve. The same could be true of those closely associated with such victims. To avoid this, trial judges are advised to alert the entire panel of the nature of the charges and to invite those jurors who would find it too difficult to sit to identify themselves so that they may be excused under section 632(c) of the *Criminal Code*. The Court noted that to protect their privacy, no follow-up questioning should be undertaken.

* Recently, the Ontario Court of Appeal had occasion to address the issue of the extent of the inquiry that is required where a question of partiality arises under section 632 of the *Criminal Code*. In *R.* v. *Harris* (9 September 1996), (Ont. C.A.) [unreported], the trial judge vetted the jury panel, asking potential jurors to indicate to him whether any of them was closely connected with the deceased. One of the individuals chosen as a juror came forward after the jury was selected but before the appellant had been put before the jury and indicated to the trial judge that he might have known the deceased as a result of their working together in the theatrical business. The trial judge asked the juror whether he in fact had worked with the deceased. The juror responded:

  > I had an acquaintance with Michael Boncoeur [sic the deceased]. We performed together for one evening in the same theatre in 1975, and in 1980 he acted as a dresser for three weeks at the Bayview Theatre at a play in which I was involved.

  Having heard this response, the trial judge concluded that the juror was not closely connected or related to the deceased, and he rejected the defence request to make further inquiries. The Court of Appeal dismissed this ground of appeal for the following reasons:

  > Based on the answers he received . . . the trial judge was obviously satisfied that the juror's connection with the deceased was nothing more than

> a casual passing professional contact many years earlier. Accordingly, he saw no basis for delving further into the possibility of [the] juror's partiality.
>
> Under these circumstances, while it would have been open for the trial judge to probe in somewhat greater detail the relationship between the juror and the deceased and its possible effect on the juror's ability to be impartial, we are not persuaded that the trial judge erred in failing to do so. The trial judge had a discretion to exercise and in our view it cannot be said that he erred in the exercise of his discretion.

* In *R.* v. *Faulds* (1996), 111 C.C.C. (3d) 39 (Ont. C.A.), the Court upheld the decision of the trial judge not to discharge a juror who indicated that his father was a lawyer who had some business dealings with the prosecuting Crown Attorney.

3.4 CASES OF DISPUTED PARTIALITY

* In *R.* v. *Sherratt*, [1991] 1 S.C.R. 509 at 534, the Court held that when the cause is controversial, the trial judge must follow the *Criminal Code* challenge for cause procedure:

> Once out of obvious situations of non-indifference . . . the procedure must conform to that which is set out in the *Criminal Code*. There is absolutely no room for a trial Judge to increase further his/her powers and take over the challenge process by deciding controversial questions of partiality. If there exist legitimate grounds for a challenge for cause, outside of the obvious cases addressed by the *Hubbert* procedure, it must proceed in accordance with the *Code* provisions — the threshold pre-screening mechanism is a poor, and more importantly, an illegal substitute in disputed areas of partiality.

See also *R.* v. *Guérin* (1984), 13 C.C.C. (3d) 231 (Que. C.A.); *R.* v. *Proulx* (1992), 76 C.C.C. (3d) 316 at 368–70 (Que. C.A.); *R.* v. *Tremblay* (1995), 101 C.C.C. (3d) 538 (Que. C.A.).

So serious is this kind of an error in the jury selection process that the only remedy is a new trial, even when the accused is unable to demonstrate prejudice: *R.* v. *Barrow*, [1987] 2 S.C.R. 694 at 714, and *R.* v. *Sherratt*, [1991] 1 S.C.R. 509 at 529.

* Where, however, there has been agreement or acquiescence by counsel to pre-screening by the trial judge, an appeal may not succeed. In *R.* v. *Sutherland* (1996), 112 C.C.C. (3d) 454 (Sask. C.A.), the accused sought to challenge jurors for cause based on pre-trial publicity. The trial judge invited counsel into his Chambers and indicated that he would

pose a general question about publicity to the entire panel. Counsel for the accused did not object and abandoned the challenge for cause application. An appeal based on the error by the trial judge was unsuccessful, although the conduct of counsel was considered relevant on the separate ground of appeal relating to the competence of counsel.

3.4(a) **Recent Cases of Pre-screening in Ontario**

* In light of what the Supreme Court of Canada held in *R.* v. *Sherratt*, [1991] 1 S.C.R. 509, the practice in Ontario of some trial judges pre-screening the array for controversial grounds of partiality is clearly in error. They do so in some cases as a substitute for conducting challenges for cause. If trial judges are of the view that pre-screening is justified in order to weed out potential partiality, then the "air of reality" test required before challenges for cause are allowed (see the discussion below, at 5.1) has surely been satisfied and the judge should proceed with the *Criminal Code* procedure by allowing a challenge for cause to be conducted: *R.* v. *Filion* (1992), 75 C.C.C. (3d) 83 at 96 (Que. C.A.), Fish J.

* Pre-screening has occurred in these Ontario cases:

  - In *R.* v. *Green* (1994), 34 C.R. (4th) 222 at 226 (Ont. Gen. Div.), the court refused to allow a challenge on the basis of alleged partiality concerning sexual offences and developmentally challenged individuals but indicated in its reasons:

    > [T]o offset any possible bias, I propose to put the questions embodied in challenge two and three to the jury panel as a whole, in my preliminary remarks. Potential jurors who feel they cannot be indifferent in the matter of *R.* v. *Green* can declare themselves and be excused. I am confident that this approach, coupled with the usual strong directions with respect to [the] presumption of innocence, the onus of proof, and the importance of the juror's role as judge, with neither sympathy or bias towards the accused, will ensure a fair trial.

  - In *R.* v. *Holmgren*, [1994] O.J. No. 2724 (Gen. Div.) (QL) [summarized at (1995), 25 W.C.B. (2d) 368], the court refused a challenge on the basis of alleged partiality concerning offences against young children but felt it necessary so as "to offset any possible bias," to pre-screen the panel, over the opposition of the Crown.

  - In *R.* v. *M.C.* (10 January 1994), (Ont. Gen. Div.) [unreported], the court refused a challenge on the basis of alleged partiality concerning sexual assault against children but indicated that the court would pre-screen the jury panel:

> However, as an additional safeguard . . . and just out of abundant precaution, I will ask the panel as a whole apart from any other questions arising from personal relationships to anybody in the case if the nature of the offence charged would prevent any of them from rendering a true verdict in accordance with the evidence.

* The practice is not confined to Ontario. In *R.* v. *Gareau*, [1996] M.J. No. 562 (Q.B.) (QL), a challenge was disallowed in a domestic violence case where no evidence to support the application had been presented. Mr. Justice Oliphant nonetheless undertook to invite any members of the panel who might have a bias or prejudice that would not permit them to render a verdict on the evidence to come forward and to be excused.

* But see now *R.* v. *Betker* (1997), 115 C.C.C. (3d) 421 (Ont. C.A.). In Betker, the trial judge had pre-screened the panel to determine whether any jurors felt unable to adjudicate impartially because the charges involved sexual offences by a father against his daughter. Justice Moldaver, for the court, held (at 448–49) that the trial judge had erred because he had no authority to pre-screen jurors in cases of non-obvious partiality. The trial judge's error was harmless, however, because there was no air of reality to the claim by the defence that the nature of the charges could undermine the impartiality of some prospective jurors.

CHAPTER 4

THE MEANING AND PURPOSE OF A CHALLENGE FOR CAUSE

4.1 THE MEANING OF A CHALLENGE FOR CAUSE

* A challenge for cause occurs when either a prosecutor or the accused seeks to have one or more potential jurors disqualified on one of the grounds enumerated in section 638(1) of the *Criminal Code of Canada*. It is a means by which either the Crown or the accused can "rid the jury of prospective members who are not indifferent or who otherwise fall within" one of the enumerated grounds: *R.* v. *Sherratt*, [1991] 1 S.C.R. 509 at 533.

4.2 THE GROUNDS FOR CHALLENGE FOR CAUSE

* Permissible grounds for challenge for cause are described in the *Criminal Code* as follows:

> 638.(1) A prosecutor or an accused is entitled to any number of challenges on the ground that
>
> (*a*) the name of the juror does not appear on the panel, but no misnomer or misdescription is a ground of challenge where it appears to the court that the description given on the panel sufficiently designates the person referred to;
>
> (*b*) a juror is not indifferent between the Queen and the accused;

(*c*) a juror has been convicted of an offence for which he was sentenced to death or to a term of imprisonment exceeding twelve months;

(*d*) a juror is an alien;

(*e*) a juror is physically unable to perform properly the duties of a juror; or

(*f*) a juror does not speak the official language of Canada that is the language of the accused or the official language of Canada in which the accused can best give testimony or both official languages of Canada, where the accused is required by reason of an order under section 530 to be tried before a judge and jury who speak the official language of Canada that is the language of the accused or the official language of Canada in which the accused can best give testimony or who speak both official languages of Canada, as the case may be.

* Section 638(2) of the *Criminal Code* provides, in effect, that the subsection (1) grounds are the sole available grounds of challenge for cause.

4.3 THE CHALLENGE FOR CAUSE PROCESS SUMMARIZED

* When a challenge for cause is requested, the trial judge must first determine whether the proposed challenge meets a threshold test; if it does, the challenge is permitted to take place.

* Where the challenge is that there is one or more jurors whose names are not on the jury panel, it is adjudicated by the judge: s. 640(1) of the *Criminal Code*.

* In all other cases the challenge is adjudicated by the two jurors last sworn, or where there have not been two jurors yet sworn, by two persons present whom the court appoints for this purpose.

* If the challenge is adjudged to be "true," the juror is disqualified: section 640(3) of the *Criminal Code*. If it is not, the juror shall be sworn (section 640(3) of the *Criminal Code*) unless one of the parties exercises one of its remaining peremptory challenges: *R.* v. *Cloutier*, [1979] 2 S.C.R. 709.

4.4 THE PURPOSE OF THE CHALLENGE FOR CAUSE PROCESS

* The existence of the challenge for cause process demonstrates that in some situations, other safeguards for ensuring impartial verdicts rendered on the evidence presented in the case are insufficient and must be supplemented by a challenge for cause to ensure that adjudication is done fairly and impartially, that justice is seen to be done, and that the right to a jury trial is an effective one.

* While it is common for faith to be expressed in the wisdom and ability of juries, it is worth noting that in *R.* v. *G.(R.M.)* (1996), 110 C.C.C. (3d) 26 at 34 (S.C.C.), Cory J. expressed concern that "[i]f the process is subjected to unwarranted pressures, or to unnecessary distractions, the delicate reasoning process may be thwarted." The challenge for cause assists in protecting that delicate process from the influence of partiality.

4.4(a) **The Fairness of the Trial and Impartiality**

* The underlying purpose of the challenge for cause process is to ensure that trials are conducted fairly, since "selection of an impartial jury is crucial to a fair trial": *R.* v. *Barrow*, [1987] 2 S.C.R. 694 at 710. For this reason both the common law right to a fair trial and the *Charter* rights of accused persons are implicated when a request for a challenge for cause is brought.

* "There is a denial of a fundamental right to a fair and proper trial where the accused is not allowed to challenge any number of jurors for cause, when the grounds of challenge are properly specified in accordance with . . . the *Criminal Code* [s. 638(1)] and made before the juror is sworn": *R.* v. *Zundel* (1987), 58 O.R. (2d) 129 at 166 (C.A.).

4.4(b) **The Appearance of Justice**

* This denial of a fundamental right is so whether there are reasons "to doubt the fairness of . . . [the] trial, the impartiality of . . . [the] jury or the validity of . . . [the] verdict. [Enjoyment of the statutory right to challenge for cause] . . . is essential to the appearance of fairness and the integrity of the trial. The improper denial of this right necessitates the quashing of the conviction without any demonstration of actual prejudice": *R.* v. *Parks* (1993), 15 O.R. (3d) 324 at 352 (C.A.).

* This prejudice need not be shown because, "[a]s with all trials, justice must be seen to be done, and even the appearance of partiality is to be avoided": *R.* v. *Hubbert* (1975), 11 O.R. (2d) 464 at 475 (C.A.).

4.4(c) Keeping the Right to a Jury Trial Effective

* Similarly, a denial of this statutory right will undermine the full enjoyment of the right to a jury trial enjoyed by those who are entitled to such trials pursuant to section 11(f) of the *Canadian Charter of Rights and Freedoms*. As L'Heureux-Dubé J. said in *R.* v. *Sherratt*, [1991] 1 S.C.R. 509 at 525:

> [T]he *Charter* right to jury trial is meaningless without some guarantee that it will perform its duties impartially and represent, as far as is possible and appropriate in the circumstances, the larger community.

4.4(d) The Public Interest in Impartial Verdicts

* It is not only the accused that is to be considered. The prosecutor can bring challenges for cause as well under section 638(1) of the *Criminal Code*. This is because there is a general public interest in impartial verdicts being rendered according to admissible evidence: *R.* v. *Barrow*, [1987] 2 S.C.R. 694 at 710.

> The accused, the Crown, and the public at large all have the right to be sure that the jury is impartial and the trial fair; on this depends public confidence in the administration of justice.

4.4(e) The Implications for the Construction and Application of the Challenge for Cause Provisions

* Since the challenge for cause process exists in aid of the constitutional rights of the accused, the statutory provisions must be interpreted in a broad and purposive fashion.

4.4(f) Challenges for Cause and Fitness Hearings

* Given the important role it plays, the challenge for cause procedure is available not only at the trial proper, but also at a hearing to determine the fitness of the accused to stand trial where that hearing is being conducted in front of a jury: *R.* v. *H.S.R.*, [1994] O.J. No. 1131 (Gen. Div.) (QL).

4.4(g) Challenges for Cause and Section 745 Hearings

* Challenges for cause are available, as well, in section 745 hearings: *R.* v. *Nichols* (1992), 128 A.R. 340 (Q.B.). Section 745, often referred to as the "faint hope clause," provides for jury proceedings that are intended to determine whether convicts of first-degree murder, high treason, or second-degree murder whose parole ineligibility has been set at fifteen years or greater, should have that parole ineligibility reduced.

4.4(h) **The Implications for Section 686(1)(b)(iii)**

* In *R.* v. *Keegstra* (1991), 114 A.R. 288 at 290 (C.A.), and in *R.* v. *Wilson* (1996), 47 C.R. (4th) 61 at 71 (Ont. C.A.), the courts held that the denial of a valid challenge for cause affects the fairness of the trial and the error cannot be cured by resort to section 686(1)(b)(iii) of the *Criminal Code*.

4.5 IMPROPER PURPOSES AND USES OF THE CHALLENGE FOR CAUSE PROCESS

* Given the purposes for the challenge for cause, a number of limiting principles have developed to prevent challenges being brought for improper reasons:

  - Neither party is entitled to a favourable jury; hence the procedure is not to be used in an effort to secure a favourable jury, only an impartial one: *R.* v. *Sherratt*, [1991] 1 S.C.R. 509 at 528; *R.* v. *Makow* (1974), 28 C.R.N.S. 87 at 95 (B.C.C.A.).

  - A challenge for cause cannot be brought in an effort to cause the underrepresentation of a particular class of society or to undermine the representativeness that is essential to the proper functioning of the trial: *R.* v. *Zundel* (1987), 58 O.R. (2d) 129 at 165–66 (C.A.); *R.* v. *Sherratt*, [1991] 1 S.C.R. 509 at 533.

  - The challenge for cause process cannot be used to inquire into the lifestyles, antecedents, or personal experience of the juror. It is not a procedure for wide-ranging personalized disclosure: *R.* v. *Hubbert* (1975), 11 O.R. (2d) 464 at 475 (C.A.), aff'd (*sub nom. Hubbert* v. *R.*) [1977] 2 S.C.R. 267; *R.* v. *Parks* (1993), 15 O.R. (3d) 324 at 333 (C.A.); and *R.* v. *Sherratt*, [1991] 1 S.C.R. 509 at 527–28 & 533.

  - The procedure cannot be used as a means of discovery to assist in the exercise of peremptory challenges: *R.* v. *Hubbert* (1975), 11 O.R. (2d) 464 at 475 (C.A.), aff'd (*sub nom. Hubbert* v. *R.*) [1977] 2 S.C.R. 267; *R.* v. *Parks* (1993), 15 O.R. (3d) 324 at 333 (C.A.). It is not inappropriate, however, for information obtained pursuant to an appropriately initiated but unsuccessful challenge for cause to be used in deciding whether to exercise a peremptory challenge: *R.* v. *Sherratt*, [1991] 1 S.C.R. 509 at 533; and *R.* v. *Ho* (10 May 1996), (Ont. Gen. Div.) [unreported], Watt J.: "It is inevitable that some information garnered from the responses of a prospective juror, or the manner in which he or she answers questions, may incidentally provide such assistance. What is to be avoided, however, are challenges for cause that are mere pretenses or transparencies made but for such ulterior purpose."

- The procedure cannot be used to indoctrinate the jury to a defence: *R.* v. *Hubbert* (1975), 11 O.R. (2d) 464 at 475 (C.A.), aff'd (*sub nom. Hubbert* v. *R.*) [1977] 2 S.C.R. 267; *R.* v. *Parks* (1993), 15 O.R. (3d) 324 at 333 (C.A.).

4.6 APPROPRIATE GROUNDS OF CHALLENGE FOR CAUSE EXAMINED

4.6(a) The Name of the Juror Does Not Appear on the Panel: Section 638(1)

* To be eligible for membership on a jury, the juror's name must appear on the jury panel. As discussed above in chapter 2, the fashion in which jury panels are compiled is determined by the relevant provincial legislation pertaining to juries. The *Criminal Code* provision is intended to ensure that jurors are selected impartially from these random lists. If the prospective juror's name is totally absent, as opposed to simply misdescribed or misspelled in a fashion that still enables the court to identify the juror, then the prospective juror will not be eligible and a challenge for cause will succeed.
* Unlike other challenges for cause, the trier of fact on this issue is the judge who is conducting the *voir dire*: section 640(1).
* The judge may inspect the panel list and receive such other evidence as he or she thinks fit: section 640(1).

4.6(b) Indifference or Impartiality: Section 638(1)(b)

* Section 638(1)(b), the most commonly used basis for challenges for cause, allows challenges to be made when "a juror is not indifferent between the Queen and the accused." There is no distinction to be made between a juror's being "not indifferent" and "not impartial," and it has become common to refer to the "partiality" rather than to the lack of "indifference" of the juror: *R.* v. *Sherratt*, [1991] 1 S.C.R. 509 at 513; and *R.* v. *Hubbert* (1975), 11 O.R. (2d) 464 at 476 (C.A.).
* "Partiality cannot be equated with bias." This is because "partiality" has both an "attitudinal" and a "behavioural" component. "It refers to one who has certain preconceived biases, and who will allow those biases to affect

his or her verdict . . . A partial juror is one who is biased and who will discriminate against one of the parties to the litigation based on that bias." Both aspects must be considered in determining whether a challenge for cause is to be allowed: *R.* v. *Parks* (1993), 15 O.R. (3d) 324 at 336 (C.A.); *R.* v. *Williams* (1996), 106 C.C.C. (3d) 215 (B.C.C.A.).

* Thus, for example, where the challenge for cause is based on pre-trial publicity, a juror will not necessarily be considered partial for having been exposed to that publicity: *R.* v. *Hubbert* (1975), 11 O.R. (2d) 464 at 476–77 (C.A.). The real question is whether the particular publicity or the notoriety of the accused could potentially destroy the juror's indifference between the Crown and the accused: *R.* v. *Zundel* (1987), 58 O.R. (2d) 129 at 164 (C.A.).

* Similarly, though a challenge for cause cannot be based on general grounds such as race, religion, membership in a minority group, or on mere political beliefs, or opinions (*R.* v. *Zundel* (1987), 58 O.R. (2d) 129 at 165 (C.A.)), a challenge may nonetheless be appropriate when it is directed at the ability of the jurors to set aside those opinions, beliefs, or prejudices that could render them partial when performing their duty as jurors: *R.* v. *Parks* (1993), 15 O.R. (3d) 324 at 332–33 (C.A.).

4.6(c) **The Juror's Criminal Antecedents: Section 638(1)(c)**

* The *Criminal Code of Canada* does not disentitle all persons having criminal records from jury duty. Instead, it allows those who have been sentenced to more than one year of incarceration, or who have been sentenced to death, to be challenged for cause.

* As discussed above in chapter 2, jury legislation in every province and territory disqualifies automatically some potential jurors who have been convicted of criminal offences, depending on the nature of the offence or the severity of either the possible penalty or the penalty that was imposed. In most cases, the provincial legislation is as strict or stricter than the *Criminal Code of Canada*, when the offender has not been pardoned, rendering this form of challenge for cause largely redundant save in cases where an ineligible juror is placed inappropriately on the jury panel.

4.6(d) **The Juror Is an Alien: Section 638(1)(d)**

* Although the *Criminal Code of Canada* does not define "alien," this form of challenge is also largely redundant. Provincial legislation uniformly requires eligible jurors to be Canadian citizens resident in the province, in the case of Prince Edward Island, for the prior twelve-month period (*Jury Act*, R.S.P.E.I. 1988, c. J-5). Legislation in the Territories is less demanding. Neither requires residence within the territory and neither requires

Canadian citizenship. In the Northwest Territories it is enough if the potential juror is permanently resident in Canada (*Jury Act*, R.S.N.W.T. 1988, c. J-2, s. 4(b)), and in the Yukon Territory, British subjects are eligible for jury duty (*Jury Act*, R.S.Y. 1986, c. 97, s. 4). Adherence to these eligibility requirements will make this form of challenge largely moot, as well.

4.6(e) The Physical Inability of the Juror: Section 638(1)(e)

* If a juror is unable to discharge his or her duties because of a physical disability such as inadequate hearing or because a physical infirmity disables the juror from receiving the evidence or deliberating, the juror can be challenged for cause. Typically such jurors will simply be excused by the judge pursuant to section 632 (c) without the need for a challenge for cause to be mounted. As chapter 2 explains, legislation in most provinces and territories also renders infirm and incapable jurors ineligible or allows for them to be excused from jury service.

4.6(f) The Language Ability of the Juror: Section 638(1)(f)

* Section 530 of the *Criminal Code* provides that, on application, the accused whose language is French or English has the right to be tried by a tribunal that speaks his or her language or, if circumstances warrant, that speaks both official languages of Canada. If the language of the accused is not French or English, the accused has the right to be tried by a tribunal which speaks the official language in which he or she is best able to give testimony or which, if circumstances require, speaks both official languages of Canada.
* Section 638(1)(f) enables this right to be exercised meaningfully.
* A number of provincial jury statutes also have language eligibility requirements: see 2.3(e), above.

4.7 THE BENEFITS OF BRINGING A CHALLENGE FOR CAUSE

* In *R.* v. *Parks*, (1993), 15 O.R. (3d) 324 at 352 (C.A.), Doherty J.A. had occasion to discuss the benefits of conducting challenges for cause. The self-evident reason for doing so is to rid the jury of partial jurors (s. 638(1)(b)), or of those who are unable to discharge their obligations as jurors (s. 638(1)(e) & (f)). But his Lordship spoke of other advantages in the context of challenges for partiality. In particular:

> Prospective jurors who can arrive at an impartial verdict are sensitized from the outset of the proceedings to the need to confront potential . . . bias and

> ensure that it does not impact on their verdict. In this regard, the challenge process would serve the same purpose as the trial judge's directions to the jury concerning the basis on which they must approach their task and reach their verdict. Lastly, permitting the question enhances the appearance of fairness in the mind of the accused. . . . By allowing the question, the court acknowledges the accused's perception is worthy of consideration.

* So important is the challenge for cause process in the minds of some defence counsel that their readiness to elect trial by jury is contingent on the likelihood that challenges for cause will be permitted. Several mentioned, for example, that they would not try by jury sexual assault cases involving children if they could not challenge jurors for partiality relating to the nature of the allegation facing the accused.

* Another benefit, considered important by some defence counsel, has been identified. While a number of those consulted made the point, Donald Bayne, QC, was the most committed to the view that the primary benefit of the challenge for cause process is in the strategical advantage it gives to defence counsel. In particular, defence counsel is given the first opportunity to make contact with the jury and through the challenge process can, in substance, extract a promise by those jurors who survive the process that they will give a fair and impartial trial to the accused.

* The felt need to take advantage of the process to make the first contact with the jury arises from the ordinary dynamics of the trial. Crown counsel makes its opening statement and then orchestrates the case by calling witnesses in chief, until the case for the Crown is over. The first that jurors hear from the defence counsel is when he or she gets up to cross-examine a Crown witness, a process that can, if not handled artfully, cast defence counsel in a negative light. By conducting a challenge for cause, however, defence counsel are able to introduce themselves to the jury in a proactive way. By handling the process with grace and humility they may be able to create a positive image with the jury, at an early stage.

* More important, jurors appreciate what a sombre process the challenge for cause is. As is explained below, the questioning normally asks jurors whether they are able to give the accused a fair trial, free from bias, prejudice, or partiality. By responding affirmatively to defence counsel's questions, they are effectively promising or assuring defence counsel that they can and will give the accused a fair trial and will do their best to disavow themselves of any prior impressions or biases they may have. In an era when it is perceived by many defence counsel that the presumption of innocence exists only in the imagination of lawyers and not

in the minds of members of the public, securing this promise can get the trial off on the right foot. It focuses on the particular accused as a person deserving a fair trial, reducing the risk that the jurors will see their vocation as citizens who must play their part in crime control and in protecting society.

* The notion that the challenge process establishes a rapport between counsel and the jurors who are selected is not, of course, universally accepted. Senior Assistant Crown Attorney Malcolm Lindsay, QC, would be reluctant to use the challenge process, even if the Crown had a concern about the partiality of jurors, because the process is a bothersome one. It lengthens the jury selection process, producing impatience and angst among prospective jurors. Rather than being seen positively, defence counsel, in his view, are seen to be accusatory in challenging jurors about their racist beliefs or their impartiality or fairness. They do not expect to be asked about the integrity of their belief systems and are apt to resent it if they are. Malcolm Lindsay, QC, is not alone in these concerns. Some defence counsel have sought to require the Crown to take turns asking the challenge questions for fear that defence counsel will appear in a bad light if made to carry the challenge alone.

* The challenge for cause process is not without its costs. As is discussed below, some observers see the enterprise as expensive and time consuming, producing little gain. Without question, the conduct of a challenge for cause will add time to the jury selection process.

* According to some, the challenge process has the potential to produce undesirable effects for the trial itself. Celynne Dorval, an experienced Ottawa prosecutor with particular expertise in the prosecution of child sexual offences, has observed, for example, that challenges for cause in such cases tend to result in the exclusion of a disproportionate number of women, leaving juries that are predominantly male. This, she suggests, contributes to a non-representative trier of fact.

* The view has also been expressed that the challenge for cause process results in the exclusion of honest and careful jurors. As is seen below, prospective jurors being challenged for cause are most commonly asked directly about whether they can be impartial in the case at hand, given, for example, the race of the accused or the nature of the allegation. An avowed racist, intent on harming the accused, is unlikely to disclose his or her racism. The dishonest are therefore shielded effectively from the process. Moreover, those who hesitate or qualify their answers by disclosing factors that may cause them concern are often challenged successfully. Celynne Dorval uses the example of women who respond during a challenge in sexual offence cases

that they have reservations about their ability to be impartial because they have young children at home. Women who respond in this fashion are routinely challenged successfully. Ms. Dorval is of the view that such jurors demonstrate their honesty by revealing their concerns and that this reflects that they are alive to the problem. They would undoubtedly, in her view, heed their oath and focus on the evidence if placed on a jury. In such cases, careful jurors are disqualified needlessly.

4.8 CHALLENGING PEREMPTORILY AFTER A CHALLENGE FOR CAUSE

* Some counsel, such as Donald Bayne, QC, are of the view that if a challenge for cause has been undertaken by counsel, he or she should not challenge peremptorily those jurors who are found to be acceptable by the triers. Mr. Bayne believes that to do so amounts to an open rejection of the views of the jurors who have, in effect, selected the unsuccessfully challenged jurors. Since building a rapport with the jury is essential, the cost of bringing a challenge for cause is that peremptory challenges should not be used, save in exceptional cases.

* This is not the prevailing view. Most counsel consider the challenge process to be useful in deciding which jurors to challenge peremptorily. Still, there may be wisdom in the observation that the peremptory challenges should not be used as readily by defence counsel who have brought challenges for cause. If the Crown is using peremptory challenges, the risk presented would seem to be less.

CHAPTER 5

SUCCEEDING IN OBTAINING A CHALLENGE FOR CAUSE

5.1 THE THRESHOLD TEST

5.1(a) The Burden Is Not a Substantial One

* In determining whether one or more jurors may be challenged for cause there is "little, if any, burden on the challenger": *R.* v. *Sherratt*, [1991] 1 S.C.R. 509 at 535. "The threshold for a party to exercise the right to challenge for cause is a minimal standard.": *R.* v. *Pheasant* (1995), 47 C.R. (4th) 47 at 50 (Ont. Gen. Div.), Hill J.

5.1.(b) The "Air of Reality" or "Realistic Potential" Test

* The burden is simply to provide sufficient information to convince the judge that there is an "air of reality" to the application or "a realistic *potential* for the existence of partiality, on a ground sufficiently articulated in the application." In particular, in *R.* v. *Sherratt*, [1991] 1 S.C.R. 509 at 535–36, L'Heureux-Dubé J. said for the Court:

> [W]hile there must be an "air of reality" to the application, it need not be an "extreme" case. . . .
>
> The threshold question is not whether the ground of alleged partiality will create such partiality in a juror, but rather whether it could create that partiality which would prevent a juror from being indifferent as to the result.

> In the end, there must exist a realistic *potential* for the existence of partiality, on a ground sufficiently articulated in the application, before the challenger should be allowed to proceed.

* Decisions following *Sherratt* have described the threshold test variously as follows:

> Was there a realistic possibility that one or more prospective jurors would, because of . . . [the relevant] prejudice, [opinion or belief,] not be impartial as between the Crown and the accused: *R.* v. *Parks* (1993), 15 O.R. (3d) 324 at 337 (C.A.).
>
> [T]he question . . . is whether there was, on the material before the learned trial judge, any reason to *doubt* that the impartiality of any one of the prospective jurors might have been affected irretrievably: *R.* v. *Keegstra* (1991), 114 A.R. 288 at 292 (C.A.).
>
> [T]he ground articulated for the alleged want of indifference . . . [must] show a realistic potential for partiality on the part of the prospective jurors so as to entitle defence counsel to ask that question of each juror as part of a challenge for cause: *R.* v. *Cameron* (1995), 22 O.R. (3d) 65 at 71 (C.A.).

* In *Sherratt*, [1991] 1 S.C.R. 509 at 536, the Court cited with approval, in the context of publicity cases, the following test articulated in *R.* v. *Zundel:*

> "The real question is whether the particular publicity and notoriety of the accused could potentially have the effect of destroying the prospective juror's indifference between the Crown and the accused."

5.1(c) **The Meaning of "Air of Reality"**

* The "air of reality" test is the lowest burden recognized in the law of evidence. In describing this standard of proof in the context of accused persons wishing to have defences placed before the trier of fact, Cory J. said:

> The term "air of reality" simply means that the trial judge must determine if the evidence put forward is such that, if believed, a reasonable jury properly charged could have acquitted. If the evidence meets that test then the defence must be put to the jury. This is no more than an example of the basic division of tasks between judge and jury: *R.* v. *Osolin,* [1993] 4 S.C.R. 595 at 682.

* There are parallels in both terminology and in the function of the test that can be drawn to the challenge for cause context. The threshold is intended in each case to determine whether the issue should go to the trier of fact. For this reason the threshold standard is not a high one, and judges should be cautious not to apply a strict standard that would usurp the function of the triers.

* Speaking of the air of reality test as it is applied in determining whether defences should be left with juries, the Supreme Court of Canada held in *R.* v. *Park*, [1995] 2 S.C.R. 836 at 848, that

> The requirement that the trial judge not enter into an assessment of credibility or weighing is an important factor in the application of this test. The test is the means by which a judge demarcates the limits of the jury's fact-finding responsibilities. . . . This underlying rationale must be kept first and foremost in the minds of the trial judges as they seek to apply the "air of reality" test. It is a legal threshold, not a factual one.

See also, *R.* v. *L.*, [1987] 1 S.C.R. 782 at 790.

* Applied *mutatis mutandis* to challenges for cause, this would mean that the trial judge must determine if the evidence or information put forward is such that, if it were believed, a reasonable mini-jury of the two triers, properly charged, could find that the challenged juror may not be impartial as between the Queen and the accused. Is this the appropriate approach? The language, the "air of reality," is the same, suggesting that it is. In cases where the factual question being determined by the trial judge and the two triers is the same one, there is every reason for courts to refrain from assessing the reliability of the evidence presented when deciding whether to allow the challenge to be conducted. They should refrain from prejudging the reliability of the evidence because it is for the triers to decide whether the challenge is probably true. Thus, where the challenge for cause relates to the status of a particular juror, such as where the party seeking the challenge suggests that the juror is an alien, or has been convicted of an offence for which he received a sentence of greater than twelve months' imprisonment, or has a personal interest in the case, the trial judge should not assess the reliability of the evidence presented in support of the challenge. It is up to the two triers to decide whether these assertions are probably true.

* Is the same practice appropriate where the application to conduct a challenge for cause is based upon generic or general bias? It seems that the Ontario Court of Appeal thinks not. In *R.* v. *Ly* (1997), 114 C.C.C. (3d) 279 (Ont. C.A.), and *R.* v. *Alli* (1996), 110 C.C.C. (3d) 283 (Ont. C.A.), the Court has expressed disapproval of efforts by defence counsel to establish the factual foundation for a challenge for cause for the first time on appeal, in part because the evidence is "untested" and may therefore be unreliable. If the reliability of the evidence is irrelevant at the application stage, this practice is wrong. On the other hand, concern for the reliability of the foundation evidence in a general or generic bias challenge seems defensible. In such cases the application for challenge is based on the claim that, generally,

there are persons who may not be impartial, for example, because of the race of the accused. In other words, the foundation is established by showing the court that general bias exists. This is not the issue that the triers will have to decide. They will be asked whether any particular jurors suffer from that general bias. Since the issue that the court is presented with differs from that posed to the triers of fact, there is arguably no reason why the court should not assess the reliability of the evidence presented in support of the application. Indeed, if the court refrains from examining the reliability of the evidence presented to support the application, it may end up allowing unmeritorious challenges. Having said this, courts should bear in mind that the threshold is a modest one, and that they should not be overly exacting in assessing the reliability of the evidence that has been presented.

5.1(d) **The Misuse of the "Balance of Probabilities" Standard**

* In *R.* v. *Morgan* (1995), 42 C.R. (4th) 126 at 131 (Ont. Gen. Div.), the Court said:

> There is a presumption the jurors will perform in accordance with their oath, but if a realistic potential for the existence of partiality is established through admissible evidence on a balance of probabilities, the challenge should be permitted by the court.

Other decisions, such as *R.* v. *Yashev*, [1995] O.J. No. 3598 (Gen. Div.) (QL), and *R.* v. *D'Andrea*, [1995] O.J. No. 916 (Ont. Gen. Div.) (QL), have tested challenge for cause applications according to the "balance of probabilities" standard.

* With respect, reference to the standard "the balance of probabilities" is incorrect. This describes a legal burden that is incompatible with the simple requirement that the evidence present an "air of reality." You cannot at once have a burden that is discharged by some evidence that could persuade a reasonable trier of fact of a proposition and, at the same time, require that the evidence establish that proposition on the balance of probabilities. This is as erroneous as it would be to require the Crown to establish that the accused is probably guilty in order to gain a committal at a preliminary inquiry. There should be no reference to the balance of probabilities standard in applying the threshold test. The standard enters into the challenge process only after the challenge is allowed to be conducted, when the triers of fact who are deciding the challenge are determining whether the challenge to a particular juror is true or not.

5.1(e) The Focus on Potential rather than Actual Partiality

* The focus on potential rather than on actual partiality at the threshold stage can be explained on the basis that the challenge for cause process that will be allowed if the threshold test is met is intended to inquire into the impartiality of the juror. To apply the same test at the threshold stage would involve the judge in performing the task of the trier: *R.* v. *Keegstra* (1991), 114 A.R. 288 (C.A.).

5.1(f) The Impact of the *Charter* on the Threshold Test

* The challenge for cause process is neither "extraordinary" nor "exceptional," and the cautionary remarks of the Ontario Court of Appeal in *R.* v. *Hubbert* (1975), 11 O.R. (2d) 464 (C.A.), aff'd (*sub nom. Hubbert* v. *R.*) [1977] 2 S.C.R. 267, are to be read "in light of the coming into force of the *Charter*": *R.* v. *Sherratt*, [1991] 1 S.C.R. 509 at 532 & 536.

* In particular, L'Heureux-Dubé J. said in *R.* v. *Sherratt*, [1991] 1 S.C.R. 509 at 532, about *Hubbert*'s "broad statements":

> While it is no doubt true that trial judges have a wide discretion in these matters and that jurors will usually behave in accordance with their oaths, these two principles cannot supersede the right of every accused person to a fair trial, which necessarily includes the empanelling of an impartial jury.

* But see *R.* v. *Cameron* (1995), 22 O.R. (3d) 65 at 72 (C.A.), where a panel of the Ontario Court of Appeal quoted those cautionary remarks from *Hubbert* as follows:

> The voice of caution expressed by this court almost 20 years ago in *R.* v. *Hubbert* (1975), 11 O.R. (2d) 464 at 476 . . . [aff'd] 2 S.C.R. 267 . . ., bears repeating and should be followed:
>
>> *The next principle requiring enunciation is that the trial Judge has a wide discretion and must be firmly in control of the challenge process.* We believe that from time to time, and in various parts of the Province, the process has been abused by counsel. The influence of American practices in some States has crossed the border — and sometimes not in the actual form of the prescribed practices, but as they are thought to be by Canadian imitators. The challenge process must be fair to prospective jurors as well as to the accused. Concern over undue prolongation of criminal trials has recently been voiced in England and the United States, particularly where long *voir dires* occupy substantial portions of the trial. Trials should not be unnecessarily prolonged by *speculative and sometimes suspect challenges for cause*. [Emphasis added.]

* Though speculative and suspect challenges deserve to be rejected, it has to be wondered whether the general sentiment expressed in *Cameron* is in keeping with the threshold test and with the Supreme Court of Canada's recognition of the primacy of the *Charter*. The message from *Sherratt* is clear. Courts are to err on the side of caution by allowing, rather than disallowing, challenges for cause.

* Obviously, if the threshold test has been met, the challenge for cause must be allowed to take place. In deciding whether that threshold test has been met, courts are to consider the application of a presumption relating to the ability of jurors to abide by their oath.

5.2 THE PRESUMPTION THAT JURORS WILL ABIDE BY THEIR OATH

5.2(a) The Nature and Intensity of the Presumption

* There is a presumption relating to whether duly sworn jurors will abide by their oath and decide cases on the evidence without influence from personal biases or prejudices. The following articulations are among those that have been provided by courts, and they differ materially in describing the strength of the presumption:

"[I]t is no doubt true that . . . jurors will usually behave in accordance with their oaths": *R.* v. *Sherratt*, [1991] 1 S.C.R. 509 at 532.

"[A] juror must be presumed to perform his/her duties in accordance with the oath sworn": *R.* v. *Sherratt*, [1991] 1 S.C.R. 509 at 527, describing the law as stated in *R.* v. *Hubbert* (1975), 11 O.R. (2d) 464 (C.A.).

"[T]he "presumption" [is] that jurors will do their duty in accordance with their oath": *R.* v. *Parks* (1993), 15 O.R. (3d) 324 at 335 & 338 (C.A.).

"There is an initial presumption that a juror not disqualified by the statute under which he is selected, will perform his duties in accordance with his oath": *R.* v. *Hubbert* (1975), 11 O.R. (2d) 464 at 475 (C.A.). (The Supreme Court of Canada did not comment specifically on that articulation in affirming the decision: [1977] 2 S.C.R. 267.)

"[There is a presumption] that duly chosen and sworn jurors can be relied upon to do their duty and decide the case on the evidence without regard to personal biases and prejudices" which "is well established, both as a fundamental premise of our system of trial by jury, and as an operative principle during the jury selection process": *R.* v. *Parks* (1993), 15 O.R. (3d) 324 at 332 (C.A.).

"[T]he presumption [is] that a prospective juror will deliver a true verdict on the evidence in accordance with the solemn oath he or she has taken": *R.* v. *Williams* (1996), 106 C.C.C. (3d) 215 at 232 (B.C.C.A.).

* The intensity or strength of the presumption must necessarily be qualified by the threshold test. This is because one of the functions of a presumption is to assign the burden and standard of proof on an issue; the party against whom the presumption operates must overcome it in order to succeed. In describing the standard of proof on the party wishing to conduct a challenge for cause as an "air of reality" standard that is satisfied by a realistic possibility of partiality, the Supreme Court of Canada in *Sherratt* has necessarily communicated that this presumption should not be interpreted to provide a substantial hurdle. To hold otherwise would undermine the modest burden appropriate in challenge for cause cases. Hence, it is submitted that the articulation of the presumption adopted in *Sherratt*, "that jurors will usually behave in accordance with their oaths," is more in keeping with the total scheme devised by the Supreme Court of Canada than are some of the more aggressive articulations adopted in other courts.

5.2(b) **The Role of the Presumption**

* As indicated, if the presumption can result in denial of a challenge for cause when there is evidence establishing an air of reality or realistic potential for partiality, it contradicts the threshold test. The view was expressed in *R.* v. *Parks* (1993), 15 O.R. (3d) 324 at 335 (C.A.), therefore, that:

> [T]he threshold test set down in *Sherratt* is both a recognition of the validity of the "presumption" that jurors will do their duty in accordance with their oath, and a recognition of the limits of that presumption. Where the threshold test is not met, the "presumption" is relied on. Where it is met, continued reliance on the "presumption" to the exclusion of the challenge process would negate the accused's right to a fair trial by an impartial jury.

* Similarly, in *R.* v. *Williams* (1996), 106 C.C.C. (3d) 215 at 232 (B.C.C.A.), the Court said:

> The application of the presumption, viewed in the light of such considerations [as the oath, and "diffused impartiality" of jurors], may not be sufficient if the evidence shows there is a realistic possibility of bias or prejudice influencing the judgment of a juror.

* This does not mean that the presumption has no role to play in deciding whether there is an air of reality or realistic potential for partiality. The

Parks Court explained that in deciding whether an inappropriate jury bias would lead to partial adjudication, the inquiry must take into account "[t]he nature and extent of the bias, the dynamics of jury adjudication, and the effect of directions intended to counter any jury bias." The Court then said, "In other words, the presumption that jurors will perform their duty according to their oath must be balanced against the threat of a verdict tainted by . . . bias": (1993), 15 O.R. (3d) 324 at 338 (C.A.).

* Thus, it seems that when the evidence or information suggests that there is an "air of reality" to the concern that jurors may hold inappropriate biases (the attitudinal component of partiality), the judge is to consider whether, given the nature of that bias, jury directions and the dynamics of jury adjudication can remove the threat of a verdict tainted by bias (the behavioural component of partiality). If so, the presumption that jurors will perform their duty according to their oath is sustained and the challenge denied. If not, the presumption falls aside and the challenge is to be allowed.

* In other words, the presumption plays no role in determining the existence of an attitudinal bias, but plays a part in deciding whether there is a realistic potential for behavioural bias. Before determining whether the potential exists that jurors will be influenced by their biases, the judge is to consider whether, given its nature, that potential can be defeated by jury directions and the dynamics of jury adjudication. In particular, according to the British Columbia Court of Appeal in *R.* v. *Williams* (1996), 106 C.C.C. (3d) 215 (B.C.C.A.), quoting with approval Esson C.J.B.C. in *R.* v. *Williams* (1994), 30 C.R. (4th) 277 at 281 (B.C.S.C.), the judge shall consider:

> (*a*) the jurors' oath or affirmation which can be expected to bind the conscience of most persons who might otherwise be disposed to decide on their own assumptions and preconceptions;
> (*b*) the "diffused impartiality" which results from the melding of 12 individuals of varying backgrounds into a single decision-making body, and thus tends to subdue personal prejudices;
> (*c*) the seriousness of the jury's task and the solemnity of the trial process which can be expected to have the same effect;
> (*d*) the dynamics of jury deliberations, with the minds of 12 people focused on the issues so that the views and conclusions of each must withstand the scrutiny of 11 others, also tends to subdue reliance on prejudice; [and]
> (*e*) the warnings which can be expected to be given to the jury before they hear the evidence and in the course of the final charge, including warning to guard against relying on preconceptions or biases, can be expected to be effective.

* Having said this, it should be noted that

  • His Lordship Mr. Justice Doherty noted that there has been a long-standing debate about the effectiveness of these trial safeguards: *Parks* (1993), 15 O.R. (3d) 324 at 343 (C.A.); and
  • even "[i]f one assumes 11 jurors who are responsive to their oaths, the evidence, and the law and who are of the view that a reasonable doubt exists, and one biased juror who holds out for conviction despite the oath, the evidence, and the law, the accused will be exposed to a second trial and its attendant risks, stresses, costs and delays. In such a circumstance, it could not be said that the administration of justice has provided a fair trial": *R.* v. *Griffis* (1993), 16 C.R.R. (2d) 322 at 325 (Ont. Gen. Div.).

5.3 DISCRETION AND CHALLENGES FOR CAUSE

* As indicated, trial judges have a "wide" discretion whether to allow challenges for cause to be brought. This does not mean that the judge has discretion to deny a challenge for cause that has an air of reality to it. This discretion relates to the assessment of the information or evidence. As Doherty J.A. explained in *R.* v. *Parks* (1993), 15 O.R. (3d) 324 at 335–36 (C.A.), the discretion exists because:

> [t]he assessment of whether the particular circumstances warrant a specific line of inquiry into partiality involves the pondering and balancing of intangibles and is necessarily somewhat subjective. The trial judge must be given some latitude in deciding whether to permit a proposed inquiry.

* Applied in this fashion, the discretion should be kept to the limits expressed in *Sherratt*. As the Court in that case indicated, this discretion cannot supersede the right of every accused person to a fair trial, which necessarily includes the empanelling of an impartial jury: *R.* v. *Sherratt*, [1991] 1 S.C.R. 509 at 532.

* Moreover, this discretion should always be exercised with the fairness of the trial in mind: *R.* v. *Hubbert* (1975), 11 O.R. (2d) 464 at 482 (C.A.). Hence the Court considered that it was appropriate for the judge to deny the challenge application in *Hubbert* out of concern for the fact that counsel, by asking the question, would be reinforcing the prejudicial information that at the time of the offence his client was on parole from confinement in a psychiatric hospital for the criminally insane. But see *R.* v. *Parks*, where the Court rejected the Crown submission that it would be appropriate to deny the challenge because that challenge would itself inject racism into the case, to the prejudice of the accused: (1993), 15 O.R. (3d) 324 at 333–34 (C.A.).

5.4 COST-BENEFIT ANALYSIS

* There is no room in the air of reality test, or in the discretion that is to be employed in its application, for the consideration of the cost that the process will produce in terms of lengthening trials or making them more complex, any more than there is room, for example, in the case of statements made by the accused to persons in authority for assessing the costs of conducting a *voir dire* into voluntariness. Courts that rely on cost considerations to disallow challenges for cause are erring in law.

* So important is the challenge for cause process that the *Sherratt* court, [1991] 1 S.C.R. 509 at 533, has rejected resort to cost-benefit analysis in the determination of whether a challenge should be granted:

> If the challenge [for cause] process is used in a principled fashion, according to its underlying rationales, *possible inconvenience to potential jurors or the possibility of slightly lengthening trials is not too great a price for society to pay* in ensuring that accused persons in this country have, and appear to have, a fair trial before an impartial tribunal, in this case, the jury. [Emphasis added.]

* So, too, the *Parks* court, (1993), 15 O.R. (3d) 324 at 351 (C.A.), noted:

> In reaching my conclusion I have not relied on a costs/benefit analysis. Fairness cannot ultimately be measured on a balance sheet. That kind of analysis, however, supports my conclusion. . . . The only "cost" is a small increase in the length of the trial. There is no "cost" to the prospective juror. He or she should not be embarrassed by the question; nor can the question realistically be seen as an intrusion into a juror's privacy.

* Nonetheless, some trial judges are still expressing concern about, and are allowing themselves to be influenced by, their perception that permitting challenges for cause will strain judicial resources and unduly prolong trials. For example, Chief Justice Esson in *R.* v. *Williams* (1994), 30 C.R. (4th) 277 at 290 (B.C.S.C.), said:

> "Small" and "slight" are relative terms. But where each prospective juror is subjected to challenge, our recent experience indicates that the time involved can be expected to be at least one-half day. While all too many of our criminal trials have become monsters of length requiring many weeks and months, there are still many which, as is estimated for this one, will require about three days. In relation to such a trial, even a half-day or full day increase brought about by the challenge is not slight or small. As I will explain, the cost in time and the consequent expense to the taxpayer is likely to go far beyond that.

In upholding his decision to deny the challenge for cause, the British Columbia Court of Appeal remarked, however, that Esson C.J.B.C. was simply expressing an *obiter* view and had, in fact, harkened to the law by refraining from considering cost-benefit considerations in arriving at his decision: *R.* v. *Williams* (1996), 106 C.C.C. (3d) 215 at 232 (B.C.C.A.). And see the comments of Justice Clarke in *R.* v. *Green* (1994), 34 C.R. (4th) 222 at 225 (Ont. Gen. Div.):

> If the judicial door to such challenges is left open, their number would inevitably escalate, resulting in protracted trials, a clogged criminal system, and ultimately a public revolt. When would the courts draw the line?

See, too, the comments of McIsaac J. in *R.* v. *Marquardt* (1995), 44 C.R. (4th) 353 at 357 (Ont. Gen. Div.).

* As indicated above, this kind of reasoning has been rejected by the Supreme Court of Canada. Moreover, it has not been the universal experience that properly conducted challenges for cause add unduly to the length of trials. In the United States, federal courts, where the challenge process is more restricted than in most state courts but still more extensive than in Canada, the average *voir dire* often lasts one hour or less.[1] Indeed, in an extrajudicial statement made during a round table discussion on the *Charter's* impact on the criminal justice system, Mr. Justice Casey Hill said:

> I heard hysteria when the challenge for cause came out. "This is going to lengthen trials" they said, but that has not happened.[2]

* The Canadian system for conducting challenges for cause in no way resembles the American. Despite this dissimilarity, fear of Americanization of the system still discourages some judges from allowing challenges for cause and supports the voice of caution heard in *Hubbert*, above, and *Cameron*, above. The typical questionnaire used in American trials contains more than fifty pages of questions regarding, for example, family history, residence, employment, education, activities (i.e., books read, television shows watched), criminal justice experience, law enforcement experience, legal system, and race. Indeed, it is instructive to reflect on the comments of Justice Haines some twenty-three years ago in *R.* v. *Elliott*, [1973] 3 O.R. 475 at

---

1 P. Horowitz, "Jury Selection After Dagenais: Prejudicial Pre-trial Publicity" (1996) 42 C.R. (4th) 220 at 230, citing A.W. Alshuler, "The Supreme Court and the Jury: Voir Dire, Peremptory Challenges and the Review of the Jury Verdicts" (1989) 56 U. Chi. L. Rev. 153 at 158.

2 J. Cameron, ed., *The Charter's Impact on the Criminal Justice System*, (Toronto: Carswell, 1996) at 132.

482 (H.C.J.), which undoubtedly aptly reflect the views of even the most ardent challenge for cause advocates in Canada:

> [T]he Canadian lawyer would be shocked at the unbridled questions by attorneys of prospective jurors before a permissive State or County Judge. Days and even weeks are occupied as lawyers seek to discover the juror's thought processes, his personal prejudices and ask very personal questions. They put hypothetical questions upon supported evidence they may never call, and must often leave the potential juror with the impression that he is on trial.

* In Canada the process is kept in check not by denying challenges for cause, but by controlling the questions that may be asked during the challenge process.

5.5 SPECIFIC GROUNDS OF CHALLENGE RELATING TO PARTIALITY

5.5(a) **Specific Partiality**

* Challenges for cause may be brought when there is a realistic possibility that a particular juror is "closely connected" to the case. "'Closely connected' . . . includes such prior association with the accused, a prospective witness or some person directly connected with the prosecution as to cause the prospective juror to be biased against or partial to the other person involved, to the extent it is unlikely he can render a true verdict according to the evidence": *R.* v. *Hubbert* (1975), 11 O.R. (2d) 464 at 476 (C.A.). This would include, as well, close connections with the judge (s. 632) or with an investigating officer: *R.* v. *Sherratt*, [1991] 1 S.C.R. 509 at 534; *R.* v. *Hubbert* (1975), 11 O.R. (2d) 464 at 478 (C.A.), or a personal interest in the matter to be tried: section 632(b).

* While a judge may pre-screen the panel in such obvious cases of partiality and "excuse" the juror pursuant to section 632 without using the challenge for cause process, either side can still exercise a challenge for cause on these grounds involving any juror that the judge does not exclude: *R.* v. *Barrow*, [1987] 2 S.C.R. 694 at 709–10; *R.* v. *Hubbert* (1975), 11 O.R. (2d) 464 at 478–79 (C.A.)

5.5(b) **Pre-trial Publicity about the Accused's Case**

* Save in very special circumstances, it is not enough to support a challenge for cause that there has been publicity and notoriety about the accused or the event: *R.* v. *Keegstra* (1991), 114 A.R. 288 at 292 (C.A.); *R.* v. *Makow* (1974), 28 C.R.N.S. 87 (B.C.C.A.). This is because the existence of publicity, while

it may establish attitudinal bias, will not normally, without a close examination of its nature and intensity, establish the behavioural bias necessary to partiality. As the Court said in *R.* v. *Zundel* (1987), 58 O.R. (2d) 129 at 164 (C.A.), in a passage adopted in *R.* v. *Sherratt*, [1991] 1 S.C.R. 509 at 536:

> The real question is whether the particular publicity and notoriety of the accused could potentially have the effect of destroying the prospective juror's indifference between the Crown and the accused.

* Important considerations include

- the extent of the publicity
  - the more "widespread" it is, the more likely it is that the challenge will be allowed: *R.* v. *Zundel* (1987), 58 O.R. (2d) 129 at 163–64 (C.A.); *Hubbert* (1975), 11 O.R. (2d) 464 at 477–78 (C.A.).
- the nature of the publicity

  The challenge is more likely to be allowed where
  - the media "misrepresents the evidence": *Sherratt*, [1991] 1 S.C.R. 509 at 536.
  - the media "dredges up and widely publicizes discreditable incidents from an accused's past": *Sherratt*, [1991] 1 S.C.R. 509 at 536.
  - the media characterize the accused in a pejorative fashion: *Zundel* (1987), 58 O.R. (2d) 129 at 160–61 (C.A.); but see *R.* v. *Pirozzi* (1987), 34 C.C.C. (3d) 376 at 381 (Ont. C.A.);
  - the media "engages in speculation as to the accused's guilt or innocence": *Sherratt*, [1991] 1 S.C.R. 509 at 536.
  - the media report inadmissible evidence: *R.* v. *Kray* (1969), 53 Cr. App. R. 412 at 415 (C.C.A.), quoted with approval in *R.* v. *Hubbert* (1975), 11 O.R. (2d) 464 at 478 (C.A.); and see *R.* v. *English* (1993), 111 Nfld. & P.E.I.R. 323 (Nfld. C.A.), an unsuccessful appeal by the accused relating to the results of a challenge for cause that had been allowed. Of note is that one of the factors that supported the decision to grant the challenge was that a confession by the accused had been publicized during a public inquiry into the "Mount Cashel affair." In *R.* v. *Laquant*, [1996] Y.J. No. 120 (S.C.) (QL), the criminal record of the accused had been published. For this reason the challenge for cause was allowed, despite that otherwise the reporting had been balanced.
  - the publicity relates to a finding of a board or tribunal made against the accused on a relevant matter, or a decision by a public official relating to the rights or privileges of the accused: *Keegstra* (1991), 114 A.R. 288 at 292 (C.A.); *Zundel* (1987), 58 O.R. (2d) 129 at 160 (C.A.).

- the publicity purports to recount the views of persons of influence and/or of the community: *Keegstra* (1991), 114 A.R. 288 at 292–93 (C.A.); *Zundel* (1987), 58 O.R. (2d) 129 at 160–61 (C.A.).
- the publicity relates to a "notorious episode": *Zundel* (1987), 58 O.R. (2d) 129 at 164 (C.A.).
- the publicity leads to "public outrage": *R.* v. *Guérin* (1984), 13 C.C.C. (3d) 231 (Que. C.A.).

The challenge is less likely to be allowed where

- the publicity is a mere recitation of the facts: *Sherratt*, [1991] 1 S.C.R. 509 at 536.
- the publicity does not focus on the accused: *Sherratt*, [1991] 1 S.C.R. 509 at 537; *R.* v. *Court* (1995), 23 O.R. (3d) 321 at 343–44 (C.A.); *R.* v. *Rosebush* (1992), 131 A.R. 282 at 288 (C.A.).

• the timing of the publicity

The greater the time interval between the event and the publicity, the less likely the challenge will be allowed: *Sherratt*, [1991] 1 S.C.R. 509 at 514 & 537; denied where there was a nine- to ten-month gap between publicity and trial; *R.* v. *Court* (1995), 23 O.R. (3d) 321 at 343–44 (C.A.), denied where there was a twenty-one-month gap; *R.* v. *Pirozzi* (1987), 34 C.C.C. (3d) 376 at 382 (Ont. C.A.), denied where eleven months or more elapsed between publicity and trial.

Where the publicity is of continuous duration and/or increases as related events unfold, the challenge is more likely to be allowed: *Keegstra* (1991), 114 A.R. 288 at 292–93 (C.A.).

The more short term and intermittent the publicity is, the less likely the application will succeed: *R.* v. *Ho* (10 May 1996), (Ont. Gen. Div.) [unreported], Watt J.

• the location of the publicity

R. v. *Court* (1995), 23 O.R. (3d) 321 at 343–44 (C.A.), denied where trial in Halton Region and most of the publicity was in Hamilton.

* It would be erroneous to rely on the fact that most reported appellate court cases sustain the decisions of trial judges to deny challenges for cause in the area of pre-trial publicity to conclude that such challenges are to be allowed only exceptionally. A decision by a trial judge to allow a challenge is unlikely to form the subject matter of an appeal by the Crown, since even if the jury would have been impartial without that challenge, allowing the challenge will not have rendered the

jury partial. Allowing an unnecessary challenge does not therefore provide the Crown with a realistic ground of appeal. For this reason, appeals tend to be from denials, and the issue for the appellate court in such cases is whether the judge has unreasonably exercised his or her discretion, not whether the appellate judges would have allowed that challenge had they been presiding at the trial. *Sherratt*, [1991] 1 S.C.R. 509, makes it clear that challenges for cause are not to be treated as "exceptional" or extraordinary.

* Where the nature and extent of the publicity cause the threshold test to be met, the challenge should be allowed even in the absence of an established evidentiary connection between the publicity or notoriety, on the one hand, and a lack of indifference by any of the jurors, on the other hand: *Zundel* (1987), 58 O.R. (2d) 129 at 164 (C.A.).

* While the existence of publicity about a "notorious episode" is relevant, the existence of a notorious episode is not a *sine quo non* of a challenge for cause: *Zundel* (1987), 58 O.R. (2d) 129 at 164 (C.A.).

* The fact that it is the conduct of the accused that has attracted the publicity is not a factor to be considered: *Zundel* (1987), 58 O.R. (2d) 129 at 164 (C.A.).

* Since publication bans compromise the *Charter*-protected right to free speech, it is preferable for courts to allow challenges for cause to deal with adverse pre-trial publicity rather than to order publication bans: *Dagenais* v. *Canadian Broadcasting Corp.*, [1994] 3 S.C.R. 835; *Canadian Broadcasting Corp.* v. *Giroux* (1995), 23 O.R. (3d) 621 (Gen. Div.). This suggests, arguably, that courts are not to be miserly in granting challenges for cause in publicity cases. If they were, accused persons would find greater need to seek publicity bans to preserve their right to a fair trial.

5.5(c) **Relevant Pre-trial Publicity Not about the Case of the Accused**

* Pre-trial publicity not about the case involving the accused may support a challenge for cause when that publicity is of such a nature as to threaten the impartiality of jurors. In *R.* v. *Hutton* (1992), 76 C.C.C. (3d) 476 (Ont. Gen. Div.) widespread publicity about a government-funded report on "intimate femicide," which included statistics and formed dramatic conclusions, some of which parallelled the allegation against the accused, sustained an application for challenge for cause when it occurred one week before the trial. See also *Dagenais* v. *Canadian Broadcasting Corp.*, [1994] 3 S.C.R. 835.

5.5(d) **Racial Bias**

* A challenge for cause will be allowed when the race of the accused raises a reasonable possibility that there may be jurors who will not adjudicate impartially: *R.* v. *Parks* (1993), 15 O.R. (3d) 324 (C.A.); *R.* v. *Griffis* (1993), 16 C.R.R. (2d) 322 (Ont. Gen. Div.). In some cases it is possible for judges to deny race-based challenges for cause when they have determined, as a matter of discretion, that the race of the accused does not raise a reasonable possibility that jurors will not adjudicate impartially: *R.* v. *R.(R.)* (1994), 19 O.R. (3d) 448 at 459–60 (C.A.).

* In "challenges for cause based on racial partiality, it is better to risk allowing what are in fact unnecessary challenges, than to risk prohibiting challenges which are necessary": *Parks* (1993), 15 O.R. (3d) 324 at 349 (C.A.).

5.5(d)(i) **Black Accused**

* It has been decided in Ontario that, in any trial in the province where the accused is Black and requests a challenge for cause, the right to conduct a challenge for cause must be granted and the accused should be allowed to ask each prospective juror "whether his or her ability to judge the evidence in the case without bias, prejudice or partiality might be affected by the fact that the person charged is Black": *R.* v. *Wilson* (1996), 47 C.R. (4th) 61 at 70 (Ont. C.A.). Pre-*Wilson* case law denying race-based challenges for Black accused has been overruled. See, for example, *R.* v. *Ecclestone* (29 January 1996), (Ont. Gen. Div.) [unreported], challenge denied in criminal negligence causing injury and possession of weapons charge because the incident occurred in Peterborough and the allegation did not include violence, inter-racial crime, or an allegation of illegal drug involvement; and *R.* v. *Myers* (15 September 1995), (Ont. Gen. Div.) [unreported], challenge denied because identity was the defence in a charge of robbery and unlawful confinement, with the trial occurring in Whitby.

* In some cases, more extensive questioning may be allowed so as to include reference to the circumstances of the case, such as in *R.* v. *Parks* (1993), 15 O.R. (3d) 324 (C.A.), where the question in a homicide case included reference to the fact that the accused is Black and the deceased was white, and *R.* v. *Willis* (1994), 90 C.C.C. (3d) 350 (Ont. C.A.), where the question was specific to accused persons from Jamaica, particularly with respect to a drug-related prosecution.

* In *R.* v. *Coke*, [1996] O.J. No. 2013 (Gen. Div.) (QL) [unreported], in addition to allowing the question approved in R. v. *Wilson* (1996), 47 C.R. (4th) 61 (Ont. C.A.), the Court allowed defence counsel to ask jurors specifically about whether their partiality would be affected by any beliefs, attitudes, or opinions they may have about Black men from Jamaica being involved in the commission of criminal offences. The Brampton, Ontario, application was supported by statistical evidence obtained by a random telephone poll of 400 Metropolitan Toronto residents, relating to perceptions about crime and Blacks and, in particular, West Indians. In *R.* v. *Morgan* (1995), 42 C.R. (4th) 126 (Ont. Gen. Div.) Trafford J., on similar evidence, allowed jurors to be challenged on their beliefs relating to Jamaican men and the commission of crimes involving drugs. But see *R.* v. *Tahal* (20 March 1996), (Ont. Gen. Div.) [unreported].

* In *Parks*, the Ontario Court of Appeal held that the "air of reality" supporting an automatic right to this kind of challenge in Metropolitan Toronto comes from:

(a) "[t]he existence . . . [of a growing] body of studies and reports documenting the extent and intensity of racist beliefs in contemporary Canadian society . . . [including those showing] that wide-spread anti-black racism is a grim reality in Canada and in particular in Metropolitan Toronto": *Parks* (1993), 15 O.R. (3d) 324 at 338 (C.A.);
(b) racism is manifested expressly by some, subconsciously by others, and it exists within the interstices of our institutions: *Parks*, (1993), 15 O.R. (3d) 324 at 338 (C.A.);
(c) "[e]xamination of racism as it impacts specifically on black persons suggests that they are prime victims of racial prejudice": *Parks* (1993), 15 O.R. (3d) 324 at 339 (C.A.);
(d) the Government of Ontario accepts that racism is a real and pressing problem, including in matters of advancement and in the creation of social barriers: *Parks* (1993), 15 O.R. (3d) 324 at 341 (C.A.);
(e) "attitudes which are engrained in an individual's subconscious, and reflected in both individual and institutional conduct within the community, will prove more resistant to judicial cleansing than will opinions based on yesterday's news and referable to a specific person or event": *Parks* (1993), 15 O.R. (3d) 324 at 343–44 (C.A.); and
(f) although social science research and archival data suffer from methodological weaknesses, they support the view that racially prejudicial attitudes translate into discriminatory verdicts: *Parks* (1993), 15 O.R. (3d) 324 at 344–45 (C.A.).

* In *Wilson*, the Court held that the "air of reality" supporting this kind of challenge outside Metropolitan Toronto and across all of Ontario will be assumed without the need for evidence or argument:

(a) "[a]ny distinction based on a geographical boundary between Metropolitan Toronto and communities elsewhere in Ontario is arbitrary and should not form the basis for a judicial exercise of discretion to refuse the challenge," there having been no evidence presented by the Crown to establish that problems of partiality relating to the Black race of the accused are confined to Metropolitan Toronto: *Wilson* (1996), 47 C.R. (4th) 61 at 68 & 70 (Ont. C.A.);
(b) because of the impact of the media, the influence of negative stereotyping on all of the citizens of Ontario cannot be underestimated: *Wilson* (1996), 47 C.R. (4th) 61 at 69 (Ont. C.A.); and
(c) although the largest concentration of Blacks is in Metropolitan Toronto, there is likely to be more racism where there is less interaction between Blacks and whites: *Wilson* (1996), 47 C.R. (4th) 61 at 69 (Ont. C.A.).

* In light of the decision in *Wilson*, the following comments made by Doherty J.A. in *R.* v. *R.(R.)* (1994), 19 O.R. (3d) 448 at 462 (C.A.), must be taken to have lost the significance they once had in restricting the impact of the *Parks* decision:

> In my opinion, *Parks* is consistent with pre-existing binding authority. It took the principles established in those authorities and applied them to a specific challenge for cause (partiality based on anti-Black prejudice) made in a particular setting (contemporary Metropolitan Toronto), and made in light of the specific facts of the case (an inter-racial homicide arising out of an aborted drug transaction).

Wilson (1996), 47 C.R. (4th) 61 (Ont. C.A.) has decided that regardless of the Ontario community or the nature of the charge, race-based challenges requested by Black accused persons should be allowed.

* *R.(R.)* remains good authority, however, for its central proposition — namely, that Black persons who did not request a race-based challenge for cause at their trials cannot rely on the failure of the trial judge to conduct such a challenge, even where their case was still in the system because of an outstanding appeal at the time that *Parks* was decided. This is because the decision in *Parks* to allow race-based challenges did not constitute "a dramatic shift" in the law away from a course set out by earlier eminent authority such that fairness would require allowing appellants the benefit of a change in the law: *R.* v. *R.(R.)* (1994), 19 O.R. (3d) 448 (C.A.), but see the criticism of this part of the decision in D.M. Tanovich, "Ensuring Justice for All: When Can a Change in the Law Be Raised on Appeal?" (1995) 38 C.R. (4th) 397.

* A *Parks* challenge was brought outside Ontario in *R.* v. *McPartlin*, [1994] B.C.J. No. 3101 (S.C.) (QL). Melvin J. denied the challenge for cause by a Black accused, in a trial being held in Victoria, in which the charge was sexual assault against a white woman. Melvin J. sought to confine *Parks* to Metropolitan Toronto and to its facts. He held that he was not satisfied on the evidence presented that there was a link between the race of the accused and the particular charge, or the race of the victim, that would give rise to an air of reality to partiality in Victoria, B.C.

* In Ontario, where an accused person is entitled to a race-based challenge, it is not enough that other questions asked may indirectly invite jurors to declare their inability to be impartial because of the race of the accused. The generic question must be put. In *R.* v. *Glasgow* (1996), 110 C.C.C. (3d) 57 (Ont. C.A.), the trial judge had allowed the jurors to be asked whether they had been exposed to any media reports about Black men bringing young white girls from Nova Scotia to Toronto for the purpose of forcing them to work as prostitutes. A majority of the Court of Appeal found that this question related to publicity and only indirectly to race and was not enough on its own to satisfy the requirements of *Parks*. The trial judge erred by not supplementing it with a general race-based question.

5.5(d)(ii) **Aboriginal Accused**

* In *R.* v. *Williams* (1996), 106 C.C.C. (3d) 215 (B.C.C.A.), it was held that Esson C.J.B.C. did not err in exercising his discretion to deny a challenge for cause in the retrial of an Aboriginal accused who was charged with robbing a non-Aboriginal. The British Columbia Court of Appeal accepted the principles affirmed in *Parks* but held that the trial judge applied those principles properly and did not err in concluding that, while the existence of widespread bias and prejudice towards Aboriginals in the general community was established, there was no foundation for concluding that this attitudinal bias raised a realistic possibility that a juror might fail to be indifferent between the Queen and the accused: at 225. See also *R.* v. *Morris*, [1994] Y.J. No. 98 (S.C.) (QL) where a challenge was denied where the accused was of Native ancestry and alcohol was involved, because the Court was not satisfied that an evidentiary or factual basis had been provided to establish an air of reality to the concern of behavioural bias.

* In *Williams*, the British Columbia Court of Appeal held that the evidence established dissatisfaction by Aboriginal accused persons with the administration of justice as a whole in Canada, but did not link those perceptions to juror bias. Instead, that dissatisfaction was linked to problems with

"policing, the judicial process, sentencing and the penal system — all of which aboriginals find to be inconsistent with their traditions, values and culture": (1996), 106 C.C.C. (3d) 215 at 229 (B.C.C.A.).

* The British Columbia Court of Appeal recognized in *Williams* (1996), 106 C.C.C. (3d) 215 at 230 (B.C.C.A.), the existence of stereotypes about Aboriginals, but noted that the stereotypes were different from those that impelled the Ontario Court of Appeal to allow the challenge for cause in the case of a Black accused in *Parks:*

> The stereotype upon which *Parks* was based is that of a black person, who, in the light of American and Canadian experience, is perceived as being linked with serious urban crime. The stereotype that arises from the evidence in this case is that of a disadvantaged person, often in conflict with the law, but no more inclined to serious criminal activity than any other similarly disadvantaged person.

* The British Columbia Court of Appeal in *Williams* decided that Esson C.J.B.C. was not wrong in failing to find that there was an air of reality to Williams's concern about behavioural bias. The Court did not hold, however, that the trial judge would have erred had he allowed the challenge or that the first trial judge who presided over a mistrial of Williams had been wrong to allow a race-based challenge for cause to be conducted. The decision turned on the perception of the British Columbia Court of Appeal that Esson C.J.B.C. had exercised his discretion properly, with accurate comprehension of the relevant principles.

* Even if this point is granted, it has to be wondered whether *Williams* is correct in finding that the decision of Esson C.J.B.C. represented a proper discretionary determination, for the following reasons:

    (a) Although aware of the decision in *Wilson*, above, the British Columbia Court of Appeal continued to treat *Parks* as a case in which the race-based challenge for cause occurred in a particular setting (Metropolitan Toronto), in light of the specific facts of the case (an inter-racial homicide arising from an aborted drug transaction), factors that the Ontario Court of Appeal now considers to be unimportant, at least in the case of Black accused persons: at 224–25.

    (b) As *Parks* demonstrates, partiality, including behavioural bias, is not the kind of thing that can be proved through evidence in the way that most other factual issues can. Despite this, the British Columbia Court of Appeal was profoundly influenced by the fact that there are "no studies mentioned in the evidence which conclude that persons in a jury setting may be inclined to find that an aboriginal person is more likely to have committed a crime than a non-aboriginal person" and that general statistics about such things as over-representation of Aboriginals in the criminal justice system are not linked specifically to juror bias: at 229–30 & 234. (However, in *R.* v. *Betker* (1997), 115 C.C.C. (3d) 421 at 443–44 (Ont. C.A.), the Ontario Court of Appeal used reasoning similar to the *Williams* Court in rejecting a challenge for cause based upon the nature of the sexual offence with which the accused was charged. In the absence of studies and scientifically generated statistics directed at behavioural bias, the Court characterized the challenge as "speculative.")

(c) An important consideration in determining whether there is an air of reality to a concern about partiality is the "nature and extent of the [attitudinal] bias." "[A]ttitudes which are engrained in an individual's subconscious, and reflected in both individual and institutional conduct in the community, will prove more resistant to judicial cleansing" than most other kinds of bias: *Parks*, above at 343–44, a factor arguably not given sufficient consideration by the *Williams* court. Professor Roach has argued that Esson C.J.B.C.'s decision in *Williams* is flawed because "it ignores the subconscious and institutional aspects of racial discrimination recognized in *Parks*": K. Roach, "Challenges for Cause and Racial Discrimination" (1995) 37 Crim. L.Q. 410.

(d) Although articulating all the principles and tests with accuracy, it is questionable that in the face of established racial attitudinal bias, "there was no realistic possibility of a verdict tainted by racial bias": *Williams*, above at 231.

(e) The British Columbia Court of Appeal proceeded on the erroneous basis that the pro-challenge for cause position requires detailed, Americanized questioning of prospective jurors: *Williams*, above at 230.

It is difficult to avoid concluding that while the British Columbia Court of Appeal paid lip-service to *Parks*, it is not enamoured of race-based challenges and was intent on confining the application of that decision without expressing open disapproval.

5.5(d)(iii) **Other Minorities**

* In *R.* v. *Alli* (1996), 110 C.C.C. (3d) 283 at 285 (Ont. C.A.), the trial judge refused to allow the accused, a Guyanese national, to challenge jurors on the basis that they might be prejudiced against him as a visible minority. The Ontario Court of Appeal noted that there had been no evidence to

support the request. That being so, the trial judge did not err in the exercise of his discretion. Doherty J.A. said:

> This court is now asked to extend the automatic right to challenge for cause recognized in *Parks* to a much broader concept of racial prejudice. . . . Any proposed extension of *Parks* should be approached with caution. Where, as in this case, there was no evidence offered at trial to support the proposed extension, the court should decline to interfere with the trial judge's exercise of his or her discretion. . . .
>
> In holding that the trial judge did not err in refusing to allow the questions, I do not hold that it would have been wrong for him to allow the questions. I also do not pretend any prediction as to how that discretion might be exercised in another case. I hold only that he cannot be said to have erred in the exercise of his discretion in refusing the questions in the absence of any evidence to support the proposed challenge for cause.

* In *R.* v. *Jeevaratham* (1 March 1994), (Ont. Gen. Div.) [unreported], Watt J. allowed jurors to be asked whether the fact that the person charged was a Tamil immigrant from Sri Lanka would affect their ability to adjudicate impartially, and the same line of questioning was allowed in *R.* v. *Satkunananthan*, [1996] O.J. No. 1951 (Gen. Div.) (QL). The judge indicated that even though "blackness" as contemplated by *Parks* (1993), 15 O.R. (3d) 324 (C.A.) refers to more than skin colour, concern about the impact of racism goes beyond Black accused, and where "there is any material concern about racism as to any group, then the accused from that group is equally entitled to ask a question of the *Parks* nature." In *R.* v. *Lim & Nola* (2 April 1990), (Ont. Gen. Div.) [unreported], Doherty J. allowed a challenge for cause in the case of the Vietnamese accused charged with attempted murder arising out of two bombings. In *R.* v. *Ly* (1997), 114 C.C.C. (3d) 279 (Ont. C.A.), a decision by the trial judge to deny a race-based challenge for cause in the prosecution of Vietnamese accused was upheld because no evidentiary foundation had been presented at trial.

* In *R.* v. *Shergill* (1996), 4 C.R. (5th) 28 (Ont. Gen. Div.), Ferguson J. allowed a challenge by a Sikh Indian from the Punjab because the potential prejudice might arise not simply from the colour of an accused's skin but also from other characteristics that might be associated with colour. The Crown had objected that the question asked should refer to the race of the victims and witnesses, and not only to the race of the accused, so Ferguson J. held that the Crown would also be allowed to challenge jurors on this basis. The partiality of the jury can relate to victims and witnesses as well.

* In *R.* v. *Ho* (10 May 1996), (Ont. Gen. Div.) [unreported], Watt J. allowed a challenge for cause where the accused, charged with murder, was Chinese. Relying on an affidavit from an expert witness on race relations that had been furnished by the defence, Justice Watt concluded:

> Racism exists. It is *not* confined to anti-black racism. The affidavit of Dr. Frances Henry satisfies me that racism is not unique or indigenous to anti-black racism. Racism exists in relation to persons of Asian/Chinese origin. It may not be quite so broadly based as in the case of anti-black racism, but it is nonetheless extant. Its influence is as insidious in the one case, as it is in the other.

* In *R.* v. *Yashev*, [1995] O.J. No. 3598 (Gen. Div.) (QL), Goodearle J. denied a request by defence counsel to challenge jurors for cause when two recent immigrants were charged with murder. His Honour held that he had "no convincing or realistically persuasive evidence of reports or studies that suggest a persuasive, ingrained prejudice by adult Canadians against recent immigrants generally that has any realistic prospect of derailing jurors from performing their duties in accordance with their oaths, properly instructed by [him]": at para. 19.

5.5(e) **Other Status-Based Concerns**

5.5(e)(i) **Sexual Preference**

* In *R.* v. *Alli* (1996), 110 C.C.C. (3d) 283 at 285 (Ont. C.A.), the accused had also asked to be allowed to challenge jurors for prejudice against homosexuals. Again, because no evidentiary basis had been provided, the Court declined to interfere with the trial judge's decision to deny that challenge. The Court cautioned that it should not be taken to hold that it would have been wrong for the judge to have allowed the question. The Court noted, however, that any extension of *Parks* to allow automatic challenges for other forms of "generic prejudice," such as anti-homosexual prejudice, should not be decided by the Ontario Court of Appeal absent an adequate evidentiary foundation to permit an informed determination.

* In *R.* v. *Welch* (1996), (Ont. Gen. Div.) [unreported], Humphrey J. permitted a challenge for cause in a first-degree murder prosecution relating to the homosexual lifestyle of both the accused and the deceased. In *Welch*, thirteen jurors, comprising 21 percent of those challenged, were found to be partial and were disqualified.

* In *R.* v. *Musson* (1996), 3 C.R. (5th) 61 (Ont. Gen. Div.), Clarke J. allowed a challenge for cause to be brought when jurors may conclude that the accused was homosexual. Musson had been charged with a sexual offence against another adult male. The application was also based on prejudice that may be evoked because of the sexual nature of the offence. His Honour found the issues of homophobia and sexual assault to be inextricably linked. Accepting there to be widespread homophobia on the evidence presented, he concluded that "there is a realistic potential that some jurors would hold anti homosexual views which they would be unable to set them [sic] aside and decide the case in a fair and impartial manner."

5.5(e)(ii) **HIV Status**

* Mr. Justice Hill allowed a challenge for cause to be conducted in *R.* v. *Tonye* (9 May 1996), (Ont. Gen . Div.) [unreported], relating to the HIV status of the accused. The accused had been charged with threatening to kill his step-daughter by sexually assaulting her and transmitting his HIV infection to her.

5.5(e)(iii) **Profession**

* In *R.* v. *Musson* (1996), 3 C.R. (5th) 61 (Ont. Gen. Div.), the accused also sought to challenge jurors for cause based on the fact that he was a physician charged with a sexual offence against a patient. His Honour Justice Clarke was unpersuaded that a realistic potential for the existence of partiality on this basis had been sufficiently articulated in the application.

5.5(e)(iv) **Mental Challenge**

* A challenge for cause was allowed in *R.* v. *Genereux*, [1994] O.J. No. 3095 (Gen. Div.) (QL), by Whalen J. because of the combination of the young age of the victim (eight years), the brutality of the murder (181 stab wounds with a pen knife), and the mentally challenged stature of the nineteen-year-old accused. His Honour expressed the view that together these circumstances could invite passion and irrationality to undermine the ability of some jurors to adjudicate impartially on the evidence.

5.5(e)(v) **Parole Status**

* An application for challenge for cause relating to the status of the accused as a paroled offender charged with the homicide of his son was denied by Salhany J. in *R.* v. *Neely*, [1994] O.J. No. 2983 (Gen. Div.) (QL), because he

was satisfied that jurors could disavow themselves of any inaccurate preconceptions about parolees that may have been created by the media.

* In *R.* v. *White* (1996), 108 C.C.C. (3d) 1 (Ont. C.A.), the Ontario Court of Appeal upheld the decision of a trial judge to deny a challenge for cause where the accused wished to ask jurors about their ability to disregard the fact that the accused persons had been inmates of a federal penitentiary prior to allegedly killing the victim. This fact was going to become known as part of the Crown's case, as it was relevant to the association between the victim and the accused. The Court felt that the potential prejudice that might be caused was a matter for admissibility and jury directions and that it was not wrong for the trial judge to have denied the challenge.

5.5(f) **Offence-Based Challenges**

* "Offence-based" challenges occur when the alleged partiality arises from the nature of the offence that the accused has been charged with. Offence-based challenges have been both allowed and denied in cases involving violence, particularly violence against vulnerable persons or domestic violence. They have been both allowed and denied in cases involving sexual offence allegations, especially involving young children. They have been both allowed and denied in cases involving narcotics. And they have been allowed, and criticized, in the case of politically charged offences such as abortion and obscenity.

* Speaking generally, the case in favour of offence-based challenges is premised on the belief that there are certain general or "generic" biases in the community that do not relate specifically to the accused as an individual or as a member of a particular race. Instead, it is argued that the bias emerges from a strongly held aversion to the alleged act (causing the juror to want to err on the side of conviction rather than acquittal, given the risk that the accused may be guilty despite a reasonable doubt); undue sympathy for the victim (causing the juror to see the case as involving a rejection or "validation" of the complaint, rather than a finding of guilt according to law); loss of faith in the ability or readiness of the system of justice to deal with the kind of offence alleged (causing the juror to disregard laws perceived to obstruct the "truth"); and/or the politicization of the offence (causing the juror to "cast lots" with those groups that are victimized, rather than to adjudicate the case solely on the evidence in the specific case, or to "nullify" the law because of profound disagreement with it). Proponents of offence-based challenges urge that strongly held views of this kind, while not shared by all members of the community, are sufficiently widespread and so deeply held with respect to some offences that there is a reasonable

prospect that some members of the jury panel may be unable or unwilling to adjudicate impartially, given the nature of the charges.

* There have been cases before the Ontario Court of Appeal where offence-based challenges had been allowed by the trial judge, and where the Court refrained from expressing either approval or disapproval. In *R.* v. *Joseph* (12 September 1995), (Ont. C.A.) [unreported], an appeal was allowed after the Crown conceded that the judge had taken irrelevant factors into account in denying a challenge brought by a Black accused. The Court refrained from ruling on the appropriate questions but did note, "We should not be taken as condoning a question based on the nature of the charges alone." In *R.* v. *Glasgow* (1996), 110 C.C.C. (3d) 57 (Ont. C.A.), the trial judge had allowed defence counsel, when his client was charged with pimping-related offences, to ask whether jurors had any views on prostitution or prostitution-related activities that would make it difficult for them to be impartial. The trial judge denied a race-based challenge, even though the accused was Black. The appeal concerning challenges for cause related solely to this refusal. Doherty J.A., for a majority of the Court, said that he "need not and do[es] not comment on other aspects of his [the trial judge's] ruling."

* Recently, in the case of *R.* v. *Betker* (1997), 115 C.C.C. (3d) 421 (Ont. C.A.), the Ontario Court of Appeal closed the door to general offence-based challenges, ending an emerging trend in Ontario to allow such challenges to be brought. In part because of the high level of its authority, *Betker* is likely to signal the end to offence-based challenges across Canada, even though it is binding only in Ontario. More important, offence-based challenges were predominantly an Ontario phenomenon. Given that the highest court of appeal has rejected them in the province of their birth, they are unlikely to gain a foothold elsewhere.

* The primary technical basis for the *Betker* decision is that section 638(l)(b) of the *Criminal Code* allows challenges to be brought solely on the basis that "a juror is not indifferent between The Queen and the accused." "[I]t says nothing about a lack of indifference between the Crown and the nature of the offence charged": *R.* v. *Betker* (1997), 115 C.C.C. (3d) 421 at 437 (Ont. C.A.). The Court explained that offence-based challenges are not like race-based challenges. Although both are premised upon general or "generic" attitudes in the community, racial bias is directed at the type of person the accused is and therefore represents impartiality against him. Prejudice arising from the nature of the offence, assuming such prejudice even exists, is not related to the accused and therefore does not fall within section 638(l)(b). Speaking for the Court, Moldaver J.A. said, "While this distinction might be regarded as overly simplistic, I view it as fundamental

to a proper understanding of the permissible limits within which challenges for cause based on alleged non-indifference may be brought": *R.* v. *Betker* (1997), 115 C.C.C. (3d) 421 at 437 (Ont. C.A.).

* This represents a narrow interpretation of section 638(l)(b), which may not be in keeping with its purpose. Section 638(l)(b) is intended to preserve a fair trial for the accused by ensuring that jurors are not partial. If *arguendo* there are jurors who cannot be impartial in adjudicating a particular kind of offence because of strongly held beliefs about the nature of the activity alleged, why should the source of that partiality matter? Whether partiality derives from pre-trial publicity, the race of the accused, or the nature of the allegation, the important point is that the juror is *ex hypothesi* unable to adjudicate fairly, according to law. It would do no violence to the language of section 638(l)(b) to interpret it, in all of its manifestations, so that it can fulfil its role of reducing partiality that can prejudice the accused. Arguably, a juror who cannot or will not give effect to the presumption of innocence because of the nature of the charge is partial to the Crown and thereby necessarily partial against the accused. Despite this, it is clear that, in Ontario, the narrow construction of section 638(l)(b) represents the law.

* The *Betker* decision also rests on the fact that in offence-based challenges, the risk of partiality, if it arises at all, will generally arise because of the specific allegation and not simply from the general offence charged. The real complaint in such cases, the Court said, "is not so much with pre-trial partiality occasioned by the nature of the crime as it is with strong feelings of disapprobation likely to arise in the minds of jurors as they listen to the evidence called in support of the crime": *R.* v. *Betker* (1997), 115 C.C.C. (3d) 421 at 439 (Ont. C.A.). For example, in sexual offences involving children, it is not simply the offence, sexual assault, that gives rise to the concern. It is the reaction that prospective jurors might have to the specific allegation involving a child, including the nature and extent of the sexual violation and the relationship between the accused and the complainant. In *R.* v. *Hubbert* (1975), 29 C.C.C. (2d) 279 at 295 (Ont. C.A.), the Court had held that impartiality is a state of mind to be tested at the time of the swearing of each juror. Thus, jurors' reactions to various pieces of evidence that may be elicited at trial have been said not to be the proper subject of the challenge for cause procedure. In short, challenges related to the allegation against the accused will often run afoul of the *Hubbert* principle since any partiality that may arise will do so because of the specific nature of the alleged act as revealed by the evidence, rather than from the general nature of the charge.

* In the case of *Hubbert*, the accused had been paroled from confinement in a hospital for the criminally insane, a fact that would become known to the jury when the accused sought to explain that he lied to the police because of fear of recommittal. He sought to challenge jurors who would be predisposed to finding him guilty because of his prior incarceration as a mentally disordered offender. The challenge was rejected, in part, because it related to the potential reaction of jurors to facts they would learn from the evidence. Even if this were to occur, the trial would nonetheless have commenced with an impartial jury.

* The general proposition from *R.* v. *Hubbert* that the challenge must relate to the condition of the juror prior to the calling of evidence was quoted without specific comment in *R.* v. *Sherratt* (1991), 63 C.C.C. (3d) 193 at 206 (S.C.C.), although the Court noted generally that "the reasons [for the trial judge's rejection of the challenge] are not relevant to our discussion here. Rather, it is the procedure and principles set out by the Court of Appeal that are pertinent. . . ."

* The *Betker* Court was correct to observe that often offence-based challenges are premised on the specific nature of the allegation, including details that may only become known during the presentation of evidence, and that where this is so, they would offend the *Hubbert* principle. (This is not true of all offence-based challenges. In some cases, the charge itself will disclose the information on which the prejudice is thought to be based.) It has to be wondered, however, whether the rigid position taken in *Hubbert* and affirmed in *Betker* is in keeping with the purpose of the challenge for cause process. The issue is partiality. If a juror becomes partial such that he or she will not adjudicate on the evidence, why should it matter whether that partiality is present when the trial commences, or emerges because of the nature of the evidence in the case? The crucial question should be whether, at the time of jury selection, there is an air of reality to the concern that jurors may ultimately be unable or unwilling to adjudicate impartially. Where the nature of the evidence will inevitably disclose features that may cause partiality, we would respectfully suggest that the parties should be able to reduce the risk of an unfair trial by using the challenge for cause process, particularly given the constitutionalization of fair trial principles and the right to an impartial jury that has occurred since *Hubbert* was decided.

* The *Hubbert* principle, if it remains a correct principle of law, does not only call into question offence-based challenges. It casts doubt on the propriety of all challenges for cause where the prejudice will not arise until the case begins to unfold. It casts doubt, for example, on status-based challenges

where the status that gives rise to the partiality is not visible but will become apparent as the case unfolds, such as homosexuality, mental illness, culture, or creed. It would invalidate challenges based on association by the accused with groups, and may even undermine some meritorious cases of pre-trial partiality. For example, pre-trial publicity may not predispose a juror at the outset to be partial against the accused, but may cause some jurors to evaluate the evidence in the case based on what they heard or read prior to the trial commencing.

* The *Betker* Court also expressed concern that if offence-based challenges are allowed because of strongly held views about a particular crime, it is likely that challenges for cause can be brought in virtually any criminal case, which is something Parliament could not have intended. Justice Moldaver said in the context of the specific charge before him, "If strongly held views about a particular crime are allowed to become a yardstick against which partiality is measured, then, on a principled approach, I fail to see how the crime of sexual assault can be meaningfully distinguished from other crimes such as murder, robbery, break and enter or drug trafficking, to mention but a few.": *R.* v. *Betker* (1997), 115 C.C.C. (3d) 421 at 438 (Ont. C.A.).

* Finally, the rejection of general offence-based challenges that occurred in *Betker* was also based on the absence of a "direct and logical connection that translates views about a particular crime into prejudice against a specific accused such that jurors would disregard their oath and render a verdict based on something other than the evidence and the legal instruction provided by the trial judge": *R.* v. *Betker* (1997), 115 C.C.C. (3d) 421 at 441 (Ont. C.A.). Speaking for the Court, Moldaver J.A. said, "I am of the view that strong attitudes about a particular crime, even when accompanied by intense feelings of hostility and resentment towards those who commit the crime, will rarely, if ever, translate into partiality with respect to the accused.": at 441.

* It is important to note that the *Betker* Court stopped short of holding that offence-based considerations can never support challenges for cause. Speaking of sexual offence cases in particular, Moldaver J.A. said, "[S]tanding alone, the nature of the crime will rarely if ever meet the tests of partiality under s. 638(l)(b) of the *Criminal Code*. That said, I should not be taken as suggesting that a realistic possibility of partiality can never be established in sexual assault cases.": *R.* v. *Betker* (1997), 115 C.C.C. (3d) 421 at 448 (Ont. C.A.). Justice Moldaver endorsed Professor Kent Roach's observation from "Challenges for Cause and Racial Discrimination" (1995) 37 C.L.Q. 410 at 416 that:

> The accused can always introduce evidence to establish an air of reality for the challenge on the facts of the particular case. This, however, would be

based on evidence in the particular case and not something that follows as a matter of law from *Parks*.

* Although no illustrations were provided by the Court, it would seem that where there is a foundation for believing that a particular juror may be unable to maintain impartiality, even where that problem emerges from the nature of the allegation, a challenge to that juror will be appropriate. It is difficult to imagine that a challenge for cause would not succeed, for example, if a prospective juror was known to have made comments suggesting that he or she was not going to risk turning a pervert loose by voting for an acquittal.

* Although the *Hubbert* principle could create difficulties in some cases, it is arguable that events within a community can also provide a specific basis for a challenge for cause that is premised primarily on the nature of the offence. In *R.* v. *Hutton* (1992), 76 C.C.C. (3d) 476 (Ont. Gen. Div.) for example, widespread publicity about a government-funded report on "intimate femicide," which included statistics and formed dramatic conclusions, some of which parallelled the allegation against the accused, sustained an application for challenge for cause when it occurred one week before the trial. (Given that the prejudice in *Hutton* was related, in part, to the specific allegation against the accused, including facts that would become known to the jury only on hearing evidence, it is arguable that the challenge violated the *Hubbert* principle. In our view, this should be seen as an indictment of the *Hubbert* principle rather than of the *Hutton* decision.)

* Although the door to offence-based challenges has been closed in Ontario, it may be of assistance to courts in other provinces to consider the Ontario experience with offence-based challenges. In our respectful opinion, the availability of such challenges should not turn on either a narrow interpretation of section 638(l)(b), or on an aggressive application of the *Hubbert* principle. Instead, the availability of the challenge should turn solely on whether there is an air of reality to the concern that there may be potential jurors who will be unable to adjudicate impartially, based on the nature and circumstances of the offence and the allegation.

5.5(f)(i) **Offences Involving Domestic Violence**

* Challenges for cause have been allowed in cases where men have been charged with offences of domestic violence: *R.* v. *B.(S.)* (1996), 47 C.R. (4th) 56 (Ont. Gen. Div.), Hill J. (nine counts relating to an event on a particular day, including an allegation of sexual assault by a husband against his wife, and one count of criminal harassment covering a four-month period); *R.* v. *Pheasant* (1995), 47 C.R. (4th) 47 (Ont. Gen. Div.), Hill J. (assault causing bodily harm, uttering death threats, unlawful confinement,

and possession of a dangerous weapon involving a former girlfriend). In *R.* v. *Morgan* (27 November 1995), (Ont. Gen. Div.) [unreported], Hurley J. allowed a challenge for cause in the case of the brutal axe murder of the wife of the accused, based in part on the realistic prospect that, given the nature of the allegation, some jurors might be unable to adjudicate impartially. In *R.* v. *Jeevaratham* (1 March 1994), (Ont. Gen. Div.) [unreported], Watt J. allowed a challenge for cause where the accused was charged with the murder of a young boy and where the facts of the case would disclose allegations of spousal assault by the accused. In *R.* v. *Jaramji* (12 June 1996), (Ont. Gen. Div.) [unreported], Grossi J. allowed a challenge where the accused faced two counts of sexual assault and one count of assault against his estranged wife. In *R.* v. *Haye* (12 November 1996), (Ont. Gen. Div.) [unreported], Killeen J. allowed a challenge for cause where the accused was alleged to have sexually assaulted his estranged wife. In *R.* v. *Ghosn*, [1996] O.J. No. 4055 (Gen. Div.) (QL), Morin J. allowed a challenge for cause in a first-degree murder prosecution involving the wife of the accused. The question permitted asked:

> Do you have any beliefs or attitudes about husbands accused of violence against their wives which are so strong that you would be unable to set them aside in order to judge Mr. Haye's case fairly and impartially?[3]

* A challenge for cause application based on concern about attitudes relating to spousal abuse was denied in the assault trial in *R.* v. *Banks*, [1995] O.J. No. 831 (Ont. Gen. Div.) (QL). Logan J. expressed disagreement with the conclusions that motivated Hill J. to allow a similar challenge in *R.* v. *Pheasant*. A challenge for cause application was also denied in *R.* v. *D'Andrea*, [1995] O.J. No. 916 (Ont. Gen. Div.) (QL), by Jenkins J. in an assault causing bodily harm allegation involving the wife of the accused. The Court found that there was not an adequate foundation to find a sufficiently widespread bias to create a reasonable potential for the existence of partiality that could not be cured by appropriate instruction. While that decision may be defensible, it is respectfully submitted that the Court erred by requiring the foundation to be established on the balance of probabilities. His Honour also expressed the view that challenges are to be confined to very unusual circumstances. This is contrary to the position of the Supreme Court of Canada in *Sherratt*, [1991] 1 S.C.R. 509.

3 Reportedly, six of twenty-one jurors, or 28 percent, were challenged successfully, based on their responses to this question.

* In *R.* v. *Gareau*, [1996] M.J. No. 562 (Q.B.) (QL), a challenge for cause was denied where the accused was charged with eighteen violence-related offences involving a woman with whom he had been having a relationship. No evidence had been presented to establish a foundation for the application. Oliphant J., expressing disapproval of the increasing number of challenges for cause, observed that these applications tend to arise in cases involving spousal and sexual violence and said, "I cannot help but wonder whether the views as to gender stereotyping held by defence counsel, most of whom are men, involved in these types of cases may have some impact on this."

* In *R.* v. *Marquardt* (1995), 44 C.R. (4th) 353 (Ont. Gen. Div.), McIsaac J. denied a request for a challenge for cause where a mother was charged with smothering her two-year-old child. His Honour held that even if jurors had strongly held views about child abuse, the record did not establish that those views could not be vitiated by the juror's oath and the trial process.

* A challenge for cause was denied in *R.* v. *Holmgren*, [1994] O.J. No. 2724 (Gen. Div.) (QL) [summarized at (1995), 25 W.C.B. (2d) 368], by Clarke J. in a case where a babysitter was charged with manslaughter and aggravated assault involving two infants who allegedly sustained injuries as the result of shaken baby syndrome. The Court held that the general challenge based on the nature of the charges and the fact that the victims were young children was not supported by evidence demonstrating that the potential for bias was "of such magnitude so as to displace the presumption." His Honour considered cases to the contrary to be an unwarranted extension of *Parks*. But see *R.* v. *Musson* (1996), 3 C.R. (5th) 61 (Ont. Gen. Div.), where His Honour allowed a challenge for cause in a homosexual, sexual assault offence.

5.5(f)(ii) **Offences Involving Violence against Women**

* A challenge for cause was allowed in a case involving random, non-sexual violence against women: *R.* v. *Kitaitchik* (5 October 1993), (Ont. Gen. Div.) [unreported], (homicide involving a woman home alone during a burglary). A similar application was denied in *R.* v. *Banks*, [1995] O.J. No. 831 (Gen. Div.) (QL).

5.5.(f)(iii) **Offences Involving Violence against the Elderly**

* In *R.* v. *Challice* (1993), 26 C.R. (4th) 285 (Ont. Gen. Div.), McIsaac J. allowed jurors to be challenged on whether they held any predispositions towards the elderly that would prevent them from adjudicating impartially on the evidence in a case where a young man was charged with the brutal beating death of a diminutive elderly man during an attempted robbery. After the decision of the Ontario Court of Appeal in *Cameron* (1995), 22 O.R. (3d) 65 (C.A.), Mr. Justice McIsaac, while delivering his decision in

R. v. *Marquardt* (1995), 44 C.R. (4th) 353 (Ont. Gen. Div.), expressed regret at having allowed this challenge, saying that he had failed to appreciate the limitations of *Parks* (1993), 15 O.R. (3d) 324 (C.A.).

5.5(f)(iv) **Offences Involving Violence against the Police**

* In *R.* v. *McArthur and McArthur* (10 January 1997), (Ont. Gen. Div.) [unreported], the charge related to a bank robbery in which three police officers were seriously wounded. LaForme J. allowed defence counsel to ask whether "the fact that the crimes charged involve firearms and the attempted murder of police officers" would interfere with the impartiality of the jurors.

5.5(f)(v) **The Foundation for Violent Offence Challenges**

* Courts allowing such challenges have variously relied on:

- the inherently repulsive or emotive nature of the crime alleged: *R.* v. *Challice* (1993), 26 C.R. (4th) 285 (Ont. Gen. Div.), and *R.* v. *Genereux*, [1994] O.J. No. 3095 (Gen. Div.) (QL);
- the definite gender context of domestic assault, and its high incidence, as demonstrated by government-generated statistics: *Pheasant* (1995), 47 C.R. (4th) 47 at 51 (Ont. Gen. Div.);
- the presence of strongly held attitudes about violence against women, which, for some persons, are extreme enough to cause them to look favourably on proposals to change the legal system by removing the presumption of innocence when the victim is a woman and the accused is a man: *R.* v. *Kitaitchik* (5 October 1993), (Ont. Gen. Div.) [unreported], German J.;
- the prospect that because of the prevalence of men in the population who have committed acts of domestic violence, prospective jurors would include abusers who may not adjudicate fairly on behalf of the Crown [even though the application was brought by the defence]: *Pheasant* (1995), 47 C.R. (4th) 47 at 54 (Ont. Gen. Div.).

* In support of such applications, counsel has sought to establish that

> (1) the criminal justice system is overburdened with such complaints,
>
> (2) the criminal justice system [in the eyes of some] fails to adequately address the needs of the victim,
>
> (3) [some believe that] the police do not assign enough of their budget to control of abuse of women, [and]
>
> (4) [some believe that] sentences meted out to men who physically abuse women are not severe enough

R. v. *Pheasant* (1995), 47 C.R. (4th) 47 at 52 (Ont. Gen. Div.).

5.5(f)(vi) **Sexual Offences**

* The case of *R.* v. *Betker* (1997), 115 C.C.C. (3d) 421 (Ont. C.A.), in which the Ontario Court of Appeal rejected the legitimacy of offence-based challenges, was a sexual offence case. The accused was charged with a number of sexual offences involving his daughter, who was a child at the time of the events. The Court of Appeal held that, altogether apart from the fact that section 638(l)(b) does not allow offence-based challenges, challenges based on the nature of sexual offences are not appropriate. The Court concluded that there is no support for "the conclusion that prospective jurors may hold a generic prejudice against persons accused of sexual assault [including offences against children] which would prevent them from rendering an impartial verdict": at 442. Prior to the *Betker* decision, such challenges had been allowed in dozens of cases in Ontario (see Appendix I for a list of thirty-nine of the cases where such challenges were allowed) and denied in many others, including *R.* v. *Webber* (26 October 1994), (Ont. Gen. Div.) [unreported], Zelinski J. (But see *R.* v. *L.(R.)* (1996), 3 C.R. (5th) 70 (Ont. Gen. Div.), where Zelinski J. allowed a similar challenge based on the accumulated experience with such challenges in Ontario); *R.* v. *Green* (1994), 34 C.R. (4th) 222 (Ont. Gen. Div.), Clarke J.; *R.* v. *Holmes* (29 November 1994), (Ont. Gen. Div.) [unreported], Eberhard J.; *R.* v. *Collings* (21 August 1996), (Ont. Gen. Div.) [unreported]; *R.* v. *Bolton* (29 September 1994), (Ont. Gen. Div.) [unreported], Dunnet J.; *R.* v. *Bylow* (31 October 1994), (Ont. Gen. Div.) [unreported], Weekes J.; *R.* v. *Atkinson*, [1995] A.J. No. 289 (Q.B.) (QL); *R.* v. *Gamache*, [1994] B.C.J. No. 922 (S.C.) (QL), focusing on the publicity issue. Challenges were also denied in *R.* v. *Hillis*, [1996] O.J. No. 2739 (Gen. Div.) (QL), Whealy J., and in *R.* v. *A.C.*, [1996] O.J. No. 2905 (Gen. Div.) (QL), Eberhard J.

* Although the decisions allowing such challenges vary in identifying the bases for their conclusion that there is an air of reality to the concern that some potential jurors may be unable to maintain their impartiality as between the Crown and the accused in sexual offence cases, the following points have been made:

- The fact that these offences embrace basic issues of morality and are considered by many to be repugnant. In *R.* v. *Daviault*, [1994] 3 S.C.R. 63 at 119–20, Sopinka J. remarked, "Sexual assault is a heinous crime of violence . . . [Offenders, including intoxicated ones] deserve to be stigmatized." [The issue is whether all jurors can set aside their repugnance on hearing the allegation and adjudicate the case based solely on the evidence.]

- The prevalence of sexual offence victims in the population, coupled with the broad recognition that sexual offence victims frequently suffer from harmful sequelae of the assault. [Can this produce inappropriate and distorting "victim sympathy"?]

- The nature of the views about sexual offences held by some, including
  - the gender-based nature of the crime, coupled with the strong conviction held by some that the system of justice remains male-biased despite recent reforms;
  - the belief that the system produces unacceptably low conviction rates; and
  - the belief that because of safeguards protecting accused persons, the system seems unable to address what is believed by some to be an epidemic of sexual abuse.

  These attitudes and beliefs have been noted judicially. See, for example, *R.* v. *Seaboyer*, [1991] 2 S.C.R. 577 at 648–50, 665–66, & 699–700, and *A.(L.L.)* v. *B.(A.)* (1995), 44 C.R. (4th) 91 at 115 (S.C.C.). Can jurors who have lost faith in the system of justice, or who believe that it is not gender neutral, be expected to listen to jury directions and to pay fidelity to the basic precepts of that system, such as the presumption of innocence?

- The results that have been obtained in cases where challenges for cause have been allowed. See the survey of cases in Appendix I.

- The nature of the comments made by some prospective jurors in response to challenge for cause questions.

* In *R.* v. *Betker* (1997), 115 C.C.C. (3d) 421 (Ont. C.A.), the Court had all of this information before it. While not addressing each of the points raised, Justice Moldaver agreed that while some of the evidence demonstrates an attitudinal bias in sexual offence cases, it falls short of presenting an air of reality to the concern that this may result in behavioural bias on the part of potential jurors.

* With respect to the information suggesting that repugnance relating to sexual offences, victim sympathy, and the prevalence of sexual offences in society could cause behavioural bias, His Lordship said, at 444–45:

> [T]hat evidence gives me no reason to believe that jurors' strong attitudes towards the crime of sexual assault translate into discriminatory verdicts. If it were otherwise, I would expect to see a significant percentage of sexual assault trials ending up as mistrials on account of juror disagreement . . . And yet there is no evidence of intransigent disagreement.

This is an impressive point. It is worth noting, however, that there has been no suggestion made in any of the race-based challenge for cause decisions that there is an increase in the number of mistrials where the accused is Black. Does this mean that there is no behavioural bias in such cases?

* With respect to the gender-based nature of the crime and the belief by some that the criminal justice system is unable or unwilling to address the problem of sexual abuse, Moldaver J.A. noted that there is no empirical data to support the view that there is gender-based discrimination against male accused in verdicts in sexual offence cases, nor is it clear what beliefs there are that would undermine the presumption of innocence, or how those beliefs might do so.

* The *Betker* Court had before it a survey of twelve of the cases included in Appendix I to this book. In addition, it had before it an article by Professor Neil Vidmar, "Generic Prejudice and the Presumption of Guilt in Sex Abuse Trials" (1997), 21 Law and Human Behavior 5, which lists the results of many of the other cases included in Appendix I. His Lordship said at 443–44:

> This evidence goes no further than to show that many people in our society consider the offence of sexual assault to be a despicable crime. Those same individuals unquestionably harbour intense feelings of hostility and resentment towards people who commit the crime. But that should come as no surprise. I fail to see how any responsible person in our society could think otherwise. Abhorrence of the crime, however, is one thing; inability to impartially decide whether the crime has been committed and, if it has, whether the accused is the perpetrator is another. That is where I part company with the appellant and Professor Vidmar.
>
> Speculation aside, there is simply no concrete evidence to show that any of the prospective jurors found to be partial in the various General Division cases cited could not set aside their biases and render a fair and impartial verdict based solely upon the evidence and the law as provided by the trial judge.

* With respect, the survey depicts the actual holdings of triers of fact who based their findings on the answers provided under oath by prospective jurors to questions that addressed both attitudinal and behavioural bias. Many of those jurors responded that they could not adjudicate impartially. If evidence establishing that a significant number of jurors in every case where a challenge for cause has been granted concede their own partiality when asked about behavioural bias does not provide an air of reality to the concern that there may be partial jurors, it is hard to imagine what would. Given the prohibition on interviewing jurors about the basis

for their decisions, it is our view that it is not possible to gather better evidence of behavioural bias than the actual experience in cases where challenges have been brought.

* In *R.* v. *Hillis*, [1996] O.J. No. 2739 (Gen. Div.) (QL), Whealy J. relied on an affidavit of Professor Freedman that had been prepared in connection with another case to conclude that the twelve-case survey has "been discredited as unscientific, unsupported and purely anecdotal," an assessment adopted in *R.* v. *A.C.*, [1996] O.J. No. 2905 (Gen. Div.) (QL), Eberhard J. See also *R.* v. *Holmes* (29 November 1994), (Ont. Gen. Div.) [unreported]. While the survey is not a scientific study, the accuracy of the information it contains has not been questioned. A scientific survey would necessarily be a simulated study. It is difficult to understand why such a study would provide more significant findings than the experience of courts in dozens of cases involving hundreds of subjects who have answered questions under oath about their behavioural bias.

* An earlier version of the survey material contained in Appendix I has been embraced by some courts. Mr. Justice Taliano, for example, in *R.* v. *Cox* (1994), 25 C.R.R. (2d) 278 (Ont. Gen. Div.), with reference to a survey of twelve of the cases included in Appendix I, said that this was "an astounding survey . . . [whose] results graphically demonstrate that the public have strong opinions on the subject of child sexual abuse." Based on that survey, he said: "[I]f a potential juror holds such beliefs it is entirely possible that he or she might be unable or unwilling to adjudicate the case impartially." See also *R.* v. *Henderson* (19 January 1995), (Ont. Gen. Div.) [unreported], West J.

* In *R.* v. *L.(R.)* (1996), 3 C.R. (5th) 70 (Ont. Gen. Div.), the prevalence of successful challenges persuaded Zelinski J. to allow a challenge in a sexual offence case involving a seven-year-old complainant. His Honour said:

> Crown counsel adopts the language from an unreported decision of the Honourable Mr. Justice Eberhard in *Regina v. Holmes* November 29th 1994, in which Mr. Skurka's analysis [the survey of twelve cases] was considered along with other evidence. The learned justice concluded that the survey lacked "clarity of result and scientific process."
>
> I am of the view based upon the admissions of Crown counsel that the results as they apply to this trial could be no more clear. The survey indicates, that in those trials referred to in which challenges for cause were granted, there was an average of 33 per cent of potential jurors who were found on the trial of the issue of cause, to be partial. Crown counsel accepts the accuracy of that statistic but rejects its relevance.

> Crown counsel has indicated that the scientific basis of that study would, as indicated by Justice Eberhard, be significantly altered if a more scientific approach was adopted. She suggests that an analysis should be made of the answers given by potential jurors and the findings of the triers of fact, suggesting that if I did that, I would find that the jurors did not properly apply the answers given to the result. The result would be perverse in each and every instance.
>
> Just as in *Webber* where I enunciated the oft stated belief that we all have, that jurors can, and do, implement the proper instructions given to them by trial judges, I must state that my confidence in the jury system must also extend to the conclusions of the jurors even in a mini-trial on a challenge for cause.
>
> That juror selection process is set out in the Code. It would be inappropriate, in my view, to look behind the consequences to see whether the results are skewed.
>
> I am of the belief that even if that resulted in discounting a significant portion of the percentage of jurors found to be partial, it does not detract from the fact that a number of potential jurors have been found in that process, involving similar trials, to be wanting, to be partial.
>
> In the result, it would be a serious diminution of the potential for a fair trial even if the 33 per cent number who were found to be partial in the results of the Skurka analysis were reduced by the process of examining the answers and the juror's use of those answers, which I would not do. Five per cent of the jurors would be equally an inappropriate prospect. We are attempting to achieve fairness. We do not know where the discounting would end. I am prepared to accept, as I stated, the findings of the triers, but any potential bias that can be avoided by the challenge for cause process suggests the process is warranted.
>
> . . . I can think of no evidentiary foundation for the challenge for cause that would be better than the transcripts of the results of the process being implemented.

* A sampling of responses provided during challenges for cause in sexual offence cases include:

  "I would tend towards guilty. It would be problematic for me": *McBirnie* (5 April 1994), (Ont. Gen. Div.) [unreported], Meehan J.

  "No, because I have a nine year old daughter at home": *Thomas* (22 November 1993), (Ont. Gen. Div.) [unreported], Humphrey J.

  "Anyone who would do that to a youngster should be strung up": *Thomas* (22 November 1994), (Ont. Gen. Div.) [unreported], Humphrey J.

"Yes, I think I would be [influenced]; I've been raised strict Baptist": *M. & M.* (21 September 1994), (Ont. Gen. Div.) [unreported], Crossland J.

"I'm very prejudiced against child molesters, rapists and wife-beaters, and I think they should be lashed, in my opinion": *M. & M.* (21 September 1994), (Ont. Gen. Div.) [unreported], Crossland J.

* In other cases, jurors have come forward unsolicited and have indicated that they could not give the accused a fair trial, given the nature of the allegation: *R.* v. *Jackson* (22 October 1991), (Ont. Gen. Div.) [unreported], Poulin J., precipitating an inquiry by the judge in which three other jurors expressed their belief that they might not be impartial; and *R.* v. *Lalonde* (24 April 1995), (Ont. Gen. Div.) [unreported], where a juror came forward and said the following:

> I thought when I came in yesterday, I thought, you know, I could keep an open mind and listen to both sides. But I have children. Whether these kids were — are now all grown up, or whatever, if my child came to me and told me, you know "Somebody was touching me," I believe my child first. I just can't — I can't sit there, because all that I'm thinking, like, all I'm thinking right now is that I've already convicted this man even though I haven't listened to either side. So I don't think it would be fair to me and the family and the Court": at 9 and 10.

5.5(f)(vii) **Drug Offences or Drug Involvement**

* In a number of early cases, challenges for cause have been allowed to determine whether any prospective jurors hold strongly held opinions about narcotics such that they would be unable to return a verdict solely on the evidence. A challenge was allowed in the last of the three trials involving the accused, Rowbotham. In *R.* v. *Rowbotham* (22 April 1991), (Ont. Gen. Div.) [unreported], Lane J. referred to similar challenges in *R.* v. *Neeb*, Watt J., and *R.* v. *Faulls*, H. Smith J., in allowing the challenge. A challenge had also been allowed in the first of the three *Rowbotham* trials: (1984), 12 C.C.C. (3d) 189 (Ont. H.C.J.), Ewaschuk J. In *R.* v. *Salvador* (1981), 45 N.S.R. (2d) 192 (C.A.), however, the Court refused to interfere with the discretion of the trial judge, who chose to disallow a similar question in a major drug-importation prosecution. Recently the Ontario Court of Appeal has expressed disapproval over such questioning. In *R.* v. *Hollwey* (1992), 8 O.R. (3d) 114 (C.A.), Arbour J.A. expressed agreement with the decision of Galligan J. made in the second of the three *Rowbotham* trials (15 November 1988), (Ont. H.C.J.) [unreported]. Her Ladyship quoted with approval Galligan J.'s comment that "such [general] questioning [unrelated to publicity] is not permitted in this province." The comment by Arbour J. was

obiter in *Hollwey* because the trial judge had allowed the question, and the issue related to the way in which the challenge process was conducted. More recently, in *R.* v. *Cameron* (1995), 22 O.R. (3d) 65 (C.A.), the Ontario Court of Appeal denied a general challenge relating to the involvement of the accused in drugs. Cameron was charged with a murder which occurred allegedly because of a cocaine transaction in which Cameron was involved. Galligan J.A., for the Court of Appeal this time, said that there was no evidence before the trial judge to show a "realistic potential" for bias against the appellant based on the fact that he was selling cocaine. There was therefore nothing on the record to displace the presumption. Perhaps of more significance are the general comments of Galligan J.A., on behalf of the panel that decided *Cameron*. His Lordship said, at 71:

> Before leaving this ground of appeal I should recount the concern expressed by counsel for the Crown that the decision in *Parks* has been followed by a dramatic increase in the number and breadth of questions which trial judges have been allowing counsel to put to jurors upon challenges for cause. *Parks* has been badly misinterpreted if it is being taken as authorization for using the challenge for cause process to ask wide-ranging questions of prospective jurors. *Parks* reaffirmed the presumption that duly sworn jurors can be relied upon to do their duty and decide cases on the evidence without regard to personal biases or prejudices.

See also *R.* v. *Pop* (11 February 1992), (Ont. Gen. Div.) [unreported] [summarized at 15 W.C.B. (2d) 618], denying the challenge.

* In *Parks* (1993), 15 O.R. (3d) 324 (C.A.), the Ontario Court of Appeal endorsed the decision of the trial judge to deny Parks the right to ask jurors whether learning of the involvement of witnesses in the cocaine trade would affect their ability to judge these witnesses without bias or prejudice. Doherty J.A. appropriately denied this aspect of the appeal, since involvement by witnesses in the drug trade provides legitimate data for assessing their credibility.

5.5(f)(viii) **Drugs and Race**

* In *R.* v. *Coke*, [1996] O.J. No. 2013 (Gen. Div.) (QL), Caswell J. denied a question relating to bias about Jamaicans and their involvement in the sale and use of drugs, where the Jamaican accused was charged with a murder that arose out of a drug transaction. The Court held that the defence evidence, while linking the race of the accused with prejudicial attitudes about crime in general, did not relate specifically to drug offences and therefore failed to provide an air of reality to the request. In *R.* v. *Morgan* (1995), 42 C.R. (4th) 126 (Ont. Gen. Div.), a case involving a drug-trafficking charge,

Trafford J. allowed the question to be asked after considering the evidence before him and finding that it did establish that a significant number of people in the Toronto area perceive a link between Black persons of Jamaican origin and crimes involving illegal drugs and tend to equate Black persons with Jamaicans. In *R.* v. *Willis* (1994), 90 C.C.C. (3d) 350 (Ont. C.A.), the question asked related specifically to the involvement in drugs of persons from Jamaica.

5.5(f)(ix) **Political Beliefs Related to the Offence Charged**

* As a general rule, "[i]t is contrary to established practice . . . to attempt to challenge jurors for cause on general grounds such as . . . political belief[s], or opinions": *R.* v. *Zundel* (1987), 58 O.R. (2d) 129 at 165 (C.A.). For this reason a proposed challenge for cause relating to the political views of jurors respecting the government's forestry policy was denied in *R.* v. *Lloyd*, [1994] B.C.J. No. 3168 (B.C.S.C.), where the accused was charged with a series of offences arising out of his alleged participation in a logging protest at the provincial Legislative Assembly.

* Nonetheless, in *R.* v. *Morgentaler* (15 October 1984), (Ont. H.C.J.) [unreported], jurors were challenged on the basis that their moral, religious, or other beliefs relating to abortion may interfere with their ability to render a true verdict, a process that was criticized implicitly by the Ontario Court of Appeal in *Zundel* (1987), 58 O.R. (2d) 129 (C.A.), when it noted that the questions in *Morgentaler* had never been subjected to appellate review. In *R.* v. *McAuslane* (1973), 23 C.R.N.S. 6 (Ont. Co. Ct.), Graburn J. allowed a challenge for cause in an obscenity case because obscenity involves a high degree of subjectivity and invites emotional responses which could cause a juror to refrain from adjudicating with an open mind.

* Despite the general prohibition on challenges based solely on political belief, it is difficult to deny that on some profound moral questions such as abortion, or perhaps obscenity, there may be jurors whose personal beliefs are so strong, or so rooted in matters of personal conscience, that they cannot adjudicate such questions according to law. It is no doubt this kind of concern that inspired the Assistant Crown Attorney in *R.* v. *Latimer* (1997), 4 C.R. (5th) 1 (S.C.C.), to have the police contact jurors to determine their views on the controversial issue of mercy killing. If offence-based challenges for cause are appropriate, a challenge for cause by the Crown would have provided a legal alternative.

5.5(g) **Attitudes about the Credibility of the Police**

* Some courts have allowed challenges for cause to be brought to determine whether prospective jurors are partial in the sense that they would prejudge, positively or negatively, the evidence provided by police officers because of the status of these witnesses. See, for example, *R.* v. *Racco (No. 2)* (1975), 29 C.R.N.S. 307 (Ont. Co. Ct.); *R.* v. *Kerr* (1995), 42 C.R. (4th) 118 (Ont. Gen. Div.); and *R.* v. *McArthur and McArthur* (10 January 1997), (Ont. Gen. Div.) [unreported]. Other courts have denied such challenges: *R.* v. *Mohamed*, [1995] O.J. No. 1788 (Gen. Div.) (QL); *R.* v. *Williams* (24 April 1995), (Ont. Gen. Div.) [unreported]; *R.* v. *Tahal* (20 March 1996), (Ont. Gen. Div.) [unreported], and *R.* v. *Satkunananthan*, [1996] O.J. No. 1951 (Gen. Div.) (QL); *R.* v. *Faiz* (25 May 1995), (Ont. Gen. Div.) [unreported] [summarized at 27 W.C.B. (2d) 415].

* In *Racco (No. 2)* (1975), 29 C.R.N.S. 307 (Ont. Co. Ct.), a decision rendered prior to recent developments in this area, such a challenge was allowed, though no foundation had been established beyond the defence assertion that the charges would be defended on the basis that the police had planted contraband on the accused.

* In *Kerr* (1995), 42 C.R. (4th) 118 (Ont. Gen. Div.), the foundation for the challenge was the recent, notorious arrest of four police officers in Toronto on charges of obstructing justice, based on allegations of fabricating evidence in a drug charge. Combined with the notoriety of the O.J. Simpson trial, and widely publicized remarks made by Professor Derschowitz that police are trained to "testilie," the application had an air of reality. Specifically, it was the prominence of the issue of police credibility at the time of the trial that persuaded Trafford J. to grant the request. His Honour expressed the view at 124–25 that

  > In ordinary cases, where the jury is called upon to assess the credibility of a police officer and of an accused, the comments by the trial judge at the outset of the trial and the instructions given to the jury at the conclusion of the trial would be sufficient to buttress the presumptive effect of the oath and to avoid any such challenge for cause.

* In *R.* v. *Pellington* (22 January 1991), (Ont. Gen. Div.) [unreported], *Racco* is referred to as an anomalous decision that should be confined to its facts. Langdon J. expressed the view that, in the absence of an evidentiary foundation to the contrary, jurors would be able to assess the credibility of the witnesses, including police officers.

* In *R.* v. *Malabre* (18 March 1997), (Ont. C.A.) [not yet reported], the Court upheld the trial judge's refusal to allow a challenge for cause relating to the

credibility of the police in a case where the defence claimed that the undercover officers had fabricated their testimony in an effort to frame him. The Court held that it was not its role to decide whether it would have allowed the challenge, but simply to determine whether the trial judge erred in exercising his discretion by denying it. The trial judge had not erred because there had been an insufficient evidentiary foundation presented.

* Nonetheless, affidavits that have been prepared by defence counsel who have been allowed to conduct such challenges reflect the fact that during those challenges, a significant percentage of the jurors were successfully challenged on this ground.

TABLE 5.1 Jury Challenges

Case	City/Date/ Judge	Jurors Questioned	Jurors Found Partial	Percent Jurors Partial
Clarke	Toronto, 1995 (Haley J.)	39	8	21
Levy	Toronto, 1995 (Roberts J.)	45	14	31
Ho-Sue	Toronto, 1995 (Chapnick J.)	25	10	40
Myers	Toronto, 1995 (Allen J.)	32	10	31
Almada	Toronto, 1995 (Trafford J.)	25	5	20
Jones & Powell	Whitby, 1994 (Hayes J.)	102	41	40

5.6 LAYING THE EVIDENTIARY FOUNDATION

5.6.(a) **Binding Precedent Resolving the Issue**

* In some cases there will be no need for the Court to consider whether an evidentiary foundation has been established. As a matter of binding precedent, courts in Ontario are required to find that there is an "air of reality" to support a race-based challenge for cause for Black accused

not only in Metropolitan Toronto: *R.* v. *R.(R.)* (1994), 19 O.R. (3d) 448 at 461–62 (C.A.), but across Ontario: *R.* v. *Wilson* (1996), 47 C.R. (4th) 61 at 70 (Ont. C.A.).

5.6(b) **The Limitations of Traditional Forms of Proof**

* Relative informality in establishing the grounds for a challenge for cause is necessary when the partiality is general in nature because, unlike challenges based on pre-trial publicity, "[t]he existence and extent of [matters such as] racial bias are not issues which can be established in the manner normally associated with the proof of adjudicative facts": *R.* v. *Parks* (1993), 15 O.R. (3d) 324 at 338 (C.A.). This reality means that, for many courts, doctrines of judicial notice play a significant role in determining whether a particular request for challenge for cause satisfies the threshold test and that the rules of evidence are not always applied with the same stringency as when the question of fact being examined is particular to the parties alone.

5.6(c) **Judicial Notice**

* In *Parks* (1993), 15 O.R. (3d) 324 (C.A.), the refusal by the trial judge to allow a race-based challenge was held to have been in error, even though no evidence had been called to support the challenge. The Ontario Court of Appeal conducted its own research and accepted documentary information supporting the contention of the applicant.

* The Ontario Court of Appeal has since made clear that it, as an appellate court, will only rarely act in the absence of evidence by conducting its own research. Doherty J.A. explained in *R.* v. *Alli* (1996), 110 C.C.C. (3d) 283 at 285 (Ont. C.A.):

> In *Parks*, this court went outside the trial record and beyond the material submitted by the parties to find sociological and empirical support for its conclusions. That form of appellate activism, while appropriate in some cases, ought to be used sparingly. . . . Appellate analysis of untested social science data should not be regarded as the accepted means by which the scope of the challenges for cause based on generic prejudice will be settled.

* The Ontario Court of Appeal made it clear in *R.* v. *Ly* (1997), 114 C.C.C. (3d) 279 (Ont. C.A.), that if an evidentiary foundation for the application has not been provided to the trial judge, counsel should not expect the Court of Appeal to allow an evidentiary foundation to be presented for the first time on appeal. The Court refused to consider the affidavit evidence of an expert that was offered as fresh evidence, affirming (at 282) that it was "not the appropriate forum in which to develop an adequate evidentiary

foundation for such applications." Where the evidence meets the fresh evidence test because it is new (i.e., studies or polls that emerge following the trial), or there have been new developments in the law and the case is still in the system, or the failure to present evidence at trial was the result of incompetent counsel, appellate courts may well be prepared to accept evidence that supports a challenge for cause, despite that it was not led at the trial.

* While the Ontario Court of Appeal was unwilling to go outside of the trial record in *Alli* (1996), 110 C.C.C. (3d) 283 to provide a foundation for the challenge, Doherty J.A. was careful to hold that the trial judge would not necessarily have erred by allowing the application. In the absence of evidence, however, it could not be said that he misapplied his discretion. This would suggest that in some cases, challenges for cause may be appropriate without the formal presentation of proof. This is consistent with earlier decisions of the Ontario Court of Appeal and the Supreme Court of Canada where the submissions by counsel have been enough to obtain a challenge. In *Hubbert* (1975), 11 O.R. (2d) 464 at 479 (C.A.), aff'd [1977] 2 S.C.R. 267, the Ontario Court of Appeal said that even though extrinsic evidence in support of the challenge is unnecessary, counsel must be prepared to state a reason for the challenge. This was quoted with approval in *R.* v. *Pirozzi* (1987), 34 C.C.C. (3d) 376 at 380 (Ont. C.A.). In *Sherratt*, [1991] 1 S.C.R. 509 at 514 & 537, counsel sought to establish the foundation by simply telling the judge about the publicity that the case had received. The Supreme Court of Canada took no issue with the manner in which the factual record was placed before the court, simply affirming the trial judge's conclusion that the pre-trial publicity in the case was not shown to be of such a nature as to meet the test. In *Wilson* (1996), 47 C.R. (4th) 61 (Ont. C.A.), counsel did not call any evidence but rather referred to media reports emanating from Metropolitan Toronto with respect to the prevalence of Blacks in the drug trade, which would have been available to the citizens of Whitby.

* Since there must be a factual basis for the decisions, where successful applications have been brought on the basis of submissions, the judges have necessarily taken judicial notice of the existence of the relevant partiality referred to in those submissions.

* In *R.* v. *Tonye* (9 May 1996), (Ont. Gen. Div.) [unreported], Hill J. said at 5:

> The threshold showing or demonstration of the existence of a realistic potential for an attitudinal and behavioural risk to impartiality may be established by evidence filed or by judicial recognition of notorious facts, sufficiently notorious to raise the concern regarding juror's state of indifference.

* In *R.* v. *Wilson* (1996), 47 C.R. (4th) 61 (Ont. C.A.), McMurtry J.A. took judicial notice that the major concentration of Blacks is in Metropolitan Toronto and spoke of the "global village" and the "[t]he influence of negative stereotyping on all of the citizens of Ontario," thereby judicially noting not just attitudinal partiality but also behavioural partiality: at 69. Indeed, in the face of these judicially noted facts, the Court held that the Crown had failed to call any evidence to establish its contention that the problem was confined to Metropolitan Toronto: at 68.

* In *Kitaitchik* (5 October 1993), (Ont. Gen. Div.) [unreported], at 8, German J. took judicial notice that "there are, in Ontario . . . people who are extremely concerned about violence towards women. By that I do not mean that there is anyone in favour of violence towards women, but that there are those who would look favourably, I am satisfied, on a proposal to change our legal system to remove the presumption of innocence when the victim is a woman and the accused is a man." In *R.* v. *Pheasant* (1995), 47 C.R. (4th) 47 at 53 & 54, Hill J. indicated that he would not have been prepared to note judicially that same "fact."

* Judicial notice of the possibility that prospective jurors may be partial to the Crown in sexual offence prosecutions involving children was also taken, for example, in *R.* v. *Mattingly* (1994), 28 C.R. (4th) 262 (Ont. Gen. Div.) and *R.* v. *Griffin* (28 September 1993), (Ont. Gen. Div.) [unreported], Marshall J.

* In *R.* v. *Genereux*, [1994] O.J. No. 3095 (Gen. Div.) (QL), at para 24, Whalen J. said: "I do not need studies, treatises or experts to inform me of the passion and irrationality that these issues [the brutal murder of an eight-year-old, allegedly by a mentally challenged accused] can cause in human behaviour. Judges see that every day and struggle to maintain their own equilibria and reasoned distance."

* In *R.* v. *Williams* (1996), 106 C.C.C. (3d) 215 (B.C.C.A.), the British Columbia Court of Appeal was prepared to note judicially that attitudinal bias exists in British Columbia with respect to Aboriginal Canadians, but was not prepared to take judicial notice that the nature of that bias would predispose jurors to adjudicate partially in the case of Aboriginal accused.

* Despite the readiness of some courts to take judicial notice of the foundation for the challenge for cause application, it would be extremely unwise tactically for counsel to seek to rely on the readiness of a judge to do so. It will virtually remove any prospect of appealing a denial of the challenge, and may well undermine the ability to persuade. Although inconsistent

with other Ontario Court of Appeal authority where the foundation for challenges based on mere submissions by counsel has been recognized, Moldaver J.A. went so far as to say recently in *R.* v. *Betker* (1997), 115 C.C.C. (3d) 421 at 435–36 (Ont. C.A.):

> Proving the behavioural component of partiality requires evidence that despite the trial safeguards — the juror's oath or affirmation, the solemnity of the occasion, the dynamics of jury deliberations including "diffused impartiality," and the trial judge's warnings and instructions — a juror will be unable to put that bias aside and decide the case solely on the evidence before the court. Evidence of the behavioural component of partiality is crucial.

Even if this passage is not to be taken to mean that evidence is now required to support any challenge for cause, it does underscore the importance of a properly presented foundation.

5.6(c)(i) **Judicial Notice of Adjudicative Facts**

* The most familiar form of judicial notice is sometimes referred to as "judicial notice of adjudicative facts." "Adjudicative facts are those that concern the immediate parties": *Canada Post Corp.* v. *Smith* (1994), 20 O.R. (3d) 173 at 185 (Div. Ct.). They address such questions as "who did what, where, when, how and with what motive or intent . . . Such facts are specific . . .": *Canada Post Corp.* v. *Smith* (1994), 20 O.R. (3d) 173 at 185 (Div. Ct.). The doctrine of judicial notice relating to adjudicative facts enables courts to accept without evidence those facts that are indisputable and notorious in the community where the issue is being litigated: *R.* v. *Zundel* (1987), 58 O.R. (2d) 129 at 181–82 (C.A.); *R.* v. *Potts* (1982), 36 O.R. (2d) 195 (C.A.). The indisputability requirement ensures the accuracy of factual findings made in the absence of evidence and preserves the repute of the administration of justice. If a court decides a case contrary to indisputable facts, the integrity of the administration of justice would suffer. The notoriety requirement, in turn, answers concerns about the appearance of justice. If the fact that is judicially noticed is notorious, a judge will not appear to be deciding the issue with partiality by making that factual finding in the absence of evidence.

* Because of the notoriety requirement, it is a mistake for trial judges to base their decision on their own personal observations and experiences. Hence the trial judge erred in *Wilson* (1996), 47 C.R. (4th) 61 at 70 (Ont. C.A.) in taking into account his "personal observation and experience" that jurors had not returned a racially biased verdict in any case in which he was involved, since "[t]his experience could not be objectively verified and therefore represents a very difficult area for the exercise of judicial discre-

tion." Thus, even though judges called upon to take judicial notice are left "to rely on . . . [their] personal assessment of the nature and extent of . . . [the] prejudice and its potential impact on prospective jurors' ability to act impartially" (*Parks* (1993), 15 O.R. (3d) 324 at 336 (C.A.)), they are to make that assessment based on facts that can properly be noted judicially.

* Judicial notice of adjudicative facts is particularly well suited to publicity cases, since the essence of the contention by the party seeking the challenge is that the publicity that the case received is so notorious in the community that a fair trial is not possible. Where the publicity is in fact extensive enough to support a challenge, a court may take judicial notice of it. In *R.* v. *Keegstra* (1991), 114 A.R. 288 at 292 (C.A.), for example, the trial judge said:

> . . . I take judicial notice of the fact that throughout Alberta . . . the accused has been the subject of wide media attention right up to the date of the trial . . . This has been a matter of continuing widespread public debate. Few, if any, members of the public escaped the onslaught. Most members of the public, if they're honest, must have some kind of tentative opinion about the accused.

See also *R.* v. *Ross* (18 July 1996), (Ont. Gen. Div.) [unreported], where Salhany J. allowed a challenge for cause relating to publicity in a prosecution arising from the Grandview investigation. His Honour took judicial notice that "the Grandview investigation has been the subject of a considerable amount of publicity since it began a couple of years [before] and [was] the subject of editorial comment": at 2–3.

5.6(c)(ii) **Judicial Notice of Matters Frequently before the Courts**

* A subspecies of the notorious-fact doctrine allows courts to take judicial notice of facts that are commonly before the courts and resolved to be true, such as the function of a breathalyser, or that police officers take notes. In *R.* v. *Cobham*, [1994] 3 S.C.R. 360 at 372, the Court denied the Crown's submission that a *Charter* complainant had not established a section 10(b) breach because he had not presented evidence as to the availability of duty counsel and the legal aid system in the province. The Court said:

> Duty counsel and legal aid services are . . . an intrinsic part of the practice of criminal law in this country and, as such, courts are entitled to take judicial notice of the broad parameters of these services, such as their existence and how they are generally accessed.

* Similarly, it is appropriate for courts to take judicial notice of the operation of court processes and of the conduct of cases before the courts. In connec-

tion with section 11(b) applications, for example, it is common for courts to apply judicial experience in determining whether there has been a *prima facie* unreasonable delay, what normal intake periods are, and causes for delay.

* It is this form of judicial notice that allowed Moldaver J.A., in *R.* v. *Betker* (1997), 115 C.C.C. (3d) 421 (Ont. C.A.), to take into account that there is not a problem with mistrials in sexual offence cases. No evidence had been presented to establish this. Similarly, while the information did not persuade the Court, it accepted statistical material reflecting the high rates at which jurors were challenged successfully in sexual offence cases involving child victims. Arguably, it was appropriate for the Court to have used this information to enable it to take judicial notice of the rates of successful challenge.

5.6(c)(iii) **Judicial Notice of Legislative Facts**

* Unlike "adjudicative facts," "legislative facts" "are of a more general nature" and relate to the "social, economic and cultural context" within which the law operates. As such, legislative facts are not easily provable and generally transcend the interests of the immediate parties: *Canada Post Corp.* v. *Smith* (1994), 20 O.R. (3d) 173 at 185–86 (Div. Ct.); *R.* v. *Bonin* (1989), 47 C.C.C. (3d) 230 at 248 (B.C.C.A.).

* The resolution of questions of law often requires knowledge about the factual milieu in which the law operates. Judges have always been able to take judicial notice of the social framework in which the law operates, including such things as the effect that breaches of solicitor-client privilege would have on the solicitor-client relationship and the general deterrent effect of sentences. The law could not be developed or applied without judges taking cognizance of the milieu in which it operates. The doctrine of judicial notice of legislative facts allows courts developing and interpreting the law to take judicial notice of the social framework within which the law operates. This form of judicial notice has taken on prominence in constitutional cases, particularly those involving section 1 determinations: *Bonin* (1989), 47 C.C.C. (3d) 230 at 247–49 (B.C.C.A.).

* In informing themselves of the social milieu in which the law operates, courts may consult a variety of extrinsic material. Provided that the other party is given notice of the materials and an opportunity to reply, a court may use extrinsic material to take judicial notice of the social framework within which the law operates, even where those facts may not be notorious: *Bonin* (1989), 47 C.C.C. (3d) 230 at 247–49 (B.C.C.A.).

* In determining whether a generic or general partiality exists, such as race-based or offence-based prejudice, courts are not determining questions of law but are instead resolving general questions of fact. Strictly speaking, when courts take judicial notice of the social framework within which the jury trial is being conducted, they are not noticing "legislative facts." Yet the nature of the factual questions about general or generic prejudice are more like legislative than adjudicative facts. The issues relate to the general social framework within which the law is being administered (for example, attitudinal and behavioural bias against Aboriginals) and do not relate in a specific way to the particular parties. Issues of generic or general prejudice, like legislative facts, "are more general in nature" and relate to the "social, economic and cultural context" in which the law operates. As such, they are not easily provable and transcend the interests of the immediate parties. For this reason, courts have been taking judicial notice of these social framework facts in challenge for cause cases and have assisted themselves in doing so by consulting government reports, learned studies, media reports, and other materials. See, for example, *R.* v. *Parks* (1993), 15 O.R. (3d) 324 (C.A.); *R.* v. *B.(S.)* (1996), 47 C.R. (4th) 56 (Ont. Gen. Div.); and *R.* v. *Williams* (1996), 106 C.C.C. (3d) 215 (B.C.C.A.)

5.6(d) *Viva Voce* Evidence

* Of course, relevant and otherwise admissible *viva voce* evidence can be presented in support of a challenge for cause application. In *R.* v. *Zundel* (1987), 58 O.R. (2d) 129 (C.A.), for example, the accused testified as to the publicity surrounding his actions and the charges against him, including of demonstrations at the courthouse, as well as to the nature of the publicity relating to the issues discussed in the publications leading to his charges.

5.6(e) Affidavit Evidence

* It is common for courts to receive, and act on, affidavit evidence in determining challenge for cause applications. In *R.* v. *McPartlin*, [1994] B.C.J. No. 3101 (S.C.) (QL), an affidavit of the Black accused attesting to his personal experiences with racism in Victoria, B.C., was admitted, though it was not found to be sufficient to establish an air of reality to his concern that his race could cause jurors to judge him with partiality. In a number of sexual offence cases, affidavit evidence from other lawyers attesting to their experiences with challenges for cause in similar cases has been received, as have copies of affidavits prepared by expert witnesses, even in connection with other cases. Because of the general or generic bases for these kinds of challenges, the information may retain its relevance from case to case.

5.6(f) **Exhibits**

* Typically, documentary evidence is filed in support of challenge for cause applications. Published articles were filed as exhibits, and media reports were produced in *R.* v. *Zundel* (1987), 58 O.R. (2d) 129 at 160–61 (C.A.), and *R.* v. *Keegstra* (1991), 114 A.R. 288 at 292 (C.A.). In *R.* v. *Pheasant* (1995), 47 C.R. (4th) 47 (Ont. Gen. Div.), the applicant filed a series of Statistics Canada publications reflecting the gendered nature of domestic violence and its high incidence. Extracts from government studies showing the rates of victimization in sexual offence cases have often been filed. In keeping with the informality normally associated with such applications, documents filed with the court are often not authenticated according to the strict rules of evidence: see, for example, *R.* v. *Court* (1995), 23 O.R. (3d) 321 (C.A.). In *R.* v. *Tonye* (9 May 1996), (Ont. Gen. Div.) [unreported], Hill J. allowed an article on HIV discrimination to be admitted, even though it was not in affidavit form and even though the Crown was not afforded an opportunity to cross-examine the author because His Honour "was satisfied that the exhibit in question . . . is sufficiently scholarly and authenticated to be filed and considered in its current form." This is similar to the practice that has developed in *Charter* challenges where section 1 is at issue.

5.6(g) **Expert Evidence**

* It is common for expert witnesses to testify. See, for example, *R.* v. *Griffis* (1993), 16 C.R.R. (2d) 322 (Ont. Gen. Div.), where a professor of anthropology and consultant in race relations testified to the nature and extent of racial prejudice in Metropolitan Toronto, and see *R.* v. *Coke*, [1996] O.J. No. 2013 (Gen. Div.) (QL); *R.* v. *Kerr* (1995), 42 C.R. (4th) 118 (Ont. Gen. Div.); and *R.* v. *Morgan* (1995), 42 C.R. (4th) 126 (Ont. Gen. Div.).

* As indicated, it is not uncommon for such evidence to be presented in affidavit form. Indeed, in *R.* v. *Ecclestone* (29 January 1996), (Ont. Gen. Div.) [unreported], MacDougall J. received a transcript of evidence from another case, *R.* v. *Myers* (15 September 1995), (Ont. Gen. Div.) [unreported], relating to the results of a telephone poll conducted under the supervision of an expert anthropologist.

* In *R.* v. *Hillis*, [1996] O.J. No. 2739 (Gen. Div.) (QL), Whealy J. relied heavily on affidavit evidence and transcripts of cross-examination of an expert that had been prepared in another case, in rejecting an offence-based challenge for cause application relating to sexual offences involving children.

* Expert evidence must be relevant and otherwise admissible to be received. Hence it will not be heard when it is not within the scope of the expert's expertise: *R.* v. *Hubbert* (1975), 11 O.R. (2d) 464 at 481 (C.A.), aff'd [1977] 2 S.C.R. 267. In *R.* v. *Yashev*, [1995] O.J. No. 3598 (Gen. Div.) (QL), the defence expert, a clinical psychologist, was held not to have the expertise necessary to comment on the prevalence of societal prejudice against recent immigrants. Also of concern was the limited extent to which the foundation for his opinion was established by admissible evidence. He had relied on a summary of a research poll contained in a human rights study commissioned by the government of Canada, without having examined, and without having determined the nature of, the database and without having conducted any personal research. He had uncovered no studies in the psychological literature and had not advised himself of the ethnic make-up of the population of York Region.

* In *R.* v. *Morgan* (1995), 42 C.R. (4th) 126 at 129 (Ont. Gen. Div.), Dr. Henry was permitted to base her opinion on her own work, which included analysing media information, studying the Carribean community, and monitoring Canadian institutions, this even though no formal studies had been conducted. She testified, unchallenged, that her methods were acceptable within her profession.

5.6(h) **Polls and Statistical Evidence**

* In *R.* v. *Coke*, [1996] O.J. No. 2013 (Gen. Div.) (QL), results of a poll conducted by a senior vice-president of Angus Reid Group Inc., obtained by a telephone survey of 400 residents of Metropolitan Toronto, considered to be statistically accurate by professional standards, were admitted and relied on to establish the existence of anti-Jamaican, crime-related bias in Brampton. See also *R.* v. *Kerr* (1995), 42 C.R. (4th) 118 (Ont. Gen. Div.); *R.* v. *Morgan* (1995), 42 C.R. (4th) 126 (Ont. Gen. Div.); and *R.* v. *Musson* (1996), 3 C.R. (5th) 61 (Ont. Gen. Div.). In *Morgan*, Trafford J. noted that the poll was conducted, in the opinion of the expert, consistently with methods accepted in the profession. The Crown failed to call any evidence challenging the methodology of the defence experts, including the pollster.

* As indicated, in *R.* v. *Ecclestone* (29 January 1996), (Ont. Gen. Div.) [unreported], MacDougall J. received a transcript of evidence from another case, *R.* v. *Myers* (15 September 1995), (Ont. Gen. Div.) [unreported], relating to the results of a telephone poll conducted under the supervision of an expert anthropologist. The Court in each case discounted the reliability of the poll, even though it was modelled closely on the Angus Reid poll accepted by Trafford J. in *R.* v. *Morgan* (1995), 42 C.R. (4th) 126 (Ont. Gen. Div.),

because the expert was not shown to have expertise and experience in conducting polls and because interviewers included articling students from the defence law firm.

* Statistical information, such as that contained in Appendix I to this book, has been relied on by a number of courts but rejected by others because it was not "scientific" — not gathered according to generally accepted polling methodology and without compliance with the scientific method.

* Statistical information based on the affidavits of lawyers as to the results of challenges for cause that had been conducted in two cases relating to partiality about the credibility of police officers was discounted by the Court as "anecdotal in nature": *R.* v. *Malabre* (18 March 1997), (Ont. C.A.) [not yet reported]. The evidence afforded "no insight as to the nature or extent of the bias that may have existed in the two cited cases." As this case demonstrates, if the statistical range is too modest, the evidence may be given no weight. The experience in two cases was simply inadequate to present a foundation for the application.

5.7 FRAMING THE QUESTION

5.7(a) **The Proper Form of Questions**

* The trial judge is to control the challenge for cause process by ensuring that any questions allowed are in keeping with the appropriate principles and are relevant in the sense that they provide information as to both the attitudinal and the behavioural aspects of partiality: *R.* v. *Parks* (1993), 15 O.R. (3d) 324 at 336–37 (C.A.).

* In *R.* v. *Morgan* (1995), 42 C.R. (4th) 126 at 131 (Ont. Gen. Div.), Trafford J. said:

  > [C]hallenging perspective [sic] jurors based only on their opinions, beliefs or prejudices is not appropriate. . . . An acceptable question must go further and focus upon the ability of the perspective [sic] juror to set aside certain opinions, beliefs or prejudices when performing as a juror.

* The question allowed in *R.* v. *Parks* (1993), 15 O.R. (3d) 324 at 331 (C.A.) is illustrative of a question that addresses both the attitudinal and the behavioural aspects of partiality:

  > As the judge will tell you, in deciding whether or not the prosecution has proven the charge against an accused, a juror must judge the evidence of the witnesses without bias, prejudice, or partiality.

> . . .
>
> Would your ability to judge the evidence in the case without bias, prejudice, or partiality be affected by the fact that the person charged is a black Jamaican immigrant and the deceased is a white man?

As can be seen, the issue of impartiality is introduced, the potential partiality that is of concern is then identified, and then the juror is asked about his or her ability to adjudicate the case impartially.

* In *R.* v. *B.(S.)* (1996), 47 C.R. (4th) 56 (Ont. Gen. Div.), Hill J. observed that the standard, *Parks*-type question confuses some jurors, prompting them to state their opinions in open court or to focus on their views rather than on their ability to adjudicate impartially. His Honour therefore developed a more extensive question, which states specifically that the juror is not being asked if he or she holds any biased views. The question is as follows:

> As His Honour will tell you, in deciding whether or not the Crown has proven the charges against . . . [S.B.] beyond a reasonable doubt, a juror must judge the evidence of all witnesses without bias, prejudice, or partiality, that is the juror must decide the case with an open and fair mind and render a true verdict based only on the evidence given in the trial.
>
> In this case, the prosecution alleges that Mr. . . . [S.B.] committed a number of offences directed against his wife.
>
> Some persons in the community, who have thought about the matter, have developed beliefs or attitudes regarding husbands who subject their wives to physical abuse and violence. Other persons do not hold any particular beliefs or attitudes relating to this subject.
>
> You are not being asked if you hold any such views or what views you hold.
>
> However, assuming you hold a belief or attitude relating to the issue of husbands who subject their wives to abuse or violence, would any such belief or attitude prevent you from giving a fair and impartial verdict in this case based solely upon the evidence and the instructions of the trial judge?

* As indicated, there are important limitations on the use to which the challenge for cause process is to be put. Those limitations that are relevant to the framing of the question include

- A challenge for cause cannot be brought in an effort to cause the under-representation of a particular class of society or the representativeness that is essential to the proper functioning of the trial: *R.* v. *Zundel* (1987), 58 O.R. (2d) 129 at 165 (C.A.); *R.* v. *Sherratt*, [1991] 1 S.C.R. 509 at 533.

- The challenge for cause process cannot be used to inquire into the lifestyles, antecedents, or personal experience of the juror. It is not a procedure for wide-ranging personalized disclosure: *R.* v. *Hubbert* (1975), 11 O.R. (2d) 464 at 475 (C.A.), aff'd [1977] 2 S.C.R. 267; *R.* v. *Parks* (1993), 15 O.R. (3d) 324 at 333 (C.A.); *R.* v. *Sherratt*, [1991] 1 S.C.R. 509 at 527–28 & 533.

* Hence, it is inappropriate to ask jurors

- Whether they are members of a particular race, or class of society: *R.* v. *Zundel* (1987), 58 O.R. (2d) 129 (C.A.).
- About their personal experiences, such as whether the juror or a member of the juror's family has been a victim of the offence that the accused is facing: *R.* v. *Cox* (1994), 25 C.R.R. (2d) 278 (Ont. Gen. Div.). But see *R.* v. *C.* (7 February 1994), (Ont. Gen. Div.) [unreported], Philp J., and *R.* v. *Williams* (3 April 1989), (Ont. Dist. Ct.) [unreported], Keenan J., as well as A.M. Cooper, "The ABCs of Challenge for Cause in Jury Trials: To Challenge or Not to Challenge and What to Ask if You Get It" (1994) 37 Crim. L.Q. 62.
- About what their attitudes and beliefs are, including whether they are members of any groups, such as victims of violence organizations or other lobbying groups: *R.* v. *Kitaitchik* (5 October 1993), (Ont. Gen. Div.) [unreported].

* The question should be phrased such that its answer does not reveal the relevant, disqualifying belief. It was of importance to the *Parks* court that jurors, in responding affirmatively to the question, would not be betraying the nature of their admitted bias. Jurors could respond affirmatively to the question whether they were harbouring pro-Black bias that would make them partial to the defence or anti-Black bias that would favour the Crown: (1993), 15 O.R. (3d) 324 at 333 (C.A.).

* In pre-trial publicity cases, it is common to allow more extensive questioning. In *Hubbert* (1975), 11 O.R. (2d) 464 (C.A.), aff'd [1977] 2 S.C.R. 267, the court approved of the kinds of questions put by counsel to prospective jurors in *R.* v. *Lesso* (1972), 23 C.R.N.S. 179 at 187–91 (Ont. H.C.J.). The questions asked in *Lesso* included:

- Have you discussed this case with anyone?
- If yes, have you expressed an opinion about the guilt or innocence of the accused?
- If no, do you have an opinion as to the guilt or innocence of the accused?
- If yes, what is that opinion?

5.7(b) **Rewording the Question**

* Where there is a foundation for allowing the challenge for cause, but where the trial judge rejects the proposed question, he or she must give counsel an opportunity to reword the question so that it is appropriate: *R.* v. *Zundel* (1987), 58 O.R. (2d) 129 at 166 (C.A.).

5.7(c) **Should All Jurors Be Questioned?**

* In *R.* v. *MacKinnon*, [1996] O.J. No. 1860 (Gen. Div.) (QL), McIsaac J., following *Wilson* (1996), 47 C.R. (4th) 61 (Ont. C.A.), allowed a challenge for cause in a first-degree murder charge of two Black accused charged with killing a Chinese Canadian. The question included reference to the race of the accused. Mr. Justice McIsaac stated that he would refuse to allow the question to be asked to a prospective Black juror, because to do so would be "unfair, illegitimate and insulting" and "patently degrading." It is questionable whether this aspect of the ruling was correct. To be appropriate, the question posed should be neutral in the sense that a respondent may be acknowledging either a pro-defence or a pro-Crown bias if responding affirmatively. Apart altogether from the prospect that Black persons may have pro-Crown bias relating to other members of their own race, the effect of Mr. Justice McIsaac's ruling is to prevent Black persons with pro-defence bias from indicating their inability to adjudicate impartially.

* In *R.* v. *Pheasant* (1995), 47 C.R. (4th) 47 at 55 (Ont. Gen. Div.), Hill J. refused to confine the challenge solely to male jurors, even though his concern was that there may be male jurors who are domestic abusers and who might adjudicate partially in favour of the accused. He said, "Once air of reality threshold is met, the challenge is at large in the sense of at the discretion of counsel."

CHAPTER 6

THE MECHANICS OF THE CHALLENGE FOR CAUSE PROCEDURE

6.1 DISCLOSING THE CHALLENGE PRIOR TO TRIAL

* The *Criminal Code of Canada* does not require that any notice of an intended challenge for cause be given by the challenging party to the court or to the non-challenging party. In some cases no notice will be possible because the events leading to the challenge will not become apparent until the jury is being selected, as when jurors who are not properly on the panel come forward or when it is discovered that particular prospective jurors may have a connection to the case. In most cases, however, particularly those involving general or generic challenges such as publicity and race-based challenges, the party seeking the challenge will know well in advance that a challenge will be requested.

* To avoid delays or adjournments while opposing counsel or the judge research the matter, it is, at the very least, prudent and courteous to provide notice. There are also practical advantages to doing so. Often the opposing party will agree that it is an appropriate case for a challenge for cause, and when this occurs the need for extensive legal argument can be avoided. It may also be possible to work out the questions in advance, if notice is provided. For these reasons the usual practice is for parties seeking to bring general or generic challenges to provide notice and supporting materials in advance of the application.

* Despite the silence of the *Criminal Code*, it may be that such notice is actually required, particularly where the party seeking to bring the challenge intends to rely on the *Charter* to buttress the claim to entitlement. While the procedure is governed by the *Criminal Code*, the application does raise constitutional considerations relating to both section 11(d) and section 11(f) of the *Charter*. Therefore, Rules of Criminal Procedure in each province governing *Charter* motions may well apply where challenges for cause are brought.

* It is also prudent for the party seeking to bring the challenge to prepare the challenge by assembling, serving, and filing copies of the cases relied on, and the supporting material. Indeed, the prospects of succeeding will be enhanced if the application is accompanied by a brief, clear factum outlining the facts relied on, as well as the relevant principles of law.

6.2 WHO IS ENTITLED TO CHALLENGE FOR CAUSE?

* Both the prosecution and defence are entitled to an unlimited number of challenges for cause: section 638(1) of the *Criminal Code*. Section 638(1) provides:

> 638.(1) A prosecutor or an accused is entitled to any number of challenges on the ground that . . .

6.3 WHEN DOES THE CHALLENGE FOR CAUSE PROCESS BEGIN?

* Immediately after the charge(s) on the indictment is (are) read out in open court and the accused has pleaded not guilty, the empanelling of a twelve-person jury begins: *R.* v. *Sherratt*, [1991] 1 S.C.R. 509 at 520. If there is a general challenge for cause to be put to each potential juror, then an application to challenge should be brought prior to the drawing of the first juror's name. Where the challenge is specific to a particular juror, it is brought when the prospective juror is called to the book to be sworn.

6.4 SHOULD THE *SHERRATT VOIR DIRE* BE CONDUCTED IN THE ABSENCE OF THE JURY PANEL?

* Most challenges for cause involve a general challenge pursuant to section 638(1)(b) of the *Criminal Code*, which provides that a challenge will be permitted on the ground that "a juror is not indifferent between the Queen

and the accused." As noted above in chapter 5, before the challenge will be allowed, the challenging party will have to satisfy the presiding judge that there is an "air of reality" to the application. This is commonly done in what is known as a *Sherratt voir dire*. For the reasons outlined below, this *voir dire* should be held in the absence of the jury panel, preferably prior to the panel being called into the courtroom, so as to avoid inconveniencing the prospective jurors.

* In *R.* v. *MacFarlane* (1973), 3 O.R. (2d) 467 (H.C.J.), Justice Hughes suggested that rulings made with regard to general challenges for cause (and presumably argument) are best made in the absence of the jury panel. This is the common practice and is obviously the appropriate approach. Whether to allow a challenge for cause process to be undertaken in a given case is a legal question in which prospective jurors have no role to play. Legal arguments can be made with more candour in the absence of the panel without fear of insulting or alienating potential jurors. Moreover, those arguments and the rulings that follow could confuse the jury as to the nature of the issues and as to the relevant underlying principles, potentially distorting the juror's comprehension about the judge's directions relating both to the conduct of the challenge, if it is allowed, and as to the case itself. Actual jurors are excluded from *voir dires* involving pure questions of law. Certainly prospective jurors should also be excluded.

6.5 THE TRIAL JUDGE'S PRELIMINARY COMMENTS TO THE JURY PANEL

* Following the *Sherratt voir dire*, the jury panel should then be called into the courtroom. The indictment should be read out loud to the accused and his or her plea recorded. The trial judge will then address the panel. The following address is suggested by Justice Then of the Ontario Court General Division (quoted from Justice Then's paper "Challenges for Cause" (Address to the National Judicial Institute, 27–29 November 1995)):

> Welcome to this courtroom on behalf of the administration of justice — my name is — — — . You have heard the charge read and the accused say that he is not guilty. In a few moments, jury selection will commence and the trial of the accused will follow.
>
> When you are selected as a juror, you become a judge just as I am a judge. Your role in a criminal trial is much more important than mine because it is the jury that determines whether an accused is guilty or not guilty.
>
> We live in and enjoy the freedom of a democratic society. One of the cornerstones of our society is the jury system. Your role as jurors is at the heart of the justice system. The guilt or innocence of an accused person is

decided by 12 of the accused's fellow citizens. Jury duty is the most serious, challenging and important function a person can be called upon to perform.

The jury system is the best system of justice ever devised. But we must always be vigilant, for it is fundamental that no innocent person ever be convicted of a crime that he or she did not commit. It is equally important that those who have committed crimes are dealt with fairly but firmly.

You are the legal guardians of the community. You stand between the public and those alleged to have committed crimes. You are the guardians of both the public and the accused.

To be a juror [in Ontario] you must be a Canadian citizen, be able to understand the English language and be able to hear without difficulty. If you have a problem in any of these areas, please advise me when your name is called. I will have more to tell you about the length of the trial and other matters during jury selection.

To qualify as a juror there are other requirements that you must meet. They will be obvious to you if you simply think about the standards that you require any judge to meet.

Firstly, the accused and the Crown are entitled to a jury that will be unbiased and approach their solemn duties without fear, without favour, without prejudice and who will decide the case solely on the evidence they hear and see in this courtroom. A jury must be able to put aside any preconceived notions or opinions that may have been formed from something they may have seen or read or heard. A jury must be indifferent and impartial. A jury must be neutral.

The question is not whether you may have an opinion or feelings because of what you have heard or seen or read. To be selected as a juror, what is crucial, is that are you able to set the opinion or feelings aside and try the case, solely on the evidence presented in the courtroom, the arguments of counsel, my directions to you on the law and on nothing else.

Jury selection will begin by the clerk of the court drawing names from the drum in front of him at random. In this case, you will come forward to the place indicated by the constable. Counsel for the crown and defence have a right to question and challenge jurors.

Do not take offence if you are challenged or questioned by counsel. They are given the right to do so by law. They are seeking to have what they judge to be a fair, open minded and impartial jury, who will try the case without bias or prejudice of any kind.

In this case, the crown and defence will challenge prospective jurors on the basis that they may not be indifferent or impartial or to put it another way, on the basis that the juror may be prejudiced or biased. The question whether a juror is likely biased is decided by two triers selected at random from the people in this courtroom.

The triers will decide whether a prospective juror is likely biased or not biased, after seeing and hearing the juror answer certain questions from counsel for the defence [and from the Crown], as well as some short instructions from me. To say the same thing another way the question is — does the juror have opinions or feelings about the case and most importantly, if the prospective juror does have opinions and feelings, can the juror set aside and render a true verdict based only on the evidence at trial.

The questions you will be asked have been approved by me. I remind you that counsel are not attempting to embarrass you in any way. The questions will not pry into your privacy, unduly. The same questions will be asked of every prospective juror. The whole purpose is to ensure a jury is empanelled, that will try the case without prejudice or bias. A jury must be impartial.

The decision of the triers must be unanimous one way or the other but they are entitled to disagree. The triers will indicate their decision by saying "not accepted" if the juror is found to be partial or biased and by saying "accepted," if the juror is found to be impartial or neutral.

If the decision is "accepted" then the lawyers may or may not challenge the juror by using one of the peremptory challenges allotted to them. If counsel do not challenge peremptorily, then the juror is sworn in and will be one of 12 jurors to preside over this trial. That juror will take a seat in the jury box and become a trier.

If the decision is "not accepted" or if a juror is challenged peremptorily, then that person is excused from further jury duty. This procedure will continue until 12 jurors are sworn.

The challenge for cause will be in this courtroom but only jurors who are triers, and the juror being questioned will be present. . . .

6.6 THE ORDER OF CHALLENGES

* Section 635 of the *Criminal Code*, which came into force in 1992, governs the order of challenges for both challenges for cause and peremptory challenges:

635.(1) The accused shall be called on before the prosecutor is called on to declare whether the accused challenges the first juror, for cause or peremptorily, and thereafter the prosecutor and the accused shall be called on alternately, in respect of each of the remaining jurors, to first make such a declaration.

(2) Subsection (1) applies where two or more accused are to be tried together, but all of the accused shall exercise the challenges of the

defence in turn, in the order in which their names appear in the indictment or in any other order agreed on by them,

(*a*) in respect of the first juror, before the prosecutor; and
(*b*) in respect of each of the remaining jurors, either before or after the prosecutor, in accordance with subsection (1).

* While section 635 does not address the matter directly, it seems clear that challenges for cause pertaining to each juror are to be dealt with before peremptory challenges. As Adams J. explained in *R.* v. *Aguilera* (1993), 87 C.C.C. (3d) 474 at 479–80 (Ont. Gen. Div.):

> the more reasonable interpretation of s. 635(1) is not to require any party to exercise one of a limited number of peremptory challenges until it is known whether or not the prospective juror otherwise qualifies to be a juror. "Cause" is specifically defined in the *Criminal Code* and this determination is most reasonably construed as a precondition to the exercise of a peremptory challenge. Adding strength to this construction is the fact that in s. 635(1) the phrase "challenge for cause" precedes the reference to peremptory challenge.

Moreover, it has been held that while the challenge for cause process cannot be brought for the purpose of deciding whether to exercise a peremptory challenge, it is appropriate for counsel to consider the conduct of a properly initiated challenge for cause in deciding whether to exercise a peremptory challenge. Necessarily then, the challenge for cause must occur first. (See paragraph 4.5, above.)

* Unfortunately, the section is not clear in describing whether the party bringing an unsuccessful challenge for cause must declare that he or she is exercising a peremptory challenge, before the other party or parties are called on to indicate whether they will be challenging a juror for cause or peremptorily. Section 635 of the *Criminal Code* is capable of two interpretations:

The first interpretation:

> The provision . . . may reasonably be interpreted to sanction the alternation of each challenge with the challenge for cause being first completed by the parties for a prospective juror before any party is called upon to declare a peremptory challenge in respect of that person. This approach permits the identification of those prospective jurors who should not serve because of a listed cause before any party is required to expend the scarce resource of one of its peremptory challenges.

> [The process then alternates] between prosecution and defence in respect of any peremptory challenge for the prospective juror should the challenge for cause fail. *R.* v. *Aguilera* (1993), 87 C.C.C. (3d) 474 at 477 & 475 (Ont. Gen. Div.)

The second interpretation:

The second interpretation requires "that a party must declare both types of challenge on each alternative occasion before the other party is called upon" to make a decision whether to challenge for cause, or to use a peremptory challenge. *R.* v. *Aguilera* (1993), 87 C.C.C. (3d) 474 at 477 (Ont. Gen. Div.). In other words, the party whose turn it is must declare whether it is bringing either or both types of challenge. Only then, if the prospective juror survives, is the next party called upon to decide whether it will be bringing either or both types of challenge.

* In *Aguilera*, Adams J. faced the question of which interpretation is to be preferred, and he sensibly chose the first, even though the second appears to be more faithful to a literal construction of the section. His Honour noted that the section is capable of the first interpretation because (at 479):

> While this section requires the parties to alternate in declaring their challenges, it does not explicitly require that the two types of challenges be dealt with by each party together or simultaneously. Rather, it uses the conjunction "or" and the singular "a declaration."

His Honour then noted that to accept the second interpretation would mean that the party whose turn it is would be required to make a decision on whether to use a peremptory challenge before even discovering whether the opposing party would have challenged for cause. This would not be in keeping with the policy of the act because it could require use of a peremptory challenge on some prospective jurors who do not even qualify to serve on a jury because of one of the enumerated grounds of challenge for cause in section 638(1) of the *Criminal Code*. Finally, this interpretation could have the effect of requiring a party to initiate a challenge for cause that it does not wish to undertake in order to preserve its peremptory challenge. This would occur where the party wishing to bring the challenge for cause might succeed in having the juror disqualified, but, because it is the opposing party's turn, that party would have to make a decision on whether to use a peremptory challenge before finding this out. The result might be that, strategically, the opposing party could have to join in the general challenge for cause by bringing that challenge itself in order to find out whether it is really necessary to use a peremptory challenge.

* As *Aguilera* indicates, a party should not be required to bring a challenge for cause that it does not wish to bring. Section 635 of the *Criminal Code* allows parties to "declare" whether they are bringing challenges for cause. Section 638 speaks of the prosecutor and the defence being "entitled to any number of challenges [for cause]." It seems to follow that a party cannot be made to bring challenges for cause that it does not support. Despite this, some judges have apparently required a party opposed to bringing a challenge to alternate in asking the approved questions so as to ensure that the party requesting the challenge is not prejudiced through any appearance that it alone is distrustful of the jury panel. This is not in keeping with the language of the provision. Moreover, that mischief can be largely cured by conducting the challenge in the absence of the jury panel when the party bringing the challenge feels that it poses a real problem.

* While it may seem self-evident that a party who does not wish to bring a challenge for cause need not do so, this assumption can have implications for the conduct of the challenge process. For example, the defence may be challenging all prospective jurors with a general or generic race-based challenge, which the prosecution has opposed unsuccessfully but which the prosecution still does not want to participate in. Since only the defence is wanting to declare a challenge for cause in such a case, it would follow from the rule that challenges for cause be dealt with before peremptory challenges, that the defence must bring the challenge in each case as the juror is called to the book, before the prosecution is called on to make any decisions on whether to challenge jurors peremptorily. As *Aguilera* indicates, however, when the challenge for cause is unsuccessful, the parties will take turns in deciding whether to bring peremptory challenges.

6.7 THE FORM OF THE CHALLENGE

* Section 639(1) of the *Criminal Code* states:

> 639.(1) Where a challenge is made on a ground mentioned in section 638, the court may, in its discretion, require the party that challenges to put the challenge in writing.

If required to be in writing, the challenge may be in Form 41: section 639(2) of the *Criminal Code*. In *R.* v. *Hubbert* (1975), 11 O.R. (2d) 464 at 479 (C.A.), aff'd [1977] 2 S.C.R. 267, it was suggested that "if the nature of the challenge may bring opprobrium to the juror (such as having been sentenced to 15 months' imprisonment, 10 years ago)" then counsel should put the challenge in writing.

6.8 CAN THE CHALLENGE BE ACCEPTED BY THE NON-CHALLENGING PARTY?

* The opposing party who is responding to the request by a party that the challenge for cause process be undertaken may agree that it is an appropriate case to allow a challenge for cause to be conducted, or may oppose that request. If the opposing party agrees that there is a foundation for the conduct of a challenge, and agrees to the questions proposed, this may significantly influence, but cannot bind, the judge. The judge must determine whether the challenge for cause should be allowed to be undertaken and whether the questions are appropriate before the challenge can be allowed.

* One of the more controversial, unresolved aspects of the challenge for cause process concerns whether, in a case where a challenge for cause is being undertaken, the non-challenging party (in most cases, the prosecution) can "accept the challenge" by agreeing that a prospective juror should be disqualified, without having to be tried by the mini-jury. The *Criminal Code* is silent on this issue, as it simply states:

> 639.(3) A challenge may be denied by the other party to the proceedings on the ground that it is not true.

* It is generally accepted that after the trial before the two triers has begun, the opposing party cannot accept the challenge. This is because once those triers are seized with the issue of whether the challenge is true, it is they who must decide. *R.* v. *Wade* (18 September 1990), (Ont. C.A.) [unreported]; *R.* v. *Worth* (1995), 23 O.R. (3d) 211 at 221–22 (C.A.), leave to appeal refused (7 November 1996), (S.C.C.) [unreported].

* The prevailing view is that prior to the triers being sworn to adjudicate the issue, the opposing party can accept the challenge by agreeing that the juror is partial and therefore ought to be disqualified. Courts following this position rely upon *R.* v. *Hubbert* (1975), 11 O.R. (2d) 464 (C.A.), aff'd [1977] 2 S.C.R. 267. In *Hubbert*, the Court of Appeal held in reference to section 639(3) of the *Criminal Code* at 479:

> By necessary inference, the other party may "admit the challenge," in which case the trial of its truth is not required, and the juror will not be sworn.

See *R.* v. *Wade* (18 September 1990), (Ont. C.A.) [unreported]; *R.* v. *Atkinson*, [1995] A.J. No. 289 (Q.B.) (QL), Lutz J.; *R.* v. *Elliott*, [1973] 3 O.R. 475 at 483–84 (H.C.J.), Haines J.; *R.* v. *Holmgren* [1994] O.J. No. 2724 (Gen. Div.) (QL), Clarke J., [summarized at (1995), 25 W.C.B. (2d) 368]; and *R.* v. *Shergill* (1996) 4 C.R. (5th) 28 (Ont. Gen. Div.), Ferguson J.

* There is a significant problem with this line of authority. As Ewaschuk J. observed in *R.* v. *Rowbotham* (1984), 12 C.C.C. (3d) 189 at 191–92 (Ont. H.C.J.):

> Where the challenge . . . is . . . in the nature of a general inquiry based on the reasonable and substantial possibility of partiality . . . then the Crown cannot admit that the juror is partial until the questioning has established grounds for that view. . . . In my view, were the Crown to be permitted to simply admit the general challenge when put, it would thereby, in effect acquire an unlimited number of peremptory challenges.

* Of course, Ewaschuk J.'s opinion that a challenge can be admitted after questioning has established grounds to show partiality has been overruled by the holding in *Wade* that once the triers are seized of the issue, it is the triers who must decide it. His objection to allowing the opposing party to admit the challenge for particular jurors where a general challenge is being conducted — that it would effectively give the opposing counsel the power to disqualify jurors at will — is nonetheless compelling. This outcome can occur if the opposing party uses the pretense of conceding the validity of the challenge to rid itself of jurors it does not like, thereby effectively acquiring an unlimited number of peremptory challenges.

* In *R.* v. *Shergill* (1996), 4 C.R. (5th) 28 (Ont. Gen. Div.), Ferguson J. recognized that this consequence is an undesirable thing, although he considered it to be unavoidable. He remarked that any party wanting to conduct a challenge for cause may want to bear in mind before deciding to do so that it will effectively be giving opposing counsel the power to rid itself of all jurors it does not want. See the annotation to *Shergill* at (1996), 4 C.R. (5th) at 28–30.

* This undesirable consequence should be enough to demonstrate that opposing counsel should not be allowed to admit challenges. The fundamental right to conduct a challenge for cause to rid the jury of partial jurors should not be discouraged by fear that the exercise of that right will give opposing counsel an unlimited power to reject jurors without cause. Courts not bound by *Wade* (18 September 1990), (Ont. C.A.) [unreported], may be able to avoid this patently undesirable result by recognizing that the practice of admitting a challenge for cause is not provided for in the *Criminal Code*, which sets out a comprehensive code for the procedure. In *R.* v. *Barrow*, [1987] 2 S.C.R. 694 at 714, the Supreme Court of Canada advised trial judges that they should not interfere in the partiality trial by usurping the function of the jurors:

> The *Code* sets out a detailed process for the selection of an impartial jury. It gives both parties substantial powers in the process and sets up a mechanism to try the partiality of a potential juror when challenged for cause. The trier of partiality is not the judge but a mini-jury of two potential or

> previously selected jurors. . . . Parliament has decided that the issue of partiality is a question of fact that must be decided by two of the jurors themselves, not by the judge . . . [A]ny judge who attempts to participate in such decisions usurps the function of the jurors.

Barrow disapproved, for this reason, of the unauthorized pre-screening of jurors by judges in cases of non-obvious partiality. This pre-screening, of course, takes place before the triers are sworn, yet the Court considered it to usurp the function of the triers. Parallel reasoning would suggest that a trial judge does not have jurisdiction to accept the concession of opposing counsel as to the partiality of a juror, and thereby to dismiss a juror. On the reasoning in *Barrow*, a judge usurps the function of the two triers when dismissing jurors because of partiality, whether or not the trial of the issue of partiality has commenced.

* Rejecting the right of opposing counsel to accept challenges also simplifies the procedure. In *R.* v. *Shergill* (1996), 4 C.R. (5th) 28 (Ont. Gen. Div.), Ferguson J. ruled that the triers must be sworn before each potential juror is challenged so as to enable opposing counsel to accept a challenge before the triers are seized of the issue. This adds needlessly to the time and complexity of the process. Once sworn, a trier should be able to adjudicate on the partiality of all potential jurors until replaced as a trier or until a jury is empanelled. This is possible only if there is no need to allow opposing counsel the opportunity to accept a challenge.

6.9 CAN THE TRIAL JUDGE ADJUDICATE THE CHALLENGE IN OBVIOUS CASES?

* In *R.* v. *D. (D)*, [1997] O.J. No. 919 (Ont. Gen. Div.) (QL), Justice Cosgrove discharged prospective jurors whom he judged to be of obvious partiality, based on their response to the challenge for cause question. After the case had commenced and substantial evidence had been led, defence counsel moved for a mistrial, claiming that Justice Cosgrove had acted without jurisdiction when discharging these jurors. The mistrial application was denied because the accused was not prejudiced by the error. Indeed, Justice Cosgrove concluded that he would have been prejudiced had the obviously partial jurors been allowed to continue. Moreover, the defence had accepted the procedure that had been adopted by failing to object in a timely manner. While these may be compelling reasons for rejecting the mistrial application, it is clear that Justice Cosgrove erred in law during the selection process by usurping the function of the two triers. While expedient, this practice should not be adopted by trial judges.

CHAPTER 7

THE TRIERS OF THE CHALLENGE FOR CAUSE

7.1 THE TRIAL JUDGE AS TRIER

* Where the ground of the challenge is that the name of the juror does not appear on the panel (section 638(1)(a) of the *Criminal Code*), the issue is tried by the judge on the *voir dire*, through the inspection of the panel and such other evidence as the judge thinks fit to receive: section 640(1) of the *Criminal Code*. This section provides:

> 640.(1) Where the ground of a challenge is that the name of a juror does not appear on the panel, the issue shall be tried by the judge on the *voir dire* by the inspection of the panel, and such other evidence that the judge thinks fit to receive.

7.2 TWO JURORS AS TRIERS

* Where the ground of the challenge is found in sections 638(1)(b)–(f) of the *Criminal Code*, then the triers of the challenge are two jurors. Either the triers can be the last two jurors sworn, or, where no jurors have been sworn, the court can appoint two prospective jurors as the triers, and they are sworn to determine whether the ground of the challenge is true: section 640(2) of the *Criminal Code*. This section provides:

> 640.(2) Where the ground of a challenge is one not mentioned in subsection (1), the two jurors who were last sworn, or if no jurors have then been sworn, two persons present whom the court may appoint for the purpose, shall be sworn to determine whether the ground of challenge is true.

When hearing the challenge, the two triers sit in the jury box.

7.2(a) **Should the Initial Triers Be Questioned to Assess Their Partiality?**

* It has been held that there is no requirement that the initial two jurors chosen to try the challenge be themselves questioned to determine their partiality: *R.* v. *English* (1993), 111 Nfld. & P.E.I.R. 323 (Nfld. C.A.). Ironically, in *English*, one of the prospective jurors first chosen as a trier was later found to be herself partial, while the other prospective juror was stood aside by the Crown after it was discovered that she was related to one of the prosecutors who had acted for the Crown at the appellant's preliminary inquiry. On appeal, the Newfoundland Court of Appeal took a careful look at the jury selection record and concluded that there was no evidence that the original triers had been partial in their decisions. This is a very difficult task for an appellate court to embark on after one or both of the original triers are later found to be partial.

* It may be more appropriate when a general challenge is going to be put to all prospective jurors to devise a procedure whereby the trial judge could make a preliminary determination of the partiality of the first two triers chosen. This would not seem to violate *R.* v. *Sherratt*, [1991], 1 S.C.R. 509, or *R.* v. *Barrow*, [1987] 2 S.C.R. 694, since the judge is making a determination of the juror's partiality not *qua* juror but instead *qua* trier.

7.2(b) **At What Point Should the Initial Triers Be Replaced?**

* It has been suggested that the first two triers sworn to determine the truth of the challenge act until two jurors are selected and sworn, at which time those two jurors become the triers: *R* v. *Brigham* (1988), 41 C.C.C. (3d) 379 (Que. C.A.).

* An alternative was suggested in *R.* v. *English* (1993), 111 Nfld. & P.E.I.R. 323 at 340 (Nfld. C.A.):

> The second . . . [option is] to have the two triers continue until one juror . . . [is] selected. That juror would then sit with the junior or second of the two triers selected by the trial judge until the second juror was chosen.

The Newfoundland Court of Appeal held in *English* that this second option seemed to be more in tune with the concept that the last two jurors chosen should be the triers.

* In *R.* v. *Brigham* (1988), 44 C.C.C. (3d) 379 (Que. C.A.), the *English* approach was rejected. The Court of Appeal reasoned that the *Criminal Code* implies that until two jurors have been sworn, the triers are the two prospective jurors picked by the trial judge. Only after two jurors have been sworn are those two triers to be replaced. A similar conclusion was reached in *R.* v. *Mathurin* (1903), 8 C.C.C. 1 (Que. C.A.). On the authority of these two cases, it would be an error for a judge to replace one of the two triers once the first juror is selected and sworn. They are to continue until two jurors are selected and sworn, at which time they are both to be replaced.
* Of course, under either approach, once there are two sworn jurors who are acting as the triers, the next juror chosen and sworn will replace the first of those two jurors, and so on.

CHAPTER 8

THE TRIAL OF THE TRUTH OF THE CHALLENGE FOR CAUSE

8.1 SHOULD THE TRIAL BE CONDUCTED IN THE ABSENCE OF THE SELECTED JURORS AND/OR THE JURY PANEL?

* In *R.* v. *English* (1993), 111 Nfld. & P.E.I.R. 323 (Nfld. C.A.), the Newfoundland Court of Appeal held that it would be preferable for the prospective jurors and those jurors selected to try the case to remain outside the courtroom during the trial of the challenge, though it did recognize that this was not a legal requirement.

* According to some counsel and trial judges (see the approval by Justice Then (Ont. Gen. Div.) above at 6.5), this is the preferred position strategically. For example, Don Bayne, QC, is strongly of the view that if prospective jurors watch the process, they will be able to figure out what is going on and may tailor their answers and demeanour to get onto, or off, the jury. The best way to ensure honest responses is to ask prospective jurors questions they do not expect to be asked. On the other hand, Austin Cooper, QC, has suggested that the prospective jurors should remain in the courtroom during the trial of the truth of the challenge because, after observing the process, prospective jurors "tend to assume that the whole process is part of the system by which they are required to be selected and do not seem to resent it." A.M. Cooper, "The ABCs of Challenge for Cause in Jury Trials: To Challenge or Not to Challenge and What to Ask if You Get It" (1994) 37 Crim. L.Q. 62 at 69.

8.2 THE TRIAL JUDGE'S PRELIMINARY COMMENTS TO THE TRIERS

* Once the two triers have been selected, the trial judge should briefly explain to them exactly what will happen in the mini-trial and what role they will play. In *R.* v. *Hubbert* (1975), 11 O.R. (2d) 464 (C.A.), aff'd [1977] 2 S.C.R. 267, it was suggested that the trial judge tell the triers the following:

  - they are to decide "whether the challenged juror is indifferent — that is, is impartial — between the Crown and the accused";
  - that the standard of proof that they are to apply in arriving at a verdict is the balance of probabilities;
  - that the decision must be that of both of them;
  - that they may retire to the jury room or discuss it right where they are;
  - and if they cannot agree within a reasonable time, they are to say so.

* Justice Then in his paper "Challenges for Cause" (Address to the National Judicial Institute, 27–29 November 1995), quotes a standard instruction given to the triers, before the trial of the challenge, by Justice Watt of the Ontario Court General Division:

> It is plainly necessary that in this and any criminal case tried by a jury, those who shall serve as jurors upon the trial must be free from partiality or bias and enter upon the case with an open mind.
>
> [WHERE EXTENSIVE PUBLICITY IS BASIS OF CHALLENGE]
>
> There is obviously nothing wrong with a person having read, listened to or watched media accounts of an event or its investigation which shall subsequently come before the courts as a criminal prosecution. It is scarcely unusual in this day and age for anyone who has heard, watched or listened to accounts of this or any other case to have formed some opinion about it. The mere fact that a prospective juror holds such an opinion does NOT, in and of itself, disqualify that person from serving as a juror, PROVIDED you are satisfied that he/she can give an IMPARTIAL verdict based wholly upon the evidence if he/she is sworn/affirmed as a juror.
>
> [WHERE CHALLENGE BASED ON NATURE OF EVIDENCE]
>
> However, there is manifestly nothing wrong with a prospective juror having/holding an opinion upon a subject matter that may be disclosed in evidence to be given in a criminal trial. There are few, in life, who do not have opinions about something. What is critical for your determination is whether the prospective juror, NOTWITHSTANDING HIS/HER OPINION, can and would give a verdict based wholly and exclusively upon the evidence adduced

at trial. The mere holding of an opinion does not, of itself, disqualify a prospective juror, PROVIDED you, as triers of the challenge, are satisfied that he/she could and would give an IMPARTIAL VERDICT based upon the evidence, and solely upon the evidence, if sworn/affirmed as a juror in this trial.

Your decision upon this ground of challenge must be an unanimous one, although you have the right to disagree.

Having heard the questions and answers, you must now decide whether X is more likely impartial or more likely not impartial between Her Majesty The Queen and the accused.

In arriving at your decision, you should bear in mind that there is nothing per se wrong with a potential juror having read or listened to or watched media accounts relating to the event in question or having discussed the case with anyone. Furthermore, it may be that having read or watched or listened to such accounts, or having discussed the case, the potential juror has even formed a tentative opinion. The mere fact that a potential juror has formed such an opinion, that is, a tentative opinion, does not, in and of itself disqualify that person from serving as a juror provided you are otherwise satisfied that the potential juror can and will render an honest and impartial verdict based solely on the evidence if sworn as a juror.

In order to arrive at your decision, you must be unanimous; that is, you must both agree. However, you do have the right to disagree and if that happens, please just indicate that to me. In arriving at your decision, you may retire to another room or you may discuss the matter right where you are.

Again, having heard the questions and answers, you are to decide whether X is more likely partial or more likely not impartial between Her Majesty The Queen and the accused.

Once you have decided, you will simply say impartial or not impartial.

Triers, X has been challenged as a prospective juror in this case on the ground that he/she does not stand indifferent, that is, that he/she is not impartial, neutral or unbiased between the Queen and the accused.

In a few moments, certain questions will be asked of X. Your function is to listen to the questions and answers given, in order to determine whether X is more likely impartial or more likely not impartial.

It is plainly necessary that in any criminal case tried by a jury, those who serve as jurors must be completely impartial. Each juror must be able, at the end of the case, to render a fair and impartial verdict based solely upon the evidence heard in this courtroom. Your task, therefore, is to determine at the outset, whether X, at this time, is more likely impartial or more likely not impartial. We will now begin with the question and after the question, you will, after conferring, say simply impartial or not impartial. I will give you further instructions after the questions have been asked and answered.

8.3 CALLING THE CHALLENGED JUROR AS A WITNESS

* Where a challenge for cause is being conducted, the challenged juror, in responding to the questions posed, is the witness of the challenging party. It has been held that the "other party" may also question this witness: *R.* v. *Hubbert* (1975), 11 O.R. (2d) 464 at 480 (C.A.), aff'd [1977] 2 S.C.R. 267. In our opinion, the nature and extent of that questioning will vary substantially, depending on the nature of the challenge. More extensive questioning may be appropriate where the allegation relates to some specific partiality personal to the prospective juror, or to pre-trial publicity, rather than where it relates to race or to an offence-based challenge.

* The most recent authority dealing with general or generic challenges for cause has emphasized the importance of controlling the process by carefully circumscribing the questions that may be asked by the challenging party. Indeed, in such cases only pre-orchestrated questions may be asked, and often only one question will be allowed. (See 5.7, above.)

* It seems inconsistent with the general exercise of pre-defining the questions to allow the opposing party to engage in a less restricted examination. It also seems inequitable to confine the challenging party to a pre-approved question only to allow opposing counsel to ask questions that are not vetted, and to go beyond the general kind of inquiry allowed to the challenging party. Moreover, a properly framed challenge for cause question will, in most cases, be one that will reveal either pro-Crown or pro-defence partiality. This reduces if not eliminates the importance of allowing the other party to question the juror. It is usual in race-based challenges for cause for no questions to be posed by the non-challenging party. Whatever the extent of questioning by the opposing party that is allowed, it must respect the same limits that apply in bringing a challenge for cause application. (See 4.5, above.)

8.4 MARSHALLING OTHER EVIDENCE IN SUPPORT OF/OR AGAINST THE CHALLENGE

* The challenging party may call other relevant evidence in support of the challenge. The "other party" can also call evidence against the challenge. With leave of the trial judge, the challenging party may call evidence in reply: *R.* v. *Hubbert* (1975), 11 O.R. (2d) 464 at 480 (C.A.), aff'd [1977] 2 S.C.R. 267.

8.5 ADDRESSING THE TRIERS

8.5(a) **By the Parties**

* The *Hubbert* court recognized that the *Criminal Code* does not provide or prohibit addresses by counsel to the triers. The Court of Appeal held that the trial judge may in his or her discretion permit it, though usually there will be no necessity for it: *R.* v. *Hubbert* (1975), 11 O.R. (2d) 464 at 480 (C.A.), aff'd [1977] 2 S.C.R. 267.

8.5(b) **By the Trial Judge**

* As for the extent of the trial judge's charge to the triers following the trial of the challenge, the Court of Appeal in *R.* v. *Hubbert* (1975), 11 O.R. (2d) 464 (C.A.), aff'd [1977] 2 S.C.R. 267, recommended:

> [The trial judge does not] need . . . [to] make any discursive "charge" to the triers. Usually some words like these will suffice:
>
> > As I told you, Mr. X has been challenged on the ground that he is not indifferent — that is, not impartial — between the Crown and the accused. You are to decide: is this ground of challenge true, or not true?
>
> In some cases further explanation by the trial Judge may be necessary, and should be given. Ordinarily it will not be necessary to review the evidence, which will usually be short and fresh in everyone's mind.

8.6 WHAT IS THE STANDARD OF PROOF TO BE APPLIED BY THE TRIERS?

* The standard of proof to be applied by the triers in reaching a verdict is the civil standard of balance of probabilities: *R.* v. *Hubbert* (1975), 11 O.R. (2d) 464 at 480 (C.A.), aff'd [1977] 2 S.C.R. 267.

8.7 THE VERDICT

8.7(a) **Does the Verdict Have to Be Unanimous?**

* The verdict of the triers must be unanimous: section 640(4) of the *Criminal Code*. Where, after what the court considers to be a reasonable time, the two triers are unable to agree, the court may discharge them from giving a verdict and direct two other persons to be sworn to determine whether the ground of challenge is true: section 640(4) of the *Criminal Code*. This section provides:

> 640.(4) Where, after what the court considers to be a reasonable time, the two persons who are sworn to determine whether the ground of challenge is true are unable to agree, the court may discharge them from giving a verdict and may direct two other persons to be sworn to determine whether the ground of challenge is true.

* It has been held to be inappropriate for the trial judge to discharge the prospective juror when the triers are unable to agree regarding the truth of the challenge, as the trial judge would then be assuming the role of the trier of the truth of the challenge: *R.* v. *Brigham* (1988), 44 C.C.C. (3d) 379 at 382 (Que. C.A.).

8.7(b) **The Consequences of the Verdict**

* Where the finding of the triers is that the ground of the challenge is not true, the juror shall be sworn, unless of course one of the parties exercises a peremptory challenge: section 640(3) of the *Criminal Code*. Where the finding of the triers is that the ground of the challenge is true, the juror will not be sworn: section 640(3) of the *Criminal Code*. This provision states:

> 640.(3) Where the finding, pursuant to subsection (1) or (2) is that the ground of challenge is not true, the juror shall be sworn, but if the finding is that the ground of challenge is true, the juror shall not be sworn.

8.7(c) **Is There an Appeal from the Verdict?**

* The decision of the triers is final, and there is no appeal: *R.* v. *Sherratt*, [1991] 1 S.C.R. 509 at 521–22. See too *R.* v. *Ataman* (1989), 70 C.R. (3d) 37 (Que. C.A.). However, an earlier decision suggests that an accused can appeal the decision of the triers as to the validity of the challenge, but only in cases where it can be demonstrated that the triers were acting on a wrong principle, or corruptly, or out of hostility to the accused, or for other improper motives. See *Richard (No.2)* v. *R.* (1957), 31 C.R. 340 (N.B.C.A.).

CHAPTER 9

THE MECHANICS OF PEREMPTORY CHALLENGES

9.1 WHAT IS A PEREMPTORY CHALLENGE?

* A peremptory challenge is a statutory vehicle to challenge and ultimately have removed from the jury panel a potential juror, without having first to give cause and without having cause to be found by a neutral trier of fact.

9.2 WHO IS ENTITLED TO PEREMPTORY CHALLENGES?

* By virtue of sections 634(1) and (2) of the *Criminal Code*, both defence counsel and Crown attorneys are entitled to challenge potential jurors peremptorily. These sections read:

> 634.(1) A juror may be challenged peremptorily whether or not the juror has been challenged for cause pursuant to section 638.
>
> (2) Subject to subsections (3) and (4), the prosecutor and the accused are each entitled to
>
> (*a*) twenty peremptory challenges, where the accused is charged with high treason or first degree murder;
>
> (*b*) twelve peremptory challenges, where the accused is charged with an offence, other than an offence mentioned in paragraph

(*a*), for which the accused may be sentenced to imprisonment for a term exceeding five years; or

(*c*) four peremptory challenges, where the accused is charged with an offence that is not referred to in paragraph (*a*) or (*b*).

9.3 THE PURPOSE OF A PEREMPTORY CHALLENGE

* In theory, the basis for the peremptory challenge appears threefold:

- First, it attempts to ensure that the accused has a good opinion of the jury.
- Second, it allows the setting aside of a juror who survives a challenge for cause but who nonetheless may be resentful or be, in the mind of the challenger, biased.
- Third, it enables lawyers to choose a jury that they believe will be most favourable to their position. Presumably, if both sides eliminate those most favourable to the other, the remaining jurors would constitute a more qualified and impartial group.

See *R.* v. *Sherratt*, [1991] 1 S.C.R. 509 at 532–33; *R.* v. *Bain*, [1992] 1 S.C.R. 91; *R.* v. *Cloutier*, [1979] 2 S.C.R. 709; *Holland* v. *Illinois*, 493 U.S. 474 at 484 (1990), and W.R. Blackstone, *Commentaries on the Laws of England*, ed. by W.P. Lewis, vol. 4 (Philadelphia: Rees Welsh & Co., 1990) at 356 and 1738. These portions of Blackstone were cited in both *Bain* and *Cloutier*. See too B.A. Babcock, "Voir Dire: Preserving Its Wonderful Power," (1975) 27 Stan. L. Rev. 545 at 552–55. Babcock, as cited by Justice Gonthier in *Bain* at 116 goes further than Blackstone and notes that not only does the peremptory challenge allow accused to dismiss prospective jurors without cause, it also "teaches the litigant, and through him the community, that the jury is a good and proper mode for deciding matters and that its decision should be followed because in a real sense the jury belongs to the litigant" (at 552).

* As Justice Pratte recognized in *R.* v. *Cloutier*, [1979] 2 S.C.R. 709 at 721, "The very nature of the right to peremptory challenges and the objectives underlying it require that its exercise be entirely discretionary." In practice, peremptory challenges permit, in many cases, the rejection of members of the community on the basis of the kind of unfounded and invidious stereotypes discussed below in chapter 10.

9.4 HOW MANY PEREMPTORY CHALLENGES CAN EACH PARTY EXERCISE?

* Each party is entitled to the same number of challenges: section 634(2) of the *Criminal Code*. The number is dependent on the seriousness of the charges facing the accused:

- 20 – where the accused is charged with first-degree murder or high treason: section 634(2)(a) of the *Criminal Code*.
- 12 – where the accused is charged with an offence (other than first-degree murder or high treason) for which he or she may be sentenced to a term of imprisonment exceeding five years: section 634(2)(b) of the *Criminal Code*.
- 4 – where the accused is charged with an offence for which he or she may be sentenced to a term of imprisonment of less than five years: section 634(2)(c) of the *Criminal Code*.

9.4(a) **Multiple Counts**

* Where two or more counts in an indictment are tried together, the accused and the prosecutor are entitled to the number of peremptory challenges relating to the most serious charge: section 634(3) of the *Criminal Code*. This section provides:

> 634.(3) Where two or more counts in an indictment are to be tried together, the prosecutor and the accused are each entitled only to the number of peremptory challenges provided in respect of the count for which the greatest number of peremptory challenges is available.

For example, if the accused were charged with sexual assault (potential for a term of imprisonment not exceeding ten years) and assaulting a peace officer (potential for a term of imprisonment not exceeding five years), then he or she would be entitled to twelve peremptory challenges

9.4(b) **Multiple Accused**

* Where two or more accused are tried together:

- Each accused is entitled to the number of peremptory challenges to which he or she would be entitled if tried alone: section 634(4)(a) of the *Criminal Code*.
- The prosecution is entitled to the total number of peremptory challenges available to all accused: section 634(4)(b) of the *Criminal Code*.

9.5 THE ORDER OF CHALLENGES

* See the discussion above at 6.6.

9.6 CAN A JUROR UNSUCCESSFULLY CHALLENGED FOR CAUSE BE PEREMPTORILY CHALLENGED?

* In *R.* v. *Cloutier*, [1979] 2 S.C.R. 709, the Supreme Court of Canada held that a juror unsuccessfully challenged for cause could be peremptorily challenged. Parliament confirmed this by legislation in section 634(1) of the *Criminal Code*, which now states:

> [a] juror may be challenged peremptorily whether or not the juror has been challenged for cause pursuant to section 638.

CHAPTER 10

PRACTICAL JURY SELECTION TIPS

10.1 THE UTILITY OF USING PEREMPTORY CHALLENGES

The jury selection process, providing as it does for peremptory challenges, is premised on the assumption that counsel can make rational decisions about who their better jurors will be. While there are no foolproof methods for selecting the ideal juror, most lawyers believe that they can increase their prospects of success in a jury trial by using their peremptory challenges wisely. They believe that they can identify the best possible type of juror for a given case, or at least that they can identify jurors who should be avoided. The routine spectacle of the jury selection process in which the lawyers study those jurors who are "called to the book" and who then pass judgment on their suitability before accepting or challenging them is ready proof that the majority of trial lawyers see utility in the process.

There are lawyers who reject this approach and simply accept the first twelve jurors who are not challenged by their opponent. They refrain from using their challenges because they are convinced that the tools of jury selection, being hunches, intuition, and "experience," are incapable of providing a rational basis for predicting how a potential juror is likely to see the evidence in the case. Or they may consider that, tactically, they will present themselves better in front of the jury panel if they look accommodating and accepting, while opposing counsel makes what may appear to be invidious judgments about the suitability of those who are answering their call to jury duty.

* The belief that rational choices can be made in a systematic way finds some support in the social science literature, though there are detractors within the social science community itself. Proponents of scientific jury selection (SJS) point out that cases are won and lost at the point at which the jury is selected. According to one jury consultant, Dr. Covington, "It is imperative for the trial attorney to master the art of jury selection. Many potential jurors have reached decisions regarding the case and the litigators within a few minutes of exposure to the participants . . . "

  M. Covington, "Jury Selection: Innovative Approaches to Both Civil and Criminal Litigation" (1985) 16 St. Mary's L.J. 575 at 580.

* Indeed, Covington points out that "research in the social sciences indicates that ninety percent of the juror's individual decisions are formed prior to jury deliberation, and that jury deliberation, contrary to popular notion, does not so much decide the case as contribute to a consensus."

  M. Covington, "Jury Selection: Innovative Approaches to Both Civil and Criminal Litigation" (1985) 16 St. Mary's L.J. 575 at 580 citing C.J. Mills & W.E. Bohannan, "Do Personality or Peer Pressures Influence the Way Jurors Decide" [1981] Champion 10.

* While social scientists have attempted to identify a "scientific" approach to jury selection, the reality is that even in the United States, where it is becoming more common to hire jury consultants, lawyers tend to apply no science whatsoever in selecting juries, relying on "instinct" and "experience" and in some cases on stereotype, often including racist or sexist generalizations, to select their juries.

* We attempt, in this chapter, to collect the accumulated experience of counsel and of social scientists in order to provide as much assistance as possible in terms of how to exercise a peremptory challenge. As will be seen, there is disagreement over most propositions. For this reason we chose not to exclude those jury selection "tips" that struck us as preposterous or even inappropriate. There is no tried and true recipe for jury selection, but we hope that the following discussion will assist counsel in arriving at the decisions that they choose to make. At the very least, it should provide food for thought and assist in providing some structure or rhyme or reason to those jury selection decisions that are made.

10.2 RATIONAL JURY SELECTION: GUESSWORK OR SCIENCE?

10.2(a) Experience and Stereotype

* Most jurors are selected on the basis of instinct and experience. There are essentially two general kinds of criteria that are employed by lawyers. First, there are the generalizations or stereotypes about people in general, assumptions about how persons of a given sex, age, occupation, social status, or even race, colour, or creed are apt to see the case that is being tried. Second, there are judgments that are made about the juror as an individual, including such characteristics as demeanour, comportment, dress, apparent intelligence, and even physique. Each kind of judgment is fuelled by the lawyer's own beliefs about what people are like, as well as the lawyer's experiences from prior cases.

* There are at least three problems with relying on these judgments. The first and most obvious is that the generalizations that are relied on may not be accurate. They may not be accurate as generalizations and in some cases may be invidious, being based on such things as race, sex, and sexual persuasion, constituting prohibited grounds of discrimination in most other contexts. Moreover, they are just that, generalizations, and they may well not apply to the prospective juror in question. It is generally considered, for example, that police officers, including retired police officers, are likely to favour the case for the Crown, perhaps even to the point of disregarding the evidence or evaluating it unfairly. So prevalent is this belief that most provincial jury statutes disqualify police officers from jury service. Yet Donald Bayne, QC, a prominent Ottawa defence counsel, tells of an experience he had that illustrates the point that such generalizations cannot always be relied on. He was selecting a jury in a case in which his client was charged with shooting a prison guard during a jail break. The defence was self-defence. Neither the shooting nor the jail break was being contested. A challenge for cause was being conducted to determine whether any jurors might, because of the nature of the offence and the status of the accused, be unable to adjudicate the case impartially on the evidence. Eleven jurors had been selected after a number were eliminated for cause. The last juror to come forward was a retired RCMP officer. To Mr. Bayne's surprise, the mini-jury adjudged the officer to be impartial. Mr. Bayne chose not to challenge this juror peremptorily, for fear that he would alienate the jurors who watched as two of their fellow jurors made the decision that the police officer could be impartial. In the end, the jury acquitted the accused after the officer had been elected its foreman.

* The second problem with relying on generalizations is the dearth of information available to counsel who is trying to decide which category to put a prospective juror into. In Ontario, for example, counsel is provided only with the name, address, and occupation of members of the jury panel. By observing the juror, other things may become apparent, such as the general age and the sex of the juror. Yet there is still little that is known about most jurors. This shortage of information can result in mischaracterization of the juror. Assistant Crown Attorney Celynne Dorval indicates that in her experience many prospective jurors "dress down" on jury selection day in the hope that they will appear to be unsuitable. Thus, things are not always as they seem. She recounts one case in which a police officer advised her that a particular juror looked familiar to him, but that he could not place him. She drew this to the attention of the judge in the absence of the jury, but defence counsel insisted, successfully, that this juror be kept. Defence counsel had earlier confided in the prosecutor that his best chance of acquittal in the child sexual offence trial of his client was to "get a pervert on the jury." He surmised that the juror was probably known to the officer through his criminal background. The jury convicted ultimately, with one juror wearing a T-shirt to court on deliberation day that said "KICK BUTT." As it happens, the familiar juror owned a cottage on the same lake as the police officer. As this illustration demonstrates, jury selection is typically done blindly, despite best efforts to make discriminating choices.

* Even where jurors are properly characterized, past experiences are an uncertain guide in forming generalizations. In Canada, jury deliberations are privileged. It is an offence for a juror to discuss the jury deliberation process. Counsel is often left to guess, therefore, as to how a particular kind of juror may have reacted to the evidence. A juror on an acquitting jury may have been the last to agree, rather than the champion of the defence case, as the lawyer may have come to believe. If the lawyer believes inaccurately that this juror was favourable and generalizes that other similar jurors will also be favourable, the entire practice of counsel can be mistaken.

* For this reason, Alan Dershowitz, a well-known American lawyer, once stated:

> Lawyers' instincts are often the least trustworthy basis on which to pick jurors. All those neat rules of thumb, but no feedback. Ten years of accumulated experiences may be ten years of being wrong. I myself, even when I trust my instincts, like to have them scientifically confirmed.

J.W. Barber, "The Jury Is Still Out: The Role of Jury Science in the Modern American Courtroom" (1994) 31 Am. Crim. L. Rev. 1225 at note 29.

* Even those who engage in the process recognize that the rules of thumb that are developed are notoriously unreliable, serving at best to reduce the risk that a given juror will be hostile.

* While the generalizations relied on are far from foolproof, many of the factors considered by counsel in deciding whether to select a juror have an intuitive appeal. Can counsel do better than relying on instinct and perceived experience? As indicated, Alan Dershowitz is one among many who would rather place their trust in science.

10.2(b) **Scientific Jury Selection**

* It is becoming more common in the United States for well-funded counsel to retain jury consultants to assist them in selecting the ideal jury. These consultants purport to use scientific jury selection (SJS) techniques. SJS involves the use of social science methods to arrive at juror profiles to assist counsel in determining who will make the ideal juror in the particular case being tried. The techniques of SJS operate on the assumption that an individual's behaviour as a juror is shaped by his or her experiences and attitudes.

* SJS first appeared in American courtrooms in the early 1970s in the notorious trial of two anti-war Catholic priests charged with conspiracy to kidnap Henry Kissinger. Sociologist Jay Schulman was retained by the defence to consult in the selection of the jury.

  S.S. Diamond, "Scientific Jury Selection: What Social Scientists Know and Do Not Know" (1990) 73 Judicature 178 at 179.

10.2(b)(i) **The Controversy over SJS**

* Not unexpectedly, prominent U.S. jury consultants boast that their methods are indeed successful and that they can, in 90 percent of cases, predict the outcomes of trials based on who is selected to serve as jurors. Jo-Ellan Dimitrius, perhaps the most recognized jury consultant in North America after having been retained in the Rodney King, Reginald Denny, and O.J. Simpson cases, claims "a 90 percent success rate in the more than 100 trials she has worked on since 1984."

  J.W. Barber, "The Jury is Still Out: The Role of Jury Science in the Modern American Courtroom" (1994) 31 Am. Crim. L. Rev. 1225 at note 33 and at 1231–32, referring to P.M. Gollner, "Consulting by Peering into the Minds of Jurors" *The New York Times* (7 January 1994) A23.

* Litigation Sciences Ltd., a consulting firm with revenues of over $25 million per year, "boasts a 96 percent accuracy rate in predicting the final outcome of its clients' cases that go to trial."

  J.W. Barber, "The Jury Is Still Out: The Role of Jury Science in the Modern American Courtroom" (1994) 31 Am. Crim. L. Rev. 1225 at note 33, quoting from M. Galen, "The Best Jurors Money Can Pick" *Business Week* (15 June 1992) 108.

* However, there are many social scientists who are of the view that the emphasis on SJS as the key social science tool in trial preparation is misplaced. Professor Diamond asserts:

  > [C]laims for predicting juror responses to trial evidence should be modest indeed. The studies reviewed . . . report [only] an ability to account for up to 15 per cent of the variation in juror verdict preferences. It is, of course, possible that more powerful attitudinal measures can be developed, but there is good reason to be skeptical about the potential of SJS to improve selection decisions substantially.

  S.S. Diamond, "Scientific Jury Selection: What Social Scientists Know and Do Not Know" (1990) 73 Judicature 178 at 180.

* The same point is made by Sahler, who notes: "Research shows that the utilization of survey based scientific selection methods yields slightly better results than . . . using conventional, intuition-based voir dire strategy or random selection." Hans and Vidmar caution: "The success rate in such cases may not be due to the jury selection techniques but rather to other features of the case."

  D. Sahler, "Scientifically Selecting Jurors while Maintaining Professional Responsibility: A Proposed Model Rule" (1996) 6 Alb. L.J. Sci. & Tech. 383 at 392; V.P. Hans & N. Vidmar, *Judging the Jury* (New York: Plenum Press, 1986) at 90.

* Professor Diamond asserts that ". . . research on jury selection indicates that the survey efforts of SJS will not improve the accuracy of jury selection in every case. In some cases, a jury consultant may even be less accurate than the trial attorney operating without consultant advice."

  S.S. Diamond, "Scientific Jury Selection: What Social Scientists Know and Do Not Know" (1990) 73 Judicature 178 at 1810.

* Sahler agrees, pointing out that it is "unclear exactly which types of cases will yield the greatest advantage to the scientific selection methods" and that "[w]ith regards to shadow jury researches, . . . [t]he accuracy of this

research is a function of the degree to which the case studied resembles the case that is tried and the extent to which the [shadow] jurors are similar to the actual jurors."

D. Sahler, "Scientifically Selecting Jurors while Maintaining Professional Responsibility: A Proposed Model Rule" (1996) 6 Alb. L.J. Sci. & Tech. 383 at 392–93, referring to and quoting from R. Hastie, "Is Attorney-Conducted Voir Dire an Effective Procedure for the Selection of Impartial Juries?" (1991) 49 Am. U. L. Rev. 703 at 720 & 721.

* Other social scientists are of the view that the vast majority of verdicts are determined by the strength of the evidence, as opposed to the personal characteristics of the particular jurors selected.

See W.F. Abbott, *Surrogate Juries* (1990), H. Kalven, Jr. & H. Zeisel, *The American Jury* (Boston: Little, Brown, 1966), and M.J. Saks & R. Hastie, *Social Psychology in Court* (New York: Van Nostrand Reinhold, 1978), cited in J.W. Barber, "The Jury Is Still Out: The Role of Jury Science in the Modern American Courtroom" (1994) 31 Am. Crim. L. Rev. 1225 at note 32.

* Indeed, one legal commentator concluded:

> Therefore, it appears that consultants cannot simply apply statistics to individuals and be able to predict the outcome. In addition, studies attempting to link demographic and personality variables directly to verdicts find weak correlations. Statistics reveal that demographic characteristics are weak predictors of verdicts and damage awards.

D. Sahler, "Scientifically Selecting Jurors While Maintaining Professional Responsibility: A Proposed Model Rule" (1996) 6 Alb. L.J. Sci. & Tech. 383 at 392–93, citing S.M. Fulero & S.D. Penrod, below at 229, and *Jury Research: Psychological Characteristics of Punitive Damage Jurors* (PLI Corp. Law & Practice Course Handbook Series No. B-833, 1993) Seventh Annual Institute on Corporate Law Department Management: Controlling and Reducing Costs, 59 at 62–63. A similar conclusion was reached by R. Hastie, S.D. Penrod, & N. Pennington, *Inside the Jury* (Cambridge, Mass.: Harvard University Press, 1983).

* Edward Greenspan, a prominent Toronto defence counsel, rejects any idea that one can predict who will make the "ideal juror" in any particular case. In *Greenspan: The Case for the Defence*, Greenspan states:

> The currently fashionable idea that by selecting juries "scientifically" — that is, by determining their individual prejudices ahead of time — one can determine the outcome of a trial is, I think, a pipe-dream. Luckily for justice, I might add. I utterly reject the cynical notion, held by some lawyers, that trials are won or lost by selecting juries for their prejudices. . . .

> . . . [I]t seems to me that social scientists have done a bit of a con job by invading the criminal process in jury selection. . . . Even if it had some statistical validity for big populations of ten thousand or more, as a basis for selecting a population of twelve, which is what a jury is, it was meaningless. Tossing a coin would have been better.
>
> . . . In practice, "scientific" jury selection boils down to picking out a few gross features, and then acting on them as if they were the whole story. This is not only unhelpful, but generally misleading.
>
> . . . Though they are less costly and probably quite harmless, I don't think much of the quirky ways in which some lawyers select juries, either. . . . There are lawyers who will avoid left-handed jurors — I'm not kidding — or women in rape cases, or Central Europeans . . . .
>
> I believe trials are won or lost primarily on the way the evidence unfolds in court. In other words, on their merits.

E.L. Greenspan & G. Jonas, *Greenspan: The Case for the Defence*, (Toronto: Macmillan, 1987) at 277–82.

* Despite reservations, some of those who are sceptical about SJS are not prepared to write off its contributions entirely. Sahler, for example, states:

> Although there is a lack of analytical data available regarding jury science selection and its effectiveness, the criteria already used have been documented as successful in psychological and scientific research. In addition, although the correlations studies have not resulted in concrete proof of the effectiveness of consulting, one should consider the number of attorneys who rely on consultants with criminology, market research, and sociology backgrounds. A former professor-turned-trial consultant claims that "a purchaser of (his) full services could be 96 percent sure of the outcome before the unwittingly manipulated jury even reached its verdict."
>
> Looking beyond the statistics, jury consulting has been heralded as winning some cases including the New York case of "subway vigilante" Bernhard Goetz, the William K. Smith trial, the 1992 acquittal of two Los Angeles police officers of assaulting Rodney King, and the Menendez and O.J. Simpson trials. In evaluating the accuracy of jury consultants in the context of the O.J. Simpson criminal trial, the side that did not use jury consultants, the prosecution, did not prevail.

D. Sahler, "Scientifically Selecting Jurors While Maintaining Professional Responsibility: A Proposed Model Rule" (1996) 6 Alb. L.J. Sci. & Tech. 383 at 394–95.

10.2(b)(ii) The Methodology of SJS

* There are a number of methods used by jury consultants in profiling jurors. The list includes:

- "ranking scales"
- "community attitudinal surveys"
- "juror investigations"
- "in-court assessment of non-verbal communication"
- "group dynamic analysis"
- "focus groups"
- "mock trial" and
- "shadow juries"

J.W. Barber, "The Jury Is Still Out: The Role of Jury Science in the Modern American Courtroom" (1994) 31 Am. Crim. L. Rev. 1225 at 1235–39.

* "Ranking scales" purport to enable prospective jurors to be ranked in order of desirability based on a number of characteristics deemed to be critical in determining the juror's potential sympathy for the accused. The characteristics are determined through telephone and in-person surveys. Barber notes: "Ranking scales are vulnerable to the charge that they are little more than a continuation of [the typical stereotyping]" relied on by some lawyers. Barber asserts: "The difference, however, is that the ranking scales are based on information gathered in scientific community attitudinal surveys and are, thus, more likely to be accurate than preferences based on generalizations and stereotypes."

J.W. Barber, "The Jury Is Still Out: The Role of Jury Science in the Modern American Courtroom" (1994) 31 Am. Crim. L. Rev. 1225 at 1235.

* "Community attitudinal surveys" are used in an attempt to discover "the local pressures and conditions that may be at work on the personalities of the prospective jurors in [a] geographical area."

J.W. Barber, "The Jury Is Still Out: The Role of Jury Science in the Modern American Courtroom" (1994) 31 Am. Crim. L. Rev. 1225 at 1235.

* "Juror investigations," as the term suggests, are simply inquiries undertaken to find out as much as possible about the particular prospective juror. This can involve a combination of personal contact with, and/or private investigation of, prospective jurors.

* Again, as is evident from its name, "group dynamic analysis" involves the study of how individuals arrive at decisions when interacting with others in an environment such as the jury deliberation. Information gained through

such analysis is believed to assist in developing generalizations that can help determine how particular jurors are apt to act during the decision-making process.

* According to Barber, "Focus groups are drawn from the area where the case is pending. The attorneys present one or two issues or approaches to the group to gauge its response. For example, an opening statement may be simulated before the mock jurors who will then be divided into small response groups. After the focus group responds, the individual members are questioned in great detail about which factors weighed in their decision, what they liked or disliked, and what they understood."

  J.W. Barber, "The Jury Is Still Out: The Role of Jury Science in the Modern American Courtroom" (1994) 31 Am. Crim. L. Rev. 1225 at 1237.

* Mock trials and shadow juries are intended to determine how different kinds of people will react to the specific case in question. Persons from a variety of backgrounds are subjected to the issues through a dry run of the trial, or a trial with similar issues, and then are asked about their reactions and conclusions. Based on these results, the profile of the ideal juror is drawn.

10.2(b)(iii) The Limited Applicability of SJS in Canada

* As can be seen, some of the methods used by those applying SJS techniques are unavailable in Canada, reducing the opportunity for Canadian jurists to employ SJS as effectively as it is used in the United States. In particular, potential jurors are not identified to counsel until shortly before the jury selection process occurs, making juror investigation impossible as a practical matter.[1]

* More important, it is considered improper or even illegal in Canada to approach potential jurors personally prior to jury selection. A number of provincial enactments make it an offence to approach those whose names appear on the jury panel. These include Alberta, *Jury Act*, R.S.A. 1990, c. J-2, s. 45; Manitoba, *The Jury Act*, R.S.M. 1987, c. J30, s. 50(2); New Brunswick, *Jury Act*, R.S.N.B. 1973, c. J-3, ss. 39.1 & 39.2; Ontario, *Juries Act*, R.S.O. 1990, c. J.3, s. 40; and Prince Edward Island, *Jury Act*, R.S.P.E.I. 1988, c. J-5, s. 25. Even in the absence of such provisions, it is considered

---

1 In *R.* v. *Fagan* (1993), 18 C.R.R. (2d) 191 (Ont. Gen. Div.), the court held that prosecutors must disclose to the defence any information they find out about prospective jurors (i.e., criminal records).

to be improper. As C. Granger, *The Criminal Jury Trial in Canada* (Toronto: Carswell, 1996) at 146 explains:

> All out-of-court communications with the members of the jury panel are improper and considered an interference with the administration of justice [*R.* v. *Caldough* (1961), 36 C.R. 248 (B.C.S.C.)], and/or contempt of court and obstructing the course of justice [*R.* v. *Papineau* (1980), 16 C.R. (3d) 56 (Que. S.C.)]. . . . This rule applies whether the juror has been sworn [*R.* v. *Tsoumas* (1973), 11 C.C.C.(2d) 344 (Ont. C.A.), discharged [*R.* v. *Papineau*], or whether the prospective juror has merely been summoned to serve [*R.* v. *Caldough*].

* Moreover, to the extent that SJS techniques are dependent on personal information about the juror, or watching jurors respond to extensive questioning, they cannot be applied effectively in Canada: See *R. v. Bain*, [1992] 1 S.C.R. 91 at 124–25, Gonthier J. Counsel is provided with limited information about panel members. Juror surveys or questionnaires, permitted in some American jurisdictions, are not allowed in Canada. Jurors are questioned only when a challenge for cause has been allowed to be conducted, and even then, the questions that can be asked are controlled tightly. Typically only one general question is asked, and it discloses nothing about the specific beliefs or opinions of the juror. Canadian courts have affirmed on numerous occasions that the challenge for cause process is not a procedure allowing for wide-ranging, personalized disclosure by the juror.

* Furthermore, some of the techniques relied on in SJS require observing the prospective jurors during the *voir dire* procedure. In Canada, jury *voir dires* are held only when a challenge for cause is being brought. Counsel will have no opportunity to rely on those techniques as part of the challenge for cause process itself, since the decision whether to accept a challenge for cause is made by a mini-jury of two triers of fact, and submissions by counsel to those jurors are not normally allowed. Counsel can use SJS techniques that depend on observing the *voir dire*, then, solely in deciding whether to exercise their peremptory challenges, should suspect jurors not be disqualified by the triers. Even then counsel will be left to base decisions on the briefest of questioning.

* Moreover, SJS is based largely on the results of demographic attitudinal surveys conducted in the United States. The findings, even if scientifically accurate in the United States, may not be translatable to the different social and political context in Canada.

* Finally, in Canada, there is no opportunity to conduct studies into the conduct of actual, as opposed to mock or simulated, juries, in an effort to

obtain jury profiles like those that have been developed in the United States. Section 649 of the *Code* provides:

> 649. Every member of a jury who, except for the purposes of
>
> (*a*) an investigation of an alleged offence under subsection 139(2) in relation to a juror, or
>
> (*b*) giving evidence in criminal proceedings in relation to such an offence,
>
> discloses any information relating to the proceedings of the jury when it was absent from the courtroom that was not subsequently disclosed in open court is guilty of an offence punishable on summary conviction.

A number of the provincial statutes make it an offence to disclose information relating to jury deliberations. See, for example, Alberta, s. 42; Manitoba, s. 49; Northwest Territories, *Jury Act*, R.S.N.W.T. 1988, c. J-2, s. 32; and Yukon Territory, *Jury Act*, R.S.Y. 1986, c. 97, s. 30.

* Notwithstanding this, much of the information used in SJS may be of assistance in the selection of Canadian jurors. Some of its contributions are discussed below.

10.3 JURY SELECTION: THE "COLLECTED WISDOM"

* In selecting jurors for a particular case, attention has to be paid to:

- general considerations about the kind of people who make desirable jurors;
- the kind of jurors one would want, given the kind of case being tried;
- the kind of jurors one would want, given who the main protagonists, namely the accused, the key witnesses, and the lawyers, are going to be; and
- the kind of person the prospective juror being considered seems to be.

* First, counsel should consider the kind of case they have, including who the accused is, who the Crown witnesses are, what the charges are, and what the evidence is like. They should attempt to define the kind of juror they would like to have. Next, counsel should obtain the jury list as soon as it is made available and examine it closely. Those jurors who are, on the face of the list, undesirable should be noted, as should those who are preferable. Only after giving serious consideration to these matters should counsel undertake the actual task of jury selection.

* When the jury is being selected, if there is any ambiguity in the occupation shown for the juror, counsel should not hesitate to ask the judge to have the juror clarify. Many simply record "retired" or "manager" or "consultant," without disclosing what it is precisely that they did, or do. A "retired" bar owner might make an ideal defence juror in an alcohol driving case, whereas a "retired" emergency room nurse might not.

10.3(a) **Speaking Generally, Who Makes a Good Juror?**

* By and large there is no one kind of ideal juror, since so much is dependent on the kind of case and the personalities involved. There are, nonetheless, some general observations that are worth considering.

10.3(a)(i) **Age: The Juror's Life Experience**

* Young people are often challenged by both the Crown and defence counsel alike. Pat McCann, a leading defence lawyer in Ottawa, is concerned that young people may not have the depth of experience required to understand that things are not always as they seem, nor to appreciate the realities of human frailty. He points out, however, that in his experience the Crown will generally challenge such people, so absent further cause for concern, he does not use his peremptory challenges on young jurors, leaving it to the Crown to waste its challenges on a mutually undesirable juror. Assistant Crown Attorney Malcolm Lindsay, QC, confirmed that, in his view, young jurors do not always have the requisite experience to adjudicate effectively. He has a bias towards "older" jurors.

* Loftus and Greene suggest that, based on American studies, it seems that "[j]urors aged less than thirty-four and over fifty-seven participated less than the middle-aged group. The over fifty-seven group took the deliberations more seriously but recalled information less accurately."

  E.F. Loftus & E. Greene, "Twelve Angry People: The Collective Mind of the Jury" (1984) 84 Colum. L. Rev. 1425 at 1431.

* Mills and Bohannon claim, based on their studies:

  - Jurors' guilty verdicts generally increased with age;
  - The relationship between verdict and age, however, was not the same for both sexes. Guilty verdicts remained high for females across all age levels . . . , but increased with age for males . . .
  - For males there were two peaks for guilty verdicts — between 26 and 35 years of age and between 50 and 64 years — with the lowest percentage occurring for males between 18 and 25 years of age.

  C.J. Mills & W.E. Bohannon, "Juror Characteristics: To What Extent Are They Related to Jury Verdicts?" (1980), 64 Judicature 23 at 27.

* However, the Mills and Bohannon study is dated. Those persons 18 to 25 when that study was completed are now 34 to 42. The results could be as much a function of the era and attitudes of the time as of the age of the respondents.

* Prosecutor Celynne Dorval expressed concern that older women tend to be followers and may be more intimidated by some crimes and therefore less able to return a guilty verdict.

10.3(a)(ii) **The Baby Boomer**

* Defence counsel Pat McCann is of the view that jurors are likely to reflect the general attitudes of their generation. He believes that the old adage "Never trust anyone over thirty" should now be modified to "Never trust anyone under thirty." He prefers jurors in their late thirties and in their forties. These people, he reasons, grew up in an era when authority was less trusted than it is now, and when there was more tolerance. Several of the defence counsel consulted suggest that today's younger generation is disproportionately afraid of crime, overly conservative, and apt to judge harshly those who do not conform. Today's radicals are not civil libertarians, but rather those who wish to change the attitudes of others. At the other extreme, these lawyers believe that older people are also apt to become more afraid of crime, and hence more likely to convict in a given case, as they lose the self-confidence that the successful middle years bring.

* A number of years ago, controversial defence counsel F. Lee Bailey recommended jurors between the ages of twenty-eight and fifty-five.

  F.L. Bailey & H.B. Rothblatt, *Successful Techniques for Criminal Trials* (Rochester, N.Y.: Lawyers Co-operative Publishing Co., 1971) at 104–5, cited in J.J. Gobert & W.E. Jordan, *Jury Selection: The Law, Art and Science of Selecting a Jury*, 2d ed. (Colorado Springs: Shepard's/McGraw-Hill, 1990) at 455.

10.3(a)(iii) **Education**

* Social scientists Mills and Bohannon found a relationship between education and verdicts in their study:

  - [A]s education level increased, so did acquittals;
  - . . . this relationship was different for males and females . . . Guilty verdicts remained relatively high across all educational levels for females . . . , but decreased as educational level increased for males;

- It appears that females are more conviction-prone across all education levels, whereas males with post-high school education are less likely to convict than males with less education.

C.J. Mills & W.E. Bohannon, "Juror Characteristics: To What Extent Are They Related to Jury Verdicts?" (1980) 64 Judicature 23 at 27.

10.3(a)(iv) The Expert Juror

* Hastie, Penrod, and Pennington, in their study of the jury, advise counsel to "avoid jurors having a special knowledge of areas about which expert witnesses will testify, for these jurors will think that they know more than the other jurors and more than the experts." This can have a distorting effect on the case presented.

R. Hastie, S.D. Penrod, & N. Pennington, *Inside the Jury* (Cambridge, Mass.: Harvard University Press, 1983) at 122.

* The wisdom in this is obvious. Malcolm Lindsay, QC, recounts an experience in which he accepted a "professor" on the jury. The homicide case, in which a husband shot his wife's lover to death, featured a diminished responsibility defence that was based on expert defence evidence. Mr. Lindsay's pitch to the jury not to be fooled by psychological "mumbo-jumbo" failed to impress the professor, who as it turned out was a doctor of psychology, and the defence succeeded.

10.3(a)(v) The Forceful Juror

* It is common for defence counsel and Crown counsel alike to wish to avoid jurors who, through their occupation or comportment, would appear to make strong group leaders. There is concern that such jurors will dominate the deliberations and may be more difficult to persuade. While this can work to the advantage or disadvantage of either side, the extent to which such people are perceived to be able to influence others is unsettling. As one counsel put it: "If you lose them, you lose everybody." Counsel prefer to have the case decided on their own submissions, rather than on the arguments of an aggressive juror, which cannot be answered by counsel when made in the privacy of the jury room. For this reason, many ascribe to the view that teachers should be avoided. As Assistant Crown Attorney Celynne Dorval put it, "I do not want teachers exercising their leadership skills in the jury room." Some lawyers apply the same reasoning to managers, senior civil servants, and financial consultants.

* This general wisdom finds some support in the scientific literature. Loftus and Greene observe that studies demonstrate that "[j]urors in high status

occupations — professional or managerial as opposed to blue collar — played a larger role in deliberations."

E.F. Loftus & E. Greene, "Twelve Angry People: The Collective Mind of the Jury" (1984) 84 Colum. L. Rev. 1425 at 1431.

* In contrast to this prevailing wisdom, it has elsewhere been suggested that the Crown should prefer strong minded individuals.

> You are not looking for a fair juror, but rather a strong, biased and sometimes hypocritical individual who believes that defendants are different from them in kind, rather than degree.

J.W. Barber, "The Jury is Still Out: The Role of Jury Science in the Modern American Courtroom" (1994) 31 Am. Crim. L. Rev. 1225 at note 101, referring to A.W. Alschuler, "The Supreme Court and the Jury: Voir Dire Peremptory Challenges and the Review of Jury Verdicts" (1989) 56 U. Chi. L. Rev. 153 at 156.

10.3(a)(vi) **Occupation and Social Status**

* It is believed by many that the occupation of a prospective juror can assist in determining whether that juror has a "law and order" mentality, or is more compassionate and accepting. Social scientists R. Hastie, S.D. Penrod, and N. Pennington note that "the unemployed, pensioners, and people on relief are thought to be generous, but teachers, clergy and lawyers should generally be rejected." They observe, as well, "Unless the defendant is a veteran with a good military service record, retired police, military men, and wives are undesirable, for they adhere to strict codes."

R. Hastie, S.D. Penrod, & N. Pennington, *Inside the Jury* (Cambridge, Mass.: Harvard University Press, 1983) at 122–23.

* F. Lee Bailey recommends against taking individuals with occupations such as salespersons, actors, and writers. He further recommends against taking jurors who have trained either to give or to take orders.

F.L. Bailey & H.B. Rothblatt, *Successful Techniques for Criminal Trials* (Rochester, N.Y.: Lawyers Co-operative Publishing Co., 1971) at 104–5, cited in J.J. Gobert & W.E. Jordan, *Jury Selection: The Law, Art and Science of Selecting a Jury*, 2d ed. (Colorado Springs: Shepard's/McGraw-Hill, 1990) at 455.

* One researcher found that "in criminal cases . . . socioeconomic status, . . . was related to verdict: the higher the status, the more likely the juror was to vote 'guilty.'

D. Sahler, "Scientifically Selecting Jurors While Maintaining Professional Responsibility: A Proposed Model Rule" (1996) 6 Alb. L.J. Sci. & Tech. 383 at note 62, referring to S.M. Fulero & S.D. Penrod, below at 244.

* A similar finding, albeit a weak one, was made in the Hastie, Penrod, and Pennington study, where it was revealed that "[u]nemployed and retired jurors were more defense-oriented than working people."

R. Hastie, S.D. Penrod, & N. Pennington, *Inside the Jury* (Cambridge, Mass.: Harvard University Press, 1983) at 128.

* There is a widespread view among defence lawyers that teachers, bankers, insurance agents, and engineers make bad jurors. These groups are perceived to be "law and order" oriented and judgmental. Michael Edelson prefers such professionals, however, when the accused is a lawyer, a police officer, or a judge. Assistant Crown Attorney Celynne Dorval prefers engineers and nurses, whom she sees as being pragmatic.

10.3(a)(vii) **Race**

* An instruction manual provided to prosecutors in Dallas, Texas, states:

> You are not looking for any member of a minority group which may subject him to oppression — they almost always empathize with the accused.

J.W. Barber, "The Jury is Still Out: The Role of Jury Science in the Modern American Courtroom" (1994) 31 Am. Crim. L. Rev. 1225 at note 101, referring to A.W. Alschuler, "The Supreme Court and the Jury: Voir Dire Peremptory Challenges and the Review of Jury Verdicts" (1989) 56 U. Chi. L. Rev. 153 at 156.

* By contrast, some defence counsel consulted expressed fear that new Canadians may be anxious to demonstrate their commitment to their new country by taking a law and order attitude. They may also, it was said, judge others from their own race or culture harshly in the hope that by doing so they will not be stigmatized by the acts of others. Paradoxically, some prosecutors fear that new Canadians, particularly from countries with a history of state oppression, may be more inclined to distrust the police. The only conclusion that can safely be drawn is that for many lawyers selecting jurors, fear of the unknown can result in prospective jurors being challenged because of race.

* There would appear to be no reliable studies purporting to analyse attitudes towards crime control and the prosecution of offences along racial lines. Although the different social context certainly diminishes substantially the utility of the finding for Canadian lawyers, one American study found that Blacks favoured acquittal more than did whites. As

noted above, however, Mills and Bohannon found several years ago that Black women are more conviction-prone than Black men.

R.J. Simon, *The Jury and the Defense of Insanity* (Boston: Little, Brown, 1967). See too D.W. Broeder, "The University of Chicago Jury Project" (1959) 38 Neb. L. Rev. 744.

10.3(a)(viii) Jurors Who Relate to Counsel

* The Honourable Dan Chilcott, one of the pre-eminent trial counsel in Ontario prior to his appointment to the bench, is reputed to have advised counsel to select jurors close in age to themselves. These jurors are more apt to relate to counsel and to share counsel's attitudes and beliefs. This can only enhance the prospect that the jurors will accept counsel's submissions.

* This advice might extend not just to age, but also to other factors such as socio-economic status, ethnicity, and sex.

* Prosecutor Celynne Dorval seeks jurors who are apt to see the issues the way that she does, based on their background, profile, and appearance.

10.3(a)(ix) **Sex**

* Sex is often considered a worthy indicator of predisposition to convict. Hastie, Penrod, and Pennington suggest that "[w]omen are sympathetic and extraordinarily conscientious." They also suggest that "[w]omen forgive male criminal defendants, but men are better jurors when counsel wants to avoid intuitive and sympathetic thinking."

  R. Hastie, S.D. Penrod, & N. Pennington, *Inside the Jury* (Cambridge, Mass.: Harvard University Press, 1983) at 122–23.

* James Paul Linn, a criminal lawyer in Oklahoma City, claims to have spent the last forty-two years trying to pack his juries with women. He believes that "[g]ender makes a big difference when you're picking a jury." He feels that "[w]omen are more compassionate than men in most criminal cases, but they can be ruthless when it comes to sex crimes." He also believes that "[m]en tend to be harder on defendants."

  M.B.W. Tabor, "Stereotyping Men, Women and Juries by Trial and Error" *The New York Times* (6 February 1994) 4:3.

* One lawyer consulted expressed the view that men are more difficult to convince than women, because of their egos. They are not open to good advocacy for fear of being manipulated. To some men it is more important to be strong and certain than to be right. Women, especially older women, seem to be more open-minded and curious.

* The theory that sex is an important factor in crime control attitudes and juror propensity is a controversial one. Mills and Bohannon conducted a study in which 117 females and 80 males participated. They also obtained information on final verdicts and demographics for jurors in other court cases. When individuals who had served as jurors were questioned about their experiences on actual cases, the authors found that

- The highest percentage of guilty verdicts came from women (67 percent). This was particularly true for rape and murder cases, where females gave more initial (personal) guilty verdicts (78 percent and 71 percent, respectively) than males (53 percent and 50 percent).
- However, this appears to have more to do with the relationship between race and gender rather than simply gender. Black females reported a significantly higher percentage of initial (personal) guilty verdicts (73 percent) than black males (50 percent).
- No significant difference between white males (61 per cent) and females (69 per cent) was found.

C.J. Mills & W.E. Bohannon, "Juror Characteristics: To What Extent Are They Related to Jury Verdicts?" (1980) 64 Judicature 23 at 27.

* In another study conducted by Hastie, Penrod, and Pennington involving a mock trial experiment in Massachusetts concerning a first-degree murder prosecution, the authors discovered that "[f]emales were more defense-oriented than males."

E.F. Loftus & E. Greene, "Twelve Angry People: The Collective Mind of the Jury" (1984) 84 Colum. L. Rev. 1425 at 1430, referring to the findings of Hastie *et al.*, as reported in *Inside the Jury* (Cambridge, Mass.: Harvard University Press, 1983). Loftus and Greene point out that the relationship uncovered by Hastie *et al.* was a very weak one.

10.3(a)(x) **The Unhappy Juror**

* Jurors who resent their duty may act unpredictably. They may be inattentive, uninterested, impatient, or in extreme cases unwilling to take the process seriously, potentially even sabotaging the deliberation process. For this reason, Malcolm Lindsay, QC, Senior Assistant Crown Attorney in Ottawa, advises against selecting jurors who are in occupations or callings that will be inconvenienced unduly by jury duty. In particular, persons dependent on an hourly wage, such as tradespeople or waiters, may be losing their means of livelihood during the jury trial. If a trial is apt to be long, it may prove a serious

inconvenience to university students, who will be missing appreciable portions of their studies. Persons with day care responsibilities may be in the same situation. For similar reasons, many prosecutors make it a habit to challenge jurors who seek unsuccessfully to have the trial judge excuse them from jury duty based on claims of personal hardship. No one's interest is served by having uninterested people on the jury.

10.3(b) **The Kind of Case Being Tried**

* Social scientists acknowledge that "there is no profile of the good defense (or prosecution or plaintiff) juror that can be used across cases." Counsel agree. A crucial rule of thumb about jury selection is: "always select jurors according to the kind of case being tried."

S.S. Diamond, "Scientific Jury Selection: What Social Scientists Know and Do Not Know" (1990) 73 Judicature 178 at 181. See too S.M. Fulero & S.D. Penrod, "The Myths and Realities of Attorney Jury Selection Folklore and Scientific Jury Selection: What Works?" (1980) 17 Ohio N.U.L. Rev. 229 at 250, cited in D. Sahler, "Scientifically Selecting Jurors While Maintaining Professional Responsibility: A Proposed Model Rule" (1996) 6 Alb. L.J. Sci. & Tech. 383 at 392.

10.3(b)(i) **Juror Age and the Case Being Tried**

* In their study, Mills and Bohannon found the following relationships between age and verdicts:

  - Jurors' guilty verdicts generally increased with age, particularly for rape cases where the strongest relationship between age and number of guilty verdicts was found.
  - In rape cases, older people were more likely to convict . . .
  - In murder cases, however, older people were less likely to convict.

C.J. Mills & W.E. Bohannon, "Juror Characteristics: To What Extent Are They Related to Jury Verdicts?" (1980) 64 Judicature 23 at 27 & 30.

10.3(b)(ii) **Juror Intelligence and the Case Being Tried**

* Social scientists Loftus and Greene observe that "more educated jurors participated more frequently than less educated jurors, and they accurately recalled more evidence."

E.F. Loftus & E. Greene, "Twelve Angry People: The Collective Mind of the Jury" (1984) 84 Colum. L. Rev. 1425 at 1431.

* For this reason, as a general rule, defence counsel prefer intelligent jurors when they have a real and substantial defence to a case, and less intelligent jurors if the defence is more questionable. Crown counsel, of course, seek the more intelligent jurors when the defence is questionable.

* In a fraud prosecution, where there will be complex testimony, unless defence counsel have a clear defence that must be demonstrated through a proper understanding of the forensic record, they tend to prefer those jurors who will be left in doubt about guilt because they are left in doubt about what the Crown's case means. Not surprisingly, Crown counsel tend to prefer smart jurors for such cases.

* Where the Crown case depends on forensic scientific evidence, the defence may prefer intelligent jurors. It may need to have the jurors understand the shortcomings in the scientific techniques employed. Jurors who cannot understand the challenge may rely solely on the "bottom line" conclusions of Crown witnesses.

* For the same reason, in seriously triable circumstantial evidence cases, some defence counsel spoken to prefer intelligent jurors who can anticipate and appreciate alternative possibilities to those being suggested by the Crown.

* It has been found that "less educated jurors were more likely to convict only in rape cases" and less likely to convict for other offences.

  C.J. Mills & W.E. Bohannon, "Juror Characteristics: To What Extent Are They Related to Jury Verdicts?" (1980) 64 Judicature 23 at 30.

10.3(b)(iii) **Juror Occupation and the Case Being Tried**

* It is obvious that the occupation of the juror may predispose that juror to look more or less harshly on the crime being prosecuted. It is universally recognized that "[b]ankers are bad for criminal defendants in robbery and theft cases but are good in white-collar crime cases". Defence counsel should avoid jurors whose occupations put them at risk of being victimized by the offence being tried.

  R. Hastie, S.D. Penrod, & N. Pennington, *Inside the Jury* (Cambridge, Mass.: Harvard University Press, 1983) at 122.

* Prosecutor Celynne Dorval believes that when the Crown case is a simple one, calling on nothing more than common sense to resolve, jurors with blue-collar or working-class occupations are better. Because they tend to be less educated, they have survived on common sense alone and are less likely to look beyond that which is apparent.

10.3(b)(iv) **Juror Race and the Case Being Tried**

* In *Parks*, Justice Doherty commented:

> [E]mpirical studies in the United States using mock juries suggest that juries are more inclined to convict defendants who are not of the same race as the juror. This is especially so where the evidence against the accused is not strong, or where the victim of the offence is of the same race as the juror.

(1993), 15 O.R. (3d) 324 at 345 (C.A.), citing J.E. Pfeifer "Reviewing the Empirical Evidence on Jury Racism: Findings of Discrimination or Discriminatory Findings?" (1990) 69 Nebraska L. Rev. 230, and S.L. Johnson, "Black Innocence and the White Jury" (1985) 83 Mich. L. Rev. 1611.

10.3(b)(v) **Juror Sex and the Case Being Tried**

* It is commonly believed that women do not make good defence jurors in sexual offence cases but are ideal for the prosecution. Women, it is believed, are more apt to be frightened of sexual violence and to identify with the complainants. This is particularly true in random sexual offences or sexual offences accompanied by other physical violence.

* A number of defence lawyers expressed the view that this generalization does not hold for all sexual offence cases, in particular in "date-rape" cases and in other cases where the complainant will have exercised spectacularly poor judgment. The view was expressed that women can be harsher judges of other women, but, more important, are apt to judge the likelihood of the complainant's account based on how they would have reacted if in that situation. Men may be more protective of the complainant in such cases.

* The view was also expressed that women do not make the best defence jurors in sexual offence cases involving children, or in cases involving serious non-sexual violence. Celynne Dorval prefers men of an age where they are likely to have children at home, in child abuse cases. They are apt to be protective and disgusted and will want to express that disgust. Older men, in contrast, may have had too puritanical an upbringing and may have difficulty believing some of the things that sexual offenders do to children.

* In their study, Mills and Bohannon found that these non-scientific presuppostions were not borne out, at least not sixteen years ago in the United States. They found that "[i]n only one kind of case was the sex of a juror strongly related to a particular verdict; in robbery cases, women were more likely to convict than men."

  C.J. Mills & W.E. Bohannon, "Juror Characteristics: To What Extent Are They Related to Jury Verdicts?" (1980) 64 Judicature 23 at 30.

10.3(c) The Persona of the Accused and the Main Crown Witnesses

* Just as it is important for jurors to be able to relate to counsel, it is also important to try to select jurors who will relate to the relevant trial protagonists. Defence wants jurors who can relate to the accused, while the Crown has the easier challenge of finding jurors who will relate to the complainant and key Crown witnesses. It has been observed by social scientists that "often the critical factor in determining a juror's subconscious leaning is the juror's ability to identify with a key figure, be it a party, witness, or lawyer, in the case."

  J.J. Gobert & W.E. Jordan, *Jury Selection: The Law, Art and Science of Selecting a Jury*, 2d ed. (Colorado Springs: Shepard's/McGraw-Hill, 1990) at 456, cited in R.E. Keeton, *Trial Tactics and Methods* (Boston: Little Brown, 1954) at 239.

* More specifically, social scientists believe that "[s]electing jury members who possess some emotional commitment to a litigant's case has been identified as the best prediction of how individual jurors will determine the verdict."

  D. Sahler, "Scientifically Selecting Jurors While Maintaining Professional Responsibility: A Proposed Model Rule" (1996) 6 Alb. L.J. Sci. & Tech. 383 at 392 & 393–94, referring to Diamond at 178 and R.D. Minick, "Using Jury Consultants to Assist Voir Dire" *Mass. Law. Wkly.* (9 December 1991) S2.

* Senior Assistant Crown Attorney Malcolm Lindsay, QC, like most Crown counsel, will seek to rid the jury of persons with criminal antecedents or likely connections to those who have been convicted of offences. The concern, of course, is that these people may be sympathetic to the plight of the accused, or hostile to the authorities. In Ottawa the long-standing practice of running criminal records checks on prospective jurors has been discontinued because of its administrative costs. He therefore consults with investigating officers and calls on his knowledge of surnames in the community that have been associated with criminal behaviour. He also pays attention to the addresses of potential jurors to see whether they come from "project" areas, where there is apt to be a greater risk of criminal involvement or association.

* For this reason, defence counsel tend not to challenge those jurors who may appear to have first-hand familiarity with the system. It has been suggested that, even if such jurors may not be the best jurors for the defence, there is no point in using up a challenge on such persons because the Crown will. Defence counsel can expect the Crown to challenge the "rounders" who come forward for jury selection.

* Loftus and Greene point out that defence counsel will want to "retain jurors with the same occupation as their client, since they will identify with him more readily."

  E.F. Loftus & E. Greene, "Twelve Angry People: The Collective Mind of the Jury" (1984) 84 Colum. L. Rev. 1425 at 1430.

* Pat McCann recommends that where the accused has a criminal history that will become apparent to the jurors, counsel should attempt to find jurors from the "helping professions" in the hope that they will sympathize with the accused and view the accused with humanity. Teachers, nurses, and even social workers may prove the best jurors in such a case.

* Defence counsel will want to avoid, and Crown counsel will want to select, jurors who appear as though they will relate unduly to the complainant. Although such characteristics are often difficult to detect, defence counsel will want to avoid, for example, prospective jurors who are apt to have strong feminist leanings in a sexual offence case. Similarly, they will want to attempt to select jurors in a sexual offence prosecution who could be vulnerable to false complaints, such as persons in positions of trust over children, clergy, or men in management positions.

* Where the accused is an intimidating character, prosecutors prefer jurors who appear to have backbone or character.

* A number of experienced trial lawyers believe that it is possible to exploit jurors' biases and prejudices. For example, many believe that the sexual attractiveness of counsel, the accused, or the complainant can influence some jurors. Hastie, Penrod and Pennington suggest that, "[w]ith a woman as client, take all men."

  R. Hastie, S.D. Penrod, & N. Pennington, *Inside the Jury* (Cambridge, Mass.: Harvard University Press, 1983) at 122.

* Loftus and Greene point out that one of the rules of thumb that lawyers have over the years been told they should follow is to avoid "women, especially if the client is a young, attractive woman, but not if the client is a handsome young man."

  E.F. Loftus & E. Greene, "Twelve Angry People: The Collective Mind of the Jury" (1984) 84 Colum. L. Rev. 1425 at 1430, citing J. Kelner, "Jury Selection: The Prejudice Syndrome" (1984) 56 N.Y. St. B.J. 34, and J. Appleman, *Successful Jury Trials: A Symposium* (Indianapolis: Bobbs-Merrill, 1952).

* F. Lee Bailey also recommends female jurors when the accused or the lawyer is handsome.

  F.L. Bailey & H.B. Rothblatt, *Successful Techniques for Criminal Trials* (Rochester, N.Y.: Lawyers Co-operative Publishing Co., 1971) at 104–5, cited in J.J. Gobert & W.E. Jordan, *Jury Selection: The Law, Art and Science of Selecting a Jury*, 2d ed. (Colorado Springs: Shepard's/McGraw-Hill, 1990) at 455.

* Sexist stereotypes are not the sole ones called on by some counsel. James Paul Linn, a criminal lawyer in Oklahoma City, believes that heterosexual men tend to respond negatively to gay men, while homosexuals, men and women alike, are sympathetic to mistreatment.

M.B.W. Tabor, "Stereotyping Men, Women and Juries by Trial and Error, *The New York Times* (6 February 1994) 4:3.

10.3(d) **The Individual Juror**

* Counsel should pay careful regard to the prospective juror before deciding whether to challenge.

* Edward Greenspan offers the following observations:

> How does one select jurors? First of all, humbly. One selects them with the understanding that all human beings are feeling, thinking individuals whose behaviour cannot be predicted like a bunch of rats just because they are in the same income or ethnic bracket. You try to eliminate plain, obvious prejudice in a given case. For the rest, you simply *look* at jurors. Not in the hope of diagnosing them . . . but only to assess them on the basis of your general experience of human nature, as you do in all ordinary dealings in life.

E.L. Greenspan & G. Jonas, *Greenspan: The Case for the Defence*, (Toronto: Macmillan, 1987) at 281.

* Most counsel would agree, believing that the crucial point in jury selection is when the prospective juror is called forward and asked to look at the accused. Although the acquaintance is fleeting and superficial, this is typically the sole opportunity that counsel will have to judge the juror as an individual. For this reason experienced counsel attempt to "drink up" as much as they can about the jury panel in the time available. Many make it a practice to observe as many of the panel as possible while they are waiting for the judge, and then to watch the jurors carefully as they are called forward and line up for jury selection. They attempt to gauge personalities based on comportment, demeanour, and self-confidence.

* Others, such as Donald Bayne, warn that demeanour and the apparent friendliness of jurors are an unreliable guide.

10.3(d)(i) **Body Language**

* Apparently, according to social scientists, traits such as demeanour and posture are important, but they can be difficult to read. As Gobert and Jordan note:

> It is not difficult for prospective jurors who wish to conceal their biases to lie; it is far more difficult for them to control their facial and bodily movements,

> which may be involuntary, or their manner of response. Few even appreciate that their nonverbal responses can betray their verbal falsehoods. Fewer still would know how to control their bodies even if they were aware of the need to do so. The lawyer who is attuned to nonverbal, as well as verbal, responses is accordingly better placed to discern a juror's true leanings.

J.J. Gobert & W.E. Jordan, *Jury Selection: The Law, Art and Science of Selecting a Jury*, 2d ed. (Colorado Springs: Shepard's/McGraw-Hill, 1990) at 460.

* In assessing the body language of the juror, Gobert and Jordan stress that body language should not be evaluated in isolation but rather in context:

> Is the body movement in question appropriate in the particular context? If the answer is no, then an explanation for the incongruity should be sought. Tenseness, for example, is natural when sensitive subjects are being probed, but unnatural when the juror is asked a perfunctory question such as whether he can give the defendant a fair trial. Tenseness accompanying a positive verbal response in the latter situation may indicate that the juror is in fact not prepared to give the defendant a fair trial.
>
> Contextual analysis also requires a determination of whether a particular juror's body movement is normal or abnormal for that juror. A lawyer needs to know whether the juror's facial expression or body movement is a response to the lawyer's question or part of the juror's natural character. To this end, the juror should be observed while engaged in casual conversation (perhaps during recesses or out of court), and when asked routine, nonthreatening questions at outset of voir dire. It is the departures from normal responses which indicate situational anxiety brought on by the lawyer's questioning. It is atypical responses which are significant.
>
> Body language must be evaluated comparatively: do the juror's body movements differ depending on which side is asking the questions? The side with which the juror appears more at ease as indicated by general posture, body movements, and physical reactions is likely to be the side which the juror will favour in deliberations. To fail to do a comparative analysis, however, could lead to the inappropriate challenge of a naturally fidgety juror.

J.J. Gobert & W.E. Jordan, *Jury Selection: The Law, Art and Science of Selecting a Jury*, 2d ed. (Colorado Springs: Shepard's/McGraw-Hill, 1990) at 464.

* Some of the findings relating to body language include:

> The potential juror who sits rigidly and responds in a laconic tone with monosyllabic answers to the voir dire might be an "authoritarian" personality and thus likely to side with the prosecution.

J.W. Barber, "The Jury is Still Out: The Role of Jury Sciences in the Modern American Courtroom" (1994) 31 Am. Crim. L. Rev. 1225 at 1236, referring to the work of S.H. Peskin, "Non-Verbal Communication in the Courtroom, (1980) Trial Dipl. J. 4 at 6.

> [P]eople who touch their noses while speaking are liars.

D. Sahler, "Scientifically Selecting Jurors While Maintaining Professional Responsibility: A Proposed Model Rule" (1996) 6 Alb. L.J. Sci. & Tech. 383 at 389, citing E. Oliver, "Use of Trial Consultants: Will It Ruin the Role of the Jury" *Mich. Law. Wkly.* (16 January 1995) 3, who in turn cited G.I. Nierenberg & H.H. Colero, *How to Read a Person Like a Book* (New York: Hawthorn Books, 1971).

> Other signs of "excessive or agitated body movements" such as "hand wringing and finger tapping, are signs of anxiety and may indicate hostility or deception."

J.J. Gobert & W.E. Jordan, *Jury Selection: The Law, Art and Science of Selecting a Jury*, 2d ed. (Colorado Springs: Shepard's/McGraw-Hill, 1990) at 463, citing P. Ekman & W.V. Friesen, "Hand Movements" (1972) 22 J. Comm. 353, and D. Suggs & B.D. Sales, "Using Communication Cues to Evaluate Prospective Jurors During the Voir Dire" (1978) 20 Ariz. L. Rev. 629.

> [A] juror biased against the defense might become "tense, evasive, or hostile when questioned by the defense lawyer."

J.W. Barber, "The Jury is Still Out: The Role of Jury Sciences in the Modern American Courtroom" (1994) 31 Am. Crim. L. Rev. 1225 at 1243, citing S. Seyfert, "The New Science of Jury Selection" *Boston Globe* (5 August 1984) 3.

> [C]rossed legs, tightened neck muscles, folded arms, and clenched fists may signify hostility. A sudden buttoning of a coat or the thrusting of hands into one's pocket may indicate that the juror feels threatened and has decided to resist.

J.J. Gobert & W.E. Jordan, *Jury Selection: The Law, Art and Science of Selecting a Jury*, 2d ed. (Colorado Springs: Shepard's/McGraw-Hill, 1990) at 463.

> A juror who is relaxed is an indicator that the juror is comfortable with the lawyer and potentially with the lawyer's position.

J.J. Gobert & W.E. Jordan, *Jury Selection: The Law, Art and Science of Selecting a Jury*, 2d ed. (Colorado Springs: Shepard's/McGraw-Hill, 1990) at 463, citing Blinder, "Picking Juries" (1972) 1 Trial Dipl. J. 12–13.

10.3(d)(ii) **Eye Contact**

* Most lawyers place great stock in the apparent reaction of the juror to the accused. Most defence counsel will not take a juror who will not look the accused in the eye, interpreting the juror's reluctance to do so as a sign that the juror may feel uncomfortable in the presence of a "criminal." There are also prosecutors who follow the same creed, believing that a juror without the confidence to look the accused in the eye may not have the considerable courage that it takes to convict. Malcolm Lindsay, QC, reads little into this. He points out, accurately, that the last thing the juror is expecting when called forward is to be told to look into the face of the accused. It is an unfamiliar situation and may tell little about the juror's actual character. When the reaction is clear, however — for example, when the juror glares at the accused — it is obvious that the defence will not want to take a chance with that juror.

* Similarly, eye contact with counsel is also considered significant by many practitioners.

* Eye contact with both the accused and counsel is, in fact, considered by some social scientists to be an important consideration. Research indicates that "people maintain eye contact with those from whom they seek approval." Gobert and Jordan recommend that "[c]omparisons of the juror's eye contact during the voir dire with the lawyers on each side may indicate the side from whom the juror wants approval and with whom the juror desires a positive relationship." They also note that "[e]ye contact with the client may be as important as eye contact with the lawyer."

  J.J. Gobert & W.E. Jordan, *Jury Selection: The Law, Art and Science of Selecting a Jury*, 2d ed. (Colorado Springs: Shepard's/McGraw-Hill, 1990), at 462, citing J.S. Efran, "Looking for Approval: Effects on Visual Behaviour of Approbation from Persons Differing in Importance" (1968) 10 J. Personality & Soc. Psychology 21.

  > The juror who avoids eye contact with the lawyer may not be entirely truthful in his or her verbal response. Conversely, increased eye contact may indicate a positive feeling toward the lawyer to whom the juror is speaking.

J.J. Gobert & W.E. Jordan, *Jury Selection: The Law, Art and Science of Selecting a Jury*, 2d ed. (Colorado Springs: Shepard's/McGraw-Hill, 1990) at 461–62, citing M. Argyle & J. Dean, "Eye-Contact, Distance and Affiliation" (1965) 28 Sociometry 289.

10.3(d)(iii) **The Apparent Personality of the Juror**

* Defence counsel are looking for a pleasant, natural look. They want their client tried by people with humanity and kindness, who will remember that the accused is a human being despite the charges faced. To the extent that this can be judged based on comportment, demeanour, and apparent attitude, most counsel will rely on their impressions.

10.3(d)(iv) **The Reaction to Counsel**

* The reaction of the juror to counsel is also considered to be important to most laywers. Pat McCann stresses that if it is unrealistic to expect jurors to relate well to the accused, try to choose jurors who, by their appearance, would seem to relate well to you as counsel. Try to pick jurors who look like the kind of people you might be able to sit down and have a chat with. By the same token, counsel should be wary of jurors who appear to be charmed by opposing counsel.

* It has been observed that "[t]he potential juror who looks into the attorney's eyes and smiles engagingly when answering the voir dire will probably be malleable and open to the defense's case."

  J.W. Barber, "The Jury is Still Out: The Role of Jury Selection in the Modern American Courtroom" (1994) 31 Am. Crim. L. Rev. 1225 at 1236, referring to the work of S.H. Peskin, "Non-Verbal Communication in the Courtroom" (1980) Trial Dipl. J. 4 at 6.

* Hastie, Penrod, and Pennington warn counsel to "[b]e wary of smiling jurors who are trying to disarm attorneys; they want to get on the jury and murder them."

  R. Hastie, S.D. Penrod, & N. Pennington, *Inside the Jury* (Cambridge, Mass.: Harvard University Press, 1983) at 123.

10.3(d)(v) **Verbal Responses**

* Although counsel will have little opportunity to observe the verbal responses of prospective jurors because of the limited *voir dire* permitted in Canada, the way that a prospective juror responds to the questions asked may be instructive. The choice of words used by a juror in answering a

question may reveal a bias or prejudice. For example, "Take two jurors who are asked whether they are prejudiced against Blacks. One responds: 'I'm not prejudiced against Blacks'; the other responds: 'I am not prejudiced against those people.' Both responses purport to deny prejudice, but the distancing use of 'those people' suggests that the second juror may be attempting to conceal his or her true feelings."

J.J. Gobert & W.E. Jordan, *Jury Selection: The Law, Art and Science of Selecting a Jury*, 2d ed. (Colorado Springs: Shepard's/McGraw-Hill, 1990) at 466, citing D. Suggs & B.D. Sales, "Using Communication Cues to Evaluate Prospective Jurors During the Voir Dire" (1978) 20 Ariz. L. Rev. 629 at 638.

10.3(d)(vi) **The Juror's Appearance**

* The dress and physical appearance of the prospective juror are also considered significant by many counsel. One prosecutor likened the process to a job interview, in which the neatly dressed person with good bearing and comportment would make a better candidate for the serious process of jury deliberation. One counsel suggested that it is useful to look at the shoes of the prospective juror. If they are unkempt, the juror is unlikely to be meticulous in other aspects of his or her life, including thinking.

* There are those who believe that the physique of a prospective juror is noteworthy. An American prosecutor offers the following advice: "Extremely overweight young men, indicates a lack of self-discipline and often time instability. I like the lean and hungry look."

  J.W. Barber, "The Jury is Still Out: The Role of Jury Selection in the Modern American Courtroom" (1994) 31 Am. Crim. L. Rev. 1225 at note 101, referring to A.W. Alschuler, "The Supreme Court and the Jury: Voir Dire Peremptory Challenges and the Review of Jury Verdicts" (1989) 56 U. Chi. L. Rev. 153 at 156.

* Well-known lawyer, F. Lee Bailey seems to agree, having once offered the following advice to defence counsel in selecting a jury:

  > Generally speaking, the heavy, roundfaced, jovial-looking person is the most desirable. The undesirable juror is quite often the slight, underweight and delicate type. His features are sharp and fragile, with that lean "Cassius" look. The athletic-looking juror is hard to categorize. Usually he is hard to convince; but that once convinced he will usually go all the way for you.

  F.L. Bailey & H.B. Rothblatt, *Successful Techniques for Criminal Trials* (Rochester, N.Y.: Lawyers Co-operative Publishing Co., 1971) at 104–5, cited in J.J. Gobert & W.E. Jordan, *Jury Selection: The Law, Art and Science of Selecting a Jury*, 2d ed. (Colorado Springs: Shepard's/McGraw-Hill, 1990) at 455.

10.3(d)(vii) **Prior Jury Service**

* Occasionally, jurors will be asked to sit on more than one jury during the session where they are called. Defence lawyers tend not to want jurors who have served on convicting juries, while Crowns tend to want to avoid jurors who have acquitted before.

* In the study by R. Hastie, S.D. Penrod, and N. Pennington, it was discovered that "[t]he more experience a juror had on previous criminal juries, the more prosecution-oriented the juror."

  R. Hastie, S.D. Penrod, & N. Pennington, *Inside the Jury* (Cambridge, Mass.: Harvard University Press, 1983) at 128.

10.4 JURY SELECTION AND THE PROSECUTOR'S DUTY

* As indicated, an instruction manual to prosecutors in Dallas, Texas, advised:

  > You are not looking for a fair juror, but rather a strong, biased and sometimes hypocritical individual who believes that defendants are different from them in kind, rather than degree.

  J.W. Barber, "The Jury is Still Out: The Role of Jury Science in the Modern American Courtroom" (1994) 31 Am. Crim. L. Rev. 1225 at note 101, referring to A.W. Alschuler, "The Supreme Court and the Jury: Voir Dire Peremptory Challenges and the Review of Jury Verdicts" (1989) 56 U. Chi. L. Rev. 153 at 156.

* This kind of advice is inappropriate for Canadian prosecutors, who, as quasi-judicial officers, are duty bound to attempt to ensure that the accused receives a fair trial. Malcolm Lindsay, QC, Senior Assistant Crown Attorney for Ottawa-Carleton, observed that his main focus in selecting jurors is to attempt to ensure that the accused gets a fair and serious hearing, not necessarily simply to gain a conviction. He observed that it would be grossly inappropriate, for example, for a prosecutor to attempt to challenge a Black juror in a trial when the accused was Black, on the basis of race. Similarly, it would be wrong to seek to

exploit prejudices to secure a conviction, by selecting those most likely to be homophobic when the accused is gay, or hostile to immigrants when the accused is a new Canadian.

* Mr. Lindsay related an incident in which he discovered after a jury trial had commenced that a juror, whose occupation showed only that he was "retired," was in fact a retired police officer. Out of concern that this juror might not adjudicate the case fairly, given his occupation, Mr. Lindsay felt duty bound to advise defence counsel and to consent to having this juror excused from further jury duty.

* This is not to say that prosecutors should not seek to empanel a jury that will be more sympathetic to the Crown case than other prospective jurors might be. They can legitimately attempt to counter efforts by defence counsel to select a jury that will be more likely to acquit, notwithstanding the evidence, but they must always remember that they are ministers of justice.

* It would do well for defence counsel as well, even though legitimately entitled to make decisions based on the best interests of their clients, to remember that as officers of the court they too should seek to obtain verdicts based on true reasonable doubt, rather than those resting on sympathy, prejudice, or hostility.

10.5 PREJUDICE AND JURY SELECTION

* As can readily be seen, the ability to challenge jurors peremptorily enables counsel to rely on invidious stereotypes or to seek to induce a perverse verdict by selecting jurors who are most likely to decide a case on their own prejudices, rather than on the evidence. Some of the advice available to counsel calls on stereotypes about jurors based on race, for example. Clarence Darrow provided extensive advice on which ethnic groups are most likely to be stubborn, or emotional, or sympathetic. He was not alone.

  See J.W. Barber, "The Jury Is Still Out: The Role of Jury Science in the Modern American Courtroom" (1994) 31 Am. Crim. L. Rev. 1225 at note 55.

* The opportunity to make decisions based on such criteria has caused some to suggest that the peremptory challenge should be abolished. At the very least, in some cases reliance on such criteria by the Crown can constitute a violation of section 15 of the *Charter of Rights and Freedoms*. Since this chapter is concerned with the process of jury selection, the prospect of *Charter* challenges is discussed further in chapter 11.

10.6 SAMPLE JURY SELECTION PROBLEMS

EXAMPLE 1: John Doe, forty-six years of age, is charged with several related sexual offences involving his daughter. The incidents are alleged to have occurred some seven to ten years ago when his daughter was between the ages of twelve and fifteen. The allegations include full intercourse and oral sex. John Doe is an insurance agent who has an alcohol problem. His wife is nonetheless supportive of him. The daughter, who left home at the age of fifteen, is the unwed mother of a daughter of her own. Before leaving home she had serious problems of truancy from school. She has been estranged from her parents since leaving home. After she left she accumulated a minor criminal record, but is now employed as a hostess at a restaurant. She is petite and attractive, though, in your opinion, comes across as hardened and unpolished. She says that she came forward because, now that she has a daughter, she realizes how important it is not to let people get away with child abuse.

* This is a case where defence counsel would attempt to bring a challenge for cause. Most, but not all, defence counsel would have sought to avoid a jury trial here. See 1.8, above.

* Given that this is a jury trial, defence counsel consulted agreed that they would attempt to select jurors who can relate to the defence theory in the case, which is obviously that the complainant has developed a hostile animus towards her parents in general and her father in particular, which has precipitated the allegation. The most likely candidates are men of approximately the same age as the accused, and those in positions where they may feel vulnerable to false allegations of sexual abuse.

* Male school teachers might be good jurors in such a case, as would clergy or those in management positions. While those who have worked with troubled adolescents might accept that such persons can be deceitful, there is also the appreciable risk that they may believe that such children are troubled because they have been abused and should therefore be avoided. By the same token, persons with similar life status and an occupation like John Doe's should be sought. Michael Edelson would want males with the same income and social status as the accused. He would also like parents on the jury, though it will be difficult, if not impossible, in most cases to know whether a prospective juror is a parent.

* Defence counsel would normally be concerned that the complainant is petite and attractive, potentially portraying a vulnerability that could cause mothers or male jurors to be protective of her. This complainant will present as hardened and unpolished, which diminishes the risk that such jurors may allow a preference for the complainant over the accused to influence their

verdict. On balance, Pat McCann suggested that he would really want men on this jury. Ideally those men should be over thirty-five and under fifty-five. Donald Bayne, QC, agrees that the defence will prefer men on the jury, but would also accept older women, as would Michael Edelson.

* Most defence lawyers would seek to avoid those who appear to have feminist leanings, or those who are known to work in, or be connected with, psychology, or who are likely to be exposed to the popular psychology relating to sexual abuse. Donald Bayne, QC, suggests that, out of an abundance of caution, younger women should be avoided. They may be strident about their views on sexual offence matters, and prudence counsels that they be avoided.

* In this case defence counsel might want more-educated, rather than less-educated jurors. Although dated, American studies suggest that less-educated jurors, though more likely to acquit generally, are more prone to convict in sexual offence cases.

* By contrast, Crown counsel would normally seek to select young women for this jury and would prefer those who are most likely to be exposed to media reports focusing on the high incidence of sexual offences, or to psychological explanations for delays in reporting. Celynne Dorval, a prosecutor, prefers young men and young women for the jury in this kind of case. In her view, young men are just as likely to have been socialized against stereotype in sexual offence cases.

* Mothers of the age of the accused may be acceptable jurors, given that the accused's wife is supportive of him. They may be apt to believe that if this was really going on, she would have done something about it.

Example 2: John Doe is twenty-six years old. He has an extensive record and is a drug abuser. He has been charged with robbery. He was initially released from custody but has been rearrested and is now being held in custody pending trial. Your defence relates to the poor quality of the identification evidence against him. There are four Crown witnesses, each providing descriptions that differ as to height (5 foot 6 to 5 foot 10), weight (140 to 170 pounds), and clothing colour. Two of the witnesses selected John Doe from a formal line-up, but had offered only tentative identifications from a photo line-up. All four identified John Doe in court. John Doe was arrested driving a motor vehicle of the same make and model as the vehicle that may have been used in the robbery, bearing the same licence plate number. After a valid search, a handgun was found in his house. A handgun was used in the robbery.

* This is a difficult case for defence counsel because the circumstantial evidence is strong, and the accused, who is likely to have to testify, is not a presentable witness. Defence counsel will wish to avoid, if possible, those jurors who would have a strong fear of crime. All defence counsel consulted agreed that they would want a well-educated, intelligent jury who may have sufficient life experience to appreciate that things are not always as they seem. The defence requires jurors who will analyse the evidence critically and who will ignore the background of the accused. According to Pat McCann, men over thirty are the best possible jurors, since they are less likely to feel vulnerable to this type of crime. Both younger women and older women should be avoided. They are most likely to feel vulnerable to urban violence. Although dated, American literature suggests that women are more likely to convict in robbery cases than men. By contrast, Donald Bayne, QC, would prefer women on this jury. Acknowledging that it is probably a "blunt dumb myth," he believes that women tend to be more careful about these kinds of issues than men. Michael Edelson expressed precisely the same view, independently.

* Persons in professions or occupations that are vulnerable to robbery should obviously be avoided. Pat McCann suggests that it may be appropriate in a case like this to select jurors in the helping professions, who may be less fearful of persons with John Doe's background. Persons with a lower socio-economic status are, based on American studies, more likely to prove better defence jurors in a case like this.

* Despite these best efforts, there is probably no "ideal" defence juror for this case. Decisions should be based primarily on the observations that can be made in court about the prospective jurors.

* The Crown should have little difficulty empanelling a receptive jury in a case like this. Ideal jurors would be those who are likely to have a greater fear of street crime, and those who would be mindful of the links between drug abuse and the crime of robbery.

EXAMPLE 3: Jane Doe is an attractive, thirty-eight-year-old accounting clerk who has been charged with fraud and theft from her employer, an automobile dealership. The dealership claims to have lost far more cash than can be accounted for in the transactions that Jane is being prosecuted for. The fraud allegations against her involve the alleged manipulation of the accounting books to hide cash receipts from the service department and body shop. There are twenty-five entries in the books that can be shown to be inaccurate, reflecting disbursements of money for false transactions. These false entries were discovered only after an audit by a forensic accountant, who will be testifying for the Crown.

Although Jane is not the firm's only accounting clerk, the Crown alleges that all twenty-five false entries can be attributed to her. You have a handwriting expert who is prepared to testify that it is impossible to identify her as the author of all the false entries. Jane had access to cash receipts, but so too did a number of other employees. In some cases she would prepare the disbursement cheques, but in other cases she would record pay-outs acting solely on "chit sheets," receipts, and even verbal instructions from department managers. You have a forensic accountant who can suggest that some of the entries not being attributed to Jane may also be "false." Jane was fired when the false entries were discovered and threatened suit for wrongful dismissal. Subsequently the criminal charges were laid.

* The ideal defence juror in this case, according to some defence counsel, would be a working-class man. They believe that since the case is bound to be complex, it might be best for the defence to have jurors who will have difficulty following the evidence of the Crown forensic witnesses, and who may attribute significance to the minor challenges that the defence will be able to make to Crown evidence. Moreover, because the accused is an attractive woman, several defence counsel suggested that middle-aged men may be less likely to judge her harshly, while the view was expressed that middle-aged women would probably do so. By contrast, Michael Edelson felt that older females who appear from their occupations to have been working for many years would be good jurors for this case because they may have experienced discrimination as women in the workplace. It was suggested by more than one counsel that men around forty-five would make the best jurors, given who the accused is. Business people, who understand accounts, would not be good defence jurors, nor would managers. Jurors from lower socio-economic backgrounds, and working-class jurors, are unlikely to be unduly sympathetic to the employer.

* The Crown would want intelligent jurors. Although "expert" jurors are normally to be avoided, those who have experience in accounting and bookkeeping would be preferable, for they could follow the evidence and would bring an understanding of how accounts can be manipulated. Self-employed business people who may be vulnerable to employee theft would also prove to be good Crown jurors.

EXAMPLE 4: John Doe is charged with the first-degree murder of his wife, who was killed by a shotgun blast to the face after having been stabbed a number of times. John Doe had cuts to his hands when he was arrested shortly after the killing. He also had gunpowder residue on his hands. He was intoxicated at the time and has two prior convictions for assaulting his wife and one for threatening her with death, which the Crown will attempt to prove as similar fact evidence.

John Doe claims that his wife was killed by two men who entered the house. He claims to have been awakened from his sleep by his wife's screams from downstairs and to have grabbed his shotgun before going to her rescue. He claims that he was jumped as he went downstairs, and the gun was taken from him. He received the cuts defending himself from the assailants. He claims that the intruder who had grabbed the gun shot his wife and then tried to shoot him, but could not as there was only one shell in the magazine. The assailants ran out the door and he called "911." No particular knife can be linked to the stabbing, although household knives could have caused the stab wounds. The gun contains John Doe's prints, and two partial, unidentifiable prints. There are no signs of forced entry and no missing property.

* Most defence counsel agreed that this is a case where male jurors are to be preferred. As Donald Bayne, QC, put it, "The case is full of stereotypes." As for the kind of men, Bayne would prefer older. Michael Edelson was specific, wanting as jurors working-class men who are more likely to be familiar with guns and hunting and who could see themselves attempting to defend their home and family with a firearm. At the same time, it will also be necessary for defence counsel to seek to have some intelligent jurors who can understand the challenges that will be made to the forensic evidence. Pat McCann observed that if the similar fact evidence is likely to go in, it will be especially important to avoid women jurors. By contrast, Edelson felt that the fact that the wife stayed with her husband would go a long way to reducing the impact of the two prior assaults, making women less dangerous as jurors than the stereotypes in the case might suggest.

  The Crown will have less of a challenge selecting jurors but will want to ensure that there are women, particularly of the age of the victim, on the jury. Persons likely to be of apparently peaceable or mild character would be preferred, to the extent that this can be determined on the limited information available.

Example 5: Jane Doe is charged with an aggravated assault against her common law partner, Howard, who lost an eye after he was stabbed by Jane in the face with a pair of scissors. He claims that he was asleep at the time. Jane claims that he had just raped her and told her that he was going to rest for a while and do it again and that she reached for the scissors that were on the night table and used them to defend herself. Jane is twenty-five and has a criminal record for minor property-related offences. Howard is a fifty-one-year-old man, who has had a prior failed marriage. Jane moved in with him when she was nineteen. At the time, she worked for him at an adults-only video rental business he was managing. There is no evidence to corroborate her claim that she has been abused by him since the relationship began.

* Defence counsel indicated that they would attempt to have as many women as possible on this jury. Ideally, Pat McCann would want women who are married or have been divorced. By contrast, Donald Bayne, QC, would prefer younger women, feeling that older women would be riskier. Persons from the helping professions, such as nurses, social workers, and teachers, would make good jurors. Those who seem likely to have feminist leanings should be selected, including those who are likely to be exposed to, and sympathetic to, campaigns against violence against women.

* Michael Edelson would also try to select men of forty or fifty years of age, who might disapprove of the complainant's conduct. He suggested that splitting the jury between younger and older jurors would be a way to hedge one's bets. The younger female jurors may empathize with her, while the younger males might disapprove of his background. Middle-aged women might disapprove of his relationship with this younger, vulnerable employee.

* Crown counsel will have to empanel this jury appreciating that the Crown will be both prosecuting the accused and defending the victim. The Crown will want to ensure that there are middle-aged men on the jury. Counsel may be cautious about jurors who are apt to judge the complainant harshly as a dirty old man, given his occupation and the age difference between him and the complainant. For this reason, middle-aged and elderly women should be avoided. Younger persons, less likely to judge him harshly for these things, might be preferable, particularly younger males.

CHAPTER 11

PEREMPTORY CHALLENGES AND THE *CHARTER*

11.1 INTRODUCTION

* As the preceding chapter revealed, peremptory challenges provide an opportunity for the state to discriminate on the basis of stereotypes and thereby exclude members of the community from serving on juries. For example, in a sexual assault case, the prosecution may decide that it wants as many women jurors as possible, or in a highly racialized case, the prosecution may decide that it does not want any Black jurors. An uncharted area of jury selection in Canada is whether a prosecutor can lawfully use his or her allotted peremptory challenges in a discriminatory fashion so as to remove male and Black jurors in these examples. One argument is that the use of discriminatory peremptory challenges may give rise to a reasonable apprehension of bias. A similar argument was made in a number of cases where the Crown used its stand aside provisions to discriminate on the basis of gender. As will be seen below, given the limited number of peremptory challenges now accorded to the Crown, it is unlikely that this type of argument would now succeed. However, there is a viable argument that the discriminatory use of peremptory challenges violates the equality provisions of section 15(1) of the *Charter*. Both of these arguments are addressed below.

* Both the Supreme Court of Canada and the Ontario Court of Appeal have implied that resort can be made to the *Charter* in this context. In *R.* v. *Bain*,

[1992] 1 S.C.R. 91, Justice Gonthier in a dissenting opinion (but not on this point), Justices McLachlin and Iacobucci concurring, noted (at 132):

> In the United States, it is true, problems have arisen with the use of peremptory challenges by the prosecution to exclude blacks from the jury. In *Batson v. Kentucky*, 476 U.S. 79 (1986), the Supreme Court of the United States has held that in these situations the accused has a recourse against the prosecution if discrimination is proven. Canada has largely been spared these prosecutorial practices, but if they occur, the common law and the *Charter* offer sufficient protection to the accused.

So too in *R.* v. *Biddle* (1993), 14 O.R. (3d) 756 (C.A.), Justice Doherty, for the Court, held that (at 769):

> Exclusion of potential jurors based on their sex may also implicate an accused's rights under s. 15 of the *Charter*: *Batson* v. *Kentucky*, 476 U.S. 79 . . . [1986]. That issue is not before this court.

11.2 THE DISCRIMINATORY USE OF THE STAND-BY PROVISIONS

* Prior to 1992, the *Criminal Code* provided the Crown with the ability to stand by up to forty-eight jurors without having to give a reason. Section 634(1) and (2) read:

> 634.(1) The prosecutor is entitled to challenge four jurors peremptorily, and may direct any number of jurors who are not challenged peremptorily by the accused to stand by until all the jurors have been called who are available for the purpose of trying the indictment.
>
> 634.(2) Notwithstanding subsection (1), the prosecutor may not direct more than forty-eight jurors to stand by unless the presiding judge, for special cause to be shown, so orders.

* In *R.* v. *Bain*, [1992] 1 S.C.R. 91 at 101, the Supreme Court of Canada held that these provisions of the *Criminal Code* violated section 11(d) of the *Charter* because the provisions "would lead a reasonable person, fully apprised of the extensive rights the Crown may exercise in the selection of a jury, to conclude that there was an apprehension of bias." The Court struck down the provisions but suspended the declaration of invalidity to provide Parliament with an opportunity to remedy the situation. Indeed shortly after *Bain*, Parliament passed an amendment to the *Criminal Code* to abolish sections 634(1) and (2): *An Act to amend the Criminal Code (jury)*, S.C. 1992, c. 41, s. 2.

* Prior to *Bain*, the Ontario Court of Appeal was faced with two sexual assault cases where the prosecution had used its stand asides to discriminate on the basis of gender in order to achieve an all-female jury. The issue on these appeals was framed in terms of "reasonable apprehension of bias."

* In *R.* v. *Pizzacalla* (1991), 5 O.R. (3d) 783 (C.A.), the Crown exercised twenty-three stand-asides during the jury selection process, twenty of which he frankly admitted were used to exclude men from the jury. In his submissions to the trial judge on the abuse of process motion that was brought at trial following the selection process, the prosecutor stated (at 784):

> "Yes, your Honour, the selection process is obviously weighted in favour of the Crown, inasmuch as, if the Crown chooses to employ its stand-asides, it can outlast the number of challenges . . . I will concede that most of the challenges I used were directed at keeping men from this jury, and preferring to have women try this particular case. I have tried, in my experience, probably 50 or 100 jury trials involving sexual assaults. I have never before used the option that I used in this case, of attempting to get a jury of all women. This is a case involving sexual harassment in the workplace. In my experience, I was of the view that I might encounter a man or more than one man who felt that, somehow, a person in the workplace has the right to fondle, make passes at, or otherwise touch people in the workplace."

In light of this frank admission by Crown counsel, the Court of Appeal ordered a new trial for the following reasons given by Morden A.C.J.O., for the Court (at 785):

> Counsel for the respondent before us agrees with the appellant's submission that the manner in which Crown counsel exercised the right to stand aside jurors gave "the appearance that the prosecutor secured a favourable jury, rather than simply an impartial one." . . .
>
> On the particular facts of this case, which include Crown counsel's candid statement of his purpose, we agree with this concession. In giving effect to the concession we are not, of course, saying that a jury composed entirely of women, or of men, cannot render an impartial verdict in a case involving an accused person of the opposite sex or in any other case. Our decision is based upon the way in which the jury selection process was used.

* In *R.* v. *Biddle* (1993), 14 O.R. (3d) 756 (C.A.), appeal allowed by the S.C.C. on other grounds, [1995] 1 S.C.R. 761, the trial Crown used twenty-eight of thirty stand-asides to exclude male jurors. However, the appellant did not have the benefit of a similar, frank statement of purpose from trial counsel or a concession from appellate counsel that a new trial was warranted as was the case in *Pizzacalla*. In its decision, the Ontario

Court of Appeal discussed in more detail the concept of "reasonable apprehension of bias." Justice Doherty, for the majority, held (at 768):

> The two judgments constituting the majority in *Bain* took different approaches to its application to cases tried before *Bain* was released. . . . Cory J., for three members of the four-person majority, held that a verdict returned by a jury empanelled under the former provisions of the *Code* could only be set aside if the appellant could demonstrate an "abuse" of the stand-aside provisions by the Crown.: . . . *R.* v. *Sedore*, released June 30, 1992 at pp. 6–11.
>
> Cory J. referred to *R.* v. *Pizzacalla* (1991), 5 O.R. (3d) 783 . . . (C.A.), as an example of a case where the stand-aside provisions had been "abused" by the Crown. In *Pizzacalla* this court looked to the effect of the prosecution's use of its stand asides on the perceived impartiality of the jury ultimately selected. I understand *Pizzacalla* to have applied the well-known reasonable apprehension of bias test in assessing whether the end product of the Crown's use of its stand-aside powers was an impartial or partial jury.
>
> In my view, the "abuse" described by Cory J. in *Bain* refers to both the misuse of the stand-aside power and the resultant negative consequences on the impartiality of the jury selected as a result of that misuse. Consequently in pre-*Bain* cases the court must address the Crown's use of its numerical advantage to shape the composition of the jury, and must also decide whether the jury selected by that process is one which would create a reasonable apprehension of bias in the mind of a reasonable observer.

* In *Biddle*, the Ontario Court of Appeal ultimately held that the prosecution's use of its stand asides to achieve an all-female jury did not rise above the level of unwarranted stereotyping and that the end result did not create a situation whereby a reasonable observer would conclude that an all-female jury would be favourably disposed to find for the Crown. It was also pointed out that trial counsel obviously did not perceive any bias as he did not object during the jury selection process. The court held (at 769–70):

> In this case both victims were women. More importantly, they were victims of the kind of random violence to which women are all too frequently exposed in our society. It is regrettable, but true, that women know all too well, and much better than men, the terror that can be associated with that nightly walk through a lonely parking area to one's apartment or home. Since women are more likely than men to be victims of the type of assault involved in this case, it is understandable that they may be more inclined to see themselves as victims of this kind of assault.
>
> This potential identification by female jurors with the victims should not, however, be overstated. A strong association with the plight of the victim

> does not equate with bias in favour of the prosecution. Any reasonable person would sympathize with these women. They were entirely innocent victims of vicious unprovoked assaults. Any juror would have to be careful not to let sympathy interfere with their objective assessment of the evidence.
>
> This case turned entirely on the question of identification. The victims' honesty was not in issue. The reliability of their identification evidence was very much in issue. I am not prepared to hold, because women may be particularly sensitive to the plight of the victims, that an all-female jury would be unable to objectively assess the reliability of the identification evidence provided by the victims. More to the point, I am not prepared to find that the reasonable, well-informed observer would reasonably apprehend that an all-female jury would be favourably disposed to find for the Crown on the issue of identification.

The Ontario Court of Appeal decision in *Biddle* is criticized by Professor Stuart in his annotation (1993) 24 C.R. (4th) 66–67.

* The appeal in *Biddle* was allowed by the Supreme Court of Canada, but for a different reason, and the majority (Sopinka J. writing for the Chief Justice, La Forest, Cory, Iacobucci, and Major JJ.) did not address the jury selection issue, since in its view, with the abolition of stand asides, the issue would not recur and was therefore of academic interest only: *R.* v. *Biddle*, [1995] 1 S.C.R. 761 at 780.

* Three Supreme Court judges in *Biddle* did, however, comment on the issue of jury selection:

- Justice Gonthier, in a concurring opinion, would have allowed the appeal on the jury selection issue. His Lordship stated (at 788):

  > As I observed in *R. v. Bain*, *supra*, representativeness is a characteristic which furthers the perception of impartiality even if not fully ensuring it. While representativeness is not an essential quality of a jury, it is one to be sought after. The surest guarantee of jury impartiality consists in the combination of the representativeness with the requirement of a unanimous verdict. Consequently, an apparent attempt by the prosecution to modify the composition of the jury so as to exclude representativeness, as occurred in this case, in itself undermines the impartiality of a jury.

- Justice McLachlin, in a concurring opinion, agreed with the majority that there was no need to address the issue of jury selection but decided to write to address the reasons of Justice Gonthier. Her Ladyship held (at 788–89):

  > I agree that representativeness may provide extra assurance of impartiality and competence. I would even go so far as to say that it is generally a good

thing. But I cannot accept that it is essential in every case, nor that its absence automatically entitles an accused person to a new trial. . . .

In the case at bar there is no evidence that the Crown used its stand-by powers to the end of achieving a jury which would be favourable to the Crown. It is at least equally open to infer, . . . that its aim was to secure a jury which would be capable of judging the issues in an impartial and unbiased manner. So the suggestion of deliberate Crown abuse of the system is not made out.

Nor is there any evidence that the jury chosen was, or could reasonably be perceived to be, other than impartial and competent.

- Justice L'Heureux-Dubé, in her dissenting opinion (at 781–84), adopted the reasons of the Court of Appeal. Her Ladyship did, however, agree with the comments of Justice McLachlin cited above, regarding the representativeness of the jury.

* As suggested by Justice Sopinka in *Biddle*, since the Crown no longer has a right to stand jurors aside, the issue of creating a reasonable apprehension of bias is not likely to arise again, since the prosecutor has only a limited number of peremptory challenges. In addition, Parliament has now provided the defence and prosecution with an equal number of peremptory challenges so as to avoid an issue of numerical inequality. Defence counsel should instead turn to section 15(1) of the *Charter*:

11.3 DOES THE *CHARTER* PROHIBIT THE EXERCISE OF DISCRIMINATORY PEREMPTORY CHALLENGES BY THE PROSECUTION?

11.3(a) The Reason for the Inquiry

* In an ideal world, there would be no need to address the issue of the state exercising unconstitutional peremptory challenges in the jury selection process. Prosecutors are not expected to seek a conviction above everything else, and therefore there would be no temptation to engage in discriminatory conduct in an attempt to secure a favourable jury. As the Supreme Court of Canada recognized in *Boucher* v. *R.*, [1955] S.C.R. 16 at 23–24:

> It cannot be over-emphasized that the purpose of a criminal prosecution is not to obtain a conviction, it is to lay before a jury what the Crown considers to be credible evidence relevant to what is alleged to be a crime. Counsel have a duty to see that all available proof of the facts is presented: it should be done firmly and pressed to its legitimate strength but it must also

> be done fairly. The role of prosecutor excludes any notion of winning or losing; his function is a matter of public duty than which in civil life there can be none charged with greater personal responsibility. It is to be efficiently performed with an ingrained sense of the dignity, the seriousness and the justness of judicial proceedings.

See too *Savion* v. *R.* (1980), 13 C.R. (3d) 259 at 275 (Ont. C.A.), and *R.* v. *Stinchcombe*, [1991] 3 S.C.R. 326.

* In *R.* v. *Bain*, [1992] 1 S.C.R. 91, Justice Gonthier, in his dissenting opinion, attempted to use the model of the prosecutor as a quasi-judicial officer of the court in order to justify his opinion that the Crown stand-aside provisions of the *Criminal Code* did not violate section 11(d) of the *Charter* (at 119):

> In keeping with this quasi-judicial role, the Crown prosecutor in the jury selection process has a duty to ensure that the jury presents the three characteristics outlined above, that is impartiality, representativeness and competence. Let it be made clear, however, that these qualities, especially impartiality, must not be sought in light of securing a conviction, but rather in light of selecting the best jury to try the case. Indeed the Crown Attorney should use the means at his or her disposal to exclude prospective jurors that could be biased in favour of the prosecution, even if the defence is not aware of this fact. The "didactic" function that was attached to the peremptory challenge for the accused is absent in the case of the Crown: it does not have to develop any sense of adherence to or acceptance of the trial process through the selection of the jury, and accordingly neither does it have any interest in excluding candidates on the basis of unsupported perceptions. The Crown Attorney's only justification for taking part in the jury selection process stems from his or her responsibilities as a public officer.

In addition, Rule 28 of the *Rules of Professional Conduct* for the Law Society of Upper Canada prohibits lawyers from engaging in discriminatory conduct. Rule 28 states:

> The lawyer has a special responsibility to respect the requirements of human rights law in force in Ontario and specifically to honour the obligation not to discriminate on the grounds of race, ancestry, place of origin, colour, ethnic origin, citizenship, creed, sex, sexual orientation, age, record of offences . . . , marital status, family status or disability with respect to professional employment of other lawyers, articled students, or any other person or in professional dealings with other members of the profession or any other person.

* Unfortunately, experience has shown that sometimes Crown attorneys do in fact abandon their ethical responsibility and quasi-judicial role in the

pursuit of a conviction. Indeed in *R.* v. *Bain*, [1992] 1 S.C.R. 91, the majority of the Supreme Court of Canada struck down the Crown stand-aside provisions out of a concern that they might be on occasion abused by the Crown. Justice Cory, writing for the majority, held (at 101–4):

> At the outset, I would agree that the Crown Attorney plays a very responsible and respected role in the criminal justice system and particularly in the conduct of criminal trials. It is true that the Crown never wins or loses a case. Yet Crown Attorneys are mortal. They are subject to all the emotional and psychological pressures that are exerted by individuals and the community. They may act for the best of motives. For example they may be moved by sympathy for a helpless victim, or by contempt for the cruel and perverted acts of an accused; they may be influenced by the righteous sense of outrage of a community at the commission of a particularly cruel and vicious crime. As a rule the conduct and competence of Crown Attorneys is exemplary. They are models for the bar and the community. *Yet they, like all of us, are subject to human frailties and occasional lapses.*
>
> Crown Attorneys have been known to make inflammatory addresses to the jury. See *R.* v. *Grover*, [1991] 3 S.C.R. 387 . . . They have been known to conduct unfair cross-examinations of parties and witnesses. See *R.* v. *Logiacco* (1984), 11 C.C.C. (3d) 374 (Ont. C.A.) . . . I do not make these observations in order to be critical of Crown Attorneys. Rather they are made to emphasize the very human frailties that are common to all, no matter what the office held. . . .
>
> *It is suggested that the Crown Attorney, as an officer of the Court would never act unfairly in the selection of a jury. Yet the most exemplary Crown might be so overwhelmed by a community pressure that just such a step might be taken. In* R. v. Pizzacalla (1991), 5 O.R. (3d) 783 . . . *it was conceded that as a result of the use made by the Crown attorney of the stand by provisions in the selection of a jury an apprehension of bias was created. I have cited this case not to illustrate or emphasize a legal principle but rather for what it demonstrates. Namely, that those acting for the Crown do, on occasion, demonstrate human frailties and that the impugned section is, on occasion, utilized for the improper purpose of obtaining a jury that appears to be favourable to the Crown.*
>
> A petition is frequently made that we not be led into temptation. The impugned provision of the *Criminal Code* provides the tempting means to obtain a jury that appears to be favourable to the Crown. . . .
>
> *Unfortunately it would seem that whenever the Crown is granted statutory power that can be used abusively then, on occasion, it will indeed be used abusively. The protection of basic rights should not be dependent upon a reliance on the continuous exemplary conduct of the Crown, something that is impossible to monitor or control. Rather the offending statutory provision should be removed.* [Emphasis added.]

* Similarly, it may be necessary to resort to the *Charter* in order to remove the temptation to discriminate that section 634(1) of the *Criminal Code* provides through the exercise of peremptory challenges.

11.3(b) **The Nature of the Inquiry**

* In considering whether the *Charter* limits the ability of prosecutors to exercise peremptory challenges, it is important to note that there is no need to challenge the constitutional validity of section 634(1) of the *Criminal Code* pursuant to section 52(1) of the *Constitution Act*, 1982. Section 634(1) states:

> A juror may be challenged peremptorily whether or not the juror has been challenged for cause pursuant to section 638.

* The *Charter* challenge is to the manner in which the challenge is being exercised, not to the legislation. As such, it is not necessary to file a notice of a constitutional question or provide notice to the Attorney General of Canada.

* In *Slaight Communications Inc.* v. *Davidson*, [1989] 1 S.C.R. 1038 at 1078–80, Chief Justice Lamer, writing for the majority on this point, held:

> As the Constitution is the supreme law of Canada and any law that is inconsistent with its provisions is, to the extent of the inconsistency, of no force or effect, it is impossible to interpret legislation conferring discretion as conferring a power to infringe the *Charter*, unless, of course, the power is expressly conferred or necessarily implied. Such an interpretation would require us to declare the legislation to be of no force and effect, unless it could be justified under s. 1. Although this Court must not add anything to legislation or delete anything from it in order to make it consistent with the *Charter*, there is no doubt in my mind that it should also not interpret legislation that is open to more than one interpretation so as to make it inconsistent with the *Charter* and hence of no force or effect. Legislation conferring an imprecise discretion must therefore be interpreted as not allowing the *Charter* rights to be infringed. . . .
>
> [Therefore] [t]he application of . . . [this principle] to the exercise of a discretion leads to one of the following two situations:
>
> 1. The . . . [action] was made pursuant to legislation which confers, either expressly or by necessary implication, the power to infringe a protected right.
>   — It is then necessary to subject the <u>legislation</u> to the test set out in s. 1 by ascertaining whether it constitutes a reasonable limit that can be demonstrably justified in a free and democratic society.

> 2. The legislation . . . confers an imprecise discretion and does not confer, either expressly or by necessary implication, the power to limit the rights guaranteed by the *Charter*,
> — It is then necessary to subject the [action] . . . to the test set out in s. 1 by ascertaining whether it constitutes a reasonable limit that can be demonstrably justified in a free and democratic society. . . .

See also *Dagenais* v. *Canadian Broadcasting Corp.*, [1994] 3 S.C.R. 835 at 878; *Canadian Broadcasting Corp.* v. *New Brunswick (A.G.)*, [1996] 3 S.C.R. 480 ("a discretionary power cannot confer the power to infringe the *Charter*").

11.3(c) Race-Based Peremptory Challenges

* Historically, peremptory challenges have been used to exclude Blacks from serving on juries in the United States (see the discussion below) and quite probably in Canada as well. As Professor Henry of York University notes in M. Henry & F. Henry, "A Challenge to Discriminatory Justice: The Parks Decision in Perspective" (1996) 38 Crim. L.Q. 333 at 337–38:

> Peremptory challenges have . . . often been used to limit the number of blacks on juries. . . . The practice of excusing or challenging prospective minority jurors without good reason and without requiring counsel to be accountable for their actions is very problematic in a racially stratified and intolerant society.
>
> Blacks are challenged more often by the Crown prosecutor when the accused is black and by the defence when the victim is black.[1] These trends reflect the rational[e] that accepts the notion that all persons who share an attribute, such as skin colour, will *ipso facto* view matters in the same way, and that minority groups are less able than whites to decide the case solely on its evidence. Clearly, these challenges are symptomatic of racist beliefs about the impartiality of black jurors and the role of race in decision-making. . . .
>
> These systematic and systemic biases in the broader society and within jury selection methods result in potential jurors from diverse backgrounds being effectively screened out of jury duty.

* Consequently, we have decided to address the issue of the effect of the *Charter* on peremptory challenges from the perspective of race-based challenges. However, a similar argument could be made with respect to any of the enumerated grounds under section 15(1) of the *Charter*.

---

1 Citing D. Hanratty, "Moving Closer to Eliminating Discrimination in Jury Selection: Challenge to the Peremptory" (1989) 7 J. Human Rights at 204.

* Notwithstanding Dr. Henry's observation, some may question whether there is a need to consider race-based peremptory challenges. Indeed, some may take the position articulated by one general division judge in Ontario:

> I strongly disagree with those who allege there is a systemic discrimination and racism in the court system in Ontario. There will always be anecdotal evidence to this effect, but the hard evidence is exactly to the contrary. My extensive experience is that judges, lawyers and court personnel treat all people coming into conflict with the law in the same way.

Report of the Commission on Systemic Racism in the Ontario Criminal Justice System (Toronto: Queen's Printer, 1995) at 222.

* However, this observation is simply inconsistent with the findings of social scientists and courts and with the concerns of the state. The findings of the *Report of the Commission on Systemic Racism in the Ontario Criminal Justice System* (Toronto: Queen's Printer, 1995) at ii, 59, 250–51 reveal:

> . . . [R]acism continues in practices that affect the lives and opportunities of people in Ontario.
>
> . . . [R]acism is still entrenched in Canadian society. The Aboriginal Justice Inquiry in Manitoba, the Donald Marshall Inquiry in Nova Scotia, the *Caswey Report* in Alberta, . . . and many other studies make the same point: racism in Canadian society continues to shape the lives of Aboriginal, black and other racialized people. . . .
>
> Many black and other racialized persons perceive members of their communities as under-represented on juries. . . . Specifically, participants stressed that under-representation on juries trying racialized accused persons or "high-profile" white accused — such as police officers — who have killed or injured a racialized victim tend to promote distrust in the system. . . .
>
> Findings from the Commission's general population survey of 417 black, 435 white and 405 Chinese residents of Metropolitan Toronto, though by no means conclusive, support the perception that black people are under-represented on Ontario juries. No black residents reported having served on a jury. By contrast, 10 white and 5 Chinese residents reported that they had served on a jury.

In addition, the Ontario Court of Appeal in *R.* v. *Parks* (1993), 15 O.R. (3d) 324 (C.A.), leave to appeal refused (1994), 28 C.R. (4th) 403n (S.C.C.) recognized and gave explicit recognition to the fact that (at 338, 341, & 342):

> There is . . . an ever-growing body of studies and reports documenting the extent and intensity of racist beliefs in contemporary Canadian society. Many deal with racism in general, others with racism directed at black persons.

> These materials lend support to counsel's submission that widespread anti-black racism is a grim reality in Canada and in particular in Metropolitan Toronto. . . .
>
> The present Government of Ontario accepts that racism, and particularly systemic racism, is a real and pressing problem. It has committed substantial resources aimed at studying, exposing and eradicating racism, especially within the criminal justice system. It is somewhat ironic, given the present policy of the Government, and the far-reaching measures it has taken, that counsel for the Crown should at the same time take the position that the very brief inquiry proposed by counsel in this case was unnecessary.
>
> . . . Racism, and in particular anti-black racism, is part of our community's psyche. A significant segment of our community holds overtly racist views. A much larger segment subconsciously operates on the basis of negative racial stereotypes. *Furthermore, our institutions, including the criminal justice system, reflect and perpetuate those negative stereotypes. These elements combine to infect our society as a whole with the evil of racism. Blacks are among the primary victims of that evil.* [Emphasis added.]

Moreover, according to D. Pomerant, *Multiculturalism, Representation and the Jury Selection Process in Canadian Criminal Cases* (Working Document) (Ottawa: Department of Justice, 1994) at 6, in 1992 the Attorney General of Ontario

> announced that Ontario would review the jury selection process, to ensure that jury panels include all members of society and to eliminate any possibility of excluding visible minorities from jury service in criminal trials. *The Attorney General also called on the federal government to review the entire jury selection process in criminal cases, including the ability of jurors to be disqualified by counsel for other than valid reasons.* [Emphasis added.]

See too the Nova Scotia, *Royal Commission on the Donald Marshall, Jr., Prosecution Report: Findings and Recommendations*, vol. 1 (Halifax: Queen's Printer, 1989) at 177, and Manitoba Aboriginal Justice Inquiry, *The Justice System and Aboriginal People* (Winnipeg: Queen's Printer, 1991), which also raise concern about the Crown's use of discriminatory peremptory challenges (cited in K. Roach, "Challenges for Cause and Racial Discrimination" (1995) 37 Crim. L.Q. 410 at 422.)

11.3(d) **Section 15(1) of the *Charter***

* In Canada, as in the United States, the equality rights provisions in section 15(1) do not guarantee an accused a jury of his or her peers: *R.* v. *Kent* (1986), 27 C.C.C. (3d) 405 (Man. C.A.). However, it is suggested that sec-

tion 15(1) and to a lesser extent sections 7 and 11(d) of the *Charter* offer protection from the discriminatory use of peremptory challenges by the prosecution as a matter of principle and policy.

* It is possible to frame a constitutional argument in the following manner:

  • the use of peremptory challenges in a discriminatory fashion violates the equality right of the accused where the discrimination is a consequence of the race or other characteristic of the accused;
  • the use of race-based peremptory challenges violates the equality right of the excluded juror; and
  • there is a principle of fundamental justice protected by sections 7 and 11(d), which recognizes the right of the accused and indeed society to a trier of fact that is selected in a non-discriminatory fashion.

11.3(d)(i) **Section 15(1): The Equality Right of the Accused**

* Section 15(1) of the *Charter* states:

> 15.(1) Every individual is equal before and under the law and has the right to the equal protection and equal benefit of the law without discrimination and, in particular, without discrimination based on race, national or ethnic origin, colour, religion, sex, age or mental or physical disability.

* Section 15(1) speaks of equality in terms of "law." This raises the question of whether section 15(1) applies only to the enabling law (i.e., section 634(1) of the *Criminal Code*) or equally to the discretion that the law provides for. It is now settled that the term "law" applies not only to a statutory provision but also to the "exercise by government of a statutory power or discretion": *McKinney* v. *University of Guelph*, [1990] 3 S.C.R. 229 at 276, LaForest J., for the majority. See too P.W. Hogg, *Constitutional Law in Canada*, 3d ed. (Toronto: Carswell, 1992) at 11-56–57. This marks a shift from an earlier *obiter* comment in *R.* v. *S.(S.)*, [1990] 2 S.C.R. 254.

* Does the exercise of race-based peremptory challenges restrict section 15(1) rights? The Supreme Court of Canada has applied a number of different approaches to the analysis of section 15. Recently, in *Benner* v. *Secretary of State* (27 February 1997), (S.C.C.) [not yet reported], Iacobucci J. describes at least three approaches that are being currently employed by different members of the Court. Sometimes the analysis is described as a two-step approach. In other cases a three-step approach is defined. All of

them have in common, however, the features described in the following threefold approach to section 15(1) inquiries:

(i) has there been a denial of one of the four equality rights protected under s. 15(1) (i.e. equality before and under the law and the equal protection and benefit of the law) as a result of a distinction made or based on a personal characteristic of the individual?

(ii) does the denial result in "discrimination"? In *Andrews* v. *Law Society of British Columbia*, [1989] 1 S.C.R. 143 at 174, the Supreme Court of Canada offered the following definition of discrimination:

> I would say then that discrimination may be described as a distinction, whether intentional or not but based on grounds relating to personal characteristics of the individual or group, which has the effect of imposing burdens, obligations or disadvantages on such individual or group not imposed upon others, or which withholds or limits access to opportunities, benefits and advantages available to other members of society.

(iii) does the personal characteristic fall within one of the enumerated or analogous grounds so as to ensure that the "claim fits within the overall purpose of s. 15 — namely, to remedy or prevent discrimination against groups subject to stereotyping, historical disadvantage and political and social prejudice in Canadian society"? (*R.* v. *Swain*, [1991] 1 S.C.R. 933 at 992, Lamer C.J)

Andrews v. *Law Society of British Columbia*, [1989] 1 S.C.R. 143 at 174, McIntyre J.
R. v. *Swain*, [1991] 1 S.C.R. 933 at 992, Lamer C.J
Rodriguez v. *British Columbia (A.G)*, [1993] 3 S.C.R. 519, Lamer C.J.
Symes v. *M.N.R.*, [1993] 4 S.C.R. 695, Iacobucci J.
Miron v. *Trudel*, [1995] 2 S.C.R. 418, McLachlin J.

* Race-based peremptory challenges appear to meet this threefold test. Race-based challenges tend to be premised on unfounded stereotypes (i.e., a Black juror may be partial towards a Black accused.) As Professor Henry notes, race-based challenges

> reflect the rational[e] that accepts the notion that all persons who share an attribute, such as skin colour, will *ipso facto* view matters in the same way, and that minority groups are less able than whites to decide the case solely on its evidence. Clearly, these challenges are symptomatic of racist beliefs about the impartiality of black jurors and the role of race in decision-making. . . .

M. Henry & F. Henry, "A Challenge to Discriminatory Justice: The Parks Decision in Perspective" (1996) 38 Crim. L.Q. 333 at 337–38.

When persons of the same race as the accused are challenged because of their race, the accused is denied the equal benefit of the law as he or she is denied both an opportunity for a representative jury and the right to have a jury selected in a non-discriminatory fashion, simply because of an ascribed personal characteristic (i.e., his or her race), which is an enumerated ground in section 15(1).

11.3(d)(ii) **Section 15(1): The Equality Right of the Juror**

* In the alternative, section 15(1) may be available to a racialized juror who is challenged simply because of his or her race. Where this happens, the juror is denied an opportunity to sit as a juror because of discriminatory state action. Since it is impracticable to expect the juror to raise this challenge, it is arguable that the accused should be granted standing in order to litigate the issue on behalf of the struck juror.

* In a quartet of cases, the Supreme Court of Canada set out the following test as to when an individual should be entitled to enforce the constitutional right of another person:

(i) there is a serious question of law to be addressed;
(ii) the accused has a genuine interest in the determination of the question; and
(iii) there is no other reasonable and effective manner in which the question may be brought before the Court.

Thorson v. *Canada (A.G.) (No. 2) (1974)*, [1975] 1 S.C.R. 138
McNeil v. *Nova Scotia (Board of Censors)*, [1976] 2 S.C.R. 265
Canada (A.G.) v. *Borowski*, [1981] 2 S.C.R. 575 at 598
Finlay v. *Canada (Minister of Finance)*, [1986] 2 S.C.R. 607

* All three prongs of the standing test appear to be met in this context. First, whether a juror's equality right has been violated by the actions of the Crown is a serious and important question of law. Second, an accused has a genuine interest in the determination of this question, as he or she wishes to have a representative jury as well as a jury that is selected in a non-discriminatory fashion. Finally, there is no other reasonable and effective manner in which the question may be determined by a court, since it is not likely that a challenged juror will hire a lawyer and seek redress.

* In addition, it is a well-established principle that an accused is entitled to challenge the constitutionality of a law under which he or she is charged even if unaffected by its unconstitutional effects: *R.* v. *DeSousa*, [1992] 2 S.C.R. 944; *R.* v. *Hess*, [1990] 2 S.C.R. 906 at 945, McLachlin J., dissenting but not on this point; *R.* v. *Morgentaler*, [1988] 1 S.C.R. 30; *R.* v. *Smith*,

[1987] 1 S.C.R. 1045; *R.* v. *Big M Drug Mart Ltd.*, [1985] 1 S.C.R. 295. The policy reason for this exception to the standing rule is that "[a] person should not be convicted under an invalid law": *R.* v. *Hess*, [1990] 2 S.C.R. 906 at 945. While a challenge to the prosecutor's exercise of its peremptory challenges is not a challenge to the charging law, it is a challenge to the manner in which the trier of fact will be selected. Arguably, the same considerations should apply in these circumstances as well. In other words, an accused person should not be convicted by a jury that was selected in an unconstitutional manner.

* But see now *R.* v. *Church of Scientology of Toronto and Jacqueline Matz* (1997), 33 O.R. (3d) 65 (C.A.), where the Court of Appeal held that an accused could not litigate the section 15(l) right of an excluded potential juror. In *Scientology*, while the Court of Appeal addressed the standing issue in terms of the *Big M Drug Mart* argument noted above, it did not consider the quartet of standing cases noted above, and for this reason the authority of the case may be diminished outside Ontario. See the criticism of *Scientology* discussed above at 1.4(c)(i).

* A more liberal standing doctrine has developed in the United States in this context: see *Batson* v. *Kentucky*, 476 U.S. 79 (1986), and *Powers* v. *Ohio*, 499 U.S. 400 (1991), discussed above at 1.4(c)(i).

11.3(d)(iii) Sections 7 and 11(d): The Right to Have a Jury Selected in a Non-discriminatory Fashion

* Section 7 of the *Charter* states:

> Everyone has the right to life, liberty and security of the person and the right not to be deprived thereof except in accordance with the principles of fundamental justice.

In the seminal section 7 case of *Reference Re s. 94(2) of the Motor Vehicle Act (British Columbia)*, [1985] 2 S.C.R. 486 at 503, Lamer J., as he then was, held that "the principles of fundamental justice are to be found in the basic tenets of our legal system." It seems clear that a fundamental tenet of Canada's criminal justice system is that the jury must be picked in a non-discriminatory fashion. As the Supreme Court recognized in *R.* v. *Sherratt*, [1991] 1 S.C.R. 509 at 524:

> The modern jury was not meant to be a tool in the hands of either the Crown or the accused and indoctrinated as such through the challenge procedure, but rather was envisioned as a representative cross-section of society, honestly and fairly chosen. Any other vision may run counter to the very rationales underlying the existence of such a body. . . . Increasingly, . . . many countries have since repealed property, sex and race qualifications for

> jurors and have legislated other expansions in the number of citizens eligible for jury duty.

So too in the United States, in *J.E.B.* v. *Alabama*, 114 S.Ct. 1419 (1994), the U.S. Supreme Court recognized (at 1427) that:

> Discrimination in jury selection, whether based on race or on gender, causes harm to the litigants, the community, and the individual jurors who are wrongfully excluded from participation in the judicial process. The litigants are harmed by the risk that the prejudice which motivated the discriminatory selection of the jury will infect the entire proceedings. . . . The community is harmed by the State's participation in the perpetuation of invidious group stereotypes and the inevitable loss of confidence in our judicial system that state-sanctioned discrimination in the courtroom engenders.

Consequently, the exercise of race-based peremptory challenges by the prosecution may restrict a fundamental principle of justice — that juries should be selected in a non-discriminatory fashion.

* In addition, the discriminatory use of peremptory challenges alters the representative nature of the jury, which may affect its ability to be impartial and carry out its functions as required by section 11(d) of the *Charter*. As Justice L'Heureux-Dubé held in *R.* v. *Sherratt*, [1991] 1 S.C.R. 509 at 525:

> The perceived importance of the *Charter* right to a jury trial is meaningless without some guarantee that it will perform its duties impartially and represent, as far as is possible and appropriate in the circumstances, the larger community. *Indeed, without the two characteristics of impartiality and representativeness, a jury would be unable to perform properly many of the functions that make its existence desirable in the first place.* [Emphasis added.]

And as Justice Doherty recognized in *R.* v. *Parks* (1993), 15 O.R. (3d) 324 at 342 (C.A.):

> The "diffused impartiality" produced by the melding of 12 diverse and individual perspectives into a single decision-making body may also counter personal prejudices.

Consequently, a potential claim may arise under section 11(d) of the *Charter*, which guarantees that:

> Any person charged with an offence has the right . . . to be presumed innocent until proven guilty according to law in a fair and public hearing by an independent and impartial tribunal.

And see now *R.* v. *Church of Scientology of Toronto and Jacqueline Matz* (1997), 33 O.R. (3d) 65 (C.A.), where the Court of Appeal held that

> [t]he right to a representative jury roll is also a means of ensuring impartiality. Exclusion of identifiable groups from the jury panel on the basis, for example, of race or religion casts doubt on the integrity of the process and risks the creation of the appearance of bias, thereby possibly violating an accused's right under s. 11(d) to trial by an independent and impartial tribunal.

11.3(d)(iv) **Section 1**

* Section 1 of the *Charter* states that:

> The *Canadian Charter of Rights and Freedoms* guarantees the rights and freedoms set out in it subject only to such reasonable limits prescribed by law as can be demonstrably justified in a free and democratic society.

* It is unlikely that the prosecution can turn to section 1 of the *Charter* in an attempt to justify the exercise of race-based peremptory challenges. The only objective of discriminating in the exercise of peremptory challenges is an attempt by the *Crown* to obtain a favourable jury. This is not the kind of objective that *R.* v. *Oakes*, [1986] 1 S.C.R. 103 contemplated as of sufficient importance to override a constitutionally protected right.

11.3(e) **What Should the Test Be for Identifying a *Charter* Breach?**

* Assuming that section 15(1) (and/or sections 7 and 11(d)) preclude race-based peremptory challenges, what test should be formulated in order to ensure that these *Charter* rights are protected? It is suggested that resort to the American experience provides a useful model.

11.3(e)(i) **The American Experience: *Batson* v. *Kentucky***

* In *Batson* v. *Kentucky*, 476 U.S. 79 at 85 & 86 (1986), the United States Supreme Court held that the Equal Protection Clause of the Fourteenth Amendment of the U.S. Constitution precludes the use of peremptory challenges in a discriminatory fashion. The issue in *Batson* was the peremptory challenge of Black jurors by the prosecutor. At trial, the prosecutor had used his peremptory challenges to strike all four Black persons on the jury panel. As a result, Batson was tried by an all-white jury. The U.S. Supreme Court held that while an accused has "no right to a 'petit jury composed in whole or in part of persons of his

own race,'" the "defendant does have the right to be tried by a jury whose members are selected pursuant to nondiscriminatory criteria."[2]

* Following *Batson*, the U.S. Supreme Court has held that the *Batson* principles concerning discriminatory peremptory challenges apply:

- irrespective of the race of the accused: *Powers* v. *Ohio*, 499 U.S. 400 (1991) [white accused];
- irrespective of whether the challenge came from the prosecution or defence: *Georgia* v. *McCollum*, 505 U.S. 42 (1992). On this topic see the scholarly paper of K. Goldwasser, "Limiting a Criminal Defendant's Use of Peremptory Challenges: On Symmetry and the Jury in a Criminal Trial" (1989) 102 Harv. L. Rev. 808;
- in both criminal and civil trials: *Edmonson* v. *Leesville Concrete Co.*, 500 U.S. 614 (1991);
- to challenges based on gender: *J.E.B.* v. *Alabama*, 114 S. Ct. 1419 (1994).

* In a post-*Batson* case, the U.S. Supreme Court further held that the individual juror also has a stake in the process and an equal protection right to "jury selection procedures that are free from state-sponsored group stereotypes rooted in, and reflective, of historical prejudice." The Court held:

> In recent cases we have emphasized that individual jurors themselves have a right to nondiscriminatory jury selection procedures. . . . All persons, when granted the opportunity to serve on the jury, have the right not to be excluded summarily because of discriminatory and stereotypical presumptions that reflect and reinforce patterns of historical discrimination. . . . Equal opportunity to participate in the fair administration of justice is fundamental to our democratic system. It not only furthers the goals of the jury system. It reaffirms the promise of equality under the law — that all citizens, regardless of race, ethnicity, or gender, have the chance to take part directly in our democracy. [Footnotes omitted.]

J.E.B. v. *Alabama*, 114 S. Ct. 1419 at 1427–28, & 1430 (1994).

---

2 *Batson* has spawned an industry of articles including the following: B.D. Underwood, "Ending Race Discrimination in Jury Selection: Whose Right Is It, Anyway?" (1992) 92 Colum. L. Rev. 725; A.W. Alschuler, "The Supreme Court and the Jury: Voir Dire, Peremptory Challenges and the Review of Jury Verdicts" (1989) 56 U. Chi. L. Rev. 153; J.R. Acker, "Exercising Peremptory Challenges After Batson" (1988) 24 Crim. L. Bull. 187; B.J. Serr & M. Maney, "Racism, Peremptory Challenges, and the Democratic Jury: The Jurisprudence of a Delicate Balance" (1988) 70 J. Crim. L. & Crim. 1.

* Under *Batson*, the defence is required to establish a *prima facie* case of purposeful discrimination by pointing to relevant circumstances that raise an inference that the prosecution has used a peremptory challenge to exclude members of a particular race. Following the showing of a *prima facie* case, the onus then shifts to the prosecution, which must establish a race-neutral reason for the challenge. The prosecutor must "articulate a neutral explanation related to the particular case to be tried." The explanation must be "clear and reasonably specific:" *Batson* v. *Kentucky*, 476 U.S. 79 at 98, n. 20 (1986).

* It has been suggested that while the state need not articulate a reason rising to the level of cause, it must nevertheless "show a genuine and reasonable ground for believing that a prospective juror might have an individual or personal bias that would make excusing him or her rational and desirable": *New Jersey* v. *Gilmore*, 489 A.2d 1175 at 1186 (N.J.S.C. 1985).[3]

11.3(e)(ii) **Establishing a *Prima Facie* Case**

* The burden of establishing a *prima facie* case should not be a heavy one. Given both the individual and the societal interests at stake, courts should err on the side of the accused's right to have a jury selected in a non-discriminatory fashion and the juror's right not to be discriminated against when deciding whether a *prima facie* case has been established: E. Krauss & B. Bonora, eds., *Jurywork: Systematic Techniques*, 2d ed. (Deerfield, Ill.: Clark Boardman Callaghan, 1983). A *prima facie* case is established where the accused can point to circumstances that demonstrate a reasonable likelihood that jurors are being excluded because of group membership: *Batson v. Kentucky*, 476 U.S. 79 (1986).

* The authors of *Jurywork: Systematic Techniques* point out the following factors that have proven the most significant in establishing a *prima facie* case:

  - number and pattern of strikes
  - heterogeneity of the challenged jurors

  The inquiry here is whether the challenged jurors share only one characteristic (i.e., race)?

---

3 A number of states adopted the reasoning in *Batson* as a matter of state constitutional law prior to its being decided in 1986 by the U.S. Supreme Court. See, for example, *People* v. *Wheeler*, 148 Cal. Rptr. 890 (S.C. 1978) and *Commonwealth* v. *Soares*, 387 N.E.2d 499 (Mass. S.C. 1979).

- the nature of *voir dire* responses

  For example, in *People* v. *Allen & Graham*, 152 Cal. Rptr. 454 (S.C. 1979), and *People* v. *Turner*, 230 Cal. Rptr. 656 (S.C. 1986), the *voir dire* records revealed that a number of Black jurors excused by the prosecution had friends or relatives in law enforcement. The *Turner* court, in reversing the conviction held (at 660): "[the excluded Black] jurors had backgrounds which suggested that, had they been white, the prosecution would not have peremptorily excused them."

- group membership of the trial participants

  Cases have suggested that the race of the accused, victim, witnesses, the nature of the crime are factors to consider. See *U.S.* v. *Clemons*, 843 F.2d 741 at 748 (3d Cir. 1988); *People* v. *Turner*, 230 Cal. Rptr. 656 at 860 (S.C. 1986); *Commonwealth* v. *Robinson*, 415 N.E.2d 805 at 810 (Mass. S.C. 1981).

- nature of the *voir dire* questioning
- prior peremptory challenge abuses by counsel
- proffered explanation prematurely volunteered

See, generally, E. Krauss & B. Bonora, eds., *Jurywork: Systematic Techniques*, vol. 1, 2d ed. (Deerfield, Ill.: Clark Boardman Callaghan, 1983) at 4-26 to 4-35.

* The most direct manner in which an accused can establish a *prima facie* case is to show a "pattern" of peremptory challenges against individuals of a particular group: *Batson* v. *Kentucky*, 476 U.S. 79 at 97 (1986). However, in some cases, a *prima facie* case has been established based on the exercise of only one peremptory challenge. For example, the Third Circuit in *U.S. v. Clemons*, 843 F.2d 741 (3d Cir. 1988) held (at 747):

> Striking a single black juror could constitute a *prima facie* case even when blacks ultimately sit on the panel and even when valid reasons exist for striking other blacks. See *U.S.* v. *Gordon*, 817 F.2d 1538, 1541 . . .

See also *U.S.* v. *Chinchilla*, 874 F.2d 695 at 697 (9th Cir. 1989); *U.S.* v. *Iron Moccasin*, 878 F.2d 226 at 228–229 (8th Cir. 1989); *U.S.* v. *Roan Eagle*, 867 F.2d 436 at 441 (8th Cir. 1989); *U.S.* v. *Clemons*, 843 F.2d 741 at 747 (3d Cir. 1988); *Commonwealth* v. *DiMatteo*, 427 N.E.2d 754 at 757 (Mass. App. Ct. 1981); *U.S.* v. *Gordon*, 817 F.2d 1538 at 1541 (11th Cir. 1987); *U.S.* v. *Horsley*, 864 F.2d 1543 (11th Cir. 1989).

The authors of *Jurywork* provide the following summary of the case law regarding patterns of peremptory challenges:

> A *prima facie* case has been established based on the exercise of as few as two or three peremptory challenges against group members, and, occasionally, on the basis of a single challenge. A *prima facie* case has been established on the basis of as few as three of six peremptory challenges against group members, and denied on the basis of as many as six of seven challenges against group members. Courts are divided on whether challenges to fifty percent, or even seventy-five percent, of group members will suffice to establish a *prima facie* case.
>
> The higher the percentage of group members challenged, particularly in relation to the percentage of non-group members challenged, the greater the inference of discrimination. The higher the percentage of peremptory challenges used against group members in comparison to non-group members, the greater the inference of discrimination, although this particular comparison is generally not accorded much weight. It has even been suggested that consideration be given to the percentage of group members in the venire, or the percentage of group members in the population of the district from which the jury is drawn.

E. Krauss & B. Bonora, eds., *Jurywork: Systematic Techniques*, vol. 1, 2d ed. (Deerfield, Ill.: Clark Boardman Callaghan, 1983) at 4-28 to 4-30

* In Canada, given the limited inquiry that is allowed of potential jurors, the establishment of a *prima facie* case will depend largely on such factors as

- The number of peremptory challenges used to exclude members of a particular group.
- The number of group members in the jury panel. For example, if there is only one member of a group in the panel and he or she is struck, it is submitted that a strong inference of discrimination exists.

See, for example, *U.S.* v. *Chinchilla*, 874 F.2d 695 at 697 (9th Cir. 1989); *U.S.* v. *Clemons*, 843 F.2d 741 at 748 (3d Cir. 1988); *Commonwealth* v. *DiMatteo*, 427 N.E.2d 754 at 757 (Mass. App. Ct. 1981); *U.S.* v. *Roan Eagle*, 867 F.2d 436 (8th Cir. 1989); *U.S.* v. *Horsley*, 864 F.2d 1543 (11th Cir. 1989).

- the nature of the case (i.e., whether there are any racial overtones to the crime, the race of the accused, witnesses, and victim).

11.4 IS THE DEFENCE PRECLUDED BY SECTION 15(1) FROM USING ITS PEREMPTORY CHALLENGES IN A DISCRIMINATORY FASHION?

* The foregoing discussion leads logically to the question of whether section 15(1) of the *Charter* equally limits the ability of the defence in the exercise of its allotted peremptory challenges.

* The argument has been made that while an accused has a right to a jury that is selected in a non-discriminatory fashion, so does society at large, and that the administration of justice would be brought into disrepute if an acquittal was won through jury selection that was conducted in a racist fashion. It is argued that the section 15 right belongs equally, if not more, to the individual juror. A juror who has been struck because of his or her colour will not likely go home less stigmatized because it was the defence exercising the challenge rather than the prosecution. See D.M. Tanovich, "Rethinking Jury Selection: Challenges for Cause and Peremptory Challenges" (1994) 30 C.R. (4th) 310 at 329–30. In *Georgia* v. *McCollum*, 505 U.S. 42 (1992), Justice Blackman, for the majority, held (at 49–50):

  > "Be it at the hands of the State or the defense," if a court allows jurors to be excluded because of group bias, "[i]t is [a] willing participant in a scheme that could only undermine the very foundation of our system of justice — our citizens' confidence in it."

  The Court held further that "[t]he exercise of a peremptory challenge differs significantly from other actions taken in support of a defendant's defense" because "[i]n exercising a peremptory challenge, a criminal defendant is wielding the power to choose a quintessential governmental body." The U.S. Supreme Court in *McCollum* was not persuaded that an accused's right to a fair trial, right to counsel, or right to an impartial jury included a right to discriminate.

* There are a number of problems with any attempt to extend section 15(1) of the *Charter* to limit the defence's ability to select a jury. Section 32(1) confines the *Charter* to state action. It provides:

  > This Charter applies
  >
  > (*a*) to the Parliament and government of Canada in respect of all matters within the authority of Parliament including all matters relating to the Yukon Territory and Northwest Territories; and
  >
  > (*b*) to the legislature and government of each province in respect of all matters within the authority of the legislature of each province.

The state action doctrine was developed by the Supreme Court of Canada in *R.W.D.S.U.* v. *Dolphin Delivery Ltd.*, [1986] 2 S.C.R. 573, where McIntyre J., for the Court, held that the *Charter*, by virtue of section 32, was limited in its application to Parliament and the legislatures and to the executive and administrative branches of government. In *McKinney* v. *University of Guelph*, [1990] 3 S.C.R. 229 at 261–62, Justice La Forest held: "This Court has repeatedly drawn attention to the fact that the *Charter* is essentially an instrument for checking the powers of government over the individual. . . . The exclusion of private activity from the *Charter* was not a result of happenstance. It was a deliberate choice which must be respected. . . . To open all private and public action to judicial review could strangle the operation of society . . ." Since the defence is not part of government and therefore not a state actor, its actions in exercising a peremptory challenge will not trigger section 32 of the *Charter*, unless the *McCollum* theory that participation in selecting a government body involves state action is accepted.

* Fairness may also dictate forgoing the extension of section 15(1) to defence challenges. As Justice O'Connor noted in *J.E.B.* v. *Alabama*, 114 S. Ct. 1419 at 1432–33 (1994):

> The peremptory challenge is "'one of the most important of the rights secured to the *accused*.'" . . . Limiting the accused's use of the peremptory is a "serious misordering of our priorities," for it means "we have exalted the right of citizens to sit on juries over the rights of the criminal defendant, even though it is the defendant, not the jurors, who faces imprisonment or even death." . . . Will we, in the name of fighting gender discrimination, hold that the battered wife — on trial for wounding her abusive husband — is a state actor? Will we preclude her from using her peremptory challenges to ensure that the jury of her peers contains as many women members as possible? I assume we will, but I hope we will not.

Similarly, in *R.* v. *Lines* (13 April 1993), (Ont. Gen. Div.) [unreported] where the prosecution sought to prohibit the defence from exercising race-based peremptory challenges, Justice Hawkins held:

> In my view, this motion can not be determined without deciding whether the accused, or his counsel, in exercising a peremptory challenge, is acting as an agent of the state. In a criminal trial the accused is pitted against the state. In my opinion it is fanciful to suggest that in the selection of a jury he doffs his adversarial role and joins the Crown in some sort of joint and concerted effort to empanel an independent and impartial tribunal. If the adversary system is thought to be the best method of discovering the truth, why must it be abandoned at the threshold of the trial in the jury selection process?

* Finally, a racialized accused may wish to exercise his or her peremptory challenges according to race, in an effort to obtain what he or she perceives to be a representative jury that includes a sufficient number of persons from his or her own race. Limiting the exercise of peremptory challenges by denying the accused the right to select jurors along racial lines could prevent that accused from succeeding.

* This is a complex issue. In spite of the strong arguments against interfering with the way the defence uses its peremptory challenges, it is difficult to accept the legitimacy of even accused persons using this procedure in a manipulative fashion according to criteria that are contrary to sound public policy and contrary to the public interest in the accurate disposition of criminal cases. The abuse of peremptory challenges in the United States by both prosecutors and defence lawyers alike has supported calls for the abolition of the procedure. Employing the *Charter* to control abuse by both parties might, in the end, save the peremptory challenge process from abolition.

APPENDIX I

CHALLENGE FOR CAUSE IN SEXUAL ASSAULT CASES

Appendix I Challenge for Cause Allowed[1]

Case	Date	Trial Judge	Location	Sex/Age of Complainant	Number of Jurors Questioned	% of Jurors Found Partial
R. v. *L.(R.)*	15 Oct. 1996	Justice Zelinski	Milton, Ont.	Female / 6 (at time of the allegations)	41	29
R. v. *Musson*	13 Sept. 1996	Justice Clarke	Milton, Ont.	Male	–	–
R. v. *Ross*	18 July 1996	Justice Salhany	Kitchener, Ont.	Female	–	–
R. v. *Williamson*	27 May 1996	Justice Cosgrove	Brockville, Ont.	–	26	42
R. v. *W.(S.)*	1 May 1996	Justice Langdon	Brampton, Ont.	(Children)	–	–
R. v. *Nixon*	29 April 1996	Justice Burke-Smith	Guelph, Ont.	Female	31	32
R. v. *Lawrence*	8 May 1995	Justice Wein	Toronto, Ont.	Female / 6	32	41

1 Note: In all of these cases, the defence was permitted at a minimum to inquire as to whether the nature of the charges would preclude the potential juror from rendering an impartial verdict. Most of the data about the cases has been collected from the following sources: D.M. Tanovich, "Rethinking Jury Selection: Challenges for Cause and Peremptory Challenges" (1994) 30 C.R. (4th) 310; D.M. Paciocco, "Challenges for Cause Based on Non-Impartiality" (1994) 1 S.O.L.R. 27; D.M. Paciocco, "Challenges for Cause: *Cameron* and Sexual Offence Cases" (1995) 1 S.O.L.R. 73–77; S. Skurka, "Challenge for Cause: Questions Allowed Since R. v. Parks" (Address to the Criminal Lawyers' Association, Annual Convention and Education Programme, 11–13 November 1994), and N. Vidmar, "Generic Prejudice and the Presumption of Guilt in Sex Abuse Trials" (1997) 21 Law and Human Behavior 5.

Case	Date	Trial Judge	Location	Sex/Age of Complainant	Number of Jurors Questioned	% of Jurors Found Partial
R. v. *Lawrence*	19 April 1995	Justice Jennings	Toronto, Ont.	Female / 11	–	59
R. v. *Olscamp*	28 March 1995	Justice Charron	Ottawa, Ont.	–	–	18
R. v. *Gallager*	27 March 1995	Justice Howden	Toronto, Ont.	Female / 8	28	50
R. v. *Webb*	27 Feb. 1995	Justice Forestall	Niagara Falls, Ont.	Female / 15 and 21 at time of allegations	56	55
R. v. *M.H.*	6 Feb. 1995	Justice Ferguson	Whitby, Ont.	Female / 7–14 at time of allegations	26	38
R. v. *Chisholm*	1995	–	Milton, Ont.	Female / 14	21	14
R. v. *Henderson*	19 Jan. 1995	Justice West	Kitchener, Ont.	Female / 9–14	41	49
R. v. *Cox*	5 Dec. 1994	Justice Taliano	Newmarket, Ont.	Female / 9–14	–	–
R. v. *Pihlberg*	19 Dec. 1994	Justice Lane	Toronto, Ont.	Female /23	43	30
R. v. *Batte*	19 Oct. 1994	Justice MacKenzie	–	Female / Adolescents	–	–
R. v. *W.J.*	6 Oct. 1994	Justice Nicholls	Welland, Ont.	Female	–	45

Case	Date	Trial Judge	Location	Sex/Age of Complainant	Number of Jurors Questioned	% of Jurors Found Partial
R. v. *M. & M.*	21 Sept. 1994	Justice Crossland	Toronto, Ont.	Female	36	47
R. v. *R.G.*	13 Sept 1994	Justice Stayshan	Hamilton, Ont.	Female / 7	22	18
R. v. *Lewis*	6 Sept. 1994	Justice Eberhard	Barrie, Ont.	Male / 16	35	26
R. v. *Pascoe*	1 Sept. 1994	Justice McIsaac	Whitby, Ont.	Male / 8 and 12	37	46
R. v. *McBirnie*	5 April 1994	Justice Meehan	London, Ont.	Female / 9 and 11 at time of allegations	35	40
R. v. *Greenwood*	21 March 1994	Justice MacKinnon	Barrie, Ont.	Female / 5	30	23
R. v. *Mattingly*	22 Feb. 1994	Justice Murphy	Whitby, Ont.	Female / 8-17	32	44
R. v. *C.*	7 Feb. 1994	Justice Philp	Hamilton, Ont.	–	34	59
R. v. *Rosler*	28 Jan. 1994	Justice McRae	Toronto, Ont.	Male / 7	35	34
R. v. *Talbot*	8 Jan. 1994	Justice MacDonald	Toronto, Ont.	Male / Teenagers	47	34
R. v. *Llorenz*	1994	Justice Wren	Toronto, Ont.	Female / 10 and 16	34	29
R. v. *Kerr*	27 Sept. 1994	Justice McCombs	Toronto, Ont.	Male / 3, "children"	37	19

Case	Date	Trial Judge	Location	Sex/Age of Complainant	Number of Jurors Questioned	% of Jurors Found Partial
R. v. *Jones*	1994	–	Hamilton, Ont.	Female / Under 14	26	31
R. v. *Kennedy et al.*	16 May 1994	Justice Logan	Newmarket, Ont.	–	–	–
R. v. *B.(W.)*	1 Dec. 1993	Justice Beaulieu	–	Female / 20	–	–
R. v. *Thomas*	22 Nov. 1993	Justice Humphrey	Toronto, Ont.	Female / 5 at time of allegation	36	11
R. v. *Higson*	1993	–	Hamilton, Ont.	Female / 10	31	42
R. v. *McGuire*	1993	–	Hamilton, Ont.	Female / 8	32	44
R. v. *Griffin*	28 Sept. 1993	Justice Marshall	–	Female	–	–
R. v. *Boardman*	5 Oct. 1992	Justice McDonald	Ottawa, Ont.	Female	36	36
R. v. *Jackson*	22 Oct. 1991	Justice Poulin	Ottawa, Ont.	Female / 14	27	48

APPENDIX II

AFFIDAVIT OF NEIL VIDMAR

ONTARIO COURT OF JUSTICE
(CENTRAL WEST REGION)

BETWEEN:

HER MAJESTY THE QUEEN

Respondent

and

Robert Scott Musson

Applicant

AFFIDAVIT OF NEIL (JOSEPH) VIDMAR
SWORN THE 20 DAY OF APRIL, 1995

I, Neil (Joseph) Vidmar, of the City of Chapel Hill, in the County of Orange, North Carolina, hereby MAKE OATH AND SAY:

1. I am a Canadian citizen holding the position of Professor of Social Science and Law in the Duke University School of Law, Durham, NC., U.S.A.; I also hold a cross-appointment in the Duke University Department of Psychology (Social and Health Sciences).

2. I was asked by Mr. David Porter, legal counsel for Dr. Robert Scott Musson, to assess the circumstances surrounding the charges against Dr. Musson and to offer my professional opinion as to whether there are reasonable grounds to believe that some of the veniremen called as potential jurors for Dr. Musson's trial might not be impartial as to his guilt or innocence. Additionally, if I did reach a conclusion that there are reasonable grounds for such a belief concern, Mr. Porter asked me to draw upon my knowledge of and experience with the challenge for cause process in Canada as well as my training as a social psychologist to offer the Court some possible questions for a challenge for cause of prospective jurors summoned for this case.

OVERVIEW

3. After undertaking research on the background and context of *R. v. Musson*, it is my professional opinion that there is a reasonable probability that some veniremen called for jury duty from the Central West Region, will hold opinions and beliefs that will preclude them from being fair and impartial jurors in the case of *R. v. Musson*. After summarizing my credentials relevant to determination of my expertise on the issue of pre-trial publicity and jury behavior, including research and testimony on the subject in the provinces of Ontario, British Columbia, Newfoundland and Prince Edward Island, I will explain in detail the reasons behind my opinion and offer the Court some questions that can be asked of prospective jurors in a challenge for cause, along with an explanation of why, in my professional opinion, I believe that they are appropriate.

PROFESSIONAL BACKGROUND AND QUALIFICATIONS

4. I received a B.A. from MacMurray College, Jacksonville, Ill. in 1962 and a M.A. in 1965 and Ph.D. in Psychology in 1967 (specializing in social psychology) from the University of Illinois, Champaign. Further information about my education and credentials enumerated below is contained in my curriculum vitae which is attached to this affidavit and marked as Exhibit A.

5. In 1967, I accepted a professorship in the Department of Psychology at the University of Western Ontario and held that position until I resigned to take my present position at Duke Law School in 1991. I attended Yale Law School as a Russell Sage Resident in Law in 1973-1974 and continued the study of law as a Fellow at the Battelle Seattle Research Center in 1975-1976. In 1979 I was cross-appointed with the School of Law at the University of Western Ontario where I taught classes that included

material relevant to pre-trial prejudice. I held visiting positions at Osgoode Hall Law School in 1984 and 1986 and similarly taught courses that considered the subject of pre-trial prejudice. I also teach about this subject at Duke Law School.

6. One of my principal scholarly endeavors is the study of jury behavior and decision-making, a subject that includes pre-trial prejudice. I have conducted empirical research on pre-trial prejudice. As a result of my writing and teaching on this subject, I am often asked to review the research of other scholars on this subject for law and social science journals and for grant foundations in Canada and the U.S. I also routinely review the professional writings of others on this subject as a member of editorial boards or as a consulting editor for both law and social science journals. I have discussed this topic in seminars held by the Law Society of Upper Canada; the Criminal Lawyer's Association (Ontario); the American Bar Association; and the Association of American Law Schools. In October 1993 I delivered an invited address to a conference entitled "Analyzing and Filtering Evidence in an Age of Diversity" for judges sponsored by the Canadian Institute for the Administration of Justice held in Vancouver (October 15-17, 1993). I was also invited to lecture to approximately 60 Canadian judges attending the Intensive Judicial Studies programme of the National Judicial Institute on matters pertaining to social science evidence on May 9, 1994. I have accepted an invitation to lecture at the second Intensive Judicial Studies programme in May, 1995. I was an invited panelist at conferences sponsored by the Criminal Lawyers Association held in Toronto on November 5-7, 1993, April 9, 1994, and November 11, 1994. In all of these latter conferences a major portion of my contribution was on the topic of pre-trial prejudice and in the November 1994 conference I was specifically asked to address the issue of challenge for cause in sexual assault cases.

7. My own publications bearing on pre-trial prejudice include, but are not limited to, the following: Valerie Hans and Neil Vidmar, *Judging the Jury*, 1986; N. Vidmar (Ed.) Is the Jury Competent? *Law and Contemporary Problems* (1989); Vidmar and Judson, The Use of Social Science Data in a Change of Venue Application, 59 *Canadian Bar Review* 76 (1981); Vidmar and Melnitzer, Juror Prejudice: An Empirical Study of a Challenge for Cause, 22 *Osgoode Hall Law Journal* 499 (1984); Hans and Vidmar, Jury Selection, in Kerr and A. Bray (Eds.) *The Psychology of the Courtroom (1982)*; Vidmar, chapter 23, Social Science Evidence, in Gary Chayko, T. Gulliver and D. MacDougall (Eds.) *Forensic Evidence in Canada* (1991).

8. I have been qualified as an expert and testified about pre-trial prejudice in the provinces of Ontario, British Columbia, Newfoundland and Prince Edward Island and in the States of Ohio, Pennsylvania and Oregon.

9. The specific Canadian cases in which I have been qualified or otherwise accepted as an expert for applications bearing on pre-trial prejudice are as follows:

a. *R. v. Brunner*, unreported, Middlesex County Court, Ont., 1979 (see Vidmar and Judson, paragraph 7 supra for a discussion of this case). (fraud)

b. *R. v. Iutzi*, unreported, Ont. S.C., 1980. (see Vidmar and Melnitzer, supra paragraph 7) (child killing)

c. *R. v. Taylor et. al.*, unreported, B.C. S.C., 1983 (also known popularly as the Squamish 5 or Litton Bombers case)

d. *R. v. Foshay*, unreported, Ont. S.C., 1986. (murder)

e. *R. v. Basker*, unreported, Middlesex Co. Ct., Ont., 1986. (assault)

f. *R. v. Bowers*, unreported, Ont. S.C., 1986. (murder)

g. *R. v. Burke*, unreported, Nfld. S.C., 1991. (sex abuse)

h. *R. v. Kenny*, unreported, Nfld. S.C., 1991. (sex abuse)

i. *R. v. McGregor*, unreported, Ont. Court of Justice (General Division), December, 1992. (murder with insanity defense)

j. *R. v. Starke*, unreported, Ont. Court of Justice (General Division), 1993. (murder)

k. *R. v. McBirnie*, unreported, Ont. C.J., April 5, 1994. (child sexual assault) (uncontested submission by affidavit)

l. *R. v. Theberge*, Ontario Court of Justice, Northeast Region, May 25, 1994. (murder with insanity defense)

m. *R. v. Cameron*, Supreme Court of Prince Edward Island, Court of Assize, County of Prince, January 9, 1995, unreported. (sexual assault) (uncontested submission by affidavit)

n. *R. v. Henderson*, Ontario Court of Justice, Central South Region, Waterloo, File No. CJ3095, unreported, January 19, 1995. (sexual offenses) (uncontested submission by affidavit)

10. I also have direct knowledge of the following Canadian cases involving pre-trial prejudice in which I submitted an affidavit addressing pre-trial prejudice, have served as a consultant and/or in which I otherwise researched pre-trial prejudice:

a. *R. v. Johnson and Kear*, unreported, Ont. S.C., 1986 (known popularly as the "Bounty Hunter" case or Sidney Jaffe case). (kidnapping)

b. *R. v. Doxtator et. al.*, unreported, Ont. S.C., 1976. (murder)

c. *R. v. Oughton*, unreported, B.C. S.C., 1986. (serial rape)

d. *R. v. Morin*, unreported, Ont. S.C., 1986 (second trial). (murder)

e. *R. v. Thomas*, unreported, Ontario Court of Justice, General Division, November, 1993. (child sexual abuse)

f. *R. v. Willis, Bishop and Champagnie*, Ontario Court of Appeal (no.'s C9833; C8861; C8802) 1994. (racial issues in trial involving murder and other offenses) (Affidavit submitted on behalf of an intervenor, The Urban Alliance on Race Relations for Metropolitan Toronto)

g. *R. v. Phillips*, Ontario Court of Justice, Central East Region, unreported, December, 1994. (murder) (Affidavit submission on survey results)

11. I am familiar with leading cases on challenge for cause: *R. v. Hubbert* (1975) 29 C.C.C. (2d) 279; *R. v. Sherratt* (1991) 63 C.C.C. (3d) 193; *R. v. Parks* (1993) 84 C.C.C. (3d) 353 (Ont. C.A.); *R. V. Williams* (1994) 90 C.C.C. (3d) 194; *R. v. Rollocks* (1994) 190 R. (3d) 446; *R. v. Zundel* (1987) 580.R (2d) 129 (CA), 31 C.C.C. (3d) 97; and *R. v. Cameron (1995)*, Ont. C.A., C 15804. I am also familiar with *R. v. Biddle* (March 2, 1995), Supreme Court of Canada, File No. 23734, which discusses issues of juror impartiality.

A I am also familiar with the Court's decisions in the following unreported Ontario cases involving challenge for cause: *R. v. Kitiatchik*, Ontario General Division, dated October 5, 1993 (involving the issue of violence toward women); *R. v. Griffin*, Ontario General Division, J-92-0636 (involving sexual violence against women); *R. v. Green*, Ontario General Division, dated September 1994 (involving sexual abuse); *R. v. Morrisey and Morrisey*, Ontario General Division, dated September 21, 1994 (involving the issue of attitudes toward sexual assault); *R. v. Cox*, Ontario Court of Justice, General Division, OC.932590, dated December 5, 1994 (involving the issue of attitudes toward sexual assault); *R. v. Jackson*, Ont. C. J., East Region, File 90-12085, October 21-22, 1991; *R. v. Neely*, O.C.J. (General Division), dated November 24, 1994 (issue: impartiality on parole eligibility after murder conviction); *R. v. Pheasant*, O.C.J. (General Division) File No. CRIM J(P) 5284/94 (dated February 7, 1995) (violence against women); *R. v. Kennedy et. al.* Ont. C.J., Central East Region, File 93-0885 (dated February 14, 1995) (sexual assault and incest).

B. I am also familiar with these recent materials bearing on the challenge for cause process: Austin Cooper, The ABC's of Challenge for Cause in Jury Trials: To Challenge or Not to Challenge and What to Ask if You Get It, 37 *Crim. L. Q.* 65 (1994); Steven Skurka, Defending A Child Sex Abuse Case, 15 *Criminal Lawyers' Association Newsletter*, 7, June 1994; Steven Skurka, Challenge for Cause Questions Allowed since *R. v. Parks*, Criminal Lawyers' Association, Annual Convention and Education Programme, November 11-13, 1994; David Tanovich, Rethinking Jury Selection: Challenges for Cause and Preemptory Challenges, 30 C.R. (4th) 311 (1994); and Chapman, Paciocco, Lafontaine, and Hutchinson, Challenge for Cause Based on Non-Impartiality 1 *The Sexual Offenses Law Reporter* 25, September 1994.

12. I was trained in the measurement of attitudes by some of the leading experts in the field of social and personality psychology. Of the more than 75 scientific and legal articles that I have published, approximately three-fourths involve measurement of attitudes or other matters relating to human cognitions and behavior. These articles have been published in "peer review" journals. "Peer review" refers to the process whereby research that is submitted for possible publication is reviewed by the journal editor and by two or three experts in the field who review the research under conditions of anonymity. Research is published only if these reviewers find the research to be theoretically and methodologically sound.

13. I have been asked, and continue to be asked, by editors and by research granting institutions to review research in the fields of psychology, sociology, and law and give my judgment about the theoretical and methodological adequacy of the research of other professionals. I served two terms each on the editorial boards of *Law and Human Behavior* and *Law and Society Review* and an eleven-year term on the editorial board of the

Journal of Applied Social Psychology. I am currently on the editorial boards of two international journals, *Psychology Crime and Law*, and *Legal and Criminological Psychology*. I review as many as three manuscripts per month for other scientific journals. In the recent past these have included, the *American Psychologist*, the *Journal of Personality and Social Psychology*, *Personality and Social Psychology Bulletin*, *Public Opinion Quarterly*, the *Journal of Communication*, the *Canadian Journal of Criminology*, the *American Journal of Sociology*, *Judicature*, and *Law and Social Inquiry*. I also review research proposals for the Social Sciences and Humanities Research Council of Canada and the U.S. National Science Foundation, and some other Canadian and U.S. granting agencies. I am a former member of the Board of Directors of the Canadian Law and Society Association and a current member of the Law and Behavior Panel of the U.S. National Research Council. My primary task in all of the above activities is to render my professional judgement about the theoretical and methodological soundness of research undertaken by my professional colleagues. Many of the issues in the manuscripts that I review include the assessment and measurement of attitudes and public opinion.

14. I am a former Fellow of Divisions 9 and 41 of the American Psychological Association and a current Fellow of the American Psychological Society. The awarding of Fellow status is based upon distinguished scholarly contribution to the field of psychology.

SPECIFIC MATERIALS REVIEWED

15. Before preparing this affidavit I reviewed the following material which was supplied to me by Mr. Porter:

(1) The Crown's disclosure brief in *R. v. Musson*

(2) A complete transcript of the preliminary inquiry in *R. v. Musson*

16. In addition, I reviewed materials on Canadian attitudes toward sexual assault and toward the responsibility of physicians that I have undertaken for accused persons in recent Canadian criminal cases. I also reviewed some original research data that I collected in interviews with North Carolina jurors about medical negligence and responsibility.

17. Finally, I undertook a review of newspapers, magazines and social science research findings on specific issues that in my professional opinion are relevant to the question of juror impartiality in this case. I conducted some of this review myself. A research assistant who is a

graduate student in psychology at York University conducted the remainder of the review under my direction. The review included the following:

a. A review of literature and research bearing on "homophobia" in Canada and the United States;

b. A search of the following newspapers for coverage of the case involving Dr. Musson: *The Burlington Spectator; The Hamilton Spectator: The Oakville Beaver; The Toronto Star;* the Toronto *Globe and Mail*; and the Toronto *Sun.*

c. A search of the Toronto *Globe and Mail*; the Toronto *Star*; and the Toronto *Sun* from 1992 to March 31, 1995 for articles involving physicians or other health care providers charged with sex abuse of male or female patients;

d. A search of the *Globe and Mail*, the *Star* and the *Sun* from 1992 to March 31, 1995 for articles pertaining to "homophobia" such as acts of discrimination, assaults on homosexuals or attitudes toward homosexuals;

e. A search of *Macleans* from 1992 to March 31, 1995 for similar stories relating to homophobia, assault and discrimination;

f. A search of social science literature, survey data and government reports on attitudes toward homosexuality in Canada.

ANALYTICAL FRAMEWORK

18. For purposes of analysis I identify three broad types of pre-trial prejudice: specific prejudice, generic prejudice, and normative prejudice:

A. Specific Prejudice: This involves attitudes or beliefs about the specific case before the Court that may cause the juror to be unable to decide the case with a fair and impartial mind. These attitudes and beliefs may exist because of (a) personal knowledge or connection to the case or persons associated with it (b) publicity through mass media such as newspaper and television coverage, (c) or discussion and rumor about the case arising through social networks within the community from which jurors are drawn. My review of the newspaper coverage of *R. v. Musson* yielded only a relatively few articles and none of these involved inflammatory writing. Mr. Porter has informed me that he has no other evidence bearing on specific prejudice in this case and thus it will not be discussed further in this affidavit.

B. Generic Prejudice: This category of prejudice involves the transferring of prejudice to the case as a result of juror stereotyping of the accused, victims, witnesses, or the nature of the crime itself based upon adverse assumptions about categories of persons or criminal charges. Such prejudices are often associated with strong and negative affective emotions that invoke reactions above and beyond mere abhorrence of the crime itself. The potential racial prejudice which was the issue in *R. v. Parks* (1993) 84 C.C.C. (3d) 353 (Ont. C.A.), is an example of generic prejudice: i.e., concern that general attitudes and beliefs about blacks might cause some jurors to be not impartial in judging any black person charged with a crime. Similar categorizing reactions in cases involving violence against women were noted by Madam Justice Germain in *R. v. Kitaitchik*, Ont. Gen. Div., dated October 5, 1993, and sexual assaults against women were recognized by Mr. Justice Marshall in *R. v. Griffin*, unreported, Ontario Gen. Div. J-92-0636. These are also examples of generic prejudice.

(1) A number of Ontario Courts have recognized general attitudes and beliefs about sexual assault as a condition that might prevent some prospective jurors from deciding a sexual assault case with a fair and impartial mind: e.g., *R. v. Thomas*, unreported, November 22, 1993 (Mr. Justice D. Humphrey); *R. v. McBirnie*, unreported, Ont. C.J., April 5, 1993 (Mr. Justice M. Meehan). Additional cases involving courts recognizing potential generic prejudice about sexual assault are described in Cooper (1994) supra paragraph 11; Skurka, (1994) supra paragraph 11; Skurka (November 11-13, 1994) supra paragraph 11b; Tanovich, supra paragraph 1b1; and Chapman et. al., supra paragraph 11b. In addition in *R. v. Grant Henderson*, Ontario Court, Central South Region, Waterloo, File CJ 3095, unreported, January 19, 1995, Mr. Justice Ernest F. West took cognizance of generic prejudice in a sexual assault case and granted an application for challenge for cause on that basis. As a result of ongoing research with Mr. Steven Skurka of the law firm of Cooper, Sandler, West and Skurka, regarding the challenge for cause process, I have learned about the results of challenges for cause in additional cases. I verily believe, that in *R. v. M. H.*, Ontario Court (General Division), Whitby, a case involving charges of sexual assault, sexual interference, and

sexual exploitation, Mr. Justice Donald S. Ferguson granted an application for a challenge for cause centered on generic prejudice relating to the charges. The Court in Prince Edward Island, in *R. v. Cameron*, Supreme Court of Prince Edward Island, County of Prince, File GSC 13385, unreported, January 9, 1995 has similarly recognized generic prejudice in a case involving sexual assault.

(2) Like specific prejudice, generic prejudice can arise out of the juror's personal experiences or interests, from mass media coverage, or from social networks within the community.

(a) As an example of generic prejudice arising out of personal experience or attitudes about sex abuse charges, consider the responses of some of the prospective jurors who were challenged for cause in *R. v. Morrissey and Morrissey*, Ont. C.J., unreported, Toronto Region, September 21, 1994. The transcript of the challenge is attached to this affidavit as Exhibit B. The prospective jurors were asked a single question: Would your ability to judge the evidence without bias, prejudice or partiality be affected by the fact that the accused are charged with sexually assaulting their daughters? In response to this question juror "O" (page 8, line 30) replied: "To tell you the truth, I will, because I was physically abused as a child, and I might have some pain as a matter as a result of that"; Juror "C" (page 16, line 10) said "I'm not sure. I got children myself; I cannot tell I will be able to do that as a jury (sic) on a very fair decision"; and juror "B" (page 56, line 16) said, "Yes. I'm very prejudiced against child molesters, rapists, and wife-beaters and I think they should be lashed, in my opinion." Other prospective jurors simply said "yes" to the question of potential bias because of the nature of the charges but the essential finding is that the triers found 18 of 37 prospective jurors to be "not impartial". Other examples of juror comments about sexual abuse charges are contained in Skurka, November 11-13, 1994, supra paragraph 11b: e.g., "As a father and grandfather, I abhor this situation. It would be difficult for me to empathize with this situation."

(b) The effect of mass media coverage of categories of crime on the attitudes of potential jurors has been discussed in Greene and Wade, Of Private Talk and Public Print:

General Pre-Trial Publicity and Juror Decision Making, 2 *Applied Cognitive Psychology* 123 (1987); Greene, Media Effects in Juror Decision-Making, 15 *Law and Human Behavior* 321 (1990). Greene discusses empirical evidence showing that publicity about other crimes can affect perceptions of guilt in an unrelated case. In *R. v. McGregor*, unreported, Ont. C.J., 1993, and *R. v. Theberge*, Ont. C.J. (Northeast Region), May 25, 1994, I testified about data from scientifically designed public opinion surveys indicating that significant percentages of the Ontario populations studied were strongly opposed to the insanity defense as a result of mass media-created impressions that guilty persons were escaping justice through false claims of insanity. In this affidavit I offer the professional opinion that there is a reasonable likelihood that media-influenced attitudes about homosexual acts, the issue of sexual assaults by physicians and sexual assault in general will similarly affect the impartiality of some jurors.

C. Normative Prejudice: The essence of this form of prejudice is that in legal cases of significant interest to the community some jurors perceive that there is a community consensus about the case or type of case and what is expected by the community as regards its outcome. In short, there is a perception, often based on reality, of community norms and values about a case. Some potential jurors, who believe that they themselves could be open-minded, indicate that if the evidence was close on the matter of guilt or innocence they might tilt their verdict in the direction of the perceived community norms to avoid the disapprobation of family, friends, or co-workers after trial. I have documented normative pressures in Canadian jurors. During challenges for cause in *R. v. Taylor et.al.*, B.C.S.C., 1983 (also known popularly as the "Squamish 5" or "Litton Bombers" case), and in *R. v. Iutzi*, unreported, Ont. S.C., 1980 some prospective jurors spontaneously mentioned that their verdict might be affected by such considerations. In paragraphs 36 and 38, infra, I reach the conclusion that jurors may perceive community norms about correct outcomes to exist in cases involving charges of sexual abuse by doctors.

19. I now turn to the issue of generic prejudice. My analysis consists of three issues: attitudes about acts of homosexuality; attitudes about the responsibility of physicians and other health care providers in treating

their patients; and attitudes toward sexual assault. These issues are intertwined in the *Musson* case and are separated only for conceptual analysis.

GENERIC PREJUDICE ABOUT HOMOSEXUAL ACTS

20. Homosexual acts are central to the charges in this case. Homosexual acts evoke very strong negative emotions and reactions in substantial numbers of Canadians. Indeed, many social scientists and other authors currently use the term "homophobia" as a general term to describe the constellation of reactions to homosexuality and the underlying attitudes and beliefs that give rise to these reactions. The reactions against homosexuality among some persons are so deep and strong that they may appropriately be labelled "aversions." Homosexuals are subject to discrimination. Further, many acts of violence against persons that are labelled "hate crimes" — acts against persons because of who they are — are directed against persons identified as homosexuals.

21. In discussing the subject of "homophobia," I want to be very clear in acknowledging that the issue of homosexuality has many dimensions including the perceived lifestyles of persons who are openly "gay," the fears evoked by the AIDS epidemic and even the possible social and economic costs of recognizing same sex relationships. These issues are to be separated from the central issue in this case, namely whether the Crown carries its burden of proving beyond a reasonable doubt that non-consensual homosexual acts occurred as the complainants allege. However, as the leading reviews of the social science and medical literature make clear, sexual acts between persons of the same sex are inextricably tied to these broader issues. Gregory Herek, a leading researcher on attitudes toward homosexuality, states in his review of the literature, On Heterosexual Masculinity: Some Psychical Consequences of the Social Construction of Gender and Sexuality, 29 *American Behavioral Scientist* 563 at 568 (1986):

> "Over the last few centuries, the view developed that what a person **does** sexually defines who the person **is**, and negative evaluations were attached to people who did not do what they were supposed to do and who thus were not what they were supposed to be. Not being what one is supposed to be receives many labels, including criminal, wicked and sick."

22. As much of the literature makes clear many of the reactions to homosexual acts involve a strong negative emotional component as typified in the endorsement of items such as "I think male homosexuality is

disgusting" (Herek, supra paragraph 21 at 565); see also Marsiglio, Attitudes Toward Homosexual Activity and Gays as Friends: A National Survey of Heterosexual 15 to 19-year-old Males, 30 *Journal of Sex Research* 12 (1993). Marsiglio reports that 89 percent of respondents endorsed the view that "homosexual acts are disgusting."

23. In the preparation of this affidavit I have reviewed approximately 11 books and five articles which review scientific literature on attitudes toward homosexuality and homosexual acts. Although some of the data about homophobia that I review in the paragraphs below may contain elements pertaining to the aforementioned other issues, it is my professional opinion that reactions to the sexual acts associated with homosexuality are at the core of the emotions and behaviors described in those data. Some of the literature that underlies my opinion includes, Herek, Heterosexuals' Attitudes Toward Lesbians and Gay Men: Correlates and Gender Differences, 25 Journal of Sex Research 451 (1988); Herek, Hate Crimes Against Lesbians and Gay Men, 44 *American Psychologist* 948 (1989); John DeCecco, *Bashers, Baiters, and Bigots: Homophobia in American Society* (1985); Canadian AIDS Society, *Homophobia, Heterosexism and AIDS* (1991); Richard Mohr, *Gays/Justice* (1992); Gary Kinsman, *The Regulation of Desire: Sexuality in Canada* (1987); Didi Herman, *Rights of Passage: Struggles for Lesbian and Gay Legal Equality* (1994); Gregory Herek and Kevin Berrill, (eds.) *Hate Crimes: confronting Violence Against Lesbians and Gay Men* (1992); Gary Comstock, *Violence Against Lesbians and Gay Men* (1991).

24. There are many social and psychological factors that give rise to "homophobia." Among the causes are religious teachings about homosexuality; social stereotypes of homosexuals and their lifestyles, including beliefs of sexual promiscuity and pedophilia; the perceived threat that homosexuality poses to the societal structures of the family; individuals' fears about their own heterosexuality; and, in recent years, their association with AIDS and the fears and dread that this disease evokes.

25. In his book, *The Regulation of Desire: Sexuality in Canada* (1987), Gary Kinsman traces the history of hostility toward homosexuality in Canada. He documents how homosexuality is negatively portrayed in the mass media; the incidence of "gay bashing;" harassment by police across Ontario and the negative impact of the AIDS epidemic on attitudes toward homosexuals. Didi Herman's book, *Rights of Passage: Struggles for Lesbian and Gay Legal Equality* (1994) also discusses the history of anti-homosexual attitudes in Canada. Herman discusses the impact of the teachings of the Catholic Church, and the protestant churches of the "New Christian Right," that

homosexuality is a deviant lifestyle. Miller and Humphreys, Lifestyles and Violence: Homosexual Victims of Assault and Murder, 3 *Qualitative Sociology* 169 (1980) discusses the fears of Canadian and American homosexual men regarding violence and the socially stigmatizing effects of homosexuality. In *Gays/Justice: A Study of Ethics, Society and Law* (1992), Richard Mohr further discusses literature about the stereotypes of homosexuals including widespread beliefs that homosexuals are "child molesters, sex-crazed maniacs, civilization destroyers."

26. Gregory Herek has reviewed social science literature on crimes of violence against people because of their sexual orientation, Hate Crimes Against Lesbians and Gay Men: Issues for Research and Policy, 44 *American Psychologist* 948 (1989). His review suggests that homosexuals are probably the most frequent victims of hate crimes. In one national study involving 654 lesbians and 1420 gay men in eight U.S. cities, "[n]early all of the respondents reported that they had experienced some type of harassment, threat, or attack; more than one fifth of the men and nearly one tenth of the women had been physically assaulted because of their sexual orientation." Herek also notes that the reports of physical assaults and verbal harassment have increased in recent years. One hypothesis to explain this increase relates to public reactions to the AIDS epidemic, although Herek cautions that there are other explanations. Other social science research documenting anti-homosexual attitudes and behavior is as follows: Harry, Derivative Deviance: The cases of extortion, fag-bashing and shakedown of gay men, 19 *Criminology* 546 (1982); Herek, On heterosexual masculinity: Some psychical consequences of the social construction of gender and sexuality, 29 *American Behavioral Scientist* 563 (1986); Herek, Heterosexuals' attitudes toward lesbians and gay men: correlates and gender differences, 25 *Journal of Sex Research* 451 (1988); see also, Kim, Are homosexuals facing an even more hostile world? *The New York Times* (July 3, 1988 p. E16).

27. In addition, Canadian data also show negative attitudes toward homosexuals. In a nationwide survey conducted in 1985 Reginald Bibby, *Fragmented Gods: The Poverty and Potential of Religion in Canada* (1987), found that 70 percent of Canadians indicated that they believed that "Two adults of the same sex having sexual relations" was "always wrong "or" almost always wrong." The Gallup Poll has assessed attitudes about employment of homosexuals in various occupations in nationwide surveys conducted in 1988, 1992 and 1994. A summary of that survey is appended as Exhibit C to this affidavit. While the data show that attitudes toward the employment of homosexuals became less negative between 1988 and 1994, Canadians still hold discriminatory attitudes toward homosexuals. For instance, in the 1994

survey 1 in 5 Canadians (20%) indicated that homosexuals should not be employed as doctors. Almost 1 in 4 (24%) were opposed to their employment as prison officer; 31 percent said homosexuals should not be employed as junior school teachers and 31 percent said they should not be employed as members of the clergy. In my professional opinion, it is likely that these results reflect the stereotypes of homosexuals discussed by Mohr, supra paragraph 23, as child molesters and sexually promiscuous persons who cannot be trusted in positions where they might use their power and status to seduce or force others into homosexual activities.

28. A detailed survey of 433 randomly selected adult residents of Edmonton, Alberta in 1989 found that 49 percent strongly disapproved of two men or two women openly living in a homosexual relationship (a total of 64 percent disagreed to at least some degree, see Herbert Northcott and Linda Reutter, *Public Opinion Regarding AIDS Policy: Fear of Contagion and Attitudes Toward Homosexual Relationships*, Population Research Laboratory, Department of Sociology, The University of Alberta (1989). A recent study of Canadian medical residents and faculty found substantial levels of prejudice: 11 percent of psychiatric residents, 23 percent of family practice residents and 26 percent of psychiatric faculty reported that they were prejudiced against homosexuals; 6.5 percent of the psychiatric faculty answered affirmatively to a question asking whether homosexuals with AIDS "got what they deserve" (this last figure could partially reflect attitudes about unsafe sex practices of homosexuals), see Chaimowitz, Homophobia Among Psychiatric Residents, Family Practice Residents and Psychiatric Faculty, 36 *Canadian Journal of Psychiatry* 206 (1991). An Angus Reid survey of a nationwide sample of Canadians in September 1994 found that 46 percent of respondents believed that a person who openly acknowledged that his or her homosexuality would face discrimination by their co-workers; the percentage for the Province of Ontario was 41 percent, see 9 *The Reid Report*, Issue No. 9 (October, 1994).

29. The search of the major newspapers that are published and/or distributed in Halton County supports the view that substantial numbers of Canadians hold strong negative attitudes about homosexuals and homosexual acts. Consider, for example, stories carried in the *Hamilton/Burlington Spectator*, a sample of which are appended as Exhibit D to this affidavit: "Gay discrimination okay: Vatican" (July 24, 1992 p. A8) reported on a Vatican document that said homosexuals could legitimately be discriminated against in employment, housing, and the adoption of children. "Church has made me an outcast" gay vicar laments (March 21, 1991 p. A1) regarding discrimination against an Anglican minister in Toronto. "Homosexuals live in

fear, conference told" (June 18, 1992 p. D4) reports that homosexuals fear losing their homes, children jobs. "Anti-violence TV messages made for gays" (June 21, 1993 p. A6) reports in videotaped messages produced by the Toronto police that are aimed at preventing violence against gays; a spokesperson for the police acknowledged that hate crimes are a "growing threat." A November 16, 1993 article (p. D11) reports on the murder and "gay bashing" of homosexuals in Montreal. A March 3, 1994 (p. A6) article titled "Anti-gay message is taken to Ottawa:" reported on the 50,000-member group called "REAL Women" being opposed to legal recognition of homosexual unions. Similar stories were contained in the Toronto *Star*, the *Sun*, the *Globe and Mail* and *Macleans*, a sample which are also contained in Exhibit E.

30. Finally, strong anti-homosexual attitudes are even expressed in public by members of Parliament, (see news stories contained in Exhibit F to this affidavit). The present federal government has proposed amending the Human Rights Code to prevent discrimination against homosexuals and Bill C-41 would allow judges to impose harder sentences when sexual discrimination plays a role in crime. MP Tom Wappel, of Toronto, is quoted as saying that: "Homosexuality is statistically abnormal, it's physically abnormal and it's morally immoral" (Toronto *Globe and Mail*, September 28, 1994 p. A1). MP Roseanne Skoke of Nova Scotia has said that homosexuality is not supported by "Canadian and Christian morals and values," that "homosexuality is not natural" and that "It is immoral and it is undermining the inherent rights and values of our Canadian families and it must not and should not be condoned" (Toronto *Globe and Mail* September 28, 1994 p. A7; *Macleans* October 10, 1994 p. 21). Similarly, MP Daniel McTeague is quoted as saying: "A lot of people come from very traditional, very strong upright communities. If the government proceeds... in blatant disregard to the values that many MP's have, we're going to find ourselves in a legislative deadlock" (Toronto *Globe and Mail*, September 28, 1994 p. A1). It should be noted that these comments were made by MP's from the governing Liberal Party. One, unnamed, MP is quoted as saying that "up to half the Liberal caucus might have qualms" about Bill C-41 (Toronto *Globe and Mail*, April 28, 1994 p. A1). Furthermore, Reform Leader Preston Manning has supported the position of MP Roseanne Skoke (Toronto *Globe and Mail* April 28, 1994 p A1) and Reform MP Paul Forseth who claimed that the inclusion of the words "sexual orientation" in Bill C-41 were creating "a national controversy" (Toronto *Star*, November 18, 1994, p. A15). Political controversy about homosexual rights has also affected the politics of the Province of Ontario: MPP Don Cousons of Markham withdrew his private members bill that would have prohibited demeaning comments about gays and lesbians after receiving a "flood of protest mail" (*Hamilton Spectator*, February 17, 1994 p. A11). A petition and

letter-writing campaign to MPP's and newspapers against any changes to the law regarding legal recognition of homosexual relationships is reported to have been organized in part by Ontario's Christian Reform churches. NDP caucus chairperson, Steven Owens, admitted that the atmosphere was so politically charged that many MPP's were feeling "pressure" (*Hamilton Spectator*, February 17, 1994 p. A11). Anti-homosexual feelings have also affected the politics of the city of Hamilton (*Hamilton Spectator*, July 8, 1994 p. A8; March 18, 1995 p. B1).

31. Based upon all of the materials discussed in paragraphs 20 to 30 supra it is my professional opinion that it is likely that a substantial number of persons called for jury duty in the case of *R. v. Musson* may harbor deep-rooted negative emotional reactions about homosexual acts that could affect their impartiality in deciding the charges against Robert Scott Musson. Because the Crown's case alleges homosexual acts by Dr. Musson, any homophobic attitudes held by those jurors would create negative emotional reactions about homosexual acts, which would likely prevent some of them from deciding the case with a fair and impartial mind. Having regard to the fact that such negative attitudes are quite common, there is a substantial likelihood that these attitudes would be found in some prospective jurors who, if permitted to become jurors, would likely be unable to be impartial in their consideration of the allegations against Dr. Musson.

32. In summary, based on a review of an extensive body of literature, it is my opinion that, for a substantial number of persons, overt sexual acts between two males evoke very strong emotional reactions of disgust and hostility; these reactions are reinforced by other persons in their social environment and by some religious and political organizations; there is a strong tendency in many persons to equate sex acts between two males as the same as homosexuality in all of its social manifestations. The evidence also shows that these attitudes are often translated into behaviors such as discrimination and violence. It is further my opinion that such reactions are likely to cause some people who hold them to exhibit reactions that would preclude them from being fair and impartial in judging the evidence in the case of *R. v. Musson*.

PREJUDICE INVOLVING SEX CHARGES AGAINST PHYSICIANS

33. In my professional opinion, the fact that Robert Scott Musson is a physician and that one of the charges against him involves allegations of sexual assault while in his role as a physician also increases the likelihood that some prospective jurors might not be able to decide the case with an impartial mind.

34. As documented in the articles contained in Exhibit G to this affidavit, concerns about physicians engaging in sex abuse have been continuously before the Canadian public for at least the past five years. In 1991, the Canadian public learned that a task force of the College of Physicians and Surgeons of Ontario estimated that about 10 percent of Ontario's practicing physicians may have taken sexual advantage of their patients (*Macleans*, June 10, 1991 p. 46). In 1992, a similar report from British Columbia documented widespread sexual abuse by physicians in that Province (Toronto *Globe and Mail*, November 10, 1992 p. A6; November 13, 1992 p. A6). In November 1992, the Ontario government introduced a bill to aid in the prosecution of sexual assaults by doctors (Toronto *Globe and Mail*, November 16, 1992 p. A4). Newspaper stories have also reported on sexual abuse by doctors in Nova Scotia (*Globe and Mail*, November 27, 1992 p. A5) and in Quebec (*Globe and Mail*, August 7, 1993). The February 1, 1993 issue of *Macleans* (at page 17) carried an article entitled "Breaking the Silence: Sexually Abused Patients are Speaking Out" about sexual abuse in doctor patient relationships. The December 12, 1994 issue of *Macleans* (at page 53) carried a story headlined "Betrayal of Trust" about a Surrey, British Columbia doctor charged with sexual misconduct who was then charged with the murder of one of the complainants. The Toronto *Star* has carried a number of bylined articles detailing the issue of doctors and sex abuse: e.g., "1 in 10 MD's Say They Know Colleague Who is a Sex Abuser" (February 25, 1992 p. A3); "MD's Want Colleagues to Identify Sex Abusers" (March 31, 1992 p. A1); "MD's Balk at Law Forcing Them to Report on Colleague's Behavior" (January 26, 1993 p. A2); "Courts Give Doctors Guilty of Sex Abuse Second Chance" (May 13, 1993 p. A1); "Jail Doctors for Sex Abuse, Colleague Says" (October 12, 1994 p. A2); Women Irate as Judge Acquits Doctor of Rape (April 11, 1995, p. A12). The *Hamilton Spectator* has similarly reported on the subject: e.g., "Doctors and Sex Abuse: Help Affiliated" (Editorial April 3, 1992 p. A19); "Prodding Snitch 'Unhealthy': Poll Shows MD's Reject Sex-Abuse Rules" (January 26, 1993 p. A8); "Professionals Urge Guidelines: Abuse by Counsellors Must be Stopped, They Say" (November 2, 1994 p. T6); "Doctors Dating Rules Explained" (December 31, 1994 p. A10). It is my professional opinion that this widespread coverage has aroused public concern about sexual abuse by physicians; furthermore, some of the articles imply that doctors are unwilling to report or sanction fellow physicians when they engage in such practices.

35. These articles reporting on widespread sexual abuse are complemented by articles reporting criminal convictions or other sanctions levied against doctors and other health care providers (see Exhibit H to this affidavit). My research of the Toronto *Globe and Mail*, the Toronto *Star* and

the *Hamilton Spectator* from 1992 through 1994 includes the following physicians and health care providers who practiced in the Toronto-Hamilton area who were criminally convicted, or otherwise adjudged guilty of sexual offenses against their patients: Douglas Murray; Chikmaglur Mohan; Michael George Thompson; Lal Boodoosingh; Frank Johnson; Maurice Genereux; John Beresford; James Tyhurst; Richard Hill; Hugh Cameron; Robert Ecclestone; John Minich; Eladio Alarcon; Morris Wynrib; Hector Warnes; Russell Grover; Kunwar Singh; Michael Rosman; Dermot Grove; Ashraf Gidi; Henry Fenigstein; Marc Bissonett; Clyde Landsdell; German Alverex; Alexandro Alvo Alfred; John Orpin. The case of Dr. John Minich of Hamilton was the subject of feature articles in the *Hamilton Spectator* that included interviews with former patients. It is my professional opinion that these convictions serve to heighten public concern about sexual abuse committed by physicians and it is likely that this may cause some persons to hold attitudes about charges of sex abuse by physicians such that they could not be impartial in deciding guilt or innocence in the case of Dr. Musson.

36. The publicity about doctors engaging in sexual assault and sexual abuse through the power they exercise in the physician-patient relationship should also be viewed in the light of what sociologists have labelled "status characteristics theory," J. Berger et.al., *Status Characteristics and Social Interaction: An Expectation States Approach* (1977). Physicians are prominent members of the community and their occupation accords them high status, see, e.g., Hodge, Siegel and Rossi, Occupational Prestige in the United States: 1925-1963, 70 *American Journal of Sociology* 286 (1964), A body of sociological and social psychological research indicates that high status creates higher expectations of responsibility, e.g., Wahrman, Status, Deviance and Sanctions, 13 *Pacific Sociological Review* 229 (1970); Vidmar and Miller, Social Psychological Processes Underlying Attitudes Toward Legal Punishment, 14 *Law & Society Review* 401 (1980); V. Lee Hamilton and Joseph Sanders, *Everyday Justice* (1992). Two experimental studies have specifically examined the implications of these social science insights. Stephen Rosoff, *Physicians as Criminal Defendants: Dr. Williams, Mr. Williams and the Ambivalence Hypothesis*, unpublished M.A. Thesis, University of California, Irvine (1984) presented identical evidence of a crime to two groups of jurors. For one group the accused was a physician and for the other group the accused was described as a member of a less prestigious occupational group. The physician condition yielded higher conviction rates than the lower status condition. In a follow-up experiment, Rosoff, Physicians as Criminal Defendants: Specialty, Sanctions, and Status Liability, 13 *Law & Human Behavior* 231 (1989) found that the degree of prestige accorded physicians as a function of their specialty area in medicine affected both perceptions of guilt and severity of recommended sanctions.

37. Over the past six years, I have conducted research on medical malpractice juries in the State of North Carolina. That research has included lengthy interviews with actual jurors who had just rendered verdicts in malpractice cases as well as realistic experimental studies in courthouses with persons who were awaiting jury duty. While the research involved civil as opposed to criminal trials many of my findings are highly consistent with the other literature bearing on the status and perceived professional responsibilities of physicians. On the whole, many jurors were inclined to give considerable deference to doctors. Nevertheless, a significant number of them expressed the view that they could not be fair and impartial in evaluating the trial evidence because of preconceived views about the special responsibilities doctors have for their patients. Many of these admissions were made under oath. This research is described in a forthcoming book: Neil Vidmar, *Medical Malpractice and the American Jury: Confronting the Myths About Jury Incompetence, Deep Pockets and Outrageous Damage Awards*, The University of Michigan Press (expected publication date: September, 1995).

38. In summary, it is my professional opinion that widely publicized reports of sexual abuse by doctors have created a climate of suspicion and hostility toward doctors accused of sexual assault. There is reason to believe that there is a widely held community belief that there should be a zero tolerance standard in judging sexual abuse by doctors; and that the courts, governing medical bodies, and ordinary doctors have been inexcusably lax in responding to the problem. It is likely that some prospective jurors may prejudge the case of *R. v. Musson* based primarily on this widespread publicity and not be able to set those notions aside and judge the evidence with a fair and impartial mind. Furthermore, if any of the prospective jurors perceive themselves to have been a victim of sexual abuse by a doctor it is even more likely that they will hold feelings that would prevent them from judging the case fairly and impartially. I hasten to add that it is **not** my opinion that anyone who perceives him or herself to have been a victim of sex abuse by a doctor will be biased. Some persons may be capable of setting those biases or prejudices aside. My opinion is that such an experience creates a substantial likelihood that the juror may be partial and express behavior consistent with those attitudes while serving as a juror.

GENERIC PREJUDICE REGARDING SEXUAL ASSAULT

39. I now turn to the issue of generic prejudice about sexual assault. At paragraph 18 B(2)(a) I provided some examples from recent Ontario cases in which, during a challenge for cause, jurors stated that they could not be impartial jurors and were found to be not impartial by the triers.

I specifically noted the male juror in *R. v. Morrissey and Morrissey* who spontaneously said that he could not be impartial because he personally had suffered abuse as a child. I offer here an additional example in the case of *R. v. Edward Henry Jackson*, unreported, Ont. C. J. (General Division), East Region, File 90-12085, October 21-22, 1991. The motion for a challenge for cause in that case and the affidavit of Mr. Jackson's lawyer, Karen Ann Reid, are appended to this affidavit as Appendix I. Briefly, the facts of the case are as follows. Mr. Jackson was charged with sexual assault and sexual interference. His lawyer requested a challenge for cause, but it was denied by the learned trial judge, Mr. Justice Poulin, and a jury was seated but then excused in order for the Court to hear procedural motions. That afternoon, the Court learned that one of the female jurors felt that she was unable to continue to be a juror in the trial. Upon questioning by Mr. Justice Poulin she stated that her difficulty arose out of things that had happened in her own past. She had also mentioned this to four other female jurors. Mr. Justice Poulin declared a mis-trial. In the subsequent re-trial of the case a challenge was allowed and 33 percent of jurors questioned were found to be not impartial More details of the case, including the candid comments of Mr. Justice Poulin, and the results of the challenge for cause in the re-trial are contained in the Reid affidavit and in the article by Chapman et. al. referred to in paragraph 11B supra.

40. As a result of the research undertaken with Mr. Skurka, I verily believe, that in *R. v. M. H.*, Ontario Court (General Division) Whitby, unreported, February 6, 1995, 26 jurors were challenged for cause on the issue of lack of impartiality regarding sexual assault charges and 10 were found to be partial. I verily believe, that in another unreported case, *R. v. Webb* Ont. Court of Justice (General Division) held in the region of Niagara, His Honor Mr. Justice Forestell, ruled that two questions could be put to the prospective jurors in a case involving a female complainant who alleged that she was sexually assaulted by the accused when she was 15 years of age and when she was 21 years of age. During the challenge 31 of 56 jurors answered affirmatively to a question of whether their ability to judge the case impartially would be affected just from knowing the facts of the charges and all were found to be partial by the triers.

41. In my professional opinion as a social psychologist the lack of impartiality of prospective jurors uncovered in the *R. v. Jackson* trials, in *R. v. Morrissey and Morrissey* and in the other cases described in the articles and cases cited in paragraphs 11A and 11B and paragraph 39 and 40 supra, are consistent with the results of social science research in this area. Social science evidence indicates that substantial numbers of persons have reported

that they have been victims of various types of sexual assault or sexual harassment. Newspapers, magazines, television programs, and television and radio talk show are filled with stories of sexual assaults and exploitation that simultaneously raise and reflect public concern about these issues. While being concerned about such matters or even being a victim does not necessarily mean that a prospective juror would be a biased juror, it is reasonable to assume that some may be biased and if questioned in a challenge for cause will state under oath that they are biased.

42. It is my professional opinion that some of the residents of the Central West Region, Ontario who will be called for jury duty in *R. v. Musson* are likely to hold similar views for reasons that I explain in the paragraphs below.

43. According to Statistics Canada's 1993 national Violence Against Women Survey, described in Volume 14, No.7 of the *Juristat Service Bulletin*, 39 percent of all Canadian women have experienced a (self-described) incident of sexual assault since the age of 16; 5 percent of women reported a sexual assault in the twelve months preceding the survey. Only 6 percent of the assaults reported in the survey were reported to the police, indicating that sexual assaults are heavily under-reported (for whatever reasons). Of the women reporting a sexual assault in the survey, 42 percent reported more than one incident, and 58 percent reported more that one experience of unwanted sexual touching. The women were more likely to be sexually assaulted by someone known to them than by a stranger.

44. The survey further uncovered the fact that 85 percent of the women who reported a sexual assault in the survey said that it had a negative emotional effect on them, including anger and fear. The Statistics Canada survey also reported that rates of reported sexual assault increased 142 percent from 1983 to 1992.

45. The Statistics Canada survey only addressed the issue of sexual assault involving women 18 years of age or older. It did not address the issue of sexual assault against men nor did it address the problem of child sex abuse. However, although the data on this issue are much less systematic we know that many Canadians, both male and female, have been victims of sexual assault or sexual abuse as children. It has been reported that statistics of the Institute for the Prevention of Child Abuse reveal that one in four Canadian girls and one in ten Canadian boys will be victims of sexual assault before they reach the age of 18, see R. Bessner, Kahn: Important Strides Made by the Supreme Court Respecting Children's Evidence, 79 C. R. (3d) 15 at 16 (1990).

The 1984 *Badgley Report on Sexual Offenses Against Children in Canada* drew nationwide attention to the problem of child sex abuse and not only helped to foster changes in the Criminal Code and the Canada Evidence Act but also resulted in the establishment of the Family Violence Prevention Division of Health and Welfare Canada. Currently, the federal government, all the provinces and territories, and many volunteer organizations have initiated public awareness programs about child sex abuse, see *Reaching for Solutions*, the Report of the Special Advisor to the Minister of National Health and Welfare on Child Sexual Abuse in Canada (1990). Other writings bearing on the incidence of child sex abuse in Canada include Martyn Kendrick, *Anatomy of a Nightmare: The Failure of Society in Dealing with Child Sex Abuse* (1988); Christopher Badgley, *Child Sex Abuse: The Search for Healing* (1990); Benjamin Schlesinger, *Sexual Abuse of Children in the 1980's* (1985). Canadian author, Sylvia Fraser's best selling book, *My Father's House* (1987) about incest continues to be popular and has been turned into a play performed in Hamilton and North York (reported in *Macleans*, February 27, 1995, page 58). The literature on child sex abuse is relevant for two reasons. First, some of the veniremen called for the Musson case may themselves have been victims of sex abuse or may be aware of family members or close friends who have been victims and may consequently hold attitudes about sexual assault such that they could not be fair and impartial jurors. Second, as Schlesinger observes in the preface to his book, "The topic of sexual abuse of children has been on the forefront of American and Canadian society in the 1980's." These concerns likely generalize to the whole topic of sexual abuse and sexual assault and may affect the attitudes of some veniremen called for duty in *R. v. Musson*.

46. In summary, it is my opinion that the widespread publicity about sexual assault and the actual fact of a large number of persons who have been, or believe themselves to have been, victims of sexual assault or child abuse increases the likelihood that some prospective jurors may hold attitudes and reactions that will prevent them from being impartial jurors.

IMPACT OF GENERIC PREJUDICE ON JUROR DECISIONS

47. There is a substantial body of literature by social scientists that has examined jury decision-making processes. See Valerie Hans and Neil Vidmar *Judging the Jury* (1986); Reid Hastie, Steven Penrod, and Nancy Pennington, *Inside the Jury* (1983); Saul Kassin and Lawrence Wrightsman, *The American Jury on Trial* (1988); Robert E. Litan (ed.) *Verdict: Assessing the Civil Jury System* (1993); Neil Vidmar, *Medical Malpractice and the American Jury* (in preparation, U. of Michigan Press); Neil Vidmar (ed.) Is the Jury

Competent? 52 *Law and Contemporary Problems* (1989) (whole issue); Kuhn, Weinstock and Flaton, How Well Do Jurors Reason? Competence Dimensions of Individual Variation in a Juror Reasoning Task, 5 *Psychological Science*, 289 (1994).

48. The empirical research has led to the development of a paradigm to understand jury decision-making processes. Called the "story model" by Hastie et. al., supra paragraph 47, it has been widely accepted as a valid model by researchers in Canada, the United States and England. The model is grounded in an extensive body of social psychological research that has studied how people develop "social schemas" to understand and interact with others in everyday life. In essence, the story model asserts that the jurors' task consists of three stages, a "story construction" stage, a "verdict category representation" stage, and a "story classification" stage. The first stage, which begins at the start of the trial and extends into deliberations, involves the jurors' active organization of the evidence into a story form that describes what happened. The jurors use their own experience and beliefs about human behavior and its underlying causes to organize the events brought out at trial to produce one or more plausible accounts, or stories, of what occurred. During the second stage, the verdict alternatives outlined by the judge at the conclusion of the trial are developed into categories with defining features and decision rules that specify how they will be combined. Finally, during the third stage, the juror searches for the best possible match between features of the stories developed in the first stage and the verdict categories elaborated in the second stage.

49. Story construction during the first stage, therefore, is crucial to the two other stages. The story model has particular relevance to understanding how pre-trial prejudices that may exist prior to the juror coming to the courtroom can have a direct effect on the way that the juror views the accused, the victim, witnesses and the nature of the crime. These prejudices colour the way that testimony and other evidence is viewed, evaluated and integrated into the juror's construction of the contested legal events. However, the story model also explains how pre-trial prejudice may have effects as the evidence unfolds at trial, such as causing the juror to give differential weight to the evidence of some witnesses based not on an impartial evaluation of the evidence but rather as a result of the prior stereotypes and expectations, e.g., see Kuhn et. al. supra paragraph 47. Third, prejudiced attitudes may be expressed during the deliberation phase of the jury's task, causing the jurors to tilt in the direction of their prejudices in reaching a verdict.

50. The story model and the research that supports it explains how generic prejudice and the attitudes associated with it can be transformed into behavioral prejudice. For example, if a juror holds deep emotional prejudices about homosexual acts, those attitudes may affect the juror's judgement at several stages of the trial process. The mere fact that the charges involve allegations of homosexual acts may tilt the juror's initial assumptions about the guilt or innocence of the accused toward guilt. Equally important, however, the biases may manifest themselves as the juror listens to various witnesses and integrates their testimony into his or her cognitive framework about what actually occurred: evidence supporting a finding of guilt will be given greater weight than evidence favoring a not guilty verdict. At the end of the evidence presentation and during deliberations, if the evidence favoring a verdict one way or another is in equipose, the juror will tilt toward a verdict favoring his or her initial prejudices. To the extent that the juror projects his or her own beliefs as being held by others in the community, the tilt will be enhanced. If the prejudice against homosexual acts is accompanied by other prejudices, such as generic prejudice involving accusations of sexual assaults against patients by their physicians, the judgmental biases will be increased further.

51. In summary, it is my professional opinion that there is a reasonable likelihood that some jurors called to serve in *R. v. Musson* will hold generic prejudices arising from attitudes about allegations of sexual acts between males, about sexual assault generally, and/or about allegations of physicians violating the doctor-patient relationship. It is further my opinion that there is a reasonable likelihood that **some** of these persons may not be able to set those prejudices aside and decide the case impartially from the evidence presented at trial, because these attitudes are so deeply held.

THE EFFECTIVENESS OF JUDICIAL ADMONITIONS

52. In previous testimony and writings I have addressed the effectiveness of judicial admonitions or questions to the whole panel of jurors in lieu of individual challenges for cause. In Vidmar and Melnitzer, supra paragraph 7, I presented empirical evidence in the case of *R. v. Iutzi* that the judge's statements to the whole panel to excuse themselves if they were biased were largely ineffective. Only 4 of 123 persons stepped forward; yet, the subsequent "challenge for cause" resulted in the dismissal of many prospective jurors on some of the same grounds set forth in the initial address to the whole panel. I confirmed this finding in two subsequent unpublished studies that I conducted in the *R. v. Foshay* (1986) and *R. v. Johnson and Kear* (1986). The case of *R. v. Jackson* described in paragraph

39, supra, appears consistent with these findings. The admonitions by the learned trial judge to the whole panel appears to have been ineffective in light of the subsequent disclosures of bias.

53. Research findings that are generally consistent with the above findings are discussed in Valerie Hans and Neil Vidmar *Judging the Jury* (1986) at 71; see also Jones, Judge versus attorney-conducted voir dire: an empirical investigation of juror candor, 11 *Law & Human Behavior* 131 (1987) (indicating that the formal courtroom environment hinders juror disclosure of prejudices); Moran, Cutler and Loftus, Jury selection in major controlled substance trials, 3 *Forensic Reports* 331 (1990).

54. In *R. v. Parks*, 24 C.R. (4th) 82 at 83 (1993), Mr. Justice Doherty also spoke to the issue of the effectiveness of judicial admonitions when he stated:

> "Attitudes which are ingrained in an individual's subconscious and are reflected by individual and institutional conduct within a community will be more resistant to judicial cleansing than the impact of yesterday's news about a specific person or event."

Mr. Justice Doherty was discussing the issue of racial prejudice but his view seems consistent with the substance of paragraphs 52 and 53 supra. Moreover, it is my opinion, based on the material already discussed in this affidavit, that as regards the issues of homosexual acts, sexual assaults by doctors and sexual assaults in general, that it is likely that similar subconscious attitudes, supported by individual and institutional conduct, exist in some Canadians.

55. An additional issue involves the efficacy of judicial instructions at the end of trial in lieu of the remedy of jury selection through a challenge for cause. Stated baldly, the issue is whether a judge's admonition to be "fair and impartial" during his or her charge to the jury is sufficient to cancel any conceived biases among jurors who have prejudices. It is my professional opinion that while judicial admonitions may have their intended impact in many cases, there is a reasonable probability that they will not be effective in this case.

56. For some jurors their attitudes about homosexuality, about allegations of sexual assaults by physicians, or sexual assaults in general are likely to be held very deeply and at a subconscious level. The biased juror may not even be aware that his or her own deeply held prejudices are relevant to the case and the legal meaning of impartiality since the issue has never been raised. Furthermore, as the research on the "story model" of

juror decision-making indicates, the damage will already have been done. The testimony and other evidence will have been evaluated and integrated in a biased way throughout the trial; even if the juror attempts to be impartial he or she will be working from impressions that have already been formed.

57. My professional opinion that there is a reasonable likelihood that judicial instructions during the jury charge will not be effective in this case is generally supported by a rather substantial body of social science research. That research indicates that when juror biases are based around intense emotional reactions, judicial admonitions to set prejudices aside are frequently ineffective. See Kramer et.al., Pre-trial Publicity, Judicial Remedies, and Jury Bias, 14 *Law and Human Behavior* 409 (1990); Tanford, The Law and Psychology of Jury Instructions, 69 *Nebraska Law Review* 71 (1990); Sue, Smith, and Pedroza, Authoritarianism, Pre-trial Publicity, and Awareness of Bias in Simulated Jurors, 37 *Psychological Reports* 1299 (1975); Kerr et.al, On the Effectiveness of Voir Dire in Criminal Cases with Pre-trial Publicity: An Empirical Study, 40 *American University Law Review* 665 (1991); Edward Bronson, *the Effectiveness of Voir Dire in Discovering Prejudice in High Publicity Cases: An Archival Study of the Minimization Effect*, Discussion Series 89, California State University, Chico, California (1989); Ogloff and Vidmar, The Impact of Pre-trial Publicity on Jurors: A Study to compare the Relative Effects of Television and Print Media in a Child Sex Abuse Case, 18 *Law and Human Behavior* 507 (1994).

PROPOSED CHALLENGE FOR CAUSE QUESTIONS

58. Drawing upon the conclusions summarized in Paragraph 51, I now turn to the issue of proposed questions for a challenge for cause. I begin by offering some observations on the rationale behind the proposed questions. First, I am cognizant of the constraints placed upon the "challenge for cause" process as set forth in the leading cases of *R. v. Hubbert* (1975) 29 C.C.C. (2d) 279 and *R. v. Sherratt* (1991) 63 C.C.C. (3d) 193. *Hubbert* proscribed the extensive "American style" questioning of jurors that often delves into prospective jurors' personal lives and attitudes, as stated by Laskin, C.J.C. at 289 90:

> Challenge for cause is not for the purpose of finding out what kind of juror the person called is likely to be — his personality, beliefs, prejudices, likes or dislikes...
>
> The challenge must never be used by counsel as a means of indoctrinating the jury panel to the proposed defence or otherwise attempting to influence the result of the eventual trial. ..."an accused is entitled to an indifferent jury not a favorable one".

In *R. v. Parks* and again in *R. v. Rollocks* Mr. Justice Doherty expressed the view that the *Hubbert* standards and constraints, as modified by *Sherratt*, remain the law in Canada. Second, I am also cognizant of Mr. Justice Doherty's enunciation of the test for partiality:

> "Partiality has both an attitudinal and a behavioral component. It refers to one who has certain preconceived biases and who will allow those biases to affect his or her verdict despite the trial safeguards designed to prevent reliance on those biases. A partial juror is one who is biased and who will discriminate against one of the parties to the litigation based on that bias, *R. v. Parks* 24 C.R. (4th) at 93."

59. I offer the Court two challenge for cause questions that are introduced with a preamble that is intended to help the prospective juror understand why the questions are being asked and to help him or her understand the specific context of the questions in order to give the most informed and honest answers. In the following paragraph I further explain the rational behind these questions.

TWO PROPOSED QUESTIONS

As His Honor will tell you, in deciding whether or not the Crown has proven charges against an accused person, a juror must judge the evidence of all witnesses without bias, prejudice, or partiality; that is, the juror must decide the case with an open and fair mind. I want to ask you some questions to determine if you believe that you can be a fair and impartial juror in this case.

Dr. Robert Scott Musson has been charged with two counts of sexual assault. The complainants in this case claim that while they were ages 18 and 22, respectively, Dr. Musson, on different occasions and without their consent, improperly touched their genital areas, performed oral sex on one of them, caused one of them to masturbate him and engage in other homosexual activities. One of the complainants alleges that some of these homosexual acts were undertaken when he was under the medical care of Dr. Musson, who is a licensed medical doctor.

1. Knowing these allegations, do you hold any personal beliefs, attitudes or prejudices about homosexual activity that you cannot set aside and that would prevent you from hearing the evidence and deciding this case in a fair and impartial manner?

2. Do you hold any beliefs, attitudes, or prejudices about charges of sexual assault in general, or charges of sexual assault involving medical doctors that you cannot set aside and that would prevent you from hearing the evidence with an open mind, and deciding this case in a fair and impartial manner?

60. Preambles to challenge for cause questions have been given in prior Ontario cases, see, e.g., Cooper, supra paragraph 11B; Vidmar and Melnitzer, supra paragraph 7; Skurka, supra paragraph 11B. such preambles are consistent with psychological and sociological research on how to get people to understand the context in which questions are being asked and thereby to elicit the most informed answers, see, e.g., Earl Babbie, *The Practice of Social Research* 6th ed., 1992; Shari Diamond, Reference Guide on Survey Research, in Federal Judicial Center, *Reference Manual on Scientific Evidence* (1994); Cannell and Kahn, Interviews, in Gardner Lindzey and Elliott Aronson, eds., *Handbook of Social Psychology*, 2nd ed., Vol. 2 (1968).

(a) Question one specifically address bias based on attitudes toward homosexual acts.

(b) Question two addresses biases arising out of media reports of sexual abuse generally and sexual abuse by doctors during their treatment of patients (as well as any juror who may have personally experienced medical treatment that was perceived as improper).

61. In my professional opinion as a social psychologist the questions are consistent with the test set forth in *Parks*. They are not solely concerned with whether any preconceived attitudes or biases exist but rather address the behavioral implications of the attitudes. They ask the juror whether any attitudes or biases that he or she holds can be set aside in order to decide the case fairly and impartially.

THE ISSUE OF ADMINISTRATIVE COSTS

62. The recent British Columbia case of *R. v. Williams* (1994) 90 C.C.C. (3d) 194 at 209 expressed concern about the administrative costs to the court of challenge for cause. However, in *R. v. Cox* (1994) Justice Taliano observed that in *R. v. Sherratt* Madam Justice L'Heureaux-Dube concluded that any inconvenience caused by the process is "not too great an inconvenience for society to pay in ensuring that accused persons in this country have, and appear to have, a fair trial before an impartial tribunal, in this case the jury." Similarly in the case of *R. v. R. G.* Ont. C. J. (Gen. Div.)

Hamilton, September 13, 1994, in approving a challenge for cause application Mr. Justice W. Stayshyn addressed the issue of time and expense by saying: "In any event when concerning the liberty of the subject, time and expense should not be and must not be a consideration" (at page 9). Nevertheless, I will report here that in my prior observations of the challenge for cause process in Ontario cases, the selection of a jury with challenges for cause consumed, on average, about three hours of court time. In recent research and correspondence with defense lawyers in preparation for my presentation to the 1994 Criminal Lawyers' Association, I obtained similar or even lower estimates for the time required to select a jury with challenges for cause.

63. I offer the opinions set forth in this affidavit on behalf of Dr. Robert Scott Musson's application for a challenge for cause and for no other purpose.

SWORN before me at the City of)
Durham, in the County of)
Durham, N.C., this _____ day of)
April, 1995.)

____

Neil (Joseph) Vidmar

____

A COMMISSIONER, ETC.

APPENDIX III

PROVINCIAL JURY ACTS

Alberta: *Jury Act*, R.S.A. 1980, c. J-2

Juror Eligibility Provisions

Qualifications as jurors

2. Subject to the exemptions and disqualifications hereinafter mentioned, a resident of Alberta who is

(a) at least 18 years of age, and

(b) a Canadian citizen or natural born British subject,

is qualified and liable to serve as a juror in all civil and criminal cases tried by a jury in the judicial district in which he resides.

Exemption from service on jury

3. A person otherwise qualified and liable to serve as a juror whose name appears on a current jury list may if over the age of 60 years claim exemption from service on a jury, and if the exemption is claimed, he shall be excused from serving on a jury.

Exemptions

4. The following persons are exempt from being returned and from serving as common jurors:

(a) members of the Privy Council, or of the Senate, or of the House of Commons, Canada;

(b) members of the Legislative Assembly and the officers thereof;
(c) all salaried officials and employees of the Governments of Canada and Alberta;
(d) mayors, reeves, councillors, salaried officials and employees of a municipality;
(e) officers of a court of justice, whether of general or local jurisdiction, including every sheriff, sheriff's officer, constable or bailiff;
(f) provincial judges and justices of the peace;
(g) members of the Royal Canadian Mounted Police force;
(h) members of the police force of any municipality;
(i) salaried firemen or members of a voluntary fire brigade of any municipality;
(j) professors, masters, teachers and other salaried officials or employees of any university, college or school;
(k) clergy of all denominations;
(l) physicians, registered nurses, dental surgeons, Dominion and Alberta land surveyors, chemists and druggists and apprentices to chemists and druggists, barristers, solicitors and students-at-law who are in good standing in the books of their respective corporations;
(m) editors, reporters and printers of any public newspaper or journal;
(n) licensed ferry-men, mail carriers and postmasters;
(o) pilots in actual service;
(p) all persons liable under contract to be required in the running of railway trains or buses, or liable to be employed in the operation of telegraph lines and telephones;
(q) millers, where owners of mills or employees under contract are liable to be required in the operation of mills;
(r) officers of the Canadian Forces when on full pay.

Disqualifications

5. No person is qualified to serve as a juror

(a) who has been convicted of a criminal offence for which he has been sentenced to death or to a term of imprisonment exceeding 12 months, or

(b) who is affected with blindness or deafness, or who is a lunatic, idiot or imbecile, or who possesses any other physical or mental infirmity incompatible with the discharge of the duties of a juror.

Period of exemption after serving

6. No person shall be compelled to serve as a juror more than once in any period of 2 years, unless there is not a sufficient number of qualified persons to serve as jurors residing within a reasonable distance of the place of trial.

British Columbia: *Jury Act*, R.S.B.C 1979, c. 210

Juror Eligibility Provisions

Jury duty

2. A person has the right and duty to serve as a juror unless disqualified or exempted under this Act.

Disqualification

3. (1) A person is disqualified from serving as a juror who is

(a) not a Canadian citizen;
(b) not resident in the Province;
(c) under the age of majority;
(d) a member or officer of the Parliament of Canada or of the Privy Council of Canada;
(e) a member or officer of the Legislature or of the Executive Council;
(f) a judge, justice or court referee;
(g) an employee of the Department of Justice or of the Solicitor General of Canada;
(h) an employee of the Ministry of the Attorney General of the Province;
(h.1) an employee of the Legal Services Society or of a funded agency, as defined by the *Legal Services Society Act*;
(i) a barrister or solicitor;
(j) a court official;
(k) a sheriff or sheriff's officer;
(l) a peace officer;
(m) a warden, correctional officer or person employed in a penitentiary, prison or correctional institution;

(n) subject to a mental or physical infirmity incompatible with the discharge of the duties of a juror;

(o) a person convicted within the previous 5 years of an offence for which the punishment could be a fine of more than $2,000 or imprisonment for one year or more, unless he has been pardoned; or

(p) under a charge for an offence for which the punishment could be a fine of more than $2,000 or imprisonment for one year or more.

(2) An officer or person regularly employed in the collection, management or accounting of revenue under the *Financial Administration Act*, or a person registered under the *Chiropractors Act*, *Dentists Act* or *Naturopaths Act* is exempt, if he so desires, from serving on a jury.

Disqualification because of language difficulty

4. Where the language in which a trial is to be conducted is one that a person is unable to understand, speak or read, he is disqualified from serving as a juror in the trial.

Interpreters and interpretative devices

4.1 Section 4 does not apply to a person who

(a) would be unable, if unaided, to see or hear adequately for the purpose of serving as a juror, and

(b) will as a juror receive the assistance of a person or device that the court considers adequate to enable the juror to serve.

Grounds for exemption

5. (1) A person may apply to the sheriff to be exempted from serving as a juror on the grounds that

(a) he belongs to a religion or a religious order that makes service as a juror incompatible with the beliefs or practices of the religion or order; or

(b) serving as a juror may cause serious hardship or loss to him or to others.

Exemption for person 65 years of age or over

6. A person over the age of 65 years, on application to the sheriff, shall be exempted from serving as a juror.

Juror exempted from jury service for 2 years

12. No person shall be required to serve on a jury for 2 years next after his having served as a juror on a trial.

Manitoba: *The Jury Act*, R.S.M. 1987, C. J30

Juror Eligibility Provisions

Jury Duty

2. Every person has the right and duty to serve as a juror unless disqualified or exempted under this Act.

Disqualification

3. Every person is disqualified from serving as a juror who is

(a) Repealed, R.S.M. 1987 (Supp.), c. 4, s. 14(l).
(b) not resident in the province; or
(c) under the age of majority; or
(d) a member or officer of the Parliament of Canada or the Privy Council of Canada; or
(e) a member or officer of the Legislature or the Executive Council; or
(f) a judge, magistrate or justice of the peace; or
(g) an officer or employee of the Department of Justice or of the Department of the Solicitor General in the Government of Canada; or
(h) an officer or employee of the Department of Justice in the Government of Manitoba; or
(i) a member of the Law Society of Manitoba; or
(j) a court official; or
(k) a sheriff or sheriff's officer; or
(l) a peace officer or a member of a police force; or
(m) a warden, correctional officer or person employed in a penitentiary, prison or correctional institution or a probation officer; or
(n) a medical examiner under The Fatality Inquiries Act; or
(o) a person afflicted with a mental or physical infirmity incompatible with the discharge of the duties of a juror; or
(p) a person convicted of an indictable offence, unless he or she has been pardoned; or
(q) a person convicted within the previous five years of an offence for which the punishment could be a fine of $5,000. or more or imprisonment for one year or more, unless he or she has been pardoned; or
(r) a person charged within the previous two years with an offence for which the punishment could be a fine of $5,000. or more or imprisonment for one year or more where the person has not been acquitted, the

charge has not been dismissed or withdrawn and a stay of proceedings has not been entered in respect of the trial or the offence.

Language difficulty

4. Where the language in which a trial is primarily to be conducted is one that a person is unable to understand, speak or read, that person is disqualified from serving as a juror in the trial.

Grounds for exemption

25 (1) A person may apply to the sheriff to be exempted from serving as a juror on the grounds that

(a) the person belongs to a religion or religious order that makes service as a juror incompatible with the beliefs or practices of the religion or order; or
(b) serving as a juror may cause serious hardship or loss to the person or others; or
(c) the person is a member of the regular force of the Canadian Forces or a member of a reserve force of the Canadian forces who is on active service under the National Defence Act (Canada).

25 (2) Repealed, R.S.M. 1987 (Supp.), c. 4, s. 14.

Exemption on resummoning

25 (3) A person who has served as a juror and who within two years after the date he or she last served as a juror is summoned again to serve as a juror shall, on application, be exempted from serving as a juror.

New Brunswick: *Jury Act*, R.S.N.B. 1973, c. J-3.1

Juror Eligibility Provisions

Qualifications

2. Except as otherwise provided, every resident of the Province who is nineteen years of age or over and a Canadian citizen is qualified and liable to serve as a juror in any judicial district.

Ineligibility

3. The following persons are ineligible to serve as jurors:

(a) members and clerks of the Senate and the House of Commons of Canada;
(b) members and clerks of the Legislative Assembly;
(c) judges of The Court of Queen's Bench of New Brunswick, The Court of Appeal of New Brunswick and the Provincial Court of New Brunswick;

(d) solicitors and other officers of the courts;
(e) peace officers referred to in paragraphs (a), (b) and (c) of the definition "peace officer" in section 2 of the *Criminal Code* (Canada);
(f) auxiliary police officers and auxiliary police constables;
(g) persons employed in the federal or provincial Office of the Attorney General or the Department of Justice;
(h) persons employed in the Department of the Solicitor General or in the Department of the Solicitor General of Canada;
(i) spouses of persons referred to in paragraphs (a) to (h);
(j) ordained ministers, priests or clergymen of any faith or worship licensed to perform marriages in the Province;
(k) persons who are members of religious orders vowed to live only in a convent, monastery or other like religious community;
(l) duly qualified medical practitioners;
(m) duly qualified dental practitioners;
(n) veterinarians;
(o) members of Her Majesty's forces on active service;
(p) firefighters;
(q) consuls and consular agents; and
(r) persons convicted of an offence under the *Criminal Code* (Canada), the *Food and Drugs Act* (Canada) or the *Narcotic Control Act* (Canada) unless they have obtained a pardon.

4. (2) Notwithstanding subsection (1), where a person who is not qualified under section 2 or ineligible under section 3 is sworn or solemnly affirmed as a juror without being challenged, he or she shall be conclusively deemed to be qualified and eligible to serve as a juror.

Exemptions

5. The following persons may be exempted from serving as jurors:

(a) a person who has served on a jury within the five years preceding the summons to serve on a jury;
(b) a person who is seventy years of age or over;

(c) a person who is unable to understand, speak or read the official language in which the proceeding is to be conducted;
(d) a person who suffers from a physical, mental or other infirmity that is incompatible with the discharge of the duties of a juror;
(e) a person for whom service on a jury would cause severe hardship because that person has the care during all or any part of the day of
  (i) a child who is under fourteen years of age,
  (ii) a person who is infirm or aged, or
  (iii) a person who is mentally incompetent; and
(f) a person for whom service on a jury would cause serious and irreparable financial loss because the proceeding is expected to last ten or more sitting days.

5.1 (1) Paragraph 5(d) does not apply to a person who suffers from a physical infirmity and wishes to serve as a juror who

(a) if aided would be able to see and hear adequately and to attend a proceeding in adequate comfort, and
(b) will receive the assistance of a person or device that the presiding judge considers adequate to enable the person to discharge the duties of a juror.

Newfoundland: *Jury Act*, R.S.N. 1990, c. J-5

Juror Eligibility Provisions

Jury duty **3.** Every person who is a Canadian citizen resident in the province and is of the age of majority has the right and duty to serve as a juror unless he or she is disqualified or exempted under this Act.

Disqualifications **4.** A person is disqualified from serving as a juror who is

(a) a member, an officer or employee of the Parliament of Canada or of the Privy Council of Canada;
(b) a member, an officer or employee of the House of Assembly or of the Executive Council of the province;
(c) a judge of the Court of Appeal, the Trial Division or Provincial Court of Newfoundland;

(d) an officer or employee of the Department of Justice or of the Solicitor General of the Government of Canada;
(e) an officer or employee of the Department of Justice of the government of the province;
(f) a barrister or solicitor;
(g) a court official;
(h) a sheriff or sheriff's officer;
(i) a member of a police force;
(j) a justice;
(k) a warden, correctional officer or person employed in a penitentiary, prison or correctional institution;
(l) a spouse of a person referred to in paragraphs (a) to (k);
(m) a person who is blind, deaf, or has an infirmity incompatible with the discharge of the duties of a juror;
(n) a person convicted within 5 years of the taking of the jury list of an offence for which the punishment could be a fine of $1,000 or more or imprisonment for 1 year or more; or
(o) a person charged with an offence for which the punishment could be a fine of $1,000 or more or imprisonment for 1 year or more.

Language difficulty

5. Where the language in which a trial is to be conducted is one that a person is unable to understand or speak, he or she is disqualified from serving as a juror in the trial.

Grounds for exemption

6. (1) A person may apply to be exempted from serving as a juror on the grounds that serving as a juror may cause serious hardship or loss to the person or others.

(2) Service as a juror may be considered to cause serious hardship to a person, for purposes of subsection (1), where a person has the sole care during all or a part of a day on which the court is in session of

(a) a person who is under the age of 7 years and not in full time attendance at a school as defined by the *Schools Act*;
(b) a person who is infirm or aged; or
(c) a person who is suffering from an incapacity.

Religious exemption

7. Where a person's pastoral or religious duties or beliefs would conflict with service as a juror, that person shall, on application, be exempted from serving as a juror.

Exemption for age

8. A person over the age of 65 years shall, on application, be exempted from serving as a juror.

16. (1) Jurors are not liable to serve on a jury more than once every 3 years.

(2) Once a person has served in the period set out in subsection (1) his or her card shall be set aside by the sheriff.

(3) Where more jurors are required at a time than there are cards remaining in the box, the cards of those who have served as jurors shall be returned to the box after all the other cards have been drawn from the box.

Northwest Territories: *Jury Act*, R.S.N.W.T. 1988, c. J-2

Juror Eligibility Provisions

Persons qualified as jurors

4. Subject to this Act, every person who

(a) has attained the age of 19 years,

(b) is a Canadian citizen or permanent resident of Canada, and

(c) is able to speak and understand either English or French,

is qualified to serve as a juror in any action or proceeding that may be tried by a jury in the Territories.

Persons qualified as jurors

5. No person is qualified to serve as a juror who

(a) has been convicted of an offence for which he or she was sentenced to a term of imprisonment exceeding one year, not having been subsequently granted a free pardon; or

(b) possesses any physical or mental disability that is incompatible with the discharge of the duties of a juror.

Persons exempt from service as jurors

6. The following persons are exempt from service as jurors:

(a) members of the Queen's Privy Council for Canada or of the Senate or House of Commons of Canada;

(b) the Commissioner and members of the Legislative Assembly;

(c) members of the Royal Canadian Mounted Police;
(d) judges of any court of record, territorial judges, justices of the peace and coroners;
(e) practising barristers and solicitors;
(f) members of the clergy of any denomination;
(g) salaried fire-fighters and active members of the fire brigade of a municipality;
(h) officers of the Court, including Sheriff's officers, constables and bailiffs;
(i) telegraph, telephone and radio operators;
(j) officers and members of the Canadian Armed Forces;
(k) physicians, surgeons, dental surgeons and druggists in active practice;
(l) nurses in active practice;
(m) persons whose duties relate to the custody and confinement of prisoners.

Persons excused from service as jurors

7. No person is required to serve as a juror more than once in any two-year period unless the service of that person as a juror is necessary by reason of there being an insufficient number of persons qualified to serve as jurors within a distance of 30 km from the place of trial.

Persons not to be entered on list

8. (3) The name of any person whose place of dwelling is more than 30 km from the place fixed for the sittings of the Court shall not be entered on the list unless the number of persons who live within a distance of 30 km from that place and who are qualified to serve as jurors is, in the opinion of the Sheriff, insufficient, having regard to subsection (2).

Summoning of jurors

16. (1) On receipt of the precept referred to in section 15, the Sheriff shall summon each person named on the panel list by serving a written summons in the prescribed form on the person or leaving it with a responsible member of his or her household.

Hardship

(2) When serving a summons on a person, the Sheriff shall ascertain or attempt to ascertain whether the service of that person as a juror will inflict on him or her undue hardship or serious inconvenience and if, in the opinion of the Sheriff, such hardship or inconvenience is likely to result, the Sheriff shall report this to the Clerk.

GENERAL

Excusing jurors **22.** The judge may for a good cause, excuse from service as a juror any person who has been summoned but has not been sworn.

Nova Scotia: *Juries Act*, R.S.N.S. 1989, c. 242

Juror Eligibility Provisions

Qualifications **4** Subject to Section 5, every person shall be qualified and liable to serve as a juror for a jury district who
(a) is a Canadian citizen;
(b) has attained the age of eighteen years; and
(c) has resided for twelve months within the jury district.

Exemption from service as juror **5** (1) The following persons shall be exempt from serving as jurors:

(a) the Lieutenant Governor of the Province;
(b) members of the Senate and the House of Commons of Canada;
(c) members of the House of Assembly and, while the House is in session, the officers thereof;
(d) judges of the Supreme and county courts;
(e) officers and men of the Canadian Forces on active service;
(f) barristers and solicitors of the Supreme Court;
(g) officers of the Supreme and any county court other than commissioners appointed under the *Notaries and Commissioners Act*;
(h) full-time salaried members of any policy force in the Province;
(i) medical practitioners;
(j) dental practitioners;
(k) clergymen and ministers of the gospel;
(l) judges of the provincial court and judges of the Family Court; and
(m) members of a jury committee.

Exemption at discretion of judge (2) The judge presiding at a session or the Chief Justice may grant to any person exemption from service as a juror at the whole or part of that session upon application by or on behalf of the person.

Jury service only once in three years

(3) No person shall be liable to serve as a juror for more than one session in any three-year period.

Disqualification

(4) No person shall serve as a juror who has been convicted of any criminal offence for which the punishment included death or for which he was sentenced to a term of imprisonment of two years or more.

One member of family unit a term

(5) No more than one member of a family unit or member or employee of a firm shall be liable to serve as a juror at a session.

Interpretation of subsection (5)

(6) For the purposes of subsection (5), "family unit" includes a husband, a wife and any relative of the husband or wife residing in one dwelling and "firm" means a person or association of persons carrying on a business or activity employing more than one and less than fifteen persons.

Ontario: *Juries Act*, R.S.O. 1990, c. J.3

Juror Eligibility Provisions

Eligible jurors

2. Subject to sections 3 and 4, every person who,

(a) resides in Ontario;

(b) is a Canadian citizen; and

(c) in the year preceding the year for which the jury is selected had attained the age of eighteen years or more,

is eligible and liable to serve as a juror on juries in the Ontario Court (General Division) in the county in which he or she resides.

Ineligible occupations

3. (1) The following persons are ineligible to serve as jurors:

1. Every member of the Privy Council of Canada or the Executive Council of Ontario.
2. Every member of the Senate, the House of Commons of Canada or the Assembly.
3. Every judge and every justice of the peace.

4. Every barrister and solicitor and every student-at-law.
5. Every legally qualified medical practitioner and veterinary surgeon who is actively engaged in practice and every coroner.
6. Every person engaged in the enforcement of law including, without restricting the generality of the foregoing, sheriffs, wardens of any penitentiary, superintendents, jailers or keepers of prisons, correctional institutions or lockups, sheriff's officers, police officers, and officers of a court of justice.

Connection with court action at same sittings

(3) Every person who has been summoned as a witness or is likely to be called as a witness in a civil or criminal proceeding or has an interest in an action is ineligible to serve as a juror at any sittings at which the proceeding or action might be tried.

Previous service

(4) Every person who, at any time within three years preceding the year for which the jury roll is prepared, has attended court for jury service in response to a summons after selection from the roll prepared under this Act or any predecessor thereof is ineligible to serve as a juror in that year.

Ineligibility for personal reasons

4. A person is ineligible to serve as a juror who,
(a) has a physical or mental disability that would seriously impair his or her ability to discharge the duties of a juror; or
(b) has been convicted of an indictable offence, unless the person has subsequently been granted a pardon.

Excusing of jurors

19.–(2) The sheriff may excuse any person summoned for a jury sittings on the ground,
(a) of illness; or
(b) that serving as a juror may cause serious hardships or loss to the person or others,

but unless a judge of the Ontario Court (General Division) directs otherwise and despite any other provision of this Act, such person shall be included in a panel to be returned for a sittings later in the year or, where there are not further sittings in that year, in a panel to be returned for a sittings in the year next following.

Excusing of juror for religious reasons

23.–(1) A person summoned for jury duty may be excused by a judge from service as a juror on the ground that service as a juror is incompatible with the beliefs or practices of a religion or religious order to which the person belongs.

Excusing of jurors for illness or hardship

(2) A person summoned for jury duty may be excused by a judge from attending the sittings on the ground,

(a) of illness; or

(b) that serving as a juror may cause serious hardships or loss to the person or others,

and the judge may excuse the person from all service as a juror, or the judge may direct that the service of a person excused be postponed and that despite any provision of this Act, the person be included in a panel to be returned for a sittings later in that year or in a panel to be returned for a sittings in the year next following.

Prince Edward Island: *Jury Act*, R.S.P.E.I. 1988, c. J-5

Juror Eligibility Provisions

Qualification for & liability to jury duty

3. Unless exempt or disqualified by this Act, every inhabitant of the age of majority who is a Canadian citizen, resident in this province for twelve months previous to his being summoned, is qualified and liable to serve in the court as a juror on the trial of civil and criminal cases in the county within which he resides.

Disqualifications for jury duty

4. A person is disqualified from serving as a juror who is

(a) a member or officer of the Parliament of Canada or of the Privy Council of Canada;

(b) a member or officer of the provincial legislature;

(c) a judge, provincial court judge, justice of the peace or coroner;

(d) an officer or employee of the Department of Justice or of the Solicitor General of the Government of Canada;

(e) an officer or employee of the Department of Justice and Attorney-General of the Government of this province;

(f) a barrister, solicitor, and attorney or an articled clerk;
(g) a court officer of any court of justice whether of general or local jurisdiction including every sheriff, sheriff's officer, constable or bailiff;
(h) a peace officer;
(i) a warden, correctional officer or person employed in a penitentiary, prison or correctional institution;
(j) a spouse of a person mentioned in clause (c), (d), (e), (f), (g), (h) or (i);
(k) afflicted with blindness or deafness or a mental or physical infirmity incompatible with the discharge of the duties of a juror;
(l) a person convicted within the previous five years of an offence for which the punishment could have been a fine of $1,000 or more or imprisonment for one year or more, unless he has been pardoned; or
(m) charged with an offence for which the punishment could be a fine of $1,000 or more or imprisonment for one year or more.

Language disqualification

5. Where the language in which a trial is to be conducted is one that a person is unable to understand, speak or read, he is disqualified from serving as a juror in the trial.

Exemption

6. A person may be excused from jury service by the presiding judge upon application by him or by a party to the proceeding in which he is called or drawn as juror on the grounds that serving as a juror may cause serious hardship or loss to that person or to others.

Limitation on Service

7. No person shall be compelled to serve as a juror more than once in two years.

Quebec: *Loi Sur Les Jurés*, R.S.Q., c. J-2

Qualités des Jurés

Qualités requises

3. Pour être juré, une personne doit:
a) être de citoyenneté canadienne;
b) être majeure; et
c) être inscrite sur la liste électorale.

Inhabilité

4. Est inhabile à être juré:

a) une personne qui ne possède pas les qualités requises par l'article 3;
b) un membre du Conseil Privé, du Sénat ou de la Chambre des communes du Canada;
c) un membre du Conseil exécutif ou de l'Assemblée nationale;
d) un juge de la Cour suprême du Canada, de la Cour fédérale, de la Cour d'appel, de la Cour supérieure, de la Cour du Québec ou d'une cour municipale, un coroner et un officier de justice;
e) un avocat ou un notaire en exercice;
f) un agent de la paix;
g) un pompier;
h) une personne souffrant d'une déficience ou d'une maladie mentale;
i) une personne qui ne parle pas couramment le français ou l'anglais, sous réserve des articles 30 et 45; ou
j) une personne sous le coup d'une accusation pour un acte criminel ou qui en a été déclarée coupable;
k) dans les districts judiciaires de Mingan, de Gaspé, d'Abitibi, dans ce dernier cas, dans les territoires d"Abitibi, de Mistassini et du Nouveau-Québec, une personne qui n'est pas domiciliée dans une municipalité située entièrement ou partiellement dans un rayon de 60 kilomètres du chef-lieu du district judiciaire ou de tout autre endroit autorisé par le gouvernement conformément aux articles 51 ou 70 de la Loi sur les tribunaux judiciaires (chapitre T-16).

Exemptions

5. Peut être exempté de servir comme juré:

a) un ministre du culte;
*a.*1) un membre du personnel de l'Assemblée nationale;
b) un fonctionnaire qui participe à l'administration de la justice;
c) une personne âgée de 65 ans et plus;
d) un membre des forces régulières canadiennes au sens de la Loi sur la défense nationale (Lois révisées du Canada (1985), chapitre N-5);
(*e*) pour les cinq années qui suivent, une personne qui a agi ou a été retenue pour agir comme juré;

f) une personne atteinte d'une infirmité;
g) une personne dont la santé ou les charges domestiques ne lui permettent pas d'être juré; ou
h) si l'intérêt public le permet, une personne qui a un motif raisonnable d'obtenir une exemption pour une cause non prévue par les paragraphes précédents.

Conjoints

6. Est également inhabile ou, selon le cas, peut être exempté de servir comme juré le conjoint d'une personne mentionnée aux paragraphes *b*, *c*, *d*, *e*, *f* ou *j* de l'article 4 ou aux paragraphes *b* ou *c* de l'article 5.

Indien ou Inuk

45. Un Indien ou un Inuk, même s'il ne parle pas couramment le français ou l'anglais, peut servir comme juré si l'accusé est un Indien ou un Inuk.

Primauté sur Charte des droits de la personne

52. Les articles 3, 4, 6, 14, 19, 30, 37 et la section VI de la présente loi ont effet malgré la Charte des droits et libertés de la personne (chapitre C-12).

Saskatchewan: *The Jury Act, 1981*, S.S. 1980–81, c. J-4.1

Juror Eligibility Provisions

Qualification of jurors

3. Every resident of Saskatchewan who is a Canadian citizen and who has reached the age of 18 years is qualified to serve as a juror in civil and criminal proceedings tried by a jury in the province.

Exemptions

4. The persons excluded from service as jurors in any civil or criminal proceeding tried by a jury in the province are:

(a) members of the Privy Council, the Senate and the House of Commons of Canada;
(b) members and officers of the Legislative Assembly;
(c) reeves, councillors and mayors;
(c.1) members of boards of education referred to in section 32 of *The Education Act*, members of conseils scolaires referred to in section 32.1 of *The Education Act*, and members of boards of trustees referred to in section 123 of *The Education Act*;
(d) persons who are, or who at any time have been:
  (i) judges;
  (ii) lawyers, whether or not in actual practice;

- (iii) members of any police force;
- (iv) justices of the peace; or
- (v) coroners;

(e) persons who are engaged in the administration of justice including, without restricting the generality of the foregoing:

- (i) officials or employees of the Department of Justice; and
- (ii) officials or employees of the Department of Justice (Canada) or the Department of the Solicitor General (Canada);

(h) spouses of persons mentioned in clauses (a) to (e);

(i) persons who are legally confined in an institution;

(j) persons who are certified incompetent; and

(k) persons who are unable to understand the language in which the trial is to be conducted.

Relief from jury service

5.–(1) A person who is summoned to serve as a juror and who wishes to seek relief from jury service shall apply to be relieved from attendance as a juror by submitting to the sheriff, at the judicial centre nearest to which the jury is to sit, an Application for Relief from Jury Service at least 10 days prior to the opening of the court for which he is summoned.

(2) Where a person applies in accordance with subsection (1) and the sheriff is satisfied that the person:

- (a) is one whose attendance would result in serious hardship, loss or inconvenience to himself, to others or to the general public;
- (b) is suffering from an illness which is likely to persist and to render him incapable of serving as a juror at the sitting of the court for which he is summoned;
- (c) is a practising member of a religion or religious order whose beliefs are incompatible with service as a juror;
- (d) has reached the age of 65 years;
- (e) has served as a juror in the preceding two years;
- (f) is incapable of discharging the duties of a Juror; or
- (g) is one of the persons mentioned in section 4;

the sheriff shall relieve the person from service as a juror for the court sitting for which he was summoned.

Yukon Territory: *Jury Act*, R.S.Y. 1986, c.97

Juror Eligibility Provisions

Persons qualified to serve as jurors

4. Subject to this Act, every person who
(a) is 21 or more years of age,
(b) is a Canadian citizen or British subject, and
(c) is able to speak and understand the English language,
is qualified to serve as a juror in any action or proceeding that may be tried by a jury in the Yukon.

Persons not qualified

5. No person is qualified to serve as a juror who
(a) has been convicted of an offence for which he was sentenced to a term of imprisonment exceeding one year, not having been subsequently granted a free pardon, or
(b) is afflicted with blindness or deafness, or is a mentally disordered person, idiot or imbecile, or possesses any other physical or mental infirmity incompatible with the discharge of the duties of a juror.

Persons exempt from service

6. The following persons are exempt from service as jurors:
(a) members of the Queen's Privy Council for Canada or of the Senate or House of Commons of Canada;
(b) the Commissioner and members of the Legislative Assembly;
(c) members of the Royal Canadian Mounted Police;
(d) judges of any court of record, justices of the peace and coroners;
(e) practising lawyers;
(f) clerics of any denomination;
(g) salaried firefighters and active members of the fire brigade of a municipality;
(h) officers of the Supreme Court, including sheriff's officers and bailiffs;
(i) persons employed in the Corrections Branch of the Department of Justice;
(j) persons employed in the public service of the Yukon classified as probation officers and social workers;
(k) telegraph, telephone and radio operators;
(l) postmasters;

(m) commissioned and non-commissioned members of the regular naval, army or air forces of Her Majesty in right of Canada;
(n) physicians, surgeons, dental surgeons and druggists in active practice;
(o) nurses in active practice;
(p) persons actually engaged in the operation of
  (i) railway trains and steamships,
  (ii) plants producing electricity for public consumption, and
  (iii) water distribution systems distributing water for public consumption.

Persons excused

7. No person is required to serve as a juror more than once in any two year period, unless the service of that person as a juror is necessary by reason of there being an insufficient number of persons qualified to serve as jurors within a distance of 20 miles from the place of trial.

Judge may excuse

20. The judge may for a good cause excuse from service as a juror any person who has been summoned but has not been sworn.

APPENDIX IV

CRIMINAL CODE PROVISIONS

TRIAL BY JURY COMPULSORY.

471. Except where otherwise expressly provided by law, every accused who is charged with an indictable offence shall be tried by a court composed of a judge and jury. R.S., c. C-34, s. 429.

TRIAL WITHOUT JURY/Joinder of other offences/Withdrawal of consent.

473. (1) Notwithstanding anything in this Act, an accused charged with an offence listed in section 469 may, with the consent of the accused and the Attorney General, be tried without a jury by a judge of a superior court of criminal jurisdiction.

(1.1) Where the consent of the accused and the Attorney General is given in accordance with subsection (1), the judge of the superior court of criminal jurisdiction may order that any offence be tried by that judge in conjunction with the offence listed in section 469.

(2) Notwithstanding anything in this Act, where the consent of an accused and the Attorney General is given in accordance with subsection (1), that consent shall not be withdrawn unless both the accused and the Attorney General agree to the withdrawal. R.S., c. C-34, s. 430; R.S.C. 1985, c. 27 (1st Supp.), s. 63; 1994, c. 44, s. 30.

ADJOURNMENT WHEN NO JURY SUMMONED/Adjournment on instruction of judge.

474. (1) Where the competent authority has determined that a panel of jurors is not to be summoned for a term or sittings of the court for the trial of criminal cases in any territorial division, the clerk of the court may, on the day of the opening of the term or sittings, if a judge is not present to preside over the court, adjourn the court and the business of the court to a subsequent day. R.S., c. C-34, s. 431.

(2) A clerk of the court of the trial of criminal cases in any territorial division may, at any time, on the instructions of the presiding judge or another judge of the court, adjourn the court and the business of the court to a subsequent day. R.S., c. C-34, s. 431; 1994, c. 44, s. 31.

REMAND BY JUSTICE TO PROVINCIAL COURT JUDGE IN CERTAIN CASES/Election before justice in certain cases/Procedure where accused elects trial by provincial court judge/Procedure where accused elects trial by judge alone or by judge and jury or deemed election/Jurisdiction.

536. (1) Where an accused is before a justice other than a provincial court judge charged with an offence over which a provincial court judge has absolute jurisdiction under section 553, the justice shall remand the accused to appear before a provincial court judge having jurisdiction in the territorial division in which the offence is alleged to have been committed.

(2) Where an accused is before a justice charged with an offence, other than an offence listed in section 469, and the offence is not one over which a provincial court judge has absolute jurisdiction under section 553, the justice shall, after the information has been read to the accused, put the accused to his election in the following words:

> You have the option to elect to be tried by a provincial court judge without a jury and without having had a preliminary inquiry; or you may elected to have a preliminary inquiry and to be tried by a judge without a jury; or you may elect to have a preliminary inquiry and to be tried by a court composed of a judge and jury. If you do not elect now, you shall be deemed to have elected to have a preliminary inquiry and to be tried by a court composed of a judge and jury. How do you elect to be tried?

(3) Where an accused elects to be tried by a provincial court judge, the justice shall endorse on the information a record of the election and shall

(a) where the justice is not a provincial court judge, remand the accused to appear and plead to the charge before a provincial court judge having jurisdiction in the territorial division in which the offence is alleged to have been committed; or

(b) where the justice is a provincial court judge, call on the accused to plead to the charge and if the accused does not plead guilty, proceed with the trial or fix a time for the trial.

(4) Where an accused elects to have a preliminary inquiry and to be tried by a judge without a jury or by a court composed of a judge and jury or does not elect when put to his election, the justice shall hold a preliminary inquiry into the charge and if the accused is ordered to stand trial, the justice shall endorse on the information and, where the accused is in custody, on the warrant of committal, a statement showing the nature of the election of the accused or that the accused did not elect, as the case may be.

(5) Where a justice before whom a preliminary inquiry is being or is to be held has not commenced to take evidence, any justice having jurisdiction in the province where the offence with which the accused is charged is alleged to have been committed has jurisdiction for the purposes of subsection (4). R.S., c. C-34, s. 464; R.S.C. 1985, c. 27 (1st Supp.), s. 96.

ABSOLUTE JURISDICTION

553. The jurisdiction of a provincial court judge to try an accused is absolute and does not depend on the consent of the accused where the accused is charged in an information

(a) with

(i) theft, other than theft of cattle,

(ii) obtaining money or property by false pretences,

(iii) unlawfully having in his possession any property or thing or any proceeds of any property or thing knowing that all or a part of the property or thing or of the proceeds was obtained by or derived directly or indirectly from the commission in Canada of an offence punishable by indictment or an act or omission anywhere that, if it had occurred in Canada, would have constituted an offence punishable by indictment,

(iv) having, by deceit, falsehood or other fraudulent means, defrauded the public or any person, whether ascertained or not, of any property, money or valuable security, or

(v) mischief under subsection 430(4),

where the subject-matter of the offence is not a testamentary instrument and the alleged value of the subject-matter of the offence does not exceed five thousand dollars;

(b) with counselling or with a conspiracy or attempt to commit or with being an accessory after the fact to the commission of

(i) any offence referred to in paragraph (a) in respect of the subject-matter and value thereof referred to in that paragraph, or

(ii) any offence referred to in paragraph (c); or

(c) with an offence under

(i) section 201 (keeping gaming or betting house),

(ii) section 202 (betting, pool-selling, book-making, etc.),

(iii) section 203 (placing bets),

(iv) section 206 (lotteries and games of chance),

(v) section 209 (cheating at play),

(vi) section 210 (keeping common bawdy-house),

(vii) subsection 259(4) (driving while disqualified),

(viii) section 393 (fraud in relation to fares), or

(viii.1) section 181 (breach of recognizance). R.S., c. C-34, s. 483; 1972, c. 13, s. 40; 1974-75-76, c. 93, s. 62; R.S.C. 1985, c. 27 (1st Supp.), s. 104; 1992, c. 1, s. 58; 1994, c. 44, s. 57.

TRIAL BY PROVINCIAL COURT JUDGE WITH CONSENT.

554. (1) Where an accused is charged in an information with an indictable offence other than an offence that is mentioned in section 469, and the offence is not one over which a provincial court judge has absolute jurisdiction under section 553, a provincial court judge may try the accused if the accused elects to be tried by a provincial court judge. R.S., c. C-34, s. 484

(2)-(4) [*Repealed.* R.S.C. 1985, c. 27 (1st Supp.), s. 105]

TRIAL BY JUDGE WITHOUT A JURY.

558. Where an accused who is charged with an indictable offence, other than an offence listed in section 469, elects under section 536 or re-elects under section 561 to be tried by a judge without a jury, the accused shall, subject to this Part, be tried by a judge without a jury. R.S., c. C-34, s. 488; R.S.C. 1985, c. 27 (1st Supp.), s. 108.

DUTY OF JUDGE/Notice by sheriff, when given/Duty of sheriff when date set for trial/Duty of accused when not in custody.

560. (1) Where an accused elects, under section 536 to be tried by a judge without a jury, a judge having jurisdiction shall,

(a) on receiving a written notice from the sheriff or other person having custody of the accused stating that the accused is in custody and setting out the nature of the charge against him, or

(b) on being notified by the clerk of the court that the accused is not in custody and of the nature of the charge against him,

fix a time and place for the trial of the accused.

(2) The sheriff or other person having custody of the accused shall give the notice mentioned in paragraph (1)(a) within twenty-four hours after the accused is ordered to stand trial, if the accused is in custody pursuant to that order or if, at the time of the order, he is in custody for any other reason.

(3) Where, pursuant to subsection (1), a time and place is fixed for the trial of an accused who is in custody, the accused

(a) shall be notified forthwith by the sheriff or other person having custody of the accused of the time and place so fixed, and

(b) shall be produced at the time and place so fixed.

(4) Where an accused is not in custody, the duty of ascertaining from the clerk of the court the time and place fixed for the trial, pursuant to subsection (1), is on the accused, and he shall attend for his trial at the time and place so fixed. R.S., c. C-34, s. 490; R.S.C. 1985, c. 27 (1st Supp.), ss. 101(3), 109(1).

(5) [*Repealed*, R.S.C. 1985, c. 27 (1st Supp.), s. 109(2).]

RIGHT TO RE-ELECT/Idem/Notice and transmitting record/Time and place for re-election/Proceedings on re-election.

561. (1) An accused who elects or is deemed to have elected a mode of trial other than trial by a provincial court judge may re-elect

(a) at any time before or after the completion of the preliminary inquiry, with the written consent of the prosecutor, to be tried by a provincial court judge;

(b) at any time before the completion of the preliminary inquiry or before the fifteenth day following the completion of the preliminary inquiry, as of right, another mode of trial other than trial by a provincial court judge; and

(c) on or after the fifteenth day following the completion of the preliminary inquiry, any mode of trial with the written consent of the prosecutor.

(2) An accused who elects to be tried by a provincial court judge may, not later than fourteen days before the day first appointed for the trial, re-elect as of right another mode of trial, and may do so thereafter with the written consent of the prosecutor.

(3) Where an accused wishes to re-elect under subsection (1) before the completion of the preliminary inquiry, the accused shall give notice in writing that he wishes to re-elect, together with the written consent of the prosecutor, where such consent is required, to the justice presiding at the preliminary inquiry who shall on receipt of the notice,

(a) in the case of a re-election under paragraph (1)(b), put the accused to his re-election in the manner set out in subsection (7); or

(b) where the accused wishes to re-elect under paragraph (1)(a) and the justice is not a provincial court judge, notify a provincial court judge or clerk of the court of the accused's intention to re-elect and send to the provincial court judge or clerk the information and any promise to appear, undertaking or recognizance given or entered into in accordance with Part XVI, or any evidence taken before a coroner, that is in the possession of the justice.

(4) Where an accused wishes to re-elect under subsection (2), the accused shall give notice in writing that he wishes to re-elect together with the written consent of the prosecutor, where such consent is required, to the provincial court judge before whom the accused appeared and pleaded or to a clerk of the court.

(5) Where an accused wishes to re-elect under subsection (1) after the completion of the preliminary inquiry, the accused shall give notice in writing that he wishes to re-elect, together with the written consent of the prosecutor, where that consent is required, to a judge or clerk of the court of his original election who shall, on receipt of

the notice, notify the judge or provincial court judge or clerk of the court by which the accused wishes to be tried of the accused's intention to re-elect and send to that judge or provincial court judge or clerk the information, the evidence, the exhibits and the statement, if any, of the accused taken down in writing under section 541 and any promise to appear, undertaking or recognizance given or entered into in accordance with Part XVI, or any evidence taken before a coroner, that is in the possession of the first-mentioned judge or clerk.

(6) Where a provincial court judge or judge or clerk of the court is notified under paragraph (3)(b) or subsection (4) or (5) that the accused wishes to re-elect, the provincial court judge or judge shall forthwith appoint a time and place for the accused to re-elect and shall cause notice thereof to be given to the accused and the prosecutor.

(7) The accused shall attend or, if he is in custody, shall be produced at the time and place appointed under section (6) and shall, after

(a) the charge on which he has been ordered to stand trial or the indictment, where an indictment has been preferred pursuant to section 556, 574 or 577 or is filed with the court before which the indictment is to be preferred pursuant to section 577, or

(b) in the case of a re-election under subsection (1) before the completion of the preliminary inquiry or under subsection (2), the information has been read to the accused, be put to his re-election in the following words or in words to the like effect:

You have given notice of your wish to re-elect the mode of your trial. You now have the option to do so. How do you wish to re-elect? R.S., c. C-34, s. 491; R.S.C. 1985, c. 27 (1st Supp.), s. 110.

PROCEEDINGS FOLLOWED RE-ELECTION/Idem.

562. (1) Where the accused re-elects under paragraph 561(1)(a) before the completion of the preliminary inquiry or under subsection 561(1) after the completion of the preliminary inquiry, the provincial court judge or judge, as the case may be, shall proceed with the trial or appoint a time and place for the trial.

(2) Where the accused re-elects under paragraph 561(1)(b) before the completion of the preliminary inquiry or under subsection 561(2), the justice shall proceed with the preliminary inquiry. R.S., c. C-34, s. 492; R.S.C. 1985, c. 27 (1st Supp.), s. 110.

PROCEEDINGS ON RE-ELECTION TO BE TRIED BY PROVINCIAL COURT JUDGE WITHOUT JURY.

563. Where an accused re-elects under section 561 to be tried by a provincial court judge,

(a) the accused shall be tried on the information that was before the justice at the preliminary inquiry, subject to any amendments thereto that may be allowed by the provincial court judge by whom the accused is tried; and

(b) the provincial court judge before whom the re-election is made shall endorse on the information a record of the re-election. R.S., c. C-34, s. 493; R.S.C. 1985, c. 27 (1st Supp.), s. 110.

ELECTION DEEMED TO HAVE BEEN MADE/Where direct indictment preferred/Notice of re-election/Application.

565. (1) Where an accused is ordered to stand trial for an offence that, under this Part, may be tried by a judge without a jury, the accused shall, for the purposes of the provisions of this Part relating to election and re-election, be deemed to have elected to be tried by a court composed of a judge and jury if

(a) the accused was ordered to stand trial by a provincial court judge who, pursuant to subsection 555(1), continued the proceedings before him as a preliminary inquiry;

(b) the justice, provincial court judge or judge, as the case may be, declined pursuant to section 567 to record the election or re-election of the accused; or

(c) the accused does not elect when put to an election under section 536.

(2) Where an accused is to be tried after an indictment has been preferred against the accused pursuant to a consent or order given under section 577, the accused shall, for the purposes of the provisions of this Part relating to election and re-election, be deemed to have elected to be tried by a court composed of a judge and jury and may, with the written consent of the prosecutor, re-elect to be tried by a judge without a jury.

(3) Where an accused wishes to re-elect under subsection (2), the accused shall give notice in writing that he wishes to re-elect, together with the written consent of the prosecutor, to a judge or

clerk of the court where the indictment has been filed or preferred who shall, on receipt of the notice, notify a judge having jurisdiction or clerk of the court by which the accused wishes to be tried of the accused's intention to re-elect and send to that judge or clerk the indictment and any promise to appear, undertaking or recognizance given or entered into in accordance with Part XVI, any summons or warrant issued under section 578, or any evidence taken before a coroner, that is in the possession of the first-mentioned judge or clerk.

(4) Subsections 561(6) and (7) apply to a re-election made under subsection (3). R.S., C. C-34, s. 495; R.S.C. 1985, c. 27 (1st Supp.), s. 111.

MODE OF TRIAL WHERE TWO OR MORE ACCUSED.

567. Notwithstanding any other provision of this Part, where two or more persons are charged with the same offence, unless all of them elect or re-elect or are deemed to have elected, as the case may be, the same mode of trial, the justice, provincial court judge or judge

(a) may decline to record any election, re-election or deemed election for trial by a provincial court judge or a judge without a jury; and

(b) if he declines to do so, shall hold a preliminary inquiry unless a preliminary inquiry has been held prior to the election, re-election or deemed election. R.S., C. C-34, s. 497; R.S.C. 1985, c. 27 (1st Supp.), s. 111.

ATTORNEY GENERAL MAY REQUIRE TRIAL BY JURY.

568. The Attorney General may, notwithstanding that an accused elects under section 536 or re-elects under section 561 to be tried by a judge or provincial court judge, as the case may be, require the accused to be tried by a court composed of a judge and jury, unless the alleged offence is one that is punishable with imprisonment for five years or less, and where the Attorney General so requires, a judge or provincial court judge has no jurisdiction to try the accused under this Part and a preliminary inquiry shall be held before a justice unless a preliminary inquiry has been held prior to the requirement by the Attorney General that the accused be tried by a court composed of a judge and jury. R.S., c. C-34, s. 498; R.S.C. 1985, c. 27 (1st Supp.), s. 111.

BENCH WARRANT/Execution/Interim release.

597. (1) Where an indictment has been preferred against a person who is at large, and that person does not appear or remain in attendance for his trial, the court before which the accused should have appeared or remained in attendance may issue a warrant in Form 7 for his arrest.

ELECTION DEEMED TO BE WAIVED/Idem.

598. (1) Notwithstanding anything in this Act, where a person to whom subsection 597(1) applies has elected or is deemed to have elected to be tried by a court composed of a judge and jury and, at the time he failed to appear or to remain in attendance for his trial, he had not re-elected to be tried by a court composed of a judge without a jury or provincial court judge without a jury, he shall not be tried by a court composed of a judge and jury unless

(a) he establishes to the satisfaction of a judge of the court in which he is indicted that there was a legitimate excuse for his failure to appear or remain in attendance for his trial; or

(b) the Attorney General requires pursuant to section 568 that the accused be tried by a court composed of a judge and jury.

(2) An accused who, pursuant to subsection (1), may not be tried by a court composed of a judge and jury is deemed to have elected under section 536 to be tried by a judge of the court in which he is indicted without a jury and section 561 does not apply in respect of the accused. 1974-76, c. 93, s. 65; R.S.C. 1985, c. 27 (1st Supp.), s. 122.

QUALIFICATION OF JURORS/No disqualification based on sex.

626. (1) A person who is qualified as a juror according to, and summoned as a juror in accordance with, the laws of a province is qualified to serve as a juror in criminal proceedings in that province.

(2) Notwithstanding any law of a province referred to in subsection (1), no person may be disqualified, exempted or excused from serving as a juror in criminal proceedings on the grounds of his or her sex. R.S., c. C-34, s. 554; 1972, c. 13, c. 46; R.S.C. 1985, c. 27 (1st Supp.), s. 128.

CHALLENGING THE JURY PANEL/In writing/Form.

629. (1) The accused or the prosecutor may challenge the jury panel only on the ground of partiality, fraud or wilful misconduct on the part of the sheriff or other officer by whom the panel was returned.

(2) A challenge under subsection (1) shall be in writing and shall state that the person who returned the panel was partial or fraudulent or that he wilfully misconducted himself, as the case may be.

(3) A challenge under this section may be in Form 40. R.S., c. C-34, s. 558; R.S.C. 1985, c. 27 (1st Supp.), s. 130.

TRYING GROUND OF CHALLENGE.

630. Where a challenge is made under section 629, the judge shall determine whether the alleged ground of challenge is true or not, and where he is satisfied that the alleged ground of challenge is true, he shall direct a new panel to be returned. R.S., c. C-34, s. 559.

EMPANELLING JURY

NAMES OF JURORS ON CARDS/To be placed in box/To be drawn by clerk of court/Juror to be sworn/Drawing additional names if necessary.

631. (1) The name of each juror on a panel of jurors that has been returned, his number on the panel and his address shall be written on a separate card, and all the cards shall, as far as possible, be of equal size.

(2) The Sheriff or other officer who returns the panel shall deliver the cards referred to in subsection (1) to the clerk of the court who shall cause them to be placed together in a box to be provided for the purpose and to be thoroughly shaken together.

(3) Where

(a) the array of jurors is not challenged, or

(b) the array of jurors is challenged but the judge does not direct a new panel to be returned,

the clerk of the court shall, in open court, draw out the cards referred to in subsection (1), one after another, and shall call out the name and number on each card as it is drawn, until the number of persons who have answered to their names is, in the opinion of the judge, sufficient to provide a full jury after allowing for orders to excuse, challenges and directions to stand by.

(4) The clerk of the court shall swear each member of the jury in the order in which the names of the jurors were drawn.

(5) Where the number of persons who answer to their names under subsection (3) is not sufficient to provide a full jury, the clerk of the court shall proceed in accordance with subsections (3) and (4) until twelve jurors are sworn. R.S. c. C-34, s. 560; R.S.C. 1985, c. 27 (1st Supp.), s. 131; 1992, c. 41, s. 1.

EXCUSING JURORS.

632. The judge may, at any time before the commencement of a trial, order that any juror be excused from jury service, whether or not the juror has been called pursuant to subsection 631(3) or any challenge has been made in relation to the juror, for reasons of

(a) personal interest in the matter to be tried;

(b) relationship with the judge, prosecutor, accused, counsel for the accused or a prospective witness; or

(c) personal hardship or any other reasonable cause that, in the opinion of the judge, warrants that the juror be excused. R.S., c. C-34, s. 561; 1992, c. 41, s. 2.

STAND BY.

633. The judge may direct a juror whose name has been called pursuant to subsection 631(3) to stand by for reasons of personal hardship or any other reasonable cause. R.S., c. C-34, s. 562; 1974-75-76, c. 105, s. 10; 1992, c. 41, s. 2.

PEREMPTORY CHALLENGES/Maximum number/Where there are multiple counts/Where there are joint trials.

634. (1) A juror may be challenged peremptorily whether or not the juror has been challenged for cause pursuant to section 638.

(2) Subject to subsections (3) and (4), the prosecutor and the accused are each entitled to

(a) twenty peremptory challenges, where the accused is charged with high treason or first degree murder;

(b) twelve peremptory challenges, where the accused is charged with an offence, other than an offence mentioned in paragraph (a), for which the accused may be sentenced to imprisonment for a term exceeding five years; or

(c) four peremptory challenges, where the accused is charged with an offence that is not referred to in paragraph (a) or (b).

(3) Where two or more counts in an indictment are to be tried together, the prosecutor and the accused are each entitled only to the number of peremptory challenges provided in respect of the count for which the greatest number of peremptory challenges is available.

(4) Where two or more accused are to be tried together,

(a) each accused is entitled to the number of peremptory challenges to which the accused would be entitled if tried alone; and

(b) the prosecutor is entitled to the total number of peremptory challenges available to all the accused. R.S., c. C-34, s. 563; 1992, c. 41, s. 2.

ORDER OF CHALLENGES/Where there are joint trials.

635. (1) The accused shall be called on before the prosecutor is called on to declare whether the accused challenges the first juror, for cause or peremptorily, and thereafter the prosecutor and the accused shall be called on alternately, in respect of each of the remaining jurors, to first make such a declaration.

(2) Subsection (1) applies where two or more accused are to be tried together, but all of the accused shall exercise the challenges of the defence in turn, in the order in which their names appear in the indictment or in any other order agreed on by them,

(a) in respect of the first juror, before the prosecutor; and

(b) in respect of each of the remaining jurors, either before or after the prosecutor, in accordance with subsection (1). 1992, c. 41, s. 2.

CHALLENGE FOR CAUSE/No other ground/Coming into force/Idem.

638. (1) A prosecutor or an accused is entitled to any number of challenges on the ground that

(a) the name of a juror does not appear on the panel, but no misnomer or misdescription is a ground of challenge where it appears to the court that the description given on the panel sufficiently designates the person referred to;

(b) a juror is not indifferent between the Queen and the accused;

(c) a juror has been convicted of an offence for which he was sentenced to death or to a term of imprisonment exceeding twelve months;

(d) a juror is an alien;

(e) a juror is physically unable to perform properly the duties of a juror; or

(f) a juror does not speak the official language of Canada that is the language of the accused or the official language of Canada in which the accused can best give testimony or both official languages of Canada, where the accused is required by reason of an order under section 530 to be tried before a judge and jury who speak the official language of Canada in which the accused can best give testimony or who speak both official languages of Canada, as the case may be.

(2) No challenge for cause shall be allowed on a ground not mentioned in subsection (1).

CHALLENGE IN WRITING/Form/Denial.

639. (1) Where a challenge is made on a ground mentioned in section 638, the court may, in its discretion, require the party that challenges to put the challenge in writing.

(2) A challenge may be in Form 41.

(3) A challenge may be denied by the other party to the proceedings on the ground that it is not true. R.S., c. C-34, s. 568.

OBJECTION THAT NAME NOT ON PANEL/Other grounds/If challenge not sustained, or if sustained/Disagreement of triers.

640. (1) Where the ground of a challenge is that the name of a juror does not appear on the panel, the issue shall be tried by the judge on the *voir dire* by the inspection of the panel, and such other evidence that the judge thinks fit to receive.

(2) Where the ground of a challenge is one not mentioned in subsection (1), the two jurors who were last sworn, or if no jurors have then been sworn, two persons present whom the court may appoint

for the purpose, shall be sworn to determine whether the ground of challenge is true.

(3) Where the finding, pursuant to subsection (1) or (2) is that the ground of challenge is not true, the juror shall be sworn, but if the finding is that the ground of challenge is true, the juror shall not be sworn.

(4) Where, after what the court considers to be a reasonable time, the two persons who are sworn to determine whether the ground of challenge is true are unable to agree, the court may discharge them from giving a verdict and may direct two other persons to be sworn to determine whether the ground of challenge is true. R.S., c. C-34, s. 569.

CALLING JURORS WHO HAVE STOOD BY/Other jurors becoming available.

(1) Where a full jury has not been sworn and no names remain to be called, the names of those who have been directed to stand by shall be called again in the order in which their names were drawn and they shall be sworn, unless excused by the judge or challenged by the accused or the prosecutor.

(2) Where, before a juror is sworn pursuant to subsection (1), other jurors in the panel become available, the prosecutor may require the names of those jurors to be put into and drawn from the box in accordance with section 631, and those jurors shall be challenged, directed to stand by, excused or sworn, as the case may be, before the names of the jurors who were originally directed to stand by are called again. R.S., c. C-34, s. 570; 1992, c. 41, s. 3.

SUMMONING OTHER JURORS WHEN PANEL EXHAUSTED/ Orally/Adding names to panel.

642. (1) Where a full jury cannot be provided notwithstanding that the relevant provisions of this Part have been complied with, the court may, at the request of the prosecutor, order the sheriff or other proper officer forthwith to summon as many persons, whether qualified jurors or not, as the court directs for the purpose of providing a full jury.

(2) Jurors may be summoned under subsection (1) by word of mouth, if necessary.

(3) The names of the persons who are summoned under this section shall be added to the general panel for the purposes of the trial, and the same proceedings shall be taken with respect to calling and challenging those persons, excusing them and directing them to stand by as are provided in this Part with respect to the persons named in the original panel, R.S., c. C-34, s. 571; 1992, c. 41, s. 4.

WHO SHALL BE JURY/Same jury may try another issue by consent/ Sections directory.

643. (1) The twelve jurors whose names are drawn and who are sworn in accordance with this Part shall be the jury to try the issues of the indictment, and the names of the jurors so drawn and sworn shall be kept apart until the jury gives its verdict or until it is discharged, whereupon the names shall be returned to the box as often as occasion arises, as long as an issue remains to be tried before a jury.

(2) The court may try an issue with the same jury in whole or in part that previously tried or was drawn to try another issue, without the jurors being sworn again, but if the prosecutor or the accused objects to any of the jurors or the court excuses any of the jurors, the court shall order those persons to withdraw and shall direct that the required number of names to make up a full jury be drawn and, subject to the provisions of this Part relating to challenges, orders to excuse and directions to stand by, the persons whose names are drawn shall be sworn.

(3) Failure to comply with the directions of this section or section 631, 635 or 641 does not affect the validity of a proceeding. R.S., c. C-34, s. 572; 1992, c. 41, s. 5.

DISCHARGE OF JUROR/Trial may continue.

644. (1) Where in the course of a trial the judge is satisfied that a juror shall not, by reason of illness or other reasonable cause, continue to act, the judge may discharge the juror.

(1.1) A judge may select another juror to take the place of a juror who by reason of illness or other reasonable cause cannot continue to act, if the jury has not yet begun to hear evidence, either by drawing a name from a panel of persons who were summoned to act as jurors and who are available to the court at the time of replacing the juror or by using the procedure referred to in section 642.

(2) Where in the course of a trial a member of the jury dies or is discharged pursuant to subsection (1), the jury shall, unless the judge otherwise directs and if the number of jurors is not reduced below ten, be deemed to remain properly constituted for all purposes of the trial and the trial shall proceed and a verdict may be given accordingly. R.S., c. C-34, s. 573; 1972, c. 13, s. 47; 1980-81-82-83, c. 47, s. 53.

SEPARATION OF JURORS/Keeping in charge/Non-compliance with subsection (2)/Empanelling new jury in certain cases/Refreshment and accommodation.

647. (1) The judge may, at any time before the jury retires to consider its verdict, permit the members of the jury to separate.

(2) Where permission to separate under subsection (1) cannot be given or is not given, the jury shall be kept under the charge of an officer of the court as the judge directs, and that officer shall prevent the jurors from communicating with anyone other than himself or another member of the jury without leave of the judge.

(3) Failure to comply with subsection (2) does not affect the validity of the proceedings.

(4) Where the fact that there has been a failure to comply with this section or section 648 is discovered before the verdict of the jury is returned, the judge may, if he considers that the failure to comply might lead to a miscarriage of justice, discharge the jury and

(a) direct that the accused be tried with a new jury during the same session or sittings of the court; or

(b) postpone the trial on such terms as justice may require.

(5) The judge shall direct the sheriff to provide the jurors who are sworn with suitable and sufficient refreshment, food and lodging while they are together until they have given their verdict. R.S., c. C-34, s. 576; 1972, c. 13, s. 48.

DISCLOSURE OF JURY PROCEEDINGS.

649. Every member of a jury who, except for the purposes of

(a) an investigation of an alleged offence under subsection 139(2) in relation to a juror, or

(b) giving evidence in criminal proceedings in relation to such an offence, discloses any information relating to the proceedings of the jury when it was absent from the courtroom that was not subsequently disclosed in open court is guilty of an offence punishable on summary conviction. 1972, c. 13, s. 49.

DISAGREEMENT OF JURY/Discretion not reviewable.

653. (1) Where the judge is satisfied that the jury is unable to agree on its verdict and that further detention of the jury would be useless, he may in his discretion discharge that jury and direct a new jury to be empanelled during the sittings of the court, or may adjourn the trial on such terms as justice may require.

(2) A discretion that is exercised under subsection (1) by a judge is not reviewable. R.S., c. C-34, s. 580.

JUDGMENT NOT TO BE STAYED ON CERTAIN GROUNDS.

670. Judgment shall not be stayed or reversed after verdict on an indictment

(a) by reason of any irregularity in the summoning or empanelling of the jury; or

(b) for the reason that a person who served on the jury was not returned as a juror by a sheriff or other officer. R.S., c. C-34, s. 598.

DIRECTIONS RESPECTING JURY OR JURORS DIRECTORY.

671. No omission to observe the directions contained in any Act with respect to the qualifications, selection, balloting or distribution of jurors, the preparation of the jurors' book, the selecting of jury lists, or the drafting of panels from the jury lists, is a ground for impeaching or quashing a verdict rendered in criminal proceedings. R.S., c. C-34, s. 599.

SAVING POWERS OF COURT.

672. Nothing in this Act alters, abridges or affects any power or authority that a court or judge had immediately before April 1, 1955, or any practice or form that existed immediately before April 1, 1955, with respect to trials by jury, jury process, juries or jurors, except where the power or authority, practice or form is expressly altered by or is inconsistent with this Act. R.S., c. C-34, s. 600.

TABLE OF CASES

INDEX

ABOUT THE AUTHORS

David M. Tanovich is a criminal appellate lawyer in Toronto practising with Pinkofsky, Lockyer. He is a former law clerk to Chief Justice Antonio Lamer of the Supreme Court of Canada and an L.L.M. graduate from New York University School of Law. He is author of numerous articles on criminal law, many of which have been cited by the Supreme Court of Canada and other appellate courts, and is co-editor of the *Criminal Appeals Law Reporter*. He is currently working on a book on criminal appeals for Irwin Law.

David M. Paciocco is a professor of law at the University of Ottawa, where he teaches Evidence, Criminal Law, and Trusts. He is counsel to the firm of Michael D. Edelson and Associates, conducting a specialized criminal defence practice, and was formerly an assistant Crown attorney. He is co-author with Lee Stuesser of the University of Manitoba of *The Law of Evidence* (1996) and author of *Charter Principles and Proof in Criminal Cases* (1987), as well as numerous articles on criminal law and the law of evidence.

Steven Skurka is a criminal lawyer in Toronto practising in association with Leslie Pringle. He is a part-time lecturer in criminal procedure at Osgoode Hall Law School, a faculty member of the Ontario College of Advocacy Training, and a director of the Criminal Lawyers' Association. He has written numerous articles on criminal law and is a regular contributor to the Bar Admission Course, as well as being co-editor of the *Criminal Appeals Law Reporter*.